KU-270-695

(12)

Economics for Business Studies: Volume 2

PORTOBELLO HIGH SCHOOL

B. J. E. Jukes

Senior Lecturer in Economics, West Bromwich College of Commerce and Technology

S. King

Senior Lecturer in Economics, West Bromwich College of Commerce and Technology

N. L. Paulus

Senior Lecturer in Economics, West Bromwich College of Commerce and Technology

A. G. Whitehouse

Lecturer in Economics, Worcester Technical College

Polytech Publishers Ltd. Stockport.

First Published August 1975

All rights reserved
No part of this publication may be reproduced, stored in a retrieval
system, or transmitted in any form or by any means, electronic,
mechanical, photocopying, recording, or otherwise, without the prior
permission of the copyright owner

©

Copyright Polytech Publishers Limited
36 Hayburn Road, Stockport SK2 5DB

SBN 85505 016 0

Printed by C. Nicholls & Company Ltd.

Gross Domestic Product

Gross domestic product (GDP) is defined as the value of all final goods and services produced within an economy during a given period, usually a year. Note that we have not said the value of all goods and services, only of final output.

Final output consists of those goods and services which are sold to final consumers and not incorporated into any further output. Those goods which are so incorporated are known as intermediate goods. Inclusion of intermediate goods in the valuation of output would lead to double, triple and quadruple counting and consequently overstate the true value of an economy's output as in the following example.

Stages of Production
Firm 1 (mining company) sells iron ore to Firm 2 (steelworks) for £200.
Firm 2 supplies steel plate to Firm 3 (body-pressing firm) for £400.
Firm 3 supplies body panels to Firm 4 (car manufacturer) for £600.
Firm 4 delivers car to Firm 5 (car dealer) for £1,500.
Firm 5 sells car to motorist for £2,000.

EXHIBIT 1.2

The value of all these transactions is £200+£400+£600+£1,500+£2,000 = £4,700. However only one car has been produced and this has been sold to the final customer, the motorist, for £2,000. Final output is therefore £2,000 (= one car). The other outputs or transactions are intermediate in that they lead to further production. Obviously it is misleading and incorrect to count the value of the iron ore and the value of the steel produced from it and the value of the body pressing produced from that and so on. All that we should include at each stage is the value added during that stage.

Value added is the difference between the gross value of a firm's output and the value of its inputs. In our example Firm 2 adds value of £200: it produces steel plate worth £400 but it has paid out £200 for the input (iron ore). Similarly Firm 3's added value is also £200: it sells body panels for £600 but has previously bought in steel plate costing £400. If we sum the values added at each stage we get £200+£200+£200+£900+£500=£2,000 which is the value of final output.

This is the basis upon which the value of GDP is determined. Each industry's production is valued on the basis of output × price. From this figure is deducted the value of that industry's inputs bought from elsewhere. The resulting "difference" figure represents the contribution of each industry in the form of value added to the product at that particular stage of output.

Recasting Exhibit 1.2 in terms of value added by each firm we have:

Added Values

Firm	Contribution in the form of value added (£)
1	200
2	200
3	200
4	900
5	500
Total Value (= sum of values added)	£2,000

EXHIBIT 1.3

In Exhibit 1.4 are shown the contributions of thirteen broad industrial sectors to GDP in 1963 and 1973.

Gross domestic product by industry, £ mn

Industry	1963	1973
Agriculture, forestry and fishing	964	1,876
Mining and quarrying	744	868
Manufacturing	8,974	19,103
Construction	1,768	4,429
Gas, electricity and water	839	1,939
Transport	1,766	3,837
Communication	522	1,623
Distributive Trades	3,145	6,122
Insurance, banking, etc.	1,771	5,774
Ownership of dwellings	1,149	3,668
Public administration and defence	1,551	4,266
Public health and educational services	1,183	3,726
Other services	3,172	6,908
Total	27,548	64,139
Adjustment for financial services	− 696	− 2,552
Residual error	35	589
Gross domestic product at factor cost	26,887	62,176

(**Source:** National Income and Expenditure 1963–1973, Table 11).

EXHIBIT 1.4

Gross National Product

Gross domestic product, remember, is the value of output produced within the economy, or by the resources or factors of production at work in the economy. GDP must not be confused with gross national product (GNP). GNP may be defined as the value of all final goods and services produced annually by resources owned by the residents of an economy wherever those resources may be at work. Residents of one country frequently own productive assets at work elsewhere. Britain, for example, has for many years invested overseas and a stream of earnings from those investments flows back to Britain each year. At the same time some of the production occurring within this country derives from assets located here but owned by overseas residents.

Therefore if we take the GDP figure, deduct from it rent, profits, interest, etc. paid to overseas residents, and add to it the overseas earnings of United Kingdom residents, we arrive at the figure for GNP.

In the national income accounts this adjustment is the item "Net property income from abroad". In the case of the United Kingdom this item is positive, producing a GNP greater than GDP; elsewhere it may be negative. For example if a developing country benefits from considerable investment by other countries and has not invested overseas itself, there may be a net outflow of earnings leaving its national product less than its domestic product.

For the United Kingdom the difference between GDP and GNP is not great; during the period 1963 – 1973 the average difference (GNP as percentage of GDP) was 1·24%, and the biggest, 1·76%.

United Kingdom gross domestic and national products, 1963 – 1973. £mn

	1963	1964	1965	1966	1967	1968	1969
GDP	26,887	29,163	31,153	33,042	34,854	37,333	39,180
GNP	27,285	29,556	31,588	33,429	35,233	37,668	39,679
GNP as % of GDP	101·48	101·34	101·39	101·17	101·08	100·89	101·27

	1970	1971	1972	1973
GDP	43,012	48,432	54,390	62,176
GNP	43,537	48,957	54,903	63,271
GNP as % of GDP	101·22	101·08	100·94	101·76

(**Source**: National Income and Expenditure 1963 – 1973, Table 1).

EXHIBIT 1.5

Market Prices and Factor Cost
Up to this point we have been concerned with the valuation of output at prices charged to buyers, hence GDP and GNP at market prices. Often the price at which output is sold includes an element of taxation, for example VAT and excise duties. Where this is so not all the revenue from the sale of the output accrues to the resources engaged in its production; productive resources will share that part of sales revenue which remains after taxation has been deducted.

In other cases certain products may be subsidised by the government so that the market price understates the real value of output. Examples include milk, a number of foods and certain outputs of the nationalised industries.

Bringing together these two points GDP at factor cost is equal to GDP at market prices less expenditure taxes plus subsidies. The same adjustment may be carried out with GNP figures. To give some idea of the difference, in 1963 GDP at market prices totalled £30,345mn and at factor cost totalled £26,887mn, a difference of £3,458 mn. Corresponding figures for 1973 were £70,726 mn. and £62,176 a difference of £8,550 mn. The use of factor cost rather than market price avoids what could otherwise be misleading changes in output valuations. For example on a market price basis the value of output may increase simply because the government levies higher expenditure taxes or reduces or withdraws existing subsidies. Conversely a reduction in expenditure taxes and an increase in subsidies would have the effect of decreasing the value of output, other things being equal. An example of an artificial increase in the value of output is provided in Exhibit 1.6 where we return to our simple economy to find that the government has introduced VAT at 8%. Compare the difference in market price output in the pre-tax and post-tax situation. (Look back to Exhibit 1.1 if you have forgotten what things were like in the idyllic pre-tax days!). Although there has been no change in actual production, on the face of it the value of output has gone up from £6,500 to £7,020.

National Output of simple economy with expenditure tax

Commodity	Output	Price per unit (£)	VAT @ 8% (£)	VAT-inclusive price (£)	Market value (£)
Bread	10,000	0·15	0·012	0·162	1,620
Cheese	5,000	0·20	0·016	0·216	1,080
Beer	20,000	0·20	0·016	0·216	4,320
Total National Output at Market Prices					£7,020

EXHIBIT 1.6

Current and Constant Prices
Valuations of output at market prices and at factor cost will both be affected by changes in the price level which in practice means inflation. In order to overcome the effects of inflation in the shape of higher prices and to give a clear picture of changes in real output, GDP or GNP, the Blue Book provides a series of figures at constant (1970) prices. GDP figures for selected years at current and constant prices are reproduced in Exhibit 1.7 below.

GDP at current and constant prices, selected years, £mn

	1953	1963	1973
GDP at factor cost, current prices	14,881	26,887	62,176
GDP at factor cost, 1970 prices	27,141	35,550	47,113

(**Source:** National Income and Expenditure, 1963 – 1973, Tables 1 and 14).

EXHIBIT 1.7

The use of constant price valuations makes it possible to concentrate on what really matters – the economy's performance.

Gross and Net Measures
Each year in the course of production some part of the nation's stock of capital equipment is used up; wear and tear occurs, fire and other accidents damage plant and equipment and machines become obsolescent.

In the absence of any replacement the stock of capital available to the nation will gradually contract and, as it does so, the productive potential of the economy will decline.

In order to avoid this, there must be replacement of that part of the capital stock used up. In the national income accounts the allowance that is made for this purpose is known as "Capital consumption" or depreciation. Capital consumption may be thought of as the portion of annual output which balances, or makes good, capital depreciation; or which maintains the stock of capital at its existing level. From this it follows that the amount of output available for purposes of consumption or net investment (additions to the capital stock) will be less than total output. The figure which is left when depreciation is allowed for is net product, domestic or national as the case may be.

Exhibit 1.8 shows diagrammatically the relationship between gross and net national product and Exhibit 1.9 shows figures of the relevant aggregates for 1963 and 1973.

Gross and Net Product

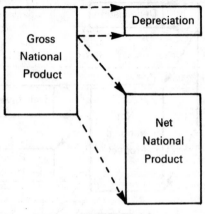

EXHIBIT 1.8

Gross and Net National Product at factor cost, current prices, £mn

	1963	1973
Gross national product	27,285	63,271
Capital consumption	2,504	7,012
Net national product	24,781	56,259

(**Source**: National Income and Expenditure, 1963–1973, Table 1).

EXHIBIT 1.9

So if GNP is regarded as a measure of the economy's total output, NNP may be regarded as a measure of the goods and services which are available to be used up for consumption and investment purposes once the capital stock has been made good. Diagrammatically this is shown in Exhibit 1·10.

In the official accounts net national product is also known as national income. Although the term national income is correctly applied only to net national product, it is worth pointing out that in some cases it is rather more loosely applied to the other measures of activity that we have introduced and which are still to be presented.

The output method gives acceptable results where there is market provision of goods and services, but not all goods and services are provided through the market; here there will not be any basis for valuation at all or at best it will only be possible to make a particular valuation on the basis of costs of provision. Examples of such goods and services include: commodities provided by the state for example defence and education; goods and services provided by the consumer himself or his family, for example vegetables grown in the back garden or allotment, interior decorating and other do-it-yourself activities; and the work of housewives and mothers, such as washing, cleaning and minding the children.

Bearing this in mind we may conclude that the national income accounts underestimate the true output of the economy. However what generally matters

Uses of GNP

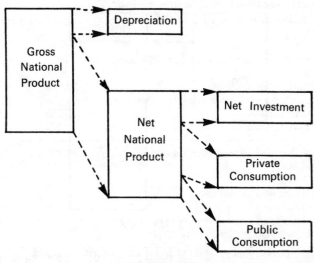

EXHIBIT 1.10

is changes in output rather than the actual level, so where the line is drawn with regard to inclusion or exclusion is of less significance.

MEASUREMENT OF EXPENDITURE

With the output approach to measuring economic activity we are primarily concerned with what the economy produces. When we look at activity from the expenditure point of view our concern is with what happens to output once it has been produced, i.e. who buys it. The expenditure approach to measuring economic activity is based on the fact that all output must either be sold for one purpose or another or be added to stocks. Therefore if we measure all expenditure on final output of goods and services and on stockbuilding we arrive at an identical valuation to that given by the output approach. (Because of statistical problems this may not be so in practice, as was mentioned earlier).

Of course there are numerous ways in which we can classify the uses of output. One simple approach is to classify output as either consumer goods, wanted for their own sake, or investment goods, required for their contribution to further output. Another approach is to classify output as being either for private or public use. When we classify in this manner all we are doing is basing our divisions on the purchasers of the output; in the first example, consumers or firms; in the second, private individuals and firms or the state. Since total spending can be equated with total demand, we are breaking down total spending into numerous components of demand.

In the national accounts five broad categories of expenditure are recognised; these are:

(1) Consumers' expenditure.
(2) Public authorities' current expenditure on goods and services.
(3) Gross domestic fixed capital formation.

(4) Value of physical increase in stocks and work in progress.

(5) Exports and property income from abroad.

In the following table expenditure figures for each category are given for 1963 and 1973.

Categories of Expenditure, 1963 and 1973, £mn

	1963	1973
Consumers' expenditure	20,118	44,855
Public authorities' current expenditure	5,176	13,270
Capital formation	5,020	13,871
Increase in stocks	168	574
Total domestic expenditure, market prices	30,482	72,570
Exports	7,217	21,542
less Imports	− 6,956	− 22,291
less Taxes on expenditure	− 4,027	− 10,006
Subsidies	569	1,456
Gross national product at factor cost	27,285	63,271

(Source: National Income and Expenditure, 1963 – 1973, Table 1).

EXHIBIT 1.11

Consumers' Expenditure

As you can see from Exhibit 1.11 consumer spending is by far the most significant element in total purchasing, accounting for 62% of total domestic expenditure in 1973. The Blue Book gives details of the various categories of personal expenditure in Table 24. Space prevents a complete listing of these but we give in Exhibit 1.12 some of the more important items, that is important in terms of magnitude.

Selected Items of Personal Consumption, 1973, £mn

Food	8,460
Alcoholic drink	3,536
Tobacco	1,945
Housing	6,190
Fuel and light	1,891
Clothing and footwear	3,774
Durable goods	4,012
Running costs of vehicles	682
Travel	1,436

(Source: National Income and Expenditure, 1963–1973, Table 24).

EXHIBIT 1.12

Two important points must be made with regard to consumers' expenditure. Firstly the total includes spending on consumer durables such as cars, washing machines and radio and television sets. Although these goods are not strictly consumption goods they are treated as such by the national income statisticians. Secondly one particular sort of consumer durable, housing, is treated as investment and is included in the category capital formation. Both these treatments are somewhat arbitrary but the student should be aware of them.

Public Authorities' Current Expenditure on Goods and Services
This item covers the expenditure of local and central government on goods
and services. In 1973 the total of £13,270 mn was split as follows: central government £7,653mn and local authorities £5,617mn; (figures from Table 45). If we
regard consumers' expenditure as private consumption, then these items can be
thought of as public consumption. Added together they form total domestic
consumption, equal to £58,125mn in 1973.

Gross Domestic Fixed Capital Formation
This is the rather long-winded term used to refer to investment. In the accounts
investment goods are those that are not used up in the accounting period, i.e. a
year; but remember the point about consumer durables. It is possible to analyse
investment by the sector undertaking it or by the type of asset acquired. Exhibits
1.13 and 1.14 show these analyses for 1963 and 1973:

Gross domestic fixed capital formation by sector, £mn

	1963	1973
Personal sector	867	2,426
Companies	2,019	5,888
Public corporations	1,024	2,029
Central government	227	773
Local authorities	883	2,755
Total	5,020	13,871

(Source: National Income and Expenditure, 1963 – 1973, Table 53).
EXHIBIT 1.13

Gross domestic fixed capital formation by type of asset, £mn

	1963	1973
Buses and coaches	29	60
Other road vehicles	318	803
Railway rolling stock	48	36
Ships	92	595
Aircraft	28	67
Plant and machinery	1,926	4,877
Dwellings	910	2,680
Other buildings and works	1,501	4,188
Transfer costs of land and buildings	168	565
Total	5,020	13,871

(Source: National Income and Expenditure, 1963–1973, Table 54).
EXHIBIT 1.14

A third breakdown of investment shows its analysis by industry, as in Exhibit
1.15 below:—
Gross domestic fixed capital formation by industry, £mn

	1963	1973
Agriculture, forestry and fishing	183	475
Mining and quarrying	90	401

Manufacturing	1,068	2,510
Construction	99	207
Gas, electricity and water	647	769
Transport and communication	495	1,834
Distributive trades	313	768
Other service industries	427	1,395
Dwellings	910	2,680
Social services	313	1,004
Other public services	307	1,263
Transfer cost of land and buildings	168	565
Total	5,020	13,871

(Source: National Income and Expenditure, 1963–1973, Table 56).
EXHIBIT 1.15

Remember that all these investment figures are gross, i.e. they include all investment purchasing whether for replacement of worn-out stock or for additions to the stock of capital (net investment). Net capital formation figures are given, analysed as above, but space precludes their insertion here.

Value of Physical Increase in Stocks and Work in Progress
Most business firms will carry stocks of raw materials, components, work in progress and finished goods as part of their normal operations. Stockholding reduces the likelihood of production hold-ups due to unavailability of supplies and the risk of lost sales due to shortage of finished goods. When firms add to stocks they are assumed to be investing; in a sense they are considered to purchase from themselves. In this way output that is not sold to customers but stocked is matched by corresponding expenditure by the stockist. Additions to stocks therefore should be thought of as a special form of investment – investment in stocks.

Do not confuse a physical increase in stocks with stock appreciation. If goods remain in stock for any length of time and there is a degree of price inflation, their value will steadily appreciate so that when they come to be sold the market value of the sales will be higher than it would have been had they been sold immediately upon completion.

The sum of the four categories of expenditure dealt with so far gives a figure for total domestic expenditure at market prices. To convert this into gross national product we have to include foreign trade activities and taxation and subsidies.

Exports and Property Income from Abroad
A significant amount of purchasing of output is undertaken by overseas individuals and companies. This additional export demand must be added to domestic demand.

Imports and Property Income paid Abroad
Conversely some of the demand represented by the expenditure figures is for overseas production in the shape of imports. This import demand has to be deducted from the total.

At this stage the figure arrived at will be GNP at market prices. To convert it into GNP at factor cost we have to deduct expenditure taxes and add on subsidies. These are shown in the last two items of Exhibit 1.11.

MEASUREMENT OF INCOME

The third and final approach to measuring the national output is by the income method. In order to produce output, resources or factors of production have to be employed and this employment generates their income. Thus if we add together all the different categories of factor incomes we shall have yet another means of estimating the value of the country's national income.

We use the term "factor income" in order to emphasise that we are only interested in those incomes earned in employment. Other forms of incomes exist in the shape of transfer payments. A transfer payment is payment made to an invidual without there being any equivalent service given in exchange. Examples of transfer payments are pensions and social security payments. These are considered as income by the recipients but for our purpose they must be omitted from the calculation or else double counting would occur. Transfer payments have already been earned by someone else before being transferred from the earner by the government via the tax or social security system to the recipient. Their value entered into the national accounts at that time.

The sum of factor incomes in a firm is equivalent to the value added to output by that firm. We have already met the concept of added value in our discussion of the output approach. Let us have another look at it. Suppose that a firm sells its annual output of 100,000 units at £1 each and suppose that there are no stocks at the beginning or the end of the year. The value of its output is thus 100,000 × £1 = £100,000. Now if it pays out £50,000 for materials and other supplies, there is another £50,000 left with which to pay wages and salaries, interest on outstanding borrowing, rent or rates on its property and dividends to its shareholders. All of these payments, of course, are forms of income to the recipients. The same applies to the whole economy.

Therefore value added can be broken down into a series of factor payments which from the factors' point of view are income for the services rendered to the firm. Earlier in the chapter we said that the sum of the added values was equal to national output or product. We can now say that the sum of the added values is also equal to national income. Therefore it follows that national product and national income are identical.

In Exhibit 1.16 are presented details of the various categories of income.

	1963	1973
Income from employment	18,195	42,890
Income from self-employment	2,207	6,244
Gross trading profits of companies	4,103	8,476
Gross trading surplus of public corporations and other public enterprises	932	2,194
Rent	1,592	4,894
Total domestic income before providing for depreciation and stock appreciation	27,029	64,698
less stock appreciation	−177	−3,111
Residual error	35	589
Gross domestic product at factor cost	26,887	62,176

(**Source:** National Income and Expenditure, 1963–1973, Table 1).

EXHIBIT 1.16

Bringing together the strands we see that conceptually the three measures of national income yield identical results; indeed we can say that there is an identity between the three: gross national product $\equiv$ gross national expenditure $=$ gross national income. All three are but different aspects of the same thing.

In this part of the chapter the student has been introduced to some of the statistics of national income and associated variables. The choice of material has to be subjective and cannot cover adequately the various aspects of the national accounts. The student is advised to get hold of the latest edition of the Blue Book and study in detail at least some of the statistical series contained therein in order to familiarise himself with the structure and coverage of the accounts. This book cannot be a substitute for such study.

Use of National Income statistics
We end this section with a brief look at some of the ways in which national income statistics can be used in a mixed economy such as the United Kingdom.

The passage of time sees successive governments increasing the degree of intervention in the economy in an attempt to attain the major objectives of full employment, price stability, balance of payments equilibrium and acceptable economic growth. If governments are going to attempt to regulate the economy it is obviously desirable that they should have as clear an idea as possible both of the present situation and also of the likely future trends. Economic planning requires fullest information. National income figures can provide valuable information about the current situation in the economy and a basis on which to make the necessary forecasts on which every plan must be based.

Use can be made of the information for purposes of reviewing performance, perhaps after a particular policy has been in operation for some time.

When preparing for the budget a Chancellor of the Exchequer will need information of the kind available in the national accounts to help him frame a relevant budget in terms of tax changes and government expenditure.

Industry too can make use of the published figures in a number of ways. Trends in expenditure and knowledge of expenditure patterns will form the basis of firms' planning for the future; who is buying and what types of things are being bought? Is the firm in a declining or an expanding industry?

Finally useful information is avilable on income distribution and changes in it. How are the various shares of the national cake changing?

We can only touch upon a small number of uses – the scope is tremendous.

THE CIRCULAR FLOW OF INCOME
Imagine a simple economy in which there is no government activity of any kind and which is not involved in any economic transaction with other countries. Because of the absence of trade between our model economy and others, in other words as all economic transactions take place within the state frontiers, such an economy is usually referred to as a closed economy. Our economy may be thought of as comprising two sectors. First there is a personal sector made up of households or consumers who own resources (factors of production) and make these available for use in production undertaken in the economy. This personal sector also performs a second important function, namely that of purchasing the goods and services produced with the income received as payment for the use of its resources in that production. Secondly there is the business or corporate sector whose job is to produce goods and provide services and whose only income or revenue is derived from the sale of those goods and services.

In our closed economy there will be generated two types of intersectoral flow. There will be flows of resources, for example manpower, from households to firms and of output from firms to households. These two are real flows represented in Exhibit 1.17 by the broken lines. Then there are income or monetary flows – household income from firms and business revenue (consumer spending) from households. These income flows are shown in the same Exhibit as unbroken lines. Following convention we use the symbol Y to denote household income and the symbol C to denote consumer expenditure or consumption as it is frequently called. H represents households – the private sector – and F represents firms – the business or corporate sector.

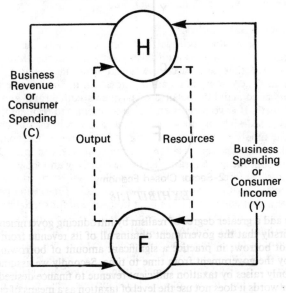

Real and Income Flows in an Economy

EXHIBIT 1.17

If we assume that each sector spends all that it receives from the other then there will be a continuous flow of income from firms to households to firms to households and so on; income will circulate throughout the economic system just as water in a central-heating system is continuously pumped from boiler to radiators and back again. Therefore at any moment the flow in any one part of the system will be exactly equal to that in any other part. (Remember that a "flow" concept relates to the value of some variable – in this case, income – over a particular period of time, so that in our system the flow would be measured as, say, £X per week, month or whatever). Thus there is equilibrium in the level of income: as long as the two sectors continue to spend all they receive there cannot be any change. In this equilibrium situation C = Y.

At this stage we can dispense with the real flows shown in Exhibit 1.17 and concentrate on the flows of income alone. In order to keep subsequent diagrams as clear and uncluttered as possible, in Exhibit 1.18 we have redrawn Exhibit 1.17

omitting the real flows and replacing the two income flow arrows with one, pointed at each end to represent flows in either direction.

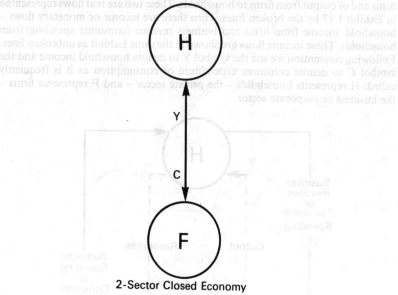

2-Sector Closed Economy

EXHIBIT 1.18

Now let us add a greater degree of realism by introducing government activity. We assume firstly that the government obtains all of its revenue from taxation, i.e. it does not borrow; in practice a significant amount of borrowing may be undertaken by the government from time to time. Secondly we assume that the government only raises by taxation sufficient revenue to finance desired expenditure – in other words it does not use the level of taxation as a means of controlling the level of activity in the economy. In real life this is an equally important function of taxation and will be dealt with in Chapter 17. Taxation may be imposed on both businesses, for example corporation tax, and on consumers, directly, for example income tax, and indirectly, for example value added tax. In Exhibit 1.19 we show tax revenue flowing to the government sector (G) from households and firms by the arrows marked T.

Government expenditure may be on goods and services purchased from the business sector such as military aircraft, construction materials, public lighting equipment, or in the form of salaries, for example to employees of central and local government such as civil servants, teachers and firemen. These flows of expenditure from the government are shown by the arrows marked G in Exhibit 1.19.

In the real world private individuals and companies will in total not spend all of their incomes, some will be saved. Let us make the simplifying assumption that all savings are invested in some way, in a building society, in a deposit account with a commercial bank, with an insurance company, unit trust and so on. We group together all such organisations and call them financial institutions (FI). This new FI sector is shown in Exhibit 1.20, the savings being channelled into this sector being represented by the S flows.

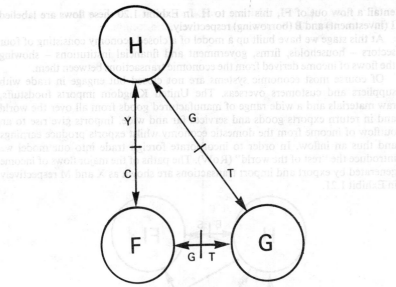

3-Sector Closed Economy

EXHIBIT 1.19

Financial institutions are at the same time sources of borrowed funds. Therefore any borrowing by firms, for example to finance investment, will be represented by a flow from FI to F. Similarly any household borrowing, such as hire purchase, bank loans and overdrafts and the use of credit cards, will also

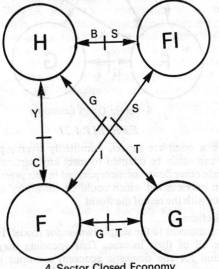

4-Sector Closed Economy

EXHIBIT 1.20

entail a flow out of FI, this time to H. In Exhibit 1.20 these flows are labelled I (investment) and B (borrowing) respectively.

At this stage we have built up a model of a closed economy consisting of four sectors – households, firms, government and financial institutions – showing the flows of income derived from the economic transactions between them.

Of course most economic systems are not closed but engage in trade with suppliers and customers overseas. The United Kingdom imports foodstuffs, raw materials and a wide range of manufactured goods from all over the world and in return exports goods and services far and wide. Imports give rise to an outflow of income from the domestic economy whilst exports produce earnings and thus an inflow. In order to incorporate foreign trade into our model we introduce the "rest of the world" (RoW). The paths of the major flows of income generated by export and import transactions are shown as X and M respectively in Exhibit 1.21.

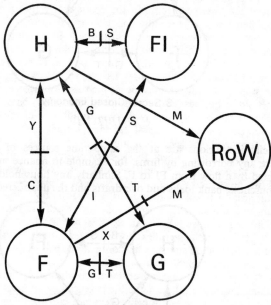

4-Sector Open Economy

EXHIBIT 1.21

Now we have a complete model, admittedly oversimplified, of a typical economy which can easily be adapted to meet any particular requirement and extended to include other flows not incorporated in this presentation, for example United Kingdom overseas aid which could be shown by an arrow linking the government sector with the rest of the world.

Leakages and Injections

Let us return for a moment to the simple two-sector model. In it we assumed that consumers spent all of their income. That spending may be thought of as generating demand for the domestic economy's output and since no other spending takes place aggregate (total) monetary demand consists only of, and is equal to, consumer expenditure; that is, $AMD = C = Y$.

If however for some reason consumers refrain from spending all of their income, then demand for output, and hence business receipts, will fall. Lower receipts will mean that firms will be unable to afford to hire factors of production in the quantities previously employed. Thus in the next period household income will fall. Given no further saving a new and lower equilibrium level of income will be established.

Suppose that the economy is initially in equilibrium with a level of consumer income and expenditure of £20m per period. Thus in any period t, households receive £20m which, we may assume, they spend in the next period, $t+1$; algebraically, $Y_t = C_{t+1} = £20m$.

If however in period $t+1$ consumers spend only £18m, then that becomes total business receipts in period $t+1$, and since firms can only spend what they have earned, the next round of firms' spending, leading to consumers' income in period $t+2$, will only total £18m. Thus the retention of £2m by individuals has reduced the level of income in the economy by that amount, and unless offset elsewhere (see later) the reduction will be permanent.

The activities of saving, spending on imports and paying out taxes all have this effect; at the time when they are undertaken they reduce the level of aggregate demand for the domestic economy's output and hence bring about a reduction in the flow of income. Such activities are known as leakages, outflows or losses from the system. A leakage may be defined as any income received by either the household or business sector and not (immediately) passed on to the other.

In a similar fashion, if initially there is equilibrium in the economy and for some reason extra, or new forms of, spending is undertaken, the effect will be to increase permanently the level of income.

Consider an economy where the level of consumer income and expenditure is again £20m per period. Now if we introduce export demand (X) aggregate demand for the economy's output will be boosted: $AMD = C + X$. The business sector will need to expand output in order to satisfy both domestic and overseas customers and to make this possible will engage extra resources (assuming that there is no spare capacity). It can do this because business revenue has increased by X. In turn the private sector will receive more income than previously, $Y + X$ rather than Y. A similar situation will occur if we introduce government spending and/or investment (borrowing).

The activities of exporting, government spending and investment are known as injections, inflows or additions to the circular flow of income, as undertaking them injects extra income, and hence demand, into the economy. An injection may be defined as any income received by either the household or business sector not directly from the other.

Equilibrium level of income in the simple two-sector model was said to exist where each sector spent all that it received. In the four-sector model equilibrium is achieved when total leakages equal total injections; algebraically, $(S+T+M) = (I+G+X)$[1]. Note that individual leakages do not have to equal corresponding injections, only that the totals must agree. If $(S+T+M)$ is less than $(I+G+X)$ there will be an increase in the flow and in activity and if $(S+T+M)$ is greater than $(I+G+X)$ there will be a reduction in the flow and in the level of activity. The application of this will be dealt with in Part 10 – The Government and the Economy – which discusses the methods by which the government may regulate the economy.

1. In a dynamic analysis, equilibrium requires that total expenditure in any one period be equal to income in the previous period: algebraically, $E_t = Y_{t-1}$.

National Income Determination

Chapter One showed how it is possible to measure national income in three ways, by totalling expenditure, income or output. The upper limit to the output (income) which a country is capable of producing at any time – the aggregate supply potential – is set by the stock of productive factors and their quality as we also saw in the same chapter. Whether or not this full potential is realised, however, will be determined by the level of aggregate demand in the economy and from overseas for its output. As Keynes demonstrated so clearly in the 1930's factories may be idle and labour unemployed simply because businessmen will sooner or later cut back on their current level of production if there is insufficient demand to justify that output. In this chapter we analyse the various components which together constitute aggregate demand in a typical economy.

CONSUMPTION

The most important component of aggregate demand is consumption or consumer spending. In the discussion of the circular flow of income it was shown that consumers' purchasing power derives directly from the income earned in employment. In addition we assumed initially, in the two-sector model, that consumers' spending accounted for all of their income. Later this assumption was dropped as we saw that saving and borrowing would occur and that taxes would be paid to, and perhaps income of some form received from, the government. So then, consumer spending is largely determined by the level of disposable income, that is income after tax. Besides disposable income, however, other factors are at work.

Many consumer purchases are not for cash but are financed by some form of credit; examples are hire purchase and credit sale transactions, use of credit cards, and straightforward borrowing from banks and other financial institutions. Credit purchasing increases over time so that one might look forward to an almost "cashless" society at some time in the future. At any particular time the amount of such purchasing will be largely determined by the availability and cost of credit: ready availability and low interest rates will encourage the use of credit.

A person's wealth, that is his stock of such assets as property, savings, and securities, is likely to influence the level of his expenditure. Wealth in a sense is a reservoir of purchasing power which can be tapped if need be. So we would expect a wealthy person to undertake higher levels of spending. Those who have at their disposal assets which may be readily turned into cash will be under less pressure to cut back on spending if they experience a reduction in their incomes.

Age also will help determine consumer spending patterns. Infants and young children spend nothing (their parents making up for it on their behalf!); schoolchildren spend but insignificantly; teenagers spend considerable amounts on a

relatively narrow range of articles, for example clothes, cosmetics, entertainment and sport; the twenties see the majority of people getting married, buying or renting accommodation and raising families, all involving great expense; finally we would expect older people to spend at relatively low levels.

Expectations have a part to play. If consumers expect future prices to be higher than present ones, current spending may be increased so that consumers benefit from today's relatively low prices. An opposite view is that current expenditure levels may be reduced so that income may be held in reserve for later purchases at higher prices.

In addition to these factors there may be other subjective or psychological pressures on spending. An example would be spending at relatively high levels for no reason other than to "keep up with the Jones's". Similarly movement into a better neighbourhood frequently results in the newcomer attempting to demonstrate his equality with existing residents through higher spending levels, particularly on ostentatious goods and services.

Of the factors mentioned by far the most important quantitatively is the level of disposable earned income and it is the relationship between spending and income that is highlighted in what follows.

The Consumption Function or Propensity to Consume

The relationship between consumer spending and the level of disposable earned income is known as the consumption function or propensity (tendency) to consume.

Average propensity to consume is the ratio of total consumption expenditure to total disposable income – the fraction of disposable income spent: $APC = \dfrac{C}{Y}$.

As any income not spent is saved, the twin concept of average propensity to save is defined as the ratio of total saving to total disposable income: $APS = \dfrac{S}{Y}$.

Marginal propensity to consume is the ratio of a change in consumer spending to a change in disposable income: $MPC = \dfrac{\Delta C}{\Delta Y}$, (" Δ " – delta – meaning "a change in . . ."). Similarly marginal propensity to save is the ratio of a change in saving to a change in disposable income: $MPS = \dfrac{\Delta S}{\Delta Y}$. It follows that, since all disposable income and any increase in it, is either disposed of by spending or by saving, $APC + APS = 1$ and $MPC + MPS = 1$. An example showing the calculation of propensities is given below in Exhibit 2.1 which summarises an individual household's income and spending behaviour in different years;

Income and Expenditure of a hypothetical Household

	Year 1	Year 2	Year 3
Y (£)	3,000	3,500	4,000
C (£)	2,800	3,000	3,100
S (£)	200	500	900
APC	$\dfrac{2,800}{3,000} = 0.93$	$\dfrac{3,000}{3,500} = 0.86$	$\dfrac{3,100}{4,000} = 0.77$

	Year 1	*Year 2*	*Year 3*
APS	$\dfrac{200}{3,000}=0.07$	$\dfrac{500}{3,500}=0.14$	$\dfrac{900}{4,000}=0.23$
MPC	—	$\dfrac{200}{500}=0.40$	$\dfrac{100}{500}=0.20$
MPS	—	$\dfrac{300}{500}=0.60$	$\dfrac{400}{500}=0.80$

EXHIBIT 2.1

In the example APC and MPC decline, and APS and MPS rise, as the absolute level of income increases. Although the figures used are hypothetical this is likely to be the case in real life. Low income families will need to spend most, if not all, of their income on the basic necessities of food, clothing and shelter whilst high income groups have no trouble in buying necessities and a range of luxuries, and still have some over for saving (perhaps the greatest luxury of them all). Exhibit 2.2 displays empirical American data showing this:

Disposable Income and Expenditure, US families, 1960's

Disposable Income ($)	Expenditure ($)	APC	APS
3,000	3,170	1·06	−0·06
4,000	4,110	1·03	−0·03
5,000	5,000	1·00	0·00
6,000	5,850	0·97	0·03
7,000	6,600	0·94	0·06
8,000	7,240	0·90	0·10
9,000	7,830	0·87	0·13
10,000	8,360	0·83	0·17
11,000	8,850	0·80	0·20

EXHIBIT 2.2

(**Source:** Adapted from P. A. Samuelson, Economics, McGraw-Hill).

Directly comparable data for the United Kingdom are not available but the periodic Family Expenditure Survey gives supporting sample data:

Household Income and Expenditure, UK families, 1972

Weekly Income (£)	Total Expenditure (£)*
Under 10	9·34
10 and under 15	14·21
15 and under 20	18·75
20 and under 25	23·47
25 and under 30	26·34
30 and under 35	29·66
35 and under 40	32·99
40 and under 45	35·19
45 and under 50	39·01

*less taxation and national insurance contributions, mortgage, life assurance and pension fund contributions and net betting payments.

Weekly Income (£)	Total Expenditure (£)*
50 and under 60	42·83
60 and under 80	52·21
Over 80	72·85

(Source: Family Expenditure Survey 1972, HMSO 1973, Table 1).

EXHIBIT 2.3

As we saw in Volume 1, Chapter 20, relationships between variables may be expressed in functional notation. Thus if consumption is linked to disposable income we write $C = f(Y_D)$. The function states only that there is a relationship, no more. An equation – an expression of equality between variables – goes one stage further than the function and specifies the manner in which the variables are related. Thus, for example, the function $r = f(s)$ is specified in the equation $r = 3s$ or, maybe, $r = s - 37$. In the same way the consumption function $C = f(Y_D)$ may be specified by an equation, for example $C = Y_D$. Here all income is spent. Instead of a ratio of 1:1 between spending and income, another consumer may spend only a fraction of his disposable income. If a constant fraction is spent the equation is of the form $C = bY_D$, where b is the fraction spent. For example if the consumer spends four-fifths of any income the equation is $C = 0·8Y_D$; in the equation $C = 0·75Y_D$ the value of b is three-quarters; in the equation $C = 0·5Y_D$ b is one-half. Given the value of either C or Y_D, it can be determined unreservedly from the relevant equation what is the value of the other variable. If disposable income is £3,000 and $C = 0·75Y_D$, spending is £2,250; if spending is £2,227 and $C = 0·5Y_D$, the level of disposable income is £4,454. An important feature of this type of relationship, $C = bY_D$, is that when disposable earned income is zero no spending at all will take place.

Observation confirms that this is unrealistic; even with zero earned income consumers will undertake spending at some level in order to maintain an acceptable minimum standard of living, such spending being financed by dissaving (using up previously accumulated savings or selling other assets), borrowing (hoping to be in a position to repay at some later date), or, in the case of many countries today, by some form of state financial assistance such as pensions, unemployment benefits, family allowances and other social security payments. To allow for this the equation of form $C = bY_D$ is expanded into the form $C = a + bY_D$ where a (some constant) represents the amount of purchasing undertaken at zero disposable income. Thus if a household with no earned income spent £600 per year and if, when it did earn, say £2,500, it spent 90% of it, its consumption function would be $C = £600 + (0·9 \times £2,500)$; £2,850 would be spent in all.

Both types of equation, $C = bY_D$ and $C = a + bY_D$, are known as linear equations because the graph depicting the values of variables in such equations is a straight line (see Exhibits 2.4 and 2.5). However as we have understood that at higher levels of income the fraction of any increase spent is less, b and Y must be inversely related. Where b varies in this way the resulting graph is non-linear (see Exhibit 2.6).

As just implied, a graph can be thought of as the geometric representation of an equation. In Exhibits 2.4, 2.5 and 2.6 are presented graphs of the three types of consumption function introduced in this chapter. Following statistical convention the dependent variable, consumption, is plotted on the ordinate and

* less taxation and national insurance contributions, mortgage, life assurance and pension fund contributions and net betting payments.

the independent variable, disposable income, on the abscissa. Common scales are used on each axis. Exhibit 2.4 shows graphs of three equations of the type $C=bY_D$, namely $C=0.5Y_D$, $C=0.75Y_D$ and $C=Y_D$. Note that all three go through the origin, illustrating what was said earlier about zero spending at zero income. The student will notice how the gradient of the consumption function curve steepens as the value of b increases.

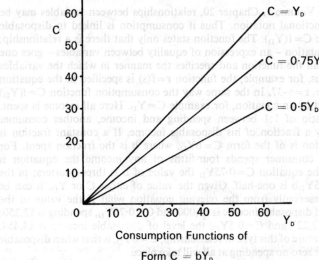

Consumption Functions of

Form $C = bY_D$

EXHIBIT 2.4

Exhibit 2.5 illustrates two equations of the form $C=a+bY_D$, namely $C=5+0.5Y_D$ and $C=10+0.75Y_D$. Note here that the graphs cut, not the origin, but the vertical axis at the values of a given in the equations.

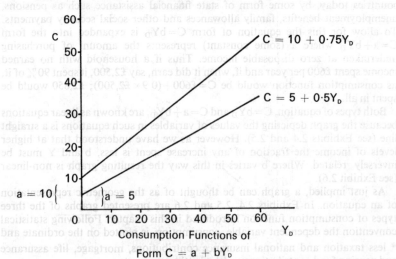

Consumption Functions of

Form $C = a + bY_D$

EXHIBIT 2.5

Finally, Exhibit 2.6 shows the graph of an equation, form $C = a + bY_D$, this time with a declining b.

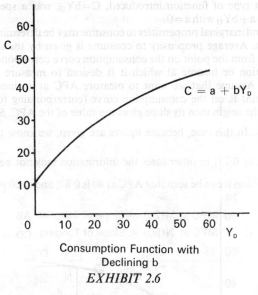

Consumption Function with
Declining b

EXHIBIT 2.6

Those readers with any statistical knowledge will have realised by now that a consumption function of the form $C = a + bY_D$ is equivalent to the general equation of a straight line, $y = a + bx$. In the equation of a straight line, a gives the value of the y variable when x is zero; a is the "y intercept" – the point where the graph meets the vertical (y) axis – and b is the slope of the line. Slope may be

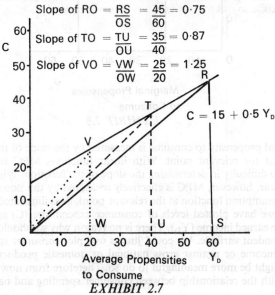

Slope of RO $= \dfrac{RS}{OS} = \dfrac{45}{60} = 0.75$

Slope of TO $= \dfrac{TU}{OU} = \dfrac{35}{40} = 0.87$

Slope of VO $= \dfrac{VW}{OW} = \dfrac{25}{20} = 1.25$

$C = 15 + 0.5\,Y_D$

Average Propensities
to Consume

EXHIBIT 2.7

thought of as the vertical distance through which the line rises for every unit move to the right along the horizontal axis. At the same time it will be realised that the first type of function introduced, $C=bY_D$, was a special case of the function $C=a+bY_D$ with $a=0$.

Average and marginal propensities to consume may be determined geometrically as follows. Average propensity to consume is given by the slope of the line to the origin from the point on the consumption curve corresponding to the level of consumption or income at which it is desired to measure APC. Consider Exhibit 2.7. Assume that we want to measure APC at an income of 60. If a line from point R on the consumption curve (corresponding to income of 60) is drawn to the origin then its slope gives the value of the APC. Slope is given by the ratio $\dfrac{RS}{OS}$. In this case, because figures are given, we know that this ratio is equal to $\dfrac{45}{60}$, or $0\cdot75$; in other cases the information may not be fully available. In similar fashion it can be seen that APC at 40 is $0\cdot87$, and at 20 is $1\cdot25$.

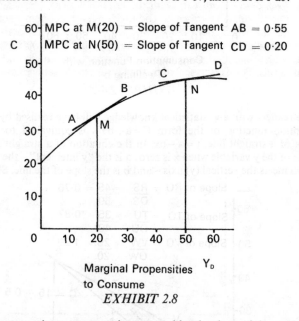

Marginal Propensities
to Consume
EXHIBIT 2.8

Marginal propensity to consume is measured by the slope of the consumption function at the relevant point. With linear functions MPC is constant, and there is no difficulty in determining the slope of the function. When the function is non-linear, however, MPC is effectively measured by the slope of the tangent to the consumption function at the relevant point, as is illustrated in Exhibit 2.8.

So far we have plotted levels of consumer expenditure (C) against levels of disposable earned income (Y_D). There is no reason why we should stick to Y_D as the independent variable. We could just as well plot consumer spending against national income or against gross national or domestic product, and in some cases it might be more meaningful to do so. Therefore from now on we shall be dealing with the relationship between consumer spending and national income.

In the diagrams we use the symbol Y to refer to national income or output. Y_F refers to that level of income produced when all of the country's productive factors are being fully utilised – Y_F is full employment income or output.

INVESTMENT

A second component of aggregate demand for an economy's output is investment demand. Remember that when economists talk about investment they are referring to that part of output that is not consumed directly but which, in the form of capital goods, will in turn help in the production of subsequent output of consumer (and other capital) goods.

As you may see from the chapter on economic growth, one of the problems faced by any society is how much present consumption should be sacrificed for investment purposes in order to enhance future output. In a sense the opportunity cost of investment is current consumption and vice versa; as resources are limited a balance has to be struck.

As with consumer spending the amount of investment which businessmen are prepared to undertake will vary with the level of activity (output). Investment is likely to be stimulated by rises in, and high levels of, economic activity, and is likely to decline when there are falls in, and low levels of, activity. Such a relationship is illustrated by the I_1 curve in Exhibit 2.9. However for simplicity we shall assume that a constant amount of investment is undertaken regardless of income levels. This is represented by the I_2 curve in the same Exhibit.

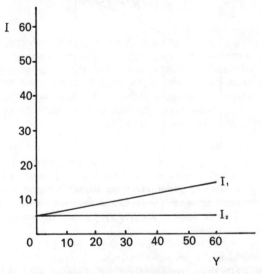

Investment Functions

EXHIBIT 2.9

The introduction of this second component means that aggregate demand now consists of consumption and investment, a situation shown in Exhibit 2.10 where the I_2 curve of Exhibit 2.9 has been added to the consumption function $C = 10 + 0.33Y$, to give the aggregate demand curve $C + I$.

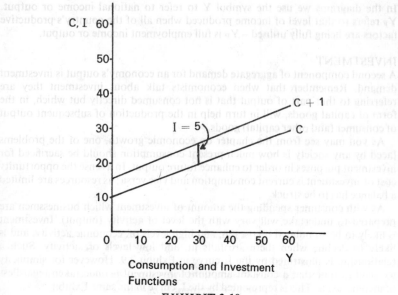

Consumption and Investment
Functions

EXHIBIT 2.10

GOVERNMENT EXPENDITURE

Apart from demand generated by the household and production sectors, further demand will be created by government expenditure. Again, for simplicity's sake, we assume that there is an unchanging level of government expenditure equal to 10. A separate government expenditure function could be drawn, as was done in the case of investment in Exhibit 2.9, but we omit this stage and show in Exhibit 2.11 the new aggregate demand function, now consisting of consumption, investment and government expenditure.

EXPORT DEMAND

If we are considering a closed economy, then aggregate demand consists of the three components so far dealt with and the C+I+G curve of Exhibit 2.11 will be the aggregate demand curve. However if the economy is an open one we must add to internal demand, C+I+G, net demand for the economy's output from overseas. This is done in Exhibit 2.12 where net export demand, X, is added to domestic demand.

EQUILIBRIUM LEVEL OF INCOME

Students will (hopefully!) remember that the graph of the function $C = Y_D$ is a straight line bisecting the origin, given that the same scales are used for plotting both C and Y_D. (Take another look at Exhibit 2.4 if you are unsure). Let us now ignore the fact that this "45° line" may be a consumption function in its own right and use it simply as a guideline to help determine the equilibrium level of income. Since any point on the 45° line represents spending equal to income, the point of intersection of a consumption function and the 45° guideline will be the "break-even" point for that consumption function; at that level all income will be spent. That particular level of income is the equilibrium level. It is

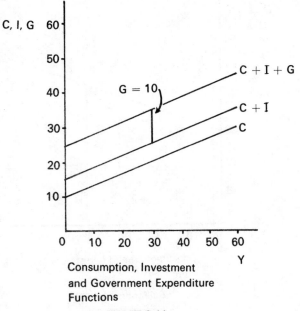

Consumption, Investment
and Government Expenditure
Functions

EXHIBIT 2.11

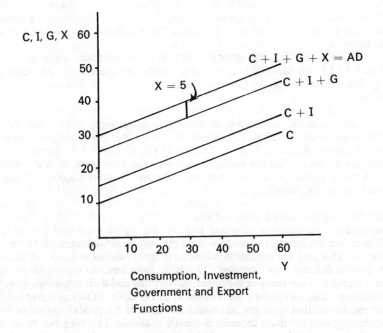

Consumption, Investment,
Government and Export
Functions

EXHIBIT 2.12

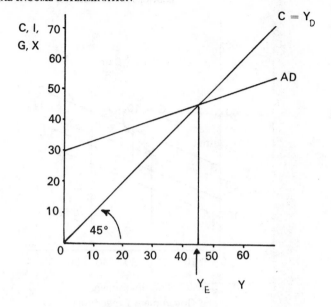

Equilibrium Income

EXHIBIT 2.13

illustrated in Exhibit 2.13 where the guideline is super-imposed upon the aggregate demand function of Exhibit 2.12. Here equilibrium income is 45, Y_E in the diagram.

To sum up so far: the aggregate demand (consumption) curve – AD in Exhibit 2.13 – shows what the level of spending (demand) in the economy will be at any level of income (output); actual output will be determined by, and equal to, spending.

Consider Exhibit 2.14. In this situation spending and output, or demand and income, are in equilibrium at Y_E. Y_E is the value of output that will be produced in the economy. Suppose for a moment that actual output is not Y_E but Y_1. Here spending, Y_1A, is insufficient to purchase all of current output OY_1 ($= Y_1M$) and output equal to AM will remain unsold. The production sector will sooner or later react to this situation of unsold stocks by cutting back on output, stage by stage, until it matches the level of demand, that is Y_E: output is eventually reduced by the amount Y_EY_1. Now consider what would happen if actual output were initially Y_2. At Y_2 aggregate demand, Y_2B, out-strips available supplies of goods and services by an amount equal to OB. The imbalance between demand and output will cause businessmen to expand output. This they will do until equilibrium is again reached at Y_E, at which level aggregate demand is just satisfied. (This is the same analysis as that put forward in Volume 1 in our study of the behaviour of firms and their customers from the microeconomic viewpoint – see Volume 1, p. 199–200). In this paragraph it has been assumed that there are no obstacles to prevent the production sector from increasing output: spare capacity is readily available. This may not be so in a particular case. If, at an output of Y_2, all of an economy's resources are being

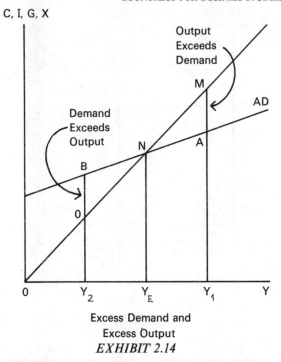

Excess Demand and
Excess Output
EXHIBIT 2.14

utilised then the effect of excess aggregate demand will be rising prices rather than increasing output.

Equilibrium level of income may also be illustrated with the aid of savings functions rather than consumption functions, although in the following diagrams the consumption function is included for comparison purposes. Where the consumption function is of the form $C = a + bY_D$ the associated savings function will be of the form $S = -a + (1 - b)Y_D$. We have seen that "a" is the amount of consumption purchasing undertaken at zero disposable income and we said that this amount could be thought of as dissaving or negative saving; hence "$-a$" in the savings function. As "b" represents the fraction of income that is spent, that is the propensity to consume, the fraction not spent, $(1 - b)$, must be the fraction saved. Therefore the propensity to save is represented by $(1 - b)$.

The consumption function $C = 10 + 0.75Y_D$ and its associated savings function $S = -10 + 0.25Y_D$ are shown in Exhibit 2.15. Equilibrium income is that income corresponding to either the intersection of the consumption function and the 45° line or the intersection of the savings function and the horizontal axis, in this case 40. Where the consumption function intersects the 45° line, $C = Y_D$ and savings must be zero; this is also shown by the fact that the savings function itself equals zero at an income level of 40.

Exhibit 2.16 shows together an aggregate demand function consisting of consumer expenditure and investment demand and the associated savings and investment functions. Here equilibrium level of income is determined by either the intersection of the aggregate demand function and the 45° line or the intersection of the savings and investment functions In this case equilibrium level

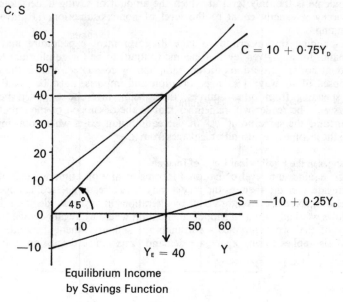

Equilibrium Income
by Savings Function

EXHIBIT 2.15

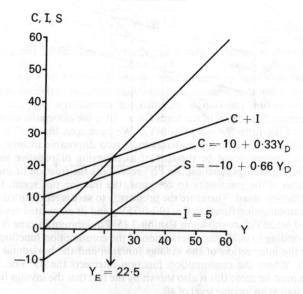

Equilibrium Income
by Savings and Investment
Functions

EXHIBIT 2.16

of income is the only level at which the amount of saving undertaken in the economy is exactly equal to the level of non-consumption (i.e. investment) spending.

Expanding this assertion to take in government expenditure and export demand, for any given level of income (output) to be the equilibrium level the amount not spent on domestic consumption by consumers, that is the amount disposed of by way of savings, taxation and imports, must be exactly offset by spending from other sources, these being investment, government and overseas. The reader will remember that in the discussion of the circular flow of income the same point was made: equilibrium exists when total injections into the income flow just offset leakages from it.[1]

Changes in the Equilibrium Level of Income

If the equilibrium level of national income at any one time is determined by aggregate demand then, as the reader may have already guessed, changes in the level of income are brought about by alterations in aggregate demand. In what follows we shall assume a simplified situation where aggregate demand consists only of the two components consumption and investment demand, but the analysis applies to any aggregate demand "mix". The discussion is linked to Exhibit 2.17.

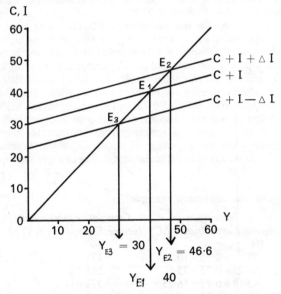

Changes in Equilibrium Income

EXHIBIT 2.17

Initially the equilibrium level of income (output) is Y_{E1}, 40, since that income corresponds to the point of intersection of the curve C+I and the 45° line. Now suppose that for some reason businessmen decide to increase their investment projects expenditure by 5. The effect on the aggregate demand curve is to

1. Or, more strictly, on a dynamic basis, equilibrium exists when expenditure in one period equals the income of the previous period.

raise it vertically through a distance equal to 5 measured on the vertical axis to the new position shown in Exhibit 2.17 as the $C+I+\Delta I$ curve. The new equilibrium point is E_2 rather than E_1 and the new equilibrium level of income is Y_{E2}, 46.6. Next consider the effect of a decline in investment. Suppose that instead of the (unspecified) investment undertaken initially, businessmen decide to cut back on investment by 7.5 at all levels of income. As a result of this change in business behaviour the aggregate demand function, $C+I$, shifts downwards by 7.5 to its new $C+I-\Delta I$ position. Consequently equilibrium income is reduced from the initial level of 40 to a new and lower level, Y_{E3}, of 30, corresponding to the new point of intersection E_3.

The Multiplier

It will be noticed from the foregoing discussion of changes in equilibrium income levels that in both cases the magnitude of the change was greater than the change in investment demand causing it. This effect is known as the multiplier: the initial change is multiplied by some factor into a final bigger change. Thus in Exhibit 2.17 an increase in investment of 5 raises national income by 6·6, and a decline in investment of 7·5 reduces national income by 10. In each case the initial change has been multiplied by 1·33 – we shall see why later. We define the multiplier as the ratio of the final overall change in national income to the initial change which caused it.

Out of any extra income received some will be spent and some will be saved; the exact proportions being determined by the marginal consumption and saving propensities. That spent will be received by others who in turn will spend a proportion and save the rest; and so the process continues until it peters out. The chain reaction of the multiplier can be shown in an arithmetic example as in Exhibit 2.18. For illustrative convenience it is assumed that all groups in the economy have a common MPC of 0·75, and hence a common MPS of 0·25; that is three-quarters of any extra income will be spent and one-quarter saved. We postulate that the economy is suffering from considerable unemployment; a new government adopts a policy of increasing unemployment and other social security payments to avoid social unrest. The chain of events is summarised below in Exhibit 2.18.

The Multiplier – an arithmetic example

Stage	Increase in Income/Expenditure (ΔC)	Cumulative increase in Income/Expenditure (ΔY)
1	100	100
2	$75 = 0·75 \times 100$	175
3	$56·25 = 0·75 \times 75$	231·25
4	$42·18 = 0·75 \times 56·25$	273·43
5	$31·63 = 0·75 \times 42·18$	305·06
6	$23·72 = 0·75 \times 31·63$	328·78
7	$17·79 = 0·75 \times 23·72$	346·57
8	$13·34 = 0·75 \times 17·79$	359·91
9	$10·00 = 0·75 \times 13·34$	369·91
10	$7·50 = 0·75 \times 10·00$	377·41 (total spending at stage 10)
↓	↓	↓
Final	399·99 recurring	399·99 recurring

EXHIBIT 2.18

To begin with there is an increase in government spending of 100. This means than 100 worth of extra purchasing power is injected into the economy for the benefit of the unemployed and their families. These people spend 75 and save 25. At stage three the recipients of the 75 spent by the unemployed and their families spend 56·25 and save 18·25. The process continues until the total new spending in the economy has reached 399·99; in practice this can be rounded off to 400.

A geometric presentation of the multiplier effect is given in Exhibit 2.19. Exhibit 2.19A repeats the above situation, showing the increase in government expenditure as a shift in the C+G function to the C+G+ ΔG position. From the horizontal axis it can be seen that income increases from 400 to 800.

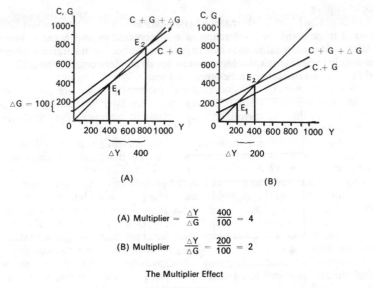

(A) Multiplier $= \dfrac{\Delta Y}{\Delta G} \quad \dfrac{400}{100} = 4$

(B) Multiplier $\dfrac{\Delta Y}{\Delta G} = \dfrac{200}{100} = 2$

The Multiplier Effect

EXHIBIT 2.19

The size of the multiplier depends upon the MPC (or MPS). The symbol "k" is frequently used to represent the multiplier and its value is given by the formula, $k = \dfrac{1}{MPS}$. Since we have already seen that MPS and MPC must always add to 1, an alternative version of the formula is $k = \dfrac{1}{1 - MPC}$. The greater the propensity to consume the more of any increased income is passed on and the greater the final increase; the smaller the propensity to consume the less any increased income is passed on to others and so the smaller the final increase. This can be shown by reworking Exhibit 2.18 with a marginal propensity to consume of 0·5, when the final increase will be equal to 200. (Rework the example and check your result). Exhibit 2.19B shows the change geometrically: income rises from 200 to 400. In Exhibit 2.19A the value of the multiplier is 4; $k = \dfrac{1}{MPS} = \dfrac{1}{0·25}$; in Exhibit 2.19B the value of the multiplier is 2; $k = \dfrac{1}{MPS} = \dfrac{1}{0·5}$. Now refer back to Exhibit

2.17; earlier it was stated that the eventual change was 1·33 times greater than the initial change – now we can see why this was so. Examination of the aggregate demand function shows that the marginal propensity to consume is 0·25; therefore the marginal propensity to save is 0·75. The value of the multiplier in this case will then be $\frac{1}{0·75}$ or 1·33.

So far we have been dealing with what is really a simplified version of the multiplier. We have assumed that whatever extra income is not saved is returned to the income flow in the domestic economy. We know that there are other leakages and a more realistic multiplier formula must be based on all of these. The major leakages recognised are savings, taxation and imports. Therefore a fuller multiplier formula is $k = \dfrac{1}{MPS + MPT + MPM}$, where MPT is the marginal propensity to be taxed, or the fraction of any increased income taken in taxes, and MPM is the marginal propensity to spend on imports, or the fraction of any increase in income that is spent on imported goods and services. Exhibit 2.20 is a diagrammatic representation of these propensities.

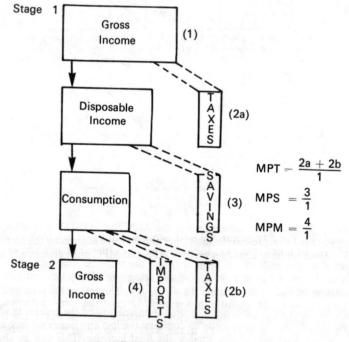

Taxation, Savings
and Import Propensities

EXHIBIT 2.20

Taken together MPS, MPT and MPM are sometimes referred to as the marginal propensity to leak or to withdraw (!), that is the marginal propensity to leak or withdraw income from the domestic flow; in other words the fraction

of an increase in income that does not find its way back to the domestic production sector. It has been estimated by M. C. Kennedy that on this basis the value of the United Kingdom multiplier is 1·45. Two final points on the multiplier: firstly, the multiplier may be described in terms of variables other than income; in fact when the concept was first introduced in 1931 by R. F. Kahn it was applied to employment, the argument being that if the government could find work for, say, an extra 100,000 men, the final increase in employment would be greater than this, say 400,000. Secondly, remember that the multiplier also works in reverse so that if for any reason there is a drop in the level of income or employment the end result will be even worse.

Full Employment and Equilibrium Income

There is no reason why equilibrium level of income should correspond with full employment income, defined as that amount of income (output) generated when the country's resources are being utilised to the fullest extent,

Consider Exhibit 2.21A. Equilibrium income (Y_E) is less than full capacity

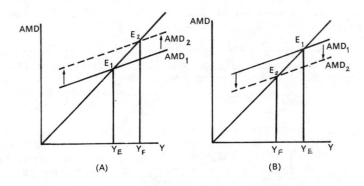

Equilibrium Income and Full Employment

EXHIBIT 2.21

output (Y_F), since aggregate demand expressed in monetary terms (AMD) is insufficient to take off the market that level of output. The implication is that potential output of $Y_E Y_F$ is being lost and the resources that would be used to produce this are either idle or, at best, are being inefficiently underutilised in the production of Y_E.

The solution to the situation is somehow to raise the level of demand from Y_E to Y_F; geometrically, the aggregate monetary demand curve needs to be raised vertically from the AMD_1 to the AMD_2 position so that it intersects the 45° guide line not at E_1 but instead at E_2, corresponding to full employment output. Measures must be undertaken which will stimulate total spending for the economy's goods.

The opposite situation is represented by Exhibit 2.21B. Here the level of aggregate demand, in terms of money, is greater than the value of output expressed in current prices by the amount $Y_F Y_E$. In order to restrain inflationary pressures (see Chapter Three) there is a need to reduce aggregate demand until equilibrium coincides with Y_F.

Part One

NATIONAL INCOME AND EXPENDITURE

Chapter Three

Inflation

REAL AND MONEY INCOMES

The value of money is measured by the quantity of goods and services that can be bought at the current price level with a given amount of it – its purchasing power in terms of commodities. A housewife may consider the value of money to mean what everyday articles she can buy with each £1 of her weekly house-keeping budget; to a businessman the value of money will be measured in terms of what labour input he can buy at a particular wage rate or what quantities of materials or advertising he can get with a given outlay. Therefore the value of money depends upon the prices of goods; in fact it will vary inversely with the general level of prices in the economy.

If prices rise the purchasing power of money falls; if prices fall, purchasing power rises. For example when the unit price of any commodity X is 4p, £1 will buy 25. If the price rises to 5p, £1 will now buy only 20 units; if it falls to 2p, the buyer can get 50 units. In the first case a 25% price increase reduces the value of money by 20%; in the second a price reduction of 50% increases the purchasing power of £1 by 100%.

In practice the value of money is measured by reference to a selection of prices rather than to just one as was done in the last paragraph. This is achieved by the use of index numbers which represent changes in the average prices of a selection of goods and services bought by the majority of households. Such an index is the United Kingdom Index of Retail Prices, published monthly. Index number changes are the key to computing changes in the value of money in an advanced economy. A discussion of index numbers is outside the scope of this book – students for whom it is primarily intended will cover, or will have covered, the topic of index numbers in a course of statistics – but a simple example may help. Suppose that an index of retail prices (a cost of living index) stands at 100 in period 1 and rises to 110 in period 2; then prices on average have risen by 10%. In order to purchase in period 2 a quantity of goods equivalent to that bought in period 1, 10% more money will be needed; alternatively a given amount of money in period 1 will buy only $\frac{100}{110}(= 90\cdot9\%)$ as much as in the earlier period.

Real income, like the real value of money, means the amount of goods and services that one's money income can purchase.

INFLATION

Inflation is said to exist when prices in general are rising. We may define inflation as a sustained and appreciable rise in the general price level. Following from this, inflation means that there will be a fall in the value or purchasing power of money. The opposite to inflation is deflation, a fall in the general price level and a consequent increase in the value of money.

As suggested a little earlier the rate of inflation can be gauged by measuring the change in the cost of living with reference to some suitable index. Exhibit 3.1 shows how the cost of living in Britain has risen over the period 1962 – 1975.

Retail Price Index, 1962–1975; figures for January each year.
(*January 1962 = 100*)

1962	1963	1964	1965	1966	1967	1968	1969	1970	1971
100·0	102·7	104·7	109·5	114·3	118·5	121·6	129·1	135·5	147·0

1972	1973	1974	1975
159·0	171·3	191·8	229·9

(**Source:** Department of Employment Gazette, February 1975).

EXHIBIT 3.1

Degrees
Economists recognise various degrees or types of inflation. Although there is no general agreement as to the precise distinction between the various degrees, a rough idea is given below.
(1) *Creeping inflation.* This is a situation where there is an underlying tendency for prices to rise steadily but continually. The annual rate of inflation is no greater than 3% or thereabouts.
(2) *Moderate inflation.* This is of the order of 3% to 6% each year. At these rates peoples' expectations of further price increases in the future stimulate their current demand for goods and services which in turn leads to further demand inflation. There is the danger that inflation at these rates will become self-generating.
(3) *Rapid or galloping inflation.* Once the rate of inflation has risen to 6% or 7%, there will be significant hardship for those whose incomes are relatively fixed such as pensioners. Export prices may rise out of line with overseas prices and lead to problems with the balance of payments. Industry will be uncertain as to the future course of events; fixed price tendering will disappear, investment plans will be shelved and perhaps production cut back as inventory levels are reduced.
(4) *Hyperinflation.* Hyperinflation probably exists when price rises are in excess of about 15% annually and getting out of hand. Business confidence will fade away. The monetary system is likely to break down as people lose faith in money's ability to perform its functions efficiently. Savings, if they occur at all, will be in non-monetary assets. Such a hyperinflation occurred in Germany in 1923. An indication of its severity is given in Exhibit 3.2, which shows how the currency unit, the mark, depreciated in value.
This is bad enough but it is not the worst that has happened. In 1945–6 Hungary experienced an even more chaotic situation. During that period prices on average rose each month by 200 times. In the worst month of all they rose by 42 thousand million million times! (For a note on this see Money International by Fred Hirsch, Allen Lane The Penguin Press, London 1967, p99).
One hopes that governments and people will never let there be a repetition of such chaos in the future. The problem is, however, that inflation feeds on itself and unless it is effectively checked from the beginning, moderate inflation may develop into hyperinflation almost before anyone realises what is happening. Recent British experience has shown that governments may not be willing to adopt effective counter-inflationary policies for various reasons including

Depreciation of the German mark, January 1920 – November 1923

Date	(1)	(2)
January 1913	1	1
January 1920	15·4	12·6
January 1921	15·4	14·4
January 1922	45·7	36·7
January 1923	4,279	2,785
July 1923	84,150	74,787
October 1923	6,014,300,000	7,095,800,000
November 1923	1,000,000,000,000	750,000,000,000

Column 1: Mark exchange rate against the American dollar.
Column 2: Wholesale price index.
(Source: Sunday Telegraph, 22 November 1970).

EXHIBIT 3.2

electoral; even when they are prepared to do so, there is opposition from a public unappreciative of the need for them.

Causes

It is widely accepted that there are three causes of inflation: increases in costs, excess demand pressure and certain government activities. However once an inflationary situation has developed it may be difficult or impossible to distinguish the cause with any precision since inflation tends to be self-generating and self-perpetuating. The well-known inflationary spiral develops, with every new cost increase or demand-induced price increase giving it a further twist.

Cost Increases

In some cases inflation is due to increases in costs, either internal or external to the economy. The resulting inflation is known as "cost inflation" or "cost-push inflation".

One internal source of cost inflation is an increase in any factor income unmatched by a corresponding improvement in productivity. Recent British figures are given in Exhibit 3.3; the student is left to draw his own conclusions.

Output and Costs in Manufacturing, 1965–1973

	1965	1966	1967	1968	1969	1970	1971	1972	1973
Output per person	100·0	101·7	105·4	113·2	116·0	117·1	120·5	127·5	137·3
Labour cost per unit output	100·0	104·6	103·0	103·4	110·3	125·3	136·8	148·5	157·1

(Source: Department of Employment Gazette, February 1975, rebased on 1965 by author).

EXHIBIT 3.3

If wages, one of a firm's production costs, rise faster than productivity the firm will adjust its prices to cover the differential. A particular group of workers may obtain a wage increase through higher productivity. In this case the increase in wages is presumably justifiable, although one should bear in mind that productivity improvements frequently do not result from more intense labour effort but rather from more and better capital equipment. However what tends to happen is that justifiable increases in one sector of industry are often the

cause of other unjustifiable ones elsewhere. The reason may be the desire to maintain comparability or differentials. Suppose that two groups of workers, A and B, initially earn equal wages. Now let A gain an increase through a productivity deal. B will want to maintain comparability with A and to this end will try to secure an equivalent rise in its wages. Again let two other groups, C and D, be initially satisfied with a wage differential; say that group C's wages are 10% higher than those of group D. Now, because of productivity gains, D gets 8% extra narrowing the gap to 2%. C may try to restore the earlier differential by asking for an extra 8% although there is no productivity justification. The pressure is even greater if the two groups work in the same firm or plant than it is if they merely work in the same industry. Each group thinks that it deserves the same as the other is getting. This "wage-wage" spiral accounts for much recent inflationary pressure in the United Kingdom. The problem is that no one group is prepared to make do with a more modest settlement. Trade union negotiators will appear weak if they accept an agreement giving lower rises than their colleagues have won.

"Wage-push" inflation may occur as wage increases gained in firms or industries where the labour force is strongly unionised spread to non-unionised firms or industries. Managements in firms whose employees do not belong to unions may feel under pressure to match union-won increases in order to prevent unrest and discontent, to discourage their employees from becoming union members ("Union members don't get any higher wages!") and to prevent their employees from leaving to join unionised firms.

Some idea of the contribution of labour costs to recent British inflation can be gained from the work of the Price Commission. In their report for the three-month period to the end of November 1974, published in January 1975, the Commission states that increases in labour costs accounted for no less than 60% of all price rises notified to it.

Certain costs may sometimes be held down at artificially low levels as a result of government policy; any policy change allowing these to rise will have inflationary consequences. In the November 1974 budget the Chancellor of the Exchequer announced that the government were anxious to remove as fast as possible the subsidies that had been made available to the nationalised industries, particularly to the nationalised energy industries, which were then running at an annual rate of £1,000mn. The subsidies had been provided for price restraint as part of earlier government anti-inflationary policy. It was now felt that the

Food Subsidies

Product	Date introduced	Rate (Jan. '75)	Annual Cost (£mn)
Bread	March '74	3p a large loaf	79
Butter	April '74	9p a lb.	60
Cheese	May '74	12p a lb.	59
Household flour	Sep. '74	1p a lb.	8
Milk	April '74	2½p a pint	335
Tea	Sep. '74	8p a lb.	30
Total			571

(**Source:** Financial Times, 22 January 1975)

EXHIBIT 3.4

artificially low prices were leading to excessive demand for energy which, in the light of the world-wide energy problem and of Britain's balance of payments situation, was undesirable. The removal of some £400mn energy subsidy would mean a transition to a more realistic pricing policy and lead to energy conservation. However it would also lead to widespread price increases and the government had to try to strike an acceptable balance between phasing out subsidies and the rate of increase in consumer prices. Other subsidies were given throughout 1974 to the food sector. Details of these are given in Exhibit 3.4.

The phasing out of these would increase the cost of living by £571mn and lead to increased pressure for wage rises to offset that increase.

Not all cost inflation is generated internally, that is by increases in domestic costs. Sometimes the initial cause lies in price increases in imported commodities. Britain imports a large proportion of her total raw material and fuel requirements and any increase in the cost of these basic inputs will work its way throughout the system.

A recent example of escalating overseas costs is the fivefold increase in oil prices that occurred during 1974. In 1974 Britain paid to the oil producers £2,500 mn extra for 5% less oil than in 1973. The result of such an increase in costs is of course widespread and serious; to quote the Chancellor of the Exchequer in his budget speech to the House of Commons on 12 November 1974:

"The effects of this colossal sum feed through directly not only into the costs of energy, light, heating and transport but also into anything made of plastic, from packaging to kitchen equipment. The indirect effects are felt in the price of almost everything we buy."

If a country devalues its currency, exports become relatively less expensive and imports become relatively more expensive; therefore devaluation will lead to cost inflation. In 1967 the British government devalued the pound by 14·3% from £1 = US $2·80 to £1 = US $2·40. Prices of our exports in dollar values fell by 14·3% whilst our imports rose in price by 16·7%, as the following example shows.[1]

Ignoring transport and other costs an article priced at £1 would have a pre-devaluation dollar price of $2·80. After devaluation its dollar price fell to $2·40. This fall of 40 cents represented a percentage reduction of $\frac{40}{280} \times 100 = 14\cdot3\%$.

On the other hand an imported American product whose dollar price before devaluation was $2·80 sold in Britain for £1. After devaluation £1 would buy only $\frac{240}{280}$ ths of it; an extra $\frac{40}{240}$ ths of £1, namely 16·7 pence, would be necessary to buy the "whole" article. In actual fact because British exports contain many previously imported inputs, and since the sterling price of these rose after devaluation, the final reduction in export prices was much less than 14·3%, probably in the 8% to 10% range.

In the same way the floating of the £ sterling in June 1972 led to an effective increase in import prices once more, as the £ floated down on the foreign exchange markets.

Cost increases need not necessarily lead to inflation; at least it may be possible to dampen their effect. If businessmen and shareholders are willing, some or all of the cost increases which a firm has to meet may be absorbed in reduced profit margins. Such a course of action is, however, unlikely; these people will be as

1. On the assumption that suppliers at home and abroad did not adjust their pre-devaluation prices to offset the effects of the devaluation.

keen to maintain their previous real earnings as any other group. So it is to be expected that firms will raise prices. This should present little difficulty to the firm in an inflationary situation unless it is operating under one or more of the following conditions:

(1) demand for its output is elastic; in this case price rises are likely to cause customers to switch to alternative suppliers;

(2) price controls have been imposed by the government, as in Britain in 1973; or

(3) much of its output is sold overseas; if this is so, the firm may be unable to raise prices and remain competitive (unless of course there is significant inflation in its export markets too).

Excess Demand

A second major cause of inflationary pressure is excess demand. The inflation so caused is known as "demand inflation" or "demand-pull inflation". Excess demand means that at the present price level the quantities that consumers are willing to buy are greater than the amounts being produced, or, more briefly, at the current price demand exceeds supply. In other words there is disequilibrium in the market and in a free market situation the disequilibrium will be corrected by a rise in the price level (inflation). Excess demand may arise in the market for labour or for goods. Let us look at its operation in the labour market first.

Where there is general full employment firms needing to fill existing vacancies will be tempted to offer wages above the going rate, thereby hoping to attract labour away from its present occupations. The same thing will happen where a particular skill is in short supply relative to the demand for it. It will probably be easy for firms to recoup these higher costs by raising the prices of their output. (This particular cause makes it difficult to distinguish between cost-push and demand-pull inflation; demand causes incomes to rise but higher incomes in turn become an increasing cost of production. Higher wages lead initially to cost-induced inflation but may later create inflationary pressure on the demand side as they are spent on goods and services).

Similar results occur in the markets for goods. An increase in aggregate demand for output, unless it is offset by an immediate and equiproportionate increase in production, will raise the price level if there is general price stability to start with or will accelerate any existing inflation. Sometimes there is spare capacity in the economy which can be brought into operation to satisfy increased demand. Pressure on prices will be less if this is so; elastic supply will expand when stimulated by demand increases to satisfy those higher levels of demand with perhaps only a small consequential rise in prices. On the other hand developed economies are likely to be operating at near-full employment most of the time; where this is so, an increase in aggregate demand will lead to only marginally higher output, there being few if any idle resources available and consequently relatively inelastic supply. The effect of higher levels of demand will make itself felt in the form of higher prices.

These two situations are illustrated in Exhibit 3.5. In Exhibit 3.5A, there is an initial equilibrium level of income at Y_{E1}, well below full-employment income Y_F. Increased aggregate demand raises output from Y_{E1} to Y_{E2} with perhaps a modest increase in the general price level. In Exhibit 3.5B, equilibrium income coincides with full-employment income, Y_{F1}, and any further increase in demand cannot bring forth extra output. Y_{F1} increases to Y_{F2}, but only in money terms – there is no real increase.

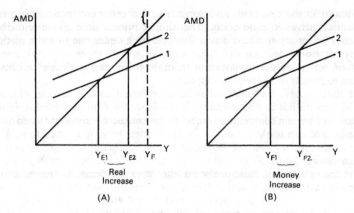

Real and Money Increases in National Income

EXHIBIT 3.5

How does an increase in aggregate demand come about? Well, although it may derive from an increase in any component of demand, the most likely source will be increases in consumer spending or in government expenditure. The public may be earning and spending higher incomes. Even with no increase in incomes a change in spending and saving behaviour may lead to an expansion in demand. For example a rise in the average propensity to consume will boost demand. Also demand may be stimulated by wider use of credit facilities. The role of the government is dealt with later.

A variation of demand-pull inflation is known as "bottleneck inflation". Here there is again an excess of demand over supply, but this time, instead of being due to increased demand, it is because of shortages in the supply sector. Shortages of labour or materials can hold back production of final goods. These bottlenecks eventually cause inflationary price increases. Lengthy strikes may have the same effect; war most certainly will. In wartime resources have to be diverted away from consumption goods to production for the war effort. The government will probably introduce rationing as a means of avoiding black market situations; this will have varying degrees of success. After the war pent-up purchasing power will be released, there will still be shortages as the economy cannot immediately return to a peacetime footing, and the result is inflation.

Government
Thirdly inflation may arise from certain government actions or policies. Taxation, although it may be used to combat inflationary pressure in the economy by reducing demand, may itself be inflationary. An increase in taxation on incomes will leave people worse off and they may react by seeking wage rises enabling them to maintain previous standards. Raising expenditure taxes will push up the cost of living and again the reaction will be in the form of pressure for extra pay to offset the rising cost of living.

Since the government controls the money supply, it may prefer to finance an increase in its expenditure by printing more money rather than by imposing higher rates of taxation. If taxation were raised the private sector's demand would be reduced and this would enable resources to be released for government

consumption. Where this does not happen, extra government spending is piled on unchanged private consumption, producing additional pressure on resources and leading to inflation. The inflation is financed by expansion of the money supply. It is widely believed that hyperinflation has its roots in the excessive creation of new money by a government that prefers to spend more without raising taxes.

Effects
In this section we shall attempt to highlight the major effects of inflation in a typical mixed economy. At the outset it must be stated that many people believe that moderate inflation may be beneficial in that it stimulates output, employment and growth and raises taxation revenue without the need for higher tax rates. On the other hand there are some less desirable effects, for example the reduction in real incomes.

Changes in Real Incomes and Redistribution of National Income
Inflation will cause a reduction in the real value of incomes but the size of the reduction will vary between groups and some groups may even be able to improve their relative position in the economy.

Not all incomes will rise at the same rate as prices. Where incomes of a particular group rise at a lower rate than prices that group will experience a decline in the real value (or purchasing power) of its income. Over time its share of the national output (income) will dimish. Low rates of increase may be due to weak economic or bargaining strength. Groups who do not possess significant economic power include salaried employees and those on (relatively) fixed incomes. Salaries generally do not rise as fast as wages of production workers; in particular salaries of those employed in the public sector, for example teachers and nurses, seem to fall far behind price increases.

Examples of fixed-income groups are those receiving social security benefits, pensioners, students on grants, landlords, and bond-holders. Those who depend on social security benefits suffer because these payments are generally fixed for a relatively long period. Although governments have recently reduced the period between pension revisions it is still true to say that pension increases are nearly always overtaken by price increases. This is even more so for members of private pension schemes; in this case the pension may not be raised at all. Students' grants are not adjusted frequently so that they suffer from higher costs of accommodation, books and other education materials, transport and so on. Landlords whose property is occupied on long term leases obviously lose in times of rising prices. At the same time governments may impose rent controls preventing them from keeping rents at a realistic economic level. People who hold government bonds or company debentures carrying fixed rates of interest find that although their money income is constant their real income is falling. They may cut their losses by switching to equities hoping that rising industrial and commercial profits will produce dividends at least high enough to offset declining money values.

Other groups may find their income and the price level rising pari passu. Certain employees such as salesman are paid on the basis of commission linked to sales; their incomes will move in line with inflation as the value of the firm's sales increases due to higher prices. Some employees have wage or salary agreements with built-in compensation for inflation; here incomes are automatically adjusted by reference to some index. The introduction of threshold payments in

1973 is an example of this. Under the government's scheme groups of workers may opt for wage settlements which include a guaranteed payment of 40p per week extra for every one point increase in the official Index of Retail Prices above a given base. Where the pay of groups keeps abreast of inflation there will be no deterioration in their real income nor in their share of the national cake. There will be no redistribution of national income in their favour nor not in their favour.

Yet others may be fortunate enough (?) to be in a situation where their incomes rise faster than the general price level. This may occur where there is strong and effective unionisation; militants may exert pressure which employers are unwilling or unable to oppose and so achieve high wage settlements, an example being the car industry. Similarly workers in so called "key" industries – is any one industry more important than any other in an interdependent industrial economy? – seemingly have the ability to push through high claims; examples include coal miners, electricity workers and dockers. Where labour is short, and particularly if there is general full employment, it may be employers who overtake price level increases by offering much higher wages in order to attract extra labour.

These groups will enjoy a greater share of the national income as time passes. Being able to overcompensate for, or perhaps anticipate, price rises will ensure that they become better off in real terms at the expense of their weaker colleagues. Indeed this is frequently considered to be one of the major problems associated with inflation; weak groups lose out in the scramble to maintain or improve relative positions from a social and economic point of view.

Consumption and Saving
Inflation is likely to boost the level of consumer purchasing in the economy. Expectations of increasing money incomes will encourage people to spend less cautiously at the present time, feeling that they will be better off in the future; expectations of continually rising prices will also increase current spending at today's lower prices.

Consumer spending will be stepped up as a result of the more widespread use of credit facilities. Inflation benefits borrowers at the expense of lenders. For example if £100 is borrowed for a year at 10% the borrower has to repay a total of £110. However if, over the year, the price level has risen also by 10% the real cost of the loan is zero; the sum borrowed and the interest is repaid in depreciated pounds.

Businesses too may gain in this respect. Much industrial and commercial activity is financed by banks and other institutions; the real cost to the business of repaying loans to these organisations declines with falling money values. The same applies to companies' debenture obligations; the real burden of interest payments is reduced with time.

One of the functions of money is as a store of value; saving allows the postponement of consumption to a later convenient date. There is controversy over the precise effect that inflation has on saving. When people realise that inflation affects the efficient performance of this function they may react by reducing their savings propensity. Those who do so will take the view that as prices are rising savings will become worth less and they may as well spend as much as possible now. If savings are invested in savings banks, building societies, insurance companies or the like, it is unlikely that the rate of interest paid by these institutions will be high enough to compensate for loss of value, therefore savings will be withdrawn.

Reduced savings by the community means that future investment plans may be thwarted. There will be a shortage of funds being channelled through the financial institutions for capital projects. In this case the community is not prepared to sacrifice as much present consumption as in a non-inflationary situation.

Other savers will take the view that since the purchasing power of savings will deteriorate as time passes, it is prudent to increase the rate of saving to compensate.

It is argued by some that total savings are unlikely to be much affected by (moderate) inflation. Research shows that in the majority of cases the total level of savings is influenced more by past, present and expected income patterns than by expected rates of return. In particular, those savings for use in the not too distant future, and most business savings fall into this category, are hardly likely to be affected at all. Where savings are for long-term use, there may be a switch from pure money-saving and low return assets into other forms of assets, for example property. Time may affect the composition, but not the total, of savings.

Output, Profits, Investment and Growth
Provided that resources are available in the economy, an increase in demand will cause businessmen to expand production, spurred on by the opportunity to increase their profits. Of course this will be impossible if the economy is already operating at full employment level of output. Many of a firm's production costs are fixed for a relatively long term; examples are rent, rates, insurance, long-term contracts with suppliers and debenture servicing costs. Prices may therefore rise faster than the firm's average costs and lead to higher profits per unit. Elementary supply theory suggests that enhanced profitability leads to an expansion of output as entrepreneurs seek to increase their profits. The extent of the rise in unit profit will depend on the ratio of fixed to total costs. The larger the proportion of fixed costs, the bigger will be the increase in unit profit; the larger the proportion of the faster rising variable costs, the smaller the increase in unit profit.

Experience shows that prices of consumer goods rise faster in an inflation than prices of capital goods. The implication here is that the production sector may divert resources to consumer goods output away from the production of investment goods. This change in the pattern of output may be reinforced by the fact that, as we have already seen, finance for investment may be in short supply due to reduced savings. This expansion of consumer goods production will have unfortunate consequences for an inflationary economy. One of the reasons for Britain's poor performance in recent years is the lack of past investment due to diversion of resources to consumption; this has reduced our present competitiveness and efficiency. However this tendency to lower investment will be partially offset by the fact that businessmen, anxious to expand output and exploit all the opportunities available, will feel it necessary to build up their capacity and this will involve investment expenditure.

Generally it is to be expected that (moderate) inflation will stimulate economic growth. As will be shown in the following Chapter, one of the determinants of growth in the economy is the level of aggregate demand. If consumer spending is rising, as is typical in an inflationary situation, this will provide a stimulus to growth.

Government
For the government inflation generates increased taxation revenues without the

need to raise tax rates which is electorally undesirable. Revenue from personal taxation will increase as people pay tax on higher incomes, some moving into income brackets where, because of the progressive nature of personal taxation, they will have to pay a bigger proportion of their earnings to the Inland Revenue. All told inflation passes to the government a bigger proportion of personal incomes. Even where the tax rate is constant, as it is at the time of writing in the case of Corporation Tax levied on companies, there will still be greater revenue for the government, companies handing over more tax on higher profits. Revenue from ad valorem expenditure taxes such as VAT will rise in line with prices; ad valorem taxes take a fixed percentage of an article's price and an increase in price means more tax revenue. At the same time extra consumer spending will also create increased revenue.

Balance of Payments

Where domestic prices are rising more rapidly than overseas prices, imports will be encouraged and exports discouraged. Imports become relatively cheaper and domestic consumers will be induced to switch their expenditure away from home-produced goods and services. Dealers will find it more profitable to buy overseas at lower prices and sell at inflated domestic prices thereby increasing their profits. Manufacturers will change to foreign suppliers of materials and components rather than continue to buy higher priced domestic supplies and similarly enhance their profits. Overseas producers will be attracted by higher prices in the inflationary economy and will seek to expand their sales in it.

Due to their higher prices exports are likely to fall, overseas clients finding it less profitable to buy. The boom situation at home will mean that domestic firms will have no difficulty in selling their products there and they may concentrate on selling in the home market rather than export. As a result of the reduction in exports and expansion in imports the economy is bound to suffer a deficit on the trade balance or, if there is already a deficit, a worsening of it. Note that this will result from higher rates of inflation at home than elsewhere. From an external point of view inflation itself is probably harmless as long as other countries are inflating at the same rate. Trouble arises when a country gets out of line as the United Kingdom has undoubtedly done in recent years.

Part One

NATIONAL INCOME AND EXPENDITURE

Chapter Four

Economic Growth

MEANING AND MEASUREMENT

The term "economic growth" is used to refer to the annual rate of increase in a country's real gross national product. Gross national product, as we have seen, is the monetary value of all goods and services produced by an economy in a year.

As time passes the purchasing power of money tends to fall so that the money value of a given amount of commodities rises. Therefore if a simple comparison is made of the money values of GNP over time, it will be impossible to tell how much, if at all, the volume of goods and services produced has changed. To overcome the problem of a decline in the purchasing power of money it is usual to express GNP at constant prices. GNP valued at current prices is deflated by reference to some suitable index of changing money values – the GNP deflator – to give a figure for real GNP. Such an index might be an index of retail prices or cost of living index.

For example, we read that the GNP at current prices of a certain country was as follows:

	1974	1975
GNP ($)	100,000,000	110,000,000

We might conclude from this that output had increased by 10%. However, unless it is known for certain that the purchasing power of a dollar had remained unchanged during 1974-5, we could not be sure of it. In fact the increase in the value of GNP in 1975 might have been entirely due to a rise of 10% in the general price level so that there was no expansion in the actual quantity of goods and services produced to satisfy the demands of residents. Alternatively there may have been only a 3% increase in GNP in real terms, the difference, 7%, being due to price rises. In Exhibit 4.1 is given a set of figures relating to the United Kingdom.

Gross National Product of the United Kingdom 1963, 1970 and 1973. £mn.

	1963	1970	1973	% change 1963–73	% change 1970–73
Current prices	27,285	43,537	63,271	132	45
Constant (1970) prices	36,069	43,537	47,944	33	10

(**Source:** National Income and Expenditure 1963–1973, HMSO 1974, Tables 1 and 14)

EXHIBIT 4.1

From the table it can be seen that GNP when valued at current prices increased by 132% over the period 1963–73 and by 45% from 1970–73. When allowance

is made for changes in the price level, the real increases were 33% and 10% respectively.

A second problem in interpretation arises from population changes and is of particular significance if one is using growth figures in an attempt to reach conclusions about improvements in living standards. In this case concern is with GNP from the viewpoint of measuring the ability of an economy to meet the demands of its residents and a more appropriate measure might be GNP per capita. Thus if over a period there has been an increase in a country's real GNP averaging 2% per year and also a corresponding increase in that country's population, then there is no increase in the amount of goods and services available to each individual (assuming that there has been no change in the distribution of output). Some examples of differences between GNP and per capita GNP figures are given in Exhibit 4.2.

Growth indices of GNP and GNP per capita, selected countries, 1963–72

Country	1972 Index (1963 = 100)	
	GNP	GNP per capita
United Kingdom	126	121
Denmark	156	146
Germany	150	140
Japan	244	221
USA	145	131

(Source: Social Trends No. 5, 1974, Table 207).

EXHIBIT 4.2

Finally the use of net rather than gross figures may be desirable in certain cases. Each year a portion of a country's GNP is used to make good capital depreciation that has occurred during the year. Obviously this is not available for consumption purposes and it may be preferable to leave it out of any calculations wherein output figures are being used to illustrate changes in, or comparisons between, living standards.

So far we have been looking at the meaning and interpretation of growth. Now we turn our attention to the question of why growth is desirable or necessary.

DESIRABILITY OF GROWTH

The basic economic problem is one of scarce resources and, following from this, scarce goods and services relative to unsatiable demands. The prime purpose of economic activity anywhere is to satisfy at least some of those demands. Therefore any increase in output that can be achieved is desirable in that it makes possible the satisfaction of more needs and wants; putting it another way, economic growth is the fundamental means by which the residents of a nation can raise their general standard of living. Living standards of an individual group may be improved without any expansion of an economy's output if redistribution of goods and services favouring that group occurs. In this way a section of the community gets a bigger slice of an unchanged "national cake". However it will be better for all if a bigger cake is produced and this is what growth achieves (given the qualifications mentioned in the first section of this chapter).

Growth also enables more resources to be channelled into investment.

Investment implies current sacrifices and communities may be unwilling to devote very much of their output to this end especially if the amount of goods and services currently available is not great anyway, as in the case of developing nations. Growth of output will allow extra consumption and investment.

As time passes we expect the state to undertake the provision of more and more goods and services such as expanded and improved transport and communications facilities, better medical care and higher standards and better conditions, for example new schools and colleges and smaller classes, in education. However as taxpayers we dislike paying out higher taxes to finance such provision. Again growth makes it possible for the state to divert extra resources into these uses without making excessive cutbacks in private consumption and investment.

The pursuit of growth as a major objective is sometimes justified for political or ideological reasons. It is argued that countries which achieve high growth rates will impress others and encourage them to adopt similar methods of organising their economies. Thus if the typical western-type mixed economy successfully maintains a high rate of growth then developing and politically uncommitted nations may decide that their interests will be best served by the evolution of a mixed economy. This argument is frequently advanced by American economists; critics point out that it implies an excessive degree of naivety on the part of such nations. In any case experience does not seem to back up the assertion.

Such ideological reasons may be closely linked with military ones. Many countries see growth as a means of acquiring military strength, influence and even domination. The United States of America believes that an adequate rate of growth is a powerful defence against the Russian challenge. When Kruschev a decade ago told the Americans that Russia would eventually "bury" them he was referring to the expected future ascendancy of the communist system over the western; since then the Americans have become even more conscious of the need to maintain a lead.

MAIN GENERATORS OF ECONOMIC GROWTH

We may say at the outset that the rate of growth of an economy broadly depends upon the rate of increase in the quantity and quality of its available resources and upon the level of aggregate demand. First we look at each category of resource in turn, secondly demand and then we round off the discussion with an examination of the other influences on the growth rate.

Labour or Human Resources

The supply of labour in an economy depends upon the following: (1) the size of the working population or labour force; (2) hours of work; and (3) the number and duration of holidays.

Economic growth may be stimulated by an increase in the total population. Population growth will in the long term generally encourage investment, employment and output as businessmen seek to produce goods in sufficient quantities to satisfy steadily expanding demand. A more direct stimulus is an increase in the size of the labour force. This may be achieved naturally over time when an earlier "bulge" in the birth-rate is translated into bigger numbers of school-leavers. Alternatively it may be achieved more rapidly by "artificial" means. The labour force may be expanded by immigration as happened in West Germany in the 1950's and '60's where large numbers of workers moved in from East Germany and Italy. A similar situation has occurred in the United Kingdom with the influx of labour from overseas, especially from Commonwealth countries.

Again expansion may be due to the entry of more women, particularly married, into employment. Recent statistics of the United Kingdom labour force are shown in Exhibit 4.3.

Labour Force Statistics – United Kingdom. Millions

	Year		
	1968	1972	1973
Total labour force	25·8	25·2	25·5
Males	16·7	16·2	16·1
Females	9·1	9·0	9·4

EXHIBIT 4.3

It is not only a matter of the number of people in the working population – it is also important to consider how long each person works. This brings in hours of work and the number and duration of holidays. Some idea of how we compare with a selection of other countries as far as hours worked are concerned is given in Exhibit 4.4, and as far as holidays in Exhibit 4.5.

Hours of Work in Manufacturing Industry

Country	Year	
	1962	1972
Belgium	41·0	37·5
France	46·2	44·4
Germany	44·7	42·9
Netherlands	46·5	43·8 (1971)
United Kingdom	46·2	45·0
United States	40·4	40·9

(**Source**: UN Statistical Yearbook 1964 and Social Trends 1973).

EXHIBIT 4.4

Number of Public Holidays per Year – 1972

Country	Holidays
Austria	11
Belgium	10
Denmark	8
France	10
Germany	13
Italy	17
Sweden	9
United Kingdom	6
United States	9

(**Source**: Adapted from Financial Times)

EXHIBIT 4.5

As the long-term trend is towards increasing leisure one must expect that hours worked will get less and holidays more. Therefore no source of increased growth is to be found here.

The amount of labour available in a particular area or for a particular use will be partially determined by the degree of mobility. Two types of mobility are recognised, geographical and occupational. Geographical mobility is the willingness to move to a different area in search of work. Occupational mobility concerns the ease with which labour is able or ready to adapt to new jobs, or the ease with which people will switch between jobs.

The degree of mobility will be influenced by such factors as:

(1). *Social and community ties.* The stronger these are the less prepared many people will be to move. This may be particularly so where families include aged parents or school-children; there will be unwillingness to leave the former and to unsettle the latter.

(2). *Age.* Generally older people are less likely to be mobile, either geographically or occupationally. It is more difficult for them to uproot and settle amongst unknown people and it is less easy for them to learn new skills – "You can't teach an old dog new tricks!"

(3). *Degree of specialisation.* Specialisation implies a narrow range of skills or maybe just one. If demand for a skill declines then a specialist worker will have nothing to offer in its place. On the other hand a person with a broad range of skills will be able to tackle numerous jobs but perhaps none with great efficiency – "Jack of all trades and master of none!"

(4). *Knowledge of opportunities.* A person may be unaware of suitable job opportunities in different areas or firms and so may remain in his present job.

(5). *Cost.* In some cases the deciding factor may be the cost of travel, or removal or of retraining. Non-financial costs too will have a bearing on mobility.

(6). *Housing and amenities.* Frequently personnel are reluctant to move to new areas and jobs because housing may not be available or suitable. The absence of adequate or desirable amenities can likewise reduce mobility.

A study undertaken by the Department of Employment and Productivity showed that well over half a million workers moved from one region to another each year and estimated that numbers moving within regions were several times this level. However there remains much mis-matching.

The implication of all this is that growth potential is reduced. Growth means change and adaptation. Old industries and trades disappear, new ones develop. Declining industries will be characterised by excess labour; this breeds inefficiency. Immobility may create labour shortages in expanding industries; this may slow down the rate of growth. Thus reallocation of labour resources to meet changed demand conditions and to facilitate growth will be retarded.

There would seem to be scope for improving the degree of labour mobility in the United Kingdom. Comparisons that have been made show that European mobility is greater; our competitors seem able to readjust and adapt more rapidly.

Before we move on to examine the quality aspect of labour it should be pointed out that (working) population growth by itself does not guarantee economic growth. In some cases increased supplies of labour will not be accompanied by increases in the nation's capital stock so that over a period the capital/labour ratio worsens: each worker on average will be working with a smaller amount of capital equipment. If this is so the principle of diminishing returns will operate; successive increments of the variable factor, labour, are being put to work with a (relatively) fixed factor, capital.

Now let us turn to the quality of labour. The quality or efficiency of the labour force will be influenced by its general educational attainment and, more

specifically, by its training. It is contended that one of the benefits of education is that it makes people aware of the need for change in an economy. As educational standards rise with time we would expect new entrants into the working population to be better educated than those already in it and those leaving it, in general. Figures in Exhibit 4.6 show how enrolments for higher education courses in the United Kingdom changed over the decade from 1960. For comparison purposes figures are also given for two other countries, each with a similar total number of enrolments in the earlier year. It can be seen that the rate of increase for this country is considerably below that of the other two.

Enrolments in Higher Education (000's)

Country	Year		% increase
	1960	1969/70	1960–69/70
United Kingdom	287·7	589·7 (1969)	105
Italy	284·3	694·2 (1970)	144
Canada	286·3	711·1 (1969)	148

(**Source**: Quantitative Trends in Post-secondary Education in OECD Countries 1960–70, OECD Observer October 1973).

EXHIBIT 4.6

General education is only part of the story. Job performance depends more heavily on skills training. One of the milestones in training this country was the passing of the 1964 Industrial Training Act which imposed a financial penalty on employers who refused to introduce properly organised training schemes and gave a financial incentive to those who did. Until this time the traditional method of learning in many industries had been "sitting by Nellie"; now a "scientific" approach was adopted. Effective job-training can reduce the amount of faulty and damaged work, abolish inefficient methods, cut labour turnover and lead to greater production and productivity in a shorter period.

Few expect labour to work physically harder as time passes – rather the trend is towards reducing the amount of physical and mental effort required in the performance of jobs. Thus the scope for increased growth from this source is non-existent. The hard work, physical and mental, is increasingly being taken over by machines and computers; this implies that improvements in productivity will derive from giving the worker a greater amount of capital equipment with which to do his job. Strictly labour productivity itself often falls when new machines and techniques are adopted, with labour putting in less effort and the investment itself creating the increase in output, but how often such so-called "productivity improvements" are used as the basis for claims for higher wages! On the other hand the introduction of labour-saving machinery and techniques frequently stirs up opposition from labour unions, criticised for being over-zealous in their attempts to project jobs and consequent over-manning.

People will not give of their best if they have to work in poor conditions. Improvements in working conditions in offices and factories seem likely to lead to higher morale and enhanced productivity as well as improvements in health, by no means unimportant in itself.

Finally, as the majority of people do work for money, a pay system whereby earnings are linked to output is desirable. Such systems are naturally enough welcomed by employers as they overcome the problem of having to pay out

regardless of what is done, whereas in daywork systems wages are paid on the basis of attendance not performance. Many companies have a wide range of incentives or perks to encourage effort; examples are company cars, luncheon voucher schemes, subsidised travel, gifts, bonuses.

Whilst on the subject of incentives it is worth noting that many regard a progressive income tax system as a discouragement to effort. Therefore a change from higher to lower marginal rates of taxation may stimulate growth in that there will be an added incentive to earn more.

Capital or Man-made Resources

Much of the increase in a nation's productive potential will stem from improvements in the quantity and quality of the capital resources available. At any time there is a stock of capital in an economy (difficult to measure in practice – but that need not worry us here) which has been built up over the years by investment, the community having decided to forego some current consumption so that resources might be devoted to the production of capital goods.

The terms gross investment or gross fixed capital formation are used to refer to the total of all investment undertaken within an economy in a given period. As capital goods are used in the production process they deteriorate, requiring attention, servicing, new parts and eventual replacement; this is known as depreciation. Gross investment less that amount used to make good depreciation gives net investment. Net investment therefore consists of additions to the nation's stock of capital – it is the rate at which an economy is building up its capital stock.

Net investment may give rise to either capital widening or capital deepening. Capital widening takes place when the nation's stock of capital is rising at a rate equal to the rate of increase in the labour force. As the two expand in line with each other there is no improvement in the capital/labour ratio; each worker on average still has the same amount of equipment with which to operate. Capital deepening occurs where the rate of capital growth is greater than the rate of increase in the labour force so that as time passes each worker on average has available for his use a greater amount of equipment; there is an improvement in the capital/labour ratio. Such situations are illustrated in Exhibit 4.7.

Investment requirements of a fictional economy

Part A.

Capital stock	£1,000,000
Depreciation rate	10%
Labour force	400
Annual growth of labour force	1%
Capital/labour ratio	£2,500

Part B.

Investment demand:		Policy 1	Policy 2
(1) Depreciation	10% × £1,000,000	£100,000	£100,000
(2) Capital widening	(400 × 1%) × £2,500	£10,000	£10,000
(3) Capital deepening	[400+(400 × 1%)] × £250	—	£101,000
Total investment demand		£110,000	£211,000
Resultant capital stock		£1,010,000	£1,111 000

EXHIBIT 4.7

In Exhibit 4.7 part A gives relevant information concerning a hypothetical economy. Part B shows components of investment demand and "final" capital stock figures for two policies, capital widening (Policy 1) and capital deepening (Policy 2). With each policy it is necessary to make good the depreciation that has occurred by purchasing £100,000 worth of new equipment and provide the extra workers with £2,500 worth of capital each. If the economy is only pursuing a capital widening policy, then the matter rests there; gross investment demand will be £110,000, of which £10,000 will represent net investment. If however a capital deepening policy is being undertaken, gross investment will be £211,000, including £111,000 of net investment to improve the capital/labour ratio of the bigger labour force from £2,500 to £2,750 per worker. With the first policy the capital stock grew by 1%; with the second it grew by 11·1%.

Measurement of the quality of a nation's capital is notoriously difficult; most economists adopt the view that quality varies inversely with age so that the most modern pieces of capital equipment are assumed to be the best. New machines embody the latest scientific and technical progress and are more efficient than the machines which they replace: one would normally expect the Mark II version to be better than the Mark I. From this it is inferred that replacement investment for depreciation is crucially important for both an individual firm and an entire economy. Unless a competitive firm exploits latest technology it is liable to lose its competitive edge. The same applies to a nation; failure to replace machines of an earlier "vintage" with those of a later can damage overall efficiency, leading to deterioration in export performance and an unfavourable increase in imports as consumers switch from domestic output to better quality or lower-priced overseas products. It is argued that much of the benefit of new investment derives from the new scientific and technical progress it brings with it and which could not be exploited without it rather than from improvements in the capital/labour ratio itself; gross investment reduces the average age of the capital stock and improves its efficiency.

Although the message of this section has clearly been "Invest in order to grow!", it is only fair to remark that a few economists give less prominence to investment as a growth source. For example, Fores in an article called "Is more investment the key to faster growth?" in the Moorgate and Wall Street Journal, Spring 1971, suggests that (1) investment may be an effect, rather than a cause, of high growth rates; (2) research has shown that increases in capital may contribute much less than half of growth rates; and (3) at least as far as the United Kingdom is concerned the best way of stimulating growth is not so much to increase the rate of investment as to improve the level of industrial skills and efficiency in the use of labour. It remains a contentious point whether investment in modern equipment is worthwhile unless there is sufficiently competent manpower to use it, adequate management expertise to exploit its potential and opportunities for its profitable deployment. In the United Kingdom the post-war record of investment has been disappointing. For example, during the period 1960–69 the ratio of gross fixed capital formation to gross domestic product averaged only 16% if investment in housing is excluded and 20% if it is included. International comparisons, too, are unfavourable as can be seen from Exhibit 4.8.

Capital formation presents a serious problem for the developing countries. In order to invest a nation must be prepared to sacrifice current consumption. In a typical developing country consumption itself is low; it will be difficult to persuade people to reduce their consumption in order to free resources for

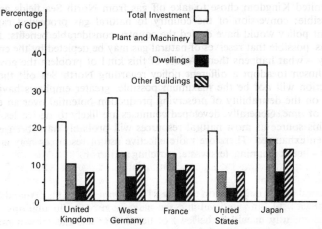

(Source: Treasury Economic Progress Report No 39, May 1973).

EXHIBIT 4.8

investment if they have an unsatisfactorily low standard of living to begin with. There will be considerable pressure on a government from consumers and voters to permit any increased output to be allocated to consumption. The aim for developing countries must be to raise output sufficiently in order to allow higher consumption and make available a surplus for investment purposes.

One leading authority on the economics of growth, the American W. W. Rostow, suggests that economies pass through five stages of development. These are:
(1) Traditional society
(2) Transitional society
(3) Self-generation or "take-off"
(4) Maturing society
(5) Mass-consumption.

The crucially important stage is the third. In order to reach the "take-off" stage, a country has to increase investment from about 5% of GNP to about 10%. This will make possible the establishment and development of growth industries; once over the threshold the country will experience self-generating growth.

Land or Natural Resources
Little can be said about natural resources as a source of growth. It is well known that there are wide variations in the quality and quantity of such resources between nations. Some may have vast reserves of coal or minerals, others none; some may have abundant supplies of fertile land, others very little; some may have plentiful timber, others hardly a tree at all; some may have considerable reserves of petroleum, others not a drop. As this is the case, all that countries can do is to ensure that discovery of latent resources and their subsequent

exploitation is undertaken with utmost speed; in this way growth will be maximised. However against this must be set the need for conservation of resources, so that an individual country must balance these clashing objectives. The United Kingdom chose to take off gas from North Sea fields as quickly as possible; conversion of the country to natural gas proceeded rapidly. A different policy would have denied the country considerable benefits. However it seems possible that reserves of natural gas may be depleted by the end of the century – what happens then? Aware of this kind of problem the government have chosen to adopt a different policy regarding North Sea oil; the rate of production will not be the maximum possible, greater emphasis having been placed on the desirability of preserving production potential over an extended period of time. Generally, developed countries are likely to derive less growth from this source as most natural resources will probably have been exploited and even exhausted. Therefore more effective use of resources may encourage growth – better planning, less waste, recycling and so on.

Demand

The second major influence on the rate of economic growth is demand from the point of view of both its level and the magnitude of its fluctuations. There is no clear-cut way in which the level of demand affects the growth rate; what happens in a particular situation is an empirical matter. The rate of growth may vary directly and indirectly with demand levels. Firstly, a high level of demand may encourage increased production and investment. It may also stimulate better methods of using existing equipment, leading to enhanced productivity. Thus one would expect better growth performance in reflationary and inflationary periods as producers try to keep up with expanding sales. When demand is running at a low level innovation, investment and growth will typically decline. The alternative view is that high levels of demand constitute a sellers' market in which businessmen will feel complacent, believing that there is no reason why they should innovate and invest. By the same token low demand pressure may stimulate investment in more efficient equipment so that the firm may cut its costs, perhaps reduce its prices, in striving to maintain, if not expand, its share of a declining market. The first view is borne out by experience of the 1930's, the second by recent "stagflation" where output and investment have failed to respond to record levels of inflation.

Turning now to fluctuations in demand pressure, it seems likely that the following will result. Cyclical variations in demand will induce businessmen to instal less-specialised equipment; this will make it easier to adapt production methods or diversify in leaner times. On the other hand consistently high demand or steadily rising demand is likely to encourage the installation of more specific rather than general purpose machines. The implication of this behaviour is that cyclical fluctuations will reduce the growth potential. Such demand variations have of course been prevalent in the United Kingdom in recent years, and have led to the introduction of "stop-go" policies by successive governments in an attempt to combat them.

Other Generators of Economic Growth

As well as the most important sources of growth mentioned earlier there are a number of subsidiary sources which will be dealt with in this section.

The first of these is the *degree of competition* in the economy. A competitive environment stimulates firms to improve productivity, to invest in the latest

techniques and equipment. It therefore follows that an economy which fosters competition will, other things being equal, enjoy a higher rate of growth. This, coupled with the following reason, may be the cause of the relatively good rates of growth achieved in the past by free enterprise and mixed economies.

Secondly existence of *incentives* will encourage growth. From the point of view of labour a system of payment-by-results will encourage effort; management will be prepared to accept promotion if higher salaries are not taken away in taxation; companies will be prepared to invest and undertake the more risky venture if any profits are not subject to high levels of tax; savings must be encouraged as a necessary base for investment finance, whether in the personal or corporate sectors. This last point may have unpalatable implications for egalitarians, a point which is admirably made in the following extract from Professor Kenneth Boulding's Economic Analysis, Vol. II, Macroeconomics: –

". . . equality can only be afforded by rich societies – in a poor society equality would condemn everyone to a miserable subsistence and the society to stagnation. A society of uniform mass poverty can hardly hope to accumulate or to concentrate resources in the hands of the innovators. At first, economic growth frequently seems to accentuate inequality, as those few who participate in it draw away toward higher incomes from the mass of the society which still remains in the primitive condition. The end result of economic growth, however, seems to be a more equal distribution at the higher level, when all members of the society have been caught up in the more productive culture. As the pioneering middle class moves out of the morass of universal and equal poverty, inequality increases; but if the progress continues, the whole society is gradually drawn up into the plateau of universal and relatively equal comfort . . ."

Next growth rates seem to vary directly with the *degree of specialisation* of productive factors. As Adam Smith wrote a couple of centuries ago specialisation is limited by the size of the market for output; potential benefits from pursuing scale economies are subject to the same constraint. Therefore a country of relatively small size is unlikely to be able fully to exploit gains from specialisation and economies of scale: feasible expansion is restricted. The same applies to self-sufficient economies, unless of considerable size.

One way in which smaller countries may overcome the problem is by joining together in some form of economic union such as a free-trade area or common market. This effectively expands the size of the "home" market in which each one operates. Another way is for them to engage in overseas trade so that foreign markets are added to the domestic one. Either way the scope for specialisation and enjoyment of scale economies is widened.

DISECONOMIES OF ECONOMIC GROWTH

The second part of this chapter looked at some of the benefits to be derived from the growth of national output, and benefits they undoubtedly are; but as always there are other aspects to consider. Continued economic growth gives rise to a number of less desirable "spillover" effects, and this section deals with a selection of them.

(1) *Exhausted resources.* As the production sector develops and expands it will require more and more inputs of raw materials. Since natural resources are not unlimited, continued exploitation will, sooner or later, result in exhaustion of supplies. At this stage, or before it if the nation is aware of the limits, alternative supplies from abroad, if available, may be imported. This temporarily solves the problem for the importing country but exacerbates the situation in the

supplying countries. An alternative policy is the development of synthetic or artificial substitutes for raw materials, as has been done with rubber and fibres. Here again, however, the problem is only shelved temporarily as artificial substitutes themselves require further raw material inputs.

(2) *Pollution*. In the course of production many firms cause pollution. Chimneys belch out into the atmosphere dirt, acid and other noxious substances. Many industrial processes are noisy. There may be uncontrolled disposal of waste products into rivers, canals and streams, with harmful effects on fish, animals and vegetation. Solid waste disposal creates unpleasant, smelly rubbish heaps. Extractive industries (mining and quarrying) create unsightly tip mounds and slag heaps, or, where opencast operations take place, lay bare whole tracts of countryside.

Pollution is not caused only by production; consumption too creates problems. Every day millions of gallons of untreated sewage are pumped into rivers and the sea. Packaging materials costing millions of pounds are discarded every year, it being considered uneconomic to recycle them; examples are plastic containers, glass bottles and aluminium beer cans. Built-in obsolescence is a feature of a number of consumer products, especially cars. Unless the old model is traded in for a new one, owners may just abandon it.

(3) *Congestion*. Industrialisation generally brings concentration of population into urban and industrial areas; people are attracted by job opportunities not present in rural districts. The result is population congestion and high density housing schemes. It has been estimated that some 40% of the entire world population live in urban areas and that 50% of all urban dwellers live in cities of at least 100,000 inhabitants. It follows that the more people are concentrated, the greater the necessary scale and expense of waste removal. Difficulties are caused by road and rail traffic congestion as people travel to and from work in relatively limited areas. Freight transport adds to congestion as it brings in and distributes materials and components and then distributes and takes out finished goods.

(4) *Change*. Economic growth implies change; the more rapid the growth the greater the change. Labour has to adjust to new industrial situations, perhaps move house, learn new skills. Many find it difficult to adapt; hardship results, social displacement occurs. A society that has an over-riding obsession with growth and progress may fail to provide adequately for those of its members who are displaced by the changes taking place. Failure to introduce acceptable and effective policies regarding, for example, redundancy and unemployment, relocation and resettlement, and retraining will generate unrest. Blind pursuit of "go-go" growth policies is a sure-fire recipe for trouble.

Part Two

RETURNS TO THE FACTORS OF PRODUCTION

Chapter Five

General Information on Returns

The factors of production on the one hand produce goods and services (economists investigate this under the Theory of Production) and on the other hand receive a return for their efforts (considered under the Theory of Distribution). Both theories, as can be seen, must be inter-related and therefore, at times, become difficult to separate into water-tight compartments. The latter theory simply theorises about the price paid to each factor; it attempts to throw light, and not give precise answers, on how incomes are distributed among the factors. In this part of the book the intention is to consider some of the aspects related to the returns to the factors of production.

Basically, when we speak about returns to the factors of production we are concerned with the way the national income is divided among the various owners of land, labour, capital and enterprise. A detailed break down of these figures would result in big differences between the rents paid to one land owner and another, between the wage packet of one unit of labour and another, etc. Figures would show that some individuals are owners of several factors thus receiving incomes such as rent and wages, or interest and profits. Explanations about mixed incomes will not be considered. Our concern will be that of looking at each form of income separately.

Before isolating each factor and their special returns it will be necessary to refresh our knowledge about the factors. Information has already been given about land, labour, capital and enterprise but not their returns.[1]

FACTORS – OUTPUT AND INCOME

Perhaps the best approach to the relationship between the factors is by showing the inter-relationship between their contribution to the output of goods and services and the incomes distributed to each factor in achieving the output. Exhibit 5.1 is an attempt to simplify this relationship.

The exhibit clearly shows that both output and income use the same set of figures. The figures calculated vertically downwards provide details about the contribution each factor makes towards output. When the figures are added horizontally, from left to right, the return to each factor for their efforts in producing goods and services is obtained. In the exhibit Firm A has produced goods and services totalling £100,000. This sum is obtained by adding up the costs of production (cost of land, labour and capital) plus profits. These costs are the incomes paid to each factor (£15,000 paid in rent to the owners of land; £60,000 paid in wages and salaries to the owners of labour, etc.). The same procedure is used for calculating the output and income of Firm B and C.

It can be noted that if we carried out this exercise for every firm in every industry in the country we would have statistics that would be incorporated

1. Refer to Volume I Chapter 2.

RELATIONSHIP BETWEEN FACTOR OUTPUT & FACTOR INCOMES

(figures £,000)

———————————————— INCOMES ————————————→

	Factors of Production		Firms			Income Values
	The Factors	Their Returns	A	B	C	
OUTPUT	Land	Rent	15	40	10	65
	Labour	Wages	60	40	20	120
	Capital	Interest	15	10	50	75
	Enterprise	Profits	10	10	20	40
	OUTPUT VALUES		100	100	100	300*

Note: * £300,000 is "total value of all incomes" and the "total value of all outputs of goods and services".

EXHIBIT 5.1

into the domestic section of the national income. In our hypothetical table adding the final production values horizontally would give us the "total value of goods and services produced" whereas the addition of the final column downwards would provide us with a figure showing the "total value of incomes received by factors in producing these goods and services",

The above information clearly shows the link between "production" and "distribution" theories, and the need to have a better understanding about the factors of production.

Another point that can be noted from the exhibit is that each firm has different combinations of the factors. Normally, there is no strict relationship between the use of factors in one firm compared to another even if the firms are in the same industry. Some firms use more of one factor than another. Firm A is labour intensive and Firm C is capital intensive. Firm A will be more conscious of changes in wages and the effect this has on the price of their units of ouptut whereas Firm C's interest payments for the use of capital will have considerable effect on their prices. In both firms the prices paid to all factors will have some effect on prices, but some prices appear to be more important than others.

PRICE OF FACTORS OF PRODUCTION

The price of factors, as well as other prices, is determined by the interaction of supply and demand.[1] The supply side relates to the total of each factor that is available at any one time (static) or it could relate to the amount that flows on to the market (dynamic). *The demand for any factor is a derived demand*, in other words it will depend upon the demand for the goods and services produced. The price is established at the equilibrium point.

To determine the price of a factor of production we need to know the conditions that affect the demand for the factor as well as the conditions that affect its supply. In the factor market firms are represented on the demand side and owners of the factors of production on the supply side. The price paid for each factor will, therefore, depend upon the factors influencing the demanders and suppliers.

1. Refer to Volume I pages 125 to 129.

Demand

The demand for factors is on the one hand a "derived demand" and on the other hand a "joint demand". The need for factors is derived from the demand for the goods (or services) produced by a firm. If there is a small demand for the firm's goods the demand for the factors will also be small. Conversely, if demand for the firm's goods increases then, normally, the demand for factors will increase.

Output is the result of a combination of factor services. Thus, the demand for goods or services will require the use of one factor in close conjunction with other factors and thus they are said to be in joint demand. Although there be joint demand it does not mean that the demand for one factor will always be equated with the demand for other factors. There is always the possibility of substituting one factor (labour saving machines) for another factor (labour).

The price of a factor will be affected by the elasticity of demand for that factor and this in turn can be related to the degree of substitutability between the factors. If it is easily possible to substitute one factor for another then the demand for that factor will tend to be elastic; the less easy it is to substitute the more the demand will tend to be inelastic.[1] So, the price of factors is affected by the degree of substitutability.

This idea of elasticity goes deeper than this. Because the demand for factors is a derived demand then the elasticity of demand for the products themselves will affect the demand for factors. For example, if the demand for good A is inelastic (buyers of that good are not very responsive to changes in price for the good) then the demand for the factors producing that good will also tend to be inelastic. The reverse situation also applies; an elastic demand for good A would imply a relatively elastic demand for the factors producing good A.

Forces, other than the availability of substitutes, that determine the degree of elasticity of demand for a product[2], such as price of the product, degree of luxury and habit, must be related back to the demand for the factors producing that product. In other words, if you can determine the shape of the demand curve for a product you would expect the corresponding shape of the demand curve for a factor to approximate the product demand curve. If buyers of the product are not responsive to price change (inelastic demand) then the firm producing the product will not be responsive to changes in the prices paid for factors (inelastic demand).

Demand, however, is only one side of the factor price situation.

Supply

Businesses are demanders of factors whereas the owners of factors are suppliers. The force that operates on suppliers is 'time'. Over a span of time specific forces, normally different for different factors, come into operation to change the supply situation. In other words, as we progress from one time period (short-run period) to another (long-run period) we would expect the supply curve to change and thus the elasticities associated with these curves. The general relationship is very similar to those for goods and we can expect (but not always, for example land), that elasticities for factors over time would become more and more elastic.

Supply curves change but the change for one factor can be different from another factor. Land, for example, is subject to small changes in supply relative to labour. Land is fairly fixed in supply and therefore normally completely inelastic.

1. Students should refresh their minds about elasticity and elasticity measurements by referring to Volume I Chapter 20 pages 179 to 184.
2. Refer to Volume I Chapter 20 page 185.

It is possible to increase supply (reclaiming land from the sea) but all of this takes *time* and the change in supply is rather small. Labour supply, on the other hand, can be increased by immigration or population growth; each takes *time*. Some 'specific areas of labour' can be increased in a very short period of time (unskilled) whereas other take weeks, months or years to train (semi-skilled to skilled). This knowledge of forces operating in the *time* periods is necessary to understand the changes in the shape of factor supply curves and the associated elasticities.

Demand and supply

All the above information is relevant to understanding the basics underlying the demand and supply for factors. The interaction of these will help us to determine the price for land, labour, capital and enterprise. They are brought together in a theory which is theoretical but not very practical.

MARGINAL PRODUCT THEORY

The marginal product theory states that the price paid for the use of any factor should be determined by the extra contribution an additional factor makes to production and the resulting revenue to the firm. In other words, the firm will employ any factor up to the point where the price of that last unit used is equal to the value of the last product produced so that the firm has maximised its profits. To put it another way: the level of wages (same wages paid to each worker in the group) will be equal to the extra output (marginal product) produced by the efforts of the last worker employed. It is this marginal worker's output that tends to govern the wages of all workers in the group. If he employed less workers his profits would be less than the maximum as it would be if he employed more than this last man. The theory uses the law of diminishing returns.[1]

This theory assumes that the firm is in a market where pure competition exists.[2] What will be the wages of labour? The wages will be determined by supply and demand. Supply refers to:
1. the number of workers having the same skills, and
2. these workers having the same satisfaction from work and leisure.

Demand by businesses for this type of worker is based upon:
1. the price of the product, and
2. the marginal product of labour.

The demand curve for labour (or for any factor) is *the marginal revenue product curve of labour* (or any other factor).

This theory is correct for any firm producing a product that is faced with 'pure competition' but not when competition is imperfect. Businessmen of today would not accept it. It falls short of what is desirable because it simply considers situations which are too perfect. It is suitable for a 'dream world' but it is definitely not suitable for determining the wage levels in the 'world of the 1970s'. It has too many shortcomings:
1. The market for products is not perfect or pure.
2. Who can measure the 'marginal product'?
3. Factors are not homogeneous.

The above applies to any factor of production. If we were to consider labour we could say that:

1. Refer to Volume I page 188.
2. Refer to Volume I pages 120 to 123. 'Pure' in the sense that the product is homogeneous, there are a large number of small firms in the industry and the price of the product is given and cannot be dictated by any firm.

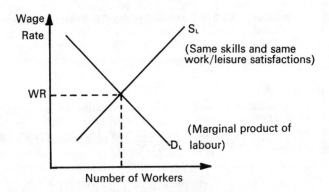

Determination of Wage Rates
(Marginal Productivity Theory)

Number of Workers

Notes: Productivity – term explained
separate chapter this part of book.

WR – Wage Rate (equilibrium price)

S_L – Supply of Labour

D_L – Demand for Labour

EXHIBIT 5.3

1. Labour is not free – workers are organised into trade unions.

2. Labour is, perhaps, the most heterogeneous of all factors of production. Even workers of the same skill are unlikely to have exactly the same attitudes to work and leisure.

3. Collective bargaining is not taken into account.

The above comments relate to the shortcomings of the theory. It does have relevance in that it does lay the foundation that no business wishes to pay a worker £1 an hour when his contribution to output is less than a £1.

In the 'world of the 1970s' there are other forces operating, especially in the field of labour, which help to determine the prices to be paid for the factors of production. The following chapters in this part of the book will look at each factor and its returns, but emphasis and details can not do justice to so complex a subject.

Part Two

RETURNS TO THE FACTORS OF PRODUCTION

Chapter Six

Rent

The return to the factor of production called land is *rent*[1] and it refers to the payment made for the *use* of land in producing goods and services. This term is used by the general public in ordinary speech when they discuss the rent of a car, caravan, television set or house. In this context the term is used in its broadest sense. Businessmen also use the term in its broadest sense when they talk about renting a machine or truck. The name often attributed to this form of rent, by economists, is 'commercial rent' or 'ordinary rent'. This is done to distinguish it from 'economic rent; a special and narrower definition which will be considered shortly.

Rent is a contractual payment fixed by agreement and therefore applies to ordinary transactions. Invariably these payments will include other payments not associated with land. The best example to show this situation would be 'house rent'; a payment which would include a contribution for the *use* of the land on which the house stands (called ground rent) as well as a contribution towards other goods and services not associated with land, for example, bricks, wood, sinks, etc.

A distinction must be made between ordinary rent and economic rent. The latter type rent applies only to those payments made for any factor, whether it be land, labour, capital or enterprise, which are for one reason or another fixed in supply. In other words it can be defined as the return to a factor over and above that payment necessary to keep it in its present use. When the term is applied to any factor other than land the tendency is to drop the word 'economic' and qualify the type of rent. Take, for example, the fact that star football players are restricted in supply and therefore command a higher return. The return to them, over and above the price paid to the general level of ability of the majority of football players is called 'rent of ability'. Notable pop groups also receive 'rent of ability'. On the other hand, if we consider a special type of machine (machinery being capital) which is fixed in supply for the short term only (more can be manufactured but it will take some time to be brought to the market) the payments may be over and above what is considered to be normal. This additional payment is given the term 'quasi rent' which simply means 'as if it were rent'. These are forms of economic rent.

An important aspect of 'economic rent' is that external forces can operate to push up the price of some good and service when it is fixed in supply. Demand for factors, it should be remembered, is a derived demand. Suppose 'cup final tickets' were issued two months before the date of play and you bought one at that time. The price of the ticket is £2. This price would presumably reflect the payment necessary to all the factors to provide the service offered. Soon all tickets

1. This subject is not required by the ONCBS and ONDBS syllabus.

have been sold, but not everyone who wanted a ticket was able to obtain one. As the day of the game grew nearer and nearer you find that you are able to sell your ticket for twice or thrice the price paid. As can be seen, the supply of tickets are fixed and you have done nothing to push up the price; external forces are operating. The difference between the price shown on the ticket (£2) and the higher price obtained nearer the date of the game (£4) is 'economic rent'.[1] *Rent, therefore, is price determined*, not price determining.

Economic rent is often described as a *surplus* because the land is fixed in supply and the land owner can obtain returns over and above what is normal without any action or effort on his part. This is simply illustrated by Exhibit 6.1.

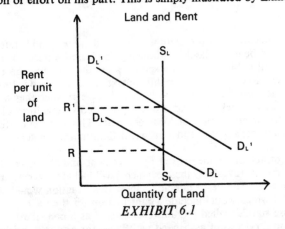

EXHIBIT 6.1

Exhibit 6·1 clearly shows that the supply of land (S_L) is fixed and thus any change in rent (R) must arise from a shift in the demand (D_L to D_L^1). The result of this shift in the demand for land is a rise in rents from R to R^1. Because supply is fixed, demand alone determines the price of land. Our demand curve is the demand for land but, as noted before, the demand for any factor is a derived demand. So, this demand curve is a reflection of what consumers want to use the land for. In our example the consumers like the produce grown on the land and shift the demand for land upwards. If they disliked the produce the shift would be downwards (from D_L^1 to D_L).

Although the exhibit was used to show 'economic rent' for the factor of production 'land', it can be applied to any factor (for example labour) which is completely inelastic in supply.

Returning to the subject of land – when land is homogeneous and scarce, as it appears to be in Exhibit 6.1, then the term given to the rent paid is 'scarcity rent'. However, we know that land can be heterogeneous, that is to say that some land is more suitable for growing vegetables than others. In this case there will be different rents paid. Higher quality land receiving higher rents than lower quality land. To note this situation the term 'differential rent' is used.

Thus, there are many types of rent and many ways in which the term is used. Economists distinguish between the ordinary usage of the word by calling it 'commercial' or 'ordinary' rent and reserve the term 'economic rent' for situations where payments are made for a factor of production which are inelastic in supply.

1. The extra £2 is the result of an increase in demand relative to fixed supply – as shown in Exhibit 6.1.

When discussing factors other than land the term rent is qualified by 'quasi' or 'of ability'. Economic rent, rightfully, is more generally used to indicate the return for the *use* of land.

Part Two

RETURNS TO THE FACTORS OF PRODUCTION

Chapter Seven

Wages — Structure and Organisation of Labour Market

Labour means all kinds of human effort undertaken for a reward. The efforts may be mental or physical, skilled or unskilled. It would include the efforts of managing directors or other managers, foremen, operators on the production line or people carrying out the paper work in the office.[1]

The reward to labour for its efforts is *wages*. Before discussing the determination of wages it would be beneficial to consider the structure and organisation of the labour market.

STRUCTURE AND ORGANISATION OF LABOUR

The Concise Oxford Dictionary defined *structure* as "the manner in which a building or organism or other complete whole is constructed, supporting framework or whole of the essential parts of something". In Economics the word is used, normally, to refer to permanent (not temporary) features; to look at the permanent features of labour which establish a pattern. *Organisation* refers to the state or the manner of being organised and often refers to a body of persons organised for some end or work.[2] Our study begins with the number, size and types of occupations in Britain.

The size of the labour force will depend, in the first place, on the number of the people that are, by law or nature, able to work. Our concern is with all forms of labour (men and women; managers and shop-floor workers; clerks, etc.) who actively participate in economic activity in producing goods and services made available to the community. Economically active persons, according to the Census of Population 1971[3] are those who are in employment plus those temporarily out of employment such as the temporary sick and those temporarily out of a job. Excluded are retired persons, students in educational establishments, persons who are permanantly sick, trainees in government training centres, housewives doing unpaid domestic duties and au pair girls. In other words it tends to exclude those never in employment and those not seeking work.

Statistical material is used to indicate the size of the labour force and their occupations. Present day figures are reasonably reliable but students are warned that the figures projected into the future have a wider margin of error. Errors are not normally the result of methods employed but are reflections by forecasters of looking into the uncertain future and the uncertain changes in social habits.

Information about the labour force can be obtained from a number of sources such as the number of national insurance cards exchanged or the details produced by the present Department of Employment. Each of these can and do give dif-

1. Further details about 'labour' can be found in Volume I pages 17 to 22.
2. Definition from 'The New Century Dictionary'.
3. Census of Population 1971 Great Britain – Summary Tables (1 % Sample), HMSO, page x.

ferent figures. For this chapter the basic source is the Census of Population, unless otherwise stated.

One point to be noted is that totals from one period of time to another may need adjustment for accurate comparisons. Some force, say a government decision, may change the structure. An example of this was the decision by the government in 1973 to raise the school leaving age from 15 to 16. This does affect the size of the labour force and such movements must be carefully considered when comparing, say 1971 with 1981 (the next Census of Population year).

Size of labour force

What is the size of the labour force in relation to the population of Great Britain? Exhibit 7.1 shows this relationship for two census years, 1961 and 1971.

RELATIONSHIP OF ECONOMICALLY ACTIVE POPULATION (EAP) TO TOTAL BRITISH POPULATION

	1961[1]			*1971*[2]			*1961–1971*	
	Totals	%	%	*Totals*	%	%	**Changes** *Totals*	%
Total Population	51,284,000	100·0	—	53,802,700	100·0	—	2,518,700	4·91
EAP[3]	23,816,000	46·44	100·0	25,002,600	46·47	100·0	1,186,600	4·98
of which								
Males	16,076,000	—	67·5	15,866,500	—	63·5	– 209,500	– 1·30
Females								
Married	3,886,000	—	16·3	5,781,100	—	23·1	1,895,100	48·77
Other	3,854,000	—	16·2	3,355,000	—	13·4	– 499,000	– 12·9

Source: 1 – Extracted from Table A1 of Census of Population 1961 entitled 'Occupation and Industry', National Summary Tables, HMSO, 1965.

2 – Based on Tables 1 and 13 of Census 1971 Great Britain, Summary Tables (1 % Sample), HMSO, 1973.

Note: 3 – Figures for both years are based on population aged 15 and over.

EXHIBIT 7.1

The 'economic active population' is not the same as the 'working population'. To obtain the working population one must *add* to the economic active population (EAP) figures the total of armed forces abroad and the 'net' figure of seamen at sea and then *substract* foreign armed forces operating in Britain. For example, in 1961:

Economically active population 23,816,000
Working population...................... 24,026,000

The figures given in Exhibit 7·1 refers to all persons economically active *within* Great Britain (including foreign armed forces) at the time of the Census and excludes those *outside* the country.

Exhibit 7·1 provides many interesting facts. The growth of population between 1961 and 1971 was of the order of 5 per cent and the EAP rose by the same percentage. The rise of the EAP represented approximately 47 per cent of the increase in total population. Where did they come from? It appears that the increase was the result of many more married women becoming economically active. A close look at the figures show that single females (including widows and

divorced) plus males, over the ten year span, fell in absolute terms; almost one-half million single females and over two hundred thousand males. The two, taken together, represents a fall of approximately 708,500; note this against the rise of EAP of 1,186,600. This loss to the EAP was filled in by the 'married female' sector; in fact, they closed this gap (708,500) and added (1,186,600) to the EAP. In other words the number of married females becoming economically active was 1,895,100.

Another significant fact is that although the EAP was increased by over one million between the two census years the percentage of EAP to the total population has remained virtually the same; 46·44 per cent in 1961 and 46·47 per cent in 1971.

Exhibit 7.1 has been broken down in a variety of ways so students can freely make comparisons. What was the make-up of those listed under the EAP?

The exhibit does not tell us many things. What part of total population are males? females? Also, it does not provide information about the future. To do this it is necessary to carry out a projection of the labour force. A fairly recent projection was carried out by the Department of Employment.[1]

There are many interesting statistics provided by the article, but the one of interest to us, at the present time, is presented as Exhibit 7.2.

PROJECTION OF
ECONOMICALLY ACTIVE POPULATION
1973 – 1991

(Figures in thousands)

Economically active population aged 16 and over	Labour force projections aged 16 and over			Changes	
	1973*	1981	1991	1973–1981	1981–1991
TOTAL	25,061	25,839	27,028	778 (3·1%)	1,189 (4·2%)
Males	15,883	16,005	16,532	122 (0·8%)	527 (3·3%)
Females	9,178	9,834	10,496	656 (7·1%)	662 (6·7%)
of whom married	6,004	6,909	7,920	905 (15·1%)	1,011 (14·6%)

EXHIBIT 7.2

Note: * 1973 figures exclude about 23,000 boys and 22,000 girls aged 15 at mid-year who were unaffected by the raising of the school leaving age and had left school.

Source: Extracted and modified from Table 2 "Labour force projections: 1973–1991" Department of Employment Gazette, April 1974, p. 305.

Exhibit 7·2 summarises the main projections of the labour force after excluding those in full time education. The figures take into account the change brought about by the raising of the school leaving age. The exhibit does substantiate the statements previously made when considering the labour force changes between the two census years. That is that the labour force in absolute terms will increase and that the number of females, especially married, constituting part of the labour force will rise. For example, for every 100 economically active persons the breakdown approximates the following:

1. "Labour force projections: 1973–1991" Department of Employment Gazette, April 1974 pages 304 to 310.

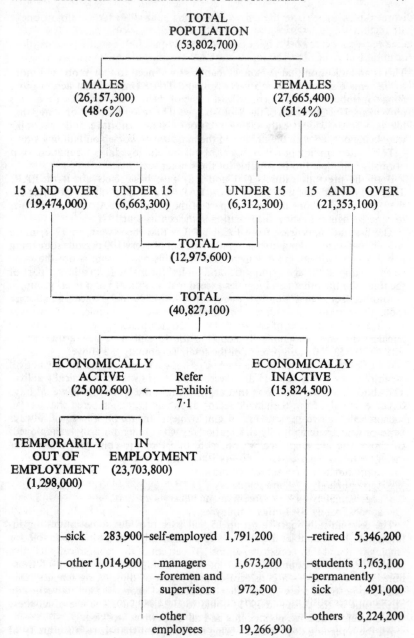

TOTAL
POPULATION
(53,802,700)

MALES
(26,157,300)
(48·6%)

FEMALES
(27,665,400)
(51·4%)

15 AND OVER
(19,474,000)

UNDER 15
(6,663,300)

UNDER 15
(6,312,300)

15 AND OVER
(21,353,100)

TOTAL
(12,975,600)

TOTAL
(40,827,100)

ECONOMICALLY
ACTIVE
(25,002,600)

Refer
Exhibit
7·1

ECONOMICALLY
INACTIVE
(15,824,500)

TEMPORARILY
OUT OF
EMPLOYMENT
(1,298,000)

IN
EMPLOYMENT
(23,703,800)

–sick   283,900
–other 1,014,900

–self-employed 1,791,200
–managers   1,673,200
–foremen and
  supervisors   972,500

–other
  employees   19,266,900

–retired   5,346,200
–students   1,763,100
–permanently
  sick   491,000
–others   8,224,200

Source: Extracted from Tables 1 and 13 of Census 1971 Great Britain, Summary
     Tables (1% Sample), 1973, HMSO.

EXHIBIT 7.3

	Males	*Females*
1961	67·5	32·5
1971	63·5	36·5
1991	61·2	38·8

This is an indication that personnel managers will need to look more and more to the female sector to fill job vacancies, and Trade Unions must accept more female members. Businessmen, at least some of them, are already aware of this movement. The Chairman of the Scottish Special Housing Association stated that his association was already facing a chronic labour shortage and that talks were being opened with the unions on the mass use of women on building sites.[1]

This statement implies that females will be employed in occupations not normally considered to be suitable for the weaker sex.

Both the previous exhibits (7·1 and 7·2) gave basic facts about the EAP. They did not indicate how many of the EAP were temporarily inactive nor did they give details about the inactive part of the population. Again, we will turn to concrete figures to show the situation in the census year 1971.

The first fact appearing from Exhibit 7·3 is that there were, in 1971, more women than men making up the population; out of every 100 persons something like 51½ were women and 48½ men. However, this relationship is not the same when looking at the age groups '15 and under' for males form a larger part of the total. On the other hand females exceed males in the '15 and over' group. ·

Another fact is that although there were 19,474,000 males aged 15 and over (potential working male force) the number that were economically active was 15,866,500; 81½ percent of the total .On the other hand there were 9,136,000 females who were economically active in the 15 and over age group which totalled 21,353,100; 42·8 percent of the total. To simplify the above:

out of every 100 males 15 and over ....81 were economically active

out of every 100 females 15 and over.........43 were economically active

The above is a clear indication that any growth in the labour force would have to come, mainly, from the female sector. It should be remembered that not all economically active persons are in employment. Invariably there will always be some who are temporarily sick and others who are temporarily unemployed. Of those who are employed we can note that they are employed under four major 'status' categories. Out of every 100 in employment:

approximately   7·5 are self-employed

approximately   7·0 are managers

approximately   4·1 are foreman and supervisors, and

approximately 81·3 other employees.

The economically inactive group 15 and over provides some interesting information. For example, the retired and permanently sick are not available for employment and they constitute, almost, 37 percent of the economically inactive total. The student population are potential employees as are many of those noted under 'others' – a considerable proportion of these being females. One can suppose from these figures that the potential economically active group, at the time of the census in 1971, would total 34,989,900. The use of all these would create problems: no students and all housewives working.

All the foregoing does seem to bring out the point that there is a scarcity of labour.

This is very interesting information but it does not recognise that labour

1. As reported in Express and Star, Oct 3, 1974 p. 13. "Building chief predicts women labourers". The Chairman of the SSH: Mr. W. A. Gordon Muir.

is a 'heterogeneous factor'. It does not answer the important question of how these people are employed. What are their occupations? How many miners and quarrymen are there? How many woodworkers or textile workers?

Occupations

According to the general explanatory notes issued at the beginning of the 1% Sample of the Census 1971 it stated that "The OCCUPATION of a person is the kind of work which he or she performs, regard being paid to the conditions under which it is performed. This alone determines the occupational group to which the person is assigned. The nature of the factory, business, or service in which the person is employed has no bearing upon the classification of his occupation, except to the extent that it enables the nature of his duties to be more clearly defined. Thus, a crane driver may be employed in a shipyard, an engineering works or in building and construction, but this has no bearing upon his occupation and all crane drivers are classified to the same occupational group."[1]

OCCUPATIONS – CHANGING STRUCTURE

Occupations are subject to change. Some occupations that exist today may have existed for hundreds of years (thatchers) and others for only a short period of time (electronic engineers). Some occupations, over time, are on the decline (agricultural occupations) whereas others are increasing in importance (manufacturing and service occupations).

At the beginning of the 19th century the greater part of the British population lived off the land; most workers were occupied on the land. Today, one and three-quarters centuries later, the occupational structure of the British labour force is quite different. Small number of workers are required for agricultural occupations, many are demanded by manufacturing and many more are required for occupations in the service sector of industry. The change has been from 'toilers' to 'blue collar' to 'white collar' cocupations.

Occupations change in relation to changes in the demand for goods and services. They reflect the use society has for the efforts of labour. There is need for occupational mobility – it has been claimed that during the life time of a worker it can be expected that he will change his occupation three times.[2]

An understanding of occupations and occupation changes is needed for manpower planning by businesses and the government. An example of this is found in the National Plan.[3] The forecast for labour indicated that there would be shortage of skilled and qualified manpower. There was need to accelerate training and retraining. There was need to provide for these becoming redundant. Above all, economic growth requires forward planning of labour as well as the other factors of production.

1971 OCCUPATIONS

The Census of Population 1971, carried out by the Office of Population Censuses and Surveys, classified occupations into 27 occupation unit groups (OUGs). Each of these were subdivided into various occupations which fitted into each OUG; all in all 223 occupations were listed.[4] Some OUGs had only 2 and others 3 or 4 or more; group XXV (Professional, Technical workers, Artists)

1. Census 1971 Great Britain – Summary Tables (1% Sample), HMSO, 1973, p. xii.
2. Factors which affect changes of occupations are noted in Vol. I page 21.
3. "The National Plan" Cmnd. 2764, HMSO, September 1965 pages 39 to 43.
4. For brief description of each occupation refer to 1% Sample publication pages xxxii to xlix.

had 40 sub groups. It would take too long to make note of all these groups and sub groups but it is worthwhile indicating the 27 groupings and the male and female make-up of each group.[1] This has been done in Exhibit 7.4.

1. Age break-down and industries using these occupations are available in the 1% Sample publication.

EXHIBIT 7.4
IMPORTANCE OF OCCUPATION GROUPS

		NUMBERS EMPLOYED			
		TOTALS			
OUG Numbers	OCCUPATION UNIT GROUPS	Actual	as %	MALES	FEMALES
	ALL Occupations of which	23,703,800	100·0	14,998,600	8,705,200
I	Farmers, foresters, fishermen	729,700	3·1	629,400	100,300
II	Miners and quarrymen	235,400	1·0	235,300	100
III	Gas, coke and chemicals makers	127,400	0·5	114,000	13,400
IV	Glass and ceramic makers	93,000	0·4	63,600	29,400
V	Furnace, forge, foundry, rolling mill workers	157,400	0·7	150,300	7,100
VI	Electrical and electronic workers	599,900	2·5	522,300	77,600
VII	Engineering and allied trades workers	2,654,800	11·2	2,373,100	281,700
VIII	Woodworkers	407,000	1·7	395,000	12,000
IX	Leather workers	110,400	0·5	55,000	55,400
X	Textile workers	292,200	1·2	134,800	156,400
XI	Clothing workers	394,600	1·7	73,600	321,000
XII	Food, drink and tobacco workers	359,400	1·5	254,100	105,300
XIII	Paper and printing workers	306,700	1·3	212,600	94,100
XIV	Makers of other products	298,200	1·3	194,200	104,000
XV	Construction workers	539,400	2·3	538,100	1,300
XVI	Painters and decorators	270,600	1·1	263,800	6,800
XVII	Drivers of stationary engines, cranes, etc.	296,800	1·3	293,500	3,300
XVIII	Labourers not elsewhere classified	1,090,100	4·6	948,100	142,000
XIX	Transport and communications workers	1,350,500	5·7	1,202,700	147,800
XX	Warehousemen, storekeepers, packers, bottlers	773,500	3·3	482,200	291,300
XXI	Clerical workers	3,498,100	14·8	1,047,600	2,450,500
XXII	Sales workers	2,194,300	9·3	1,153,400	1,040,900
XXIII	Service, sport and recreation workers	2,877,400	12·1	850,700	2,026,700

IMPORTANCE OF OCCUPATION GROUPS
NUMBERS EMPLOYED

OUG Numbers	OCCUPATION UNIT GROUPS	TOTALS Actual	as %	MALES	FEMALES
XXIV	Administrators and managers	928,100	3·9	849,100	79,000
XXV	Professional, technical workers, artists	2,686,900	11·3	1,653,300	1,033,600
XXVI	Armed forces (British and foreign)	247,200	1·0	236,400	10,800
XXVII	Inadequately described occupations	185,800	0·8	72,400	113,400

Note: Percentage figures do not add up to 100 per cent due to rounding.
Source: Extracted from Table 22 pages 118–119 of 1% Sample Summary Tables publication of 1971 Census of Population.
Percentage figures calculated by author.

EXHIBIT 7.4

Exhibit 7.4 shows that the two largest occupation units groups are in the service section of industry: Clerical workers (14·8 per cent) and Services, sport and recreation workers (12·1 per cent). These two OUGs constitute more than one-fourth the economically active persons in employment. In both these groups females out number males the ratios are as follows:

Clerical workers   1 male to 2·359 females, and
Services, etc.   1 male to 2.382 females.

Further, the number of females in these two OUGs approximate 51·43 per cent of all economically active females. In other words, more than 1 in every 2 females have occupations in these broad areas.

The next largest group of workers are occupied in the group classified as 'Professional, technical workers, artists'; more than 11 per cent of the EAP. This group is also in the service section of industry. The group is male dominated, but the ratio of men to women is approximately 1·6 males to every one female.

The fourth largest group is "Engineering and allied trades workers" having more than 11 per cent of the economically active population. This group is in the "secondary production" area and it is definitely male dominated; the ratio is approximately 6·4 males to every one female. The number of male workers in this group represents approximately 16 per cent of the total male EAP.

Thus, the four largest occupation unit groups, in terms of employment, absorb approximately:

49½ per cent of the total economically active population,
66½ per cent of all economically active females, and
39½ per cent of all economically active males.

From Exhibit 7.4 can be extracted the proportions of employment in primary, secondary and tertiary (service) areas of production[1] .Out of each 100 workers actively employed the relationship would be, approximately, as follows:

1. Actual demarcation of the OUGs into this area of production is open to debate. Refer to Volume I page 13. Exhibit 7·4 changes occupational classification into industrial classification.

4 in primary production   (OUGs 1 and 2),
34 in secondary production (OUGs 3 to 18), and
62 in tertiary production   (OUGs 19 to 27).

In terms of production Great Britain is definitely a "service" type economy.

Of the 27 OUGs listed there are only 6 where female workers outnumber the males (OUGs IX, X, XI, XXI, XXIV, XXVII); one of these by only 400 and the last group should not really be included. Now, if we were to consider the 223 occupations that make up these groups we would find that female workers dominated 40 occupations; the remander (183) are male dominated.

Exhibit 7.5 shows 18 occupations of the 183 dominated by males and Exhibit 7.6 shows the main occupations dominated by females.

MALE DOMINATED OCCUPATIONS
IN 1971

OUG Number	Occupation Number	Occupation	Males	Females*
II	007	Coal mine – workers underground	200,700	0
XV	095	Plasterers, cement finishers, terrazzo workers	45,700	0
XIX	133	Stevedores, dock labourers	43,300	0
XIX	118	Drivers, motormen, second men, railway engines	36,400	0
XVII	102	Boiler firemen	34,800	0
XVIII	106	Railway lengthmen	25,700	0
VI	026	Linesmen, cable jointers	23,700	0
XIX	115	Deck, engineering officers and pilots, ship	18,900	0
II	010	Surface workers not elsewhere classified – mines and quarries	17,900	0
III	011	Furnacemen, coal gas and coke ovens	17,900	0
XV	094	Masons, stone cutters, slate workers	15,800	0
XIX	119	Railway guards	14,500	0
VIII	058	Pattern makers	13,000	0
XIX	124	Shunters, pointsmen	10,400	0
XIX	117	Aircraft pilots, navigators and flight engineers	8,800	0
XXV	202	Metallurgists	8,000	0
XVI	101	Coach painters (so described)	7,000	0
VII	034	Steel erectors, riggers	4,100	0

Note: *figure "0" in this column signifies "nil or negligible".
Source: Extracted from Table 14 of 1% Sample, Census of Population 1971.

EXHIBIT 7.5

It is worth noting that in the 18 male dominated occupations the number of females employed is nil or negligible. A closer look at the occupations show they are of the type that normally:

require heavy lifting or
are very dirty or
are very dangerous or
are very hot.

These occupations are those typically associated with males, such as coal mining, furnacemen, dock labourers, etc. The rates of pay should take these conditions into consideration.

On the other hand, none of the 223 occupations listed showed females dominating any occupation where there were nil or negligible males employed. A selection of 18 occupations dominated by women are shown in Exhibit 7.6.

FEMALE DOMINATED OCCUPATIONS
IN 1971

OUG Number	Occupation Number	Occupation	Males	Females	Ratio*
XI	076	Hand and machine sewers and embroiderers, textile and light leather products	800	230,100	1–288
XXIII	158	Domestic housekeepers	400	34,800	1–87
XXI	141	Typists, shorthand writers, secretaries	10,700	758,900	1–71
XXV	189	Occupation therapists	200	6,000	1–30
XXIII	164	Maids, valets and related service workers not elsewhere classified	15,200	427,600	1–28
XXIII	161	Canteen assistants, counter hands	10,800	293,400	1–27
XXV	183	Nurse	37,300	394,400	1–11
XXV	188	Physiotherapists	900	7,500	1–8
XXIII	166	Charwomen, office cleaners, window cleaners, chimney sweeps	65,800	456,400	1–7
XXI	140	Office machine operators	23,900	152,700	1–6
XXIII	157	Housekeepers, stewards, matrons and housemothers	5,000	31,900	1–6
X	066	Winders, reelers	4,500	26,900	1–6
XIX	127	Telephone operators	18,600	88,700	1–5
XXIII	163	Kitchen hands	21,200	100,400	1–5
XXII	144	Shop salesmen and assistants	182,300	786,100	1–4
IV	016	Ceramics' decorators and finishers	2,200	7,800	1–4
XXIII	167	Hairdressers, manicurists, beauticians	34,600	124,200	1–4
VI	029	Electrical and electronic fitters	13,000	37,900	1–3

Note: * Ratios are taken to nearest whole number.
Source: Extracted from Table 14 of 1 % Sample, Census of Population 1971.

EXHIBIT 7.6

Exhibit 7.6 lists the top 18 occupations that are female dominated, and they have been shown from the greatest dominated occupation to the lesser ones. The first listed is, by far, the exceptional female dominated occupation when compared to the rest. A glance at these occupations seem to indicate the lack of

conditions noted for male dominated occupations, for example, they do not normally require heavy lifting. On the other hand, female occupations are the type that normally:

require neatness of handling.

This covers many aspects such as softness of touch, nimbleness of fingers, feeling towards helping others, etc.

People differ in sex but these differences are not so important as they once thought they were. The big differences in one sex performing jobs in these occupations better than others is the result of training given throughout their educational life. For example boys are trained in woodwork and metalwork whereas girls are trained in domestic work and office work.

Both exhibits clearly bring out the point that labour is not a homogeneous factor. One thing not clearly noted is that occupations can be more narrowly defined; in other words these occupations can be broken down into even more homogeneous groupings. For example, in Exhibit 7.6 the 7th occupation shown, number 183, the classification "nurse" could be divided into "hospital nurse", "district nurse", "midwife", "health visitor", etc. The ratio would be quite different. How many male midwives are there? None as far as author is aware. How many male health visitors are there? About two dozen in 1975. To be more meaningful occupations need to be classified under many more homogeneous headings.

1972 – New List of Occupations

While the Census of Population classifies occupations under one system, the Department of Employment has recently developed a new and comprehensive Classification of Occupations and Directory of Occupational Titles (CODOT). At the same time, they prepared a list of key occupations.[1]

The Department stated that "These are occupations for which it has been agreed that figures are needed and can be collected at national level. It is not possible to collect and publish statistics on a national scale about every occupation; for practical reasons it is necessary to concentrate on a fairly limited number." They also stated that "To ensure compatibility between CODOT and the key list, all key occupations are identified and defined in CODOT and grouped in the same broad structure of 18 major groups." The following Exhibit (7.7) gives these groupings and the number of occupations listed under each.

The groupings in Exhibit 7.7 appear to be a much better system of classifying occupations. Nurses are classified in the list of key occupations under several occupations, for example:

Nursing administrators and nursing executives.

State registered and state enrolled nurses and state-certified midwives.

Nursing auxiliaries and assistants.

Better, but still it does not separately classify midwives nor is there any mention of health visitors. These, evidently, are not individual key occupations. Perhaps CODOT, which contains about 3,500 coded occupations, will break such groups as nurses into even more homogeneous occupations.

1. 'List of key occupations for statistical purposes', Department of Employment Gazette, Sept 1972, pages 799–802.

CODOT GROUPING AND
NUMBER OF KEY OCCUPATIONS IN EACH GROUP

Group	Group Listing	Number of Key Occupations
I	Managerial (General Management)	2
II	Professional and related supporting management and administration	21
III	Professional and related in education, welfare and health	24
IV	Literary, artistic and sports	9
V	Professional and related in science, engineering, technology and similar fields	31
VI	Managerial (excluding general management)	26
VII	Clerical and related	15
VIII	Selling	7
IX	Security and protective services	9
X	Catering, cleaning, hairdressing and other personal service	26
XI	Farming, fishing and related	13
XII	Materials processing (excluding metal)	29
XIII	Making and repairing (excluding metal and electrical)	53
XIV	Processing, making, repairing and related (metal and electrical)	69
XV	Painting, repetitive assembling, product inspecting, packaging and related	14
XVI	Construction, mining and related not identified elsewhere	22
XVII	Transport operating, materials moving and storing and related	28
XVIII	Miscellaneous	6
	TOTAL	402

EXHIBIT 7.7

Purpose of Listing Key Occupations

The purpose of providing a list of key occupations, according to the Department of Employment, is to identify those occupations for which national statistics are most needed with the aim of helping government and industry in the light of current needs.

Occupational mobility has taken place and will take place because of the changing pattern of demand for labour. It is imperative that labour is directed into the right occupations, and that businessmen and the government establish training systems relevant to the changing occupation structure. Economic growth depends upon us making the most efficient use of our labour force and this can be achieved, partially, by ensuring specific occupational shortages do not occur. Equilibrium between the demand for and the supply of specific occupations (for all occupations) is the goal to be achieved to satisfy economic growth.

RETURNS TO THE FACTORS OF PRODUCTION

Chapter Eight

Determination of Wages

The reward to labour[1] for its efforts in the production of goods and services is *wages*.

Wages, according to Economists, refers to payments to all individuals for their skills and energy made available to an employer in producing goods and services. Normally the payments to workers on a weekly basis are usually called wages whereas payments made monthly (usually by cheque) are called salaries. However, as far as we are concerned the monies paid to all forms of labour (worker on the production floor, maintenance worker, clerk in the office, works manager, etc.) are considered as wages.[2]

All employees make a contract with their employers. It could be an oral or written contract; it could be covered by collective agreements. The contract would make note of the time employees are at the disposal of employers, stipulate benefits such as holidays, use of company car and perhaps state the elements that are to be included in the pay packet. Perhaps for one worker it consists of a basic wage plus piece work rates, for another it may be basic wage plus commissions, and for yet another it is basic wages plus overtime payments plus productivity payments.

Wages, payable weekly, may be paid on a time rate (a specified rate per hour) or on a piece rate (a specified rate per unit of work produced) or a combination of the two. Expressed differently:

Wages = hourly rate × number of hours

Wages = piece rate × number of pieces

Wages = (hourly rate × number of hours) plus (piece rate × number of pieces).

Salaries are usually paid by time or a combination of time and commission, and sometimes by commission only whereby a salesman may receive a specified percentage of the value at which each item is sold.

It can be seen that different groups of labour have their wages treated in different ways, and thus total wages can be calculated in different ways. This creates a problem in discussing how wages are determined.

CONFUSION OF TERMS

Before getting to grips with "wage determination" it is essential that certain terms be made clear.

1. Wages has already been defined in two ways: the one used by Economists and the other referring to "a contract with employers". The first is preferred by Economists and shall be used in this section unless otherwise stated.

2. Wages and wage rate should be distinguished. Wages refers to payments to

1. Information on labour is in Vol. I pages 17 to 22.
2. Countries do not normally attempt to separate these two types of labour income in their national income statistics.

labour for their skills and energy. Wage rate, for example, refers to the wage paid at the rate for the job for a specified period of time be it an hour, a day, a week, etc. Wage rates may be based on time rates, piece rates, standard rates or other forms. Thus:

Wages = *Rate* per hour × Number of hours. OR:

Wages = Rate per piece × Number of pieces.

It can be seen that two workers may do the same type of work in the same plant but receive different wages simply because one worker has worked more hours or produced more pieces than his mate.

3. Wages should be carefully distinguished from earnings. Earnings is a wider term and would include contributions to the pay packet not necessarily related to the "skill and efforts of labour", for example payments for good time keeping. Often the tendency is to include overtime (more than the basic *rate* is paid for an extra *hour* of skill and effort) and bonuses (here a firm may set output targets for a worker or group of workers to achieve and when output is greater than the target the firm gives a special payment). *Some considerations are debatable*[1] – the key for inclusion is whether they are or are not payments for skill and effort.

4. Money wages and real wages are terms that are often confused. Money wages often called nominal wages, refers to wages expressed in terms of money. Real wages are wages expressed in terms of real goods and services an employee can purchase with his money wages. For example, let us assume that one year ago a man received money wages for his weekly efforts totalling £25. At that time he paid his weekly rent of £10, bought a basket of goods (specified number of items) totalling £15 and saved nothing. Today, a year later, he still receives £25 but over this span of time prices have risen by 10 per cent. Today his weekly rent would be £11 and the same number of items in the basket of goods would now cost £16·50 – a total outlay of £27·50. The worker's money wages have not changed but his real wages have fallen because he can not purchase that which he was able to purchase one year earlier. Our worker is worse off! To offset this difference between money and real wages the worker needs an increase in money wages that will enable him to match his previous purchases.[2]

RATE DIFFERENCES

Wage rates paid to labour in one occupation can, and usually do, differ from the rates paid to labour in other occupations. The basic reasons for these differences arise because labour has many different qualities (mental abilities, physical abilities, etc.) and the rates paid tend to reflect the special contributions made by occupations to production. Some occupations require longer training (skilled) and others none (non-skilled). Rates paid evaluate these contributions. On the other hand some workers receive higher rates because their position demands responsibilities greater than others.

On the other hand some workers may receive higher rates because it reflects severe working conditions such as miners working at the coal face or spider men working at great heights. Not everyone has the desire nor mental attitudes to work in these dangerous positions. Other occupations may be restricted in supply because of certain in-born qualities (how many people have the ability to differentiate differences in acute taste (tea tasters and wine tasters) or acute smell required in certain occupations).

1. Refer to element five towards end of this chapter.
2. Refer to Chapter 9. What will be the effect of increased productivity on money wages and real wages??

Rate differences may reflect the barriers to entry into certain occupations. Some skills may restrict entry of apprentices with the intention of keeping supply low in relation to high demand. Their rates will tend to be higher than skilled occupations which do not create this artificial barrier to entry.

Perhaps the most noticeable of rate differences is that paid to men compared to women . . . even in the same occupation. To show this let us consider the rates of males and females in one section of the distributive trades, i.e. retail and food trades in England and Wales.[1] In this industry females constitute approximately 60 per cent of the labour force. At the end of March 1970 the rate for men was 226 shillings (£11·3) and that of females 175s 6d (£8·775). This meant that the wage rate for females was only 78 per cent of males. Under the Equal Pay Act 1970[2] employers are required to give equal treatment for pay (also terms and conditions of work) to men and women employed on work of the same or broadly similar nature or on work which was given the same value (although the work was different) under a job evaluation[3] scheme. At the end of March 1974 the rates were still different: the rate for males being £16·35 and that for females £15·40. The difference is now smaller; the female rate is now 94 per cent of the wage rate given to males. Even these differences must disappear when the 1970 Act comes into operation.

Rates differ for a variety of reasons.

WAGE DRIFT

Earlier it was noted that the earnings of a person are different from the rates that are negotiated. The "gap" between these two has been given a special name called "the wage drift". The gap has gradually been increasing; becoming more noticeable ever since the mid 1930s. A visual interpretation of the gap is shown in Exhibit 8.1.

1. Information for this example was extracted from "Progress towards equal pay" in Department of Employment Gazette, August 1974, Tables 2 and 3.
2. This Act comes into operation on December 29, 1975.
3. Job evaluation is briefly discussed later in this chapter.

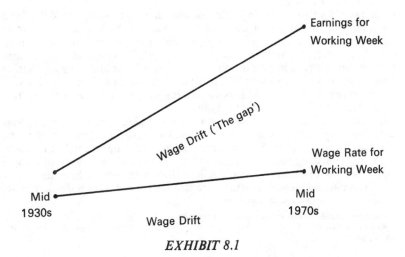

EXHIBIT 8.1

The gap, according to the Donovan report,[1] shows "a remarkable transfer of authority in collective bargaining". They stated that "Before the war it was generally assumed that industry-wide agreements could provide almost all the joint regulation that was needed, leaving only minor issues to be settled by individual managers. Today the consequences of bargaining within the factory can be more momentous than those of industry-wide agreements".

What are the major elements filling the gap? These very simply stated are:
1. incentive earnings or piecework,
2. company or factory additions, and
3. overtime earnings.

Other elements, minor in importance, also fill in the gap. Most of these will be noted when discussing the elements that make up the pay packet.

It should be noted that the gap is greater in some industries than in others. Some companies have little freedom to negotiate other rates at local levels whereas other companies are not hindered by their trade associations to exceed nationally negotiated rates. Some companies, in the face of competition, offer additions to the national rates to attract scarce labour or to keep its present labour force.

Workers, on the other hand, operate in the field by putting pressure on their employers to provide more than the wage rates. Some occupations (skilled) pressurise companies to create additions to the basic rates to maintain wage differentials.

The above statements state what have caused the gap. Underlying these forces is the fact that national agreements normally fix minimum levels and maximums are determined by negotiations carried out at the factory or the company. To close the gap it is necessary to remove the freedom of negotiating at the factory level by transferring more authority to the collective bargaining table at the national level.

SUPPLY AND DEMAND FOR LABOUR
Having explained some terms associated with wages it is necessary to consider the supply and demand for labour.

The supply of labour, previously noted,[2] is influenced by:
1. The population.
2. The proportion of the population actually forming the labour force.
3. The average number of hours the work force is prepared to work in a given period.
4. The quality of the skill and effort provided by workers.

The demand for labour is a derived demand, in other words it depends upon:
1. The existing demand for goods and services produced by a business. Also, it depends upon:
2. The availability of other factors of production.
3. The prices of other factors of production.

Like any good or service the price of labour (wages) will or should depend on the interaction of supply and demand. Later in this section it will become evident that this partially explains how wages are determined.

DETERMINATION OF WAGES
When considering how wages are determined it is best to break this section into two parts:

1. Royal Commission on Trade Unions and Employers' Associations 1965–1968, HMSO, June 1968 para 57.
2. Refer to Volume I page 17.

1. The historical or classical.
2. The modern.

Historical

Over time different theories[1] have been propounded about wages. These were usually restrictive in their assumptions; they did not consider the major role of collective bargaining nor the growing importance of trade unions in wage negotiations. One of these theories, the marginal productivity theory is classical in the sense that it related to conditions existing prior to the growth of trade unions and collective agreements.

In the 19th century, with the introduction of machines and the factory system, it was the laws of supply and demand which settled the price of labour. The idea was that "labour is dear when it is scarce and cheap when it is plentiful". Men tended to act independently when bargaining with their employer. Employers attempted to find their labour in the cheapest market; thus the exploitation of children. Laissez-faire (lack of government influence) was the key note of this day and age. However, conditions were changing.

During the 19th century trade unions had little power but their power was on an upward trend. Even though unions began organising semi-skilled workers (those needing a small amount of training) in the 1880s it was not until after the first world war that they were considered to be strong enough to balance the powers enjoyed by employers. They were now able to improve the welfare of member workers by obtaining higher wages and reducing hours of work.

During this time there were many workers who were not trade union members and who were not able to secure a fair share of the increased wealth Great Britain was enjoying. Experience was showing that low wages did not always produce the best possible output. The State recognised the need for improving the welfare of the workers who were weak and not organised to bargain for those minimum wage standards which were being agreed upon between unions and employers. So, the State stepped in to protect workers in the sweated trades (areas where labour was not organised) and established minimum wage standards.[2]

Also during this period scientific management had its beginning. In the latter 19th and early 20th centuries Frederick Winslow Taylor (so-called father of scientific management) and other pioneers were proposing schemes to reduce the time spent in performing production operations. The object was to increase output and allow both workers and managers to enjoy the benefits.

With all of these changes (recognition of trade unions, State interference, scientific management, etc.) and others not mentioned (growth of markets, speed-up of communications by rail, wire and sea, change in social attitudes, etc.) we can see the beginning of the end of simple supply and demand interactions as being the only determinants in deciding the pay packet the worker takes home.

The marginal product theory, previously discussed, did not consider these changes. It may be a satisfactory theory for the early 19th century but not for the changed world of the 1970s.

1. Suggest students read "Wages and Labour Economics" J. M. Jackson, McGraw-Hill,
2. Acts brought into operation were the 1909 and 1918 Trades Boards Acts, Coal Mines (Minimum Wages) Act 1912 and Agricultural Wages (Regulation) Act 1924.

Modern

In the 1970s, wage levels are generally determined by collective agreements. The majority of workers are covered by negotiations between trade unions and employer associations. In 1972 trade union membership was approximately 11,315,000 but it was estimated that agreements reached by trade unions covered approximately 4,000,000 non union members. To put it another way, approximately 60 out of every 100 economically active persons benefit from collective agreements arranged between trade unions and employer associations. The Trades Union Congress (TUC) gave written evidence to the Royal Commission on Trade Unions and Employers' Associations 1965-68[2] claiming the influence

2. As before and hereafter referred to simply as the Donovan Report. Written evidence appeared in para 151.

of industry-wide bargaining was as follows:

    5,000,000 employees are not covered by agreements,
    1,000,000 employees are covered mainly by company agreements,
    4,000,000 employees are in Wage Council industries,
    7,000,000 employees are in industries in which industry-wide agreements
            were closely followed at company and local level, and
    6,000,000 employees were in industries covered by industry-wide agree-
            ments where bargaining within companies has an important
            influence on actual earnings.

This evidence supports the fact that trade unions are powerful negotiators on the behalf of its members – suppliers of labour.

When arranging collective agreements there appears to be an automatic minimum and maximum wage level. The minimum is determined by the government which sets the level of unemployment benefits. It would pay a worker to become unemployed should his wages fall below this level. On the other hand, in the absence of government benefits, the minimum is determined by opportunity cost.[1]

1. Refer to Volume I page 8 for explanation.

The maximum is determined by employers. The maximum being the level at which they are not prepared to offer wages which would result in their profits being squeezed below a level which they consider to be normal.

Thus, the wage level reached from negotiations, resulting in collective agreements, must be between the acceptable minimum and maximum levels as noted.

Agreements, can basically, be of two types:
1. Individual.
2. Collective.

When an employee and his employer bargain about the employee's wages (and work conditions) we say they have negotiated an *individual agreement*. On the other hand when a group of employees (collectively represented) reach an agreement with their employer we claim that they have had their wages fixed by a *collective agreement*. This type agreement applies to all wage negotiations not carried out by individuals on their own behalf.

Collective agreements, as well as individual agreements, cover more aspects of a worker's life than wages alone.

Collective agreements not only cover wage rates but other payments which are added to the wage rate, such as threshold agreements, payments for unsocial hours, productivity arrangements and other special allowances which when totalled become the earnings of the worker. Outside the wage area, the agreements can include hours of work, employment of apprentices, entitlement to holidays and holiday pay, redundancy, guaranteed work arrangements and

general working conditions. Added to these are the procedures for settling disputes.

These agreements are the result of:

1. Voluntary action, or
2. Statutory regulations.

Voluntary agreements are those reached without governmental intervention, and constitute the greater part of all collective agreements; covering approximately 60 out of every 100 workers. *Statutory regulations* apply to those agreements reached by a wage fixing authority set up by legislation such as the Wages Councils Act of 1959 and the Agricultural Wages Act of 1948.

Regardless of how the agreements are reached they form the standards for workers and managers in their dealing with each other.

This is the background to the modern version of how wages are determined.

THE PAY PACKET – EARNINGS

Our concern will now be centred on that part of collective agreements that refers to the earnings of labour. What goes into the pay packets? How are the items making up the pay packet determined? These questions are not always easy to answer because of the varied and diverse arrangements reached under collective bargaining. A worker's pay packet may be the end result of negotiations carried out at various levels; industry, regional, district, company, work-place. It may be the result of any one or all levels.

What are the earnings of a worker? The Donovan Report stated that the average earnings of an adult male manual worker in the gas industry, a nationalised industry, in October 1966 was approximately £20.26.[1] This was made up of:

basic pay	£13·29
overtime	4·52
service increments	0·25
shift allowances	0·91
incentive payments	0·86
other payments	0·43
Earnings	**20·26**

A road haulage driver, in September 1967, had an average pay of £22·39 for an average nominal working week of 58·6 hours[2] The pay packet included the following:

basic pay	£12·67
bonus and other payments	1·29
overtime payments	8·43
Earnings	**22·39**

In this case overtime represents a considerable part of earnings. The Prices and Incomes Board said that "The large amount of overtime represents units of payments rather than hours strictly worked; in other words, the size of the pay packet is *determined* not so much by the number of hours worked as by the number of hours for which the employer is prepared to pay".

1. Donovan Report, HMSO, June 1968, Para 137. Details obtained from a Prices and Incomes Board Report. Figures changed to decimal currency, rounded to nearest new penny by author.
2. Donovan Report, para 139. From a survey carried out by the Prices and Incomes Board. Figures changed to decimal currency, rounded to nearest new penny, by author.

In both cases the *'wage drift'* is very noticeable; earnings are much higher than basic pay. The gas industry worker's drift being £6·97 and the road haulage driver's earnings that fitted into the gap was £9·72.

In comparison the Donovan Report[1] considered an area of retailing (drapery, outfitting and footwear) where little overtime is worked and noted that earnings above the minimum came mainly from higher rates than those prescribed by the Wages Council or from commission on sales. They noted that in October 1966 the statutory minimum rates for male shop assistants varied from £9 15s 0d (£9·75) to £10 16s 0d (£10·80) according to the area of the country; average earnings for a working week of 40·3 hours were £15 16s 1d (£15·80416).

The last two examples are of industries whose minimum rates of pay are subject to collective agreements covered by statutory regulations – by Wage Councils.[2] These Councils have the power to determine minimum rates of pay; they do not have the power to determine other rates of pay.

Statutory regulations results, in addition to Wage Councils, from two Agricultural Wages Boards which fix minimum remunerations for approximately 350,000 agricultural workers.

In the field of voluntary collective agreements, the Donovan Report (para 36) stated that the pay and conditions of an employee may be the result of collective bargains at one or more agreement levels; such as industry-wide, company or work-place. The following example provided by the Donovan Report (para 36) notes the level of agreements and type of payment that went into the pay packet of a skilled engineering time-rated fitter in a factory in the north-east of England in a particular pay week in December, 1967.

Money in pay packet[3]			Type payment	Negotiation Level
£	s	d		
11	1	8	Time rate	Industry level. Negotiated between Engineering Employers' Federation and the Confederation of Ship-building and Engineering Unions (rate for 40 hours' work)
4	8	8	Overtime	Industry level as above. (8 hours at double time)
3	13	11	Night shift Premium	Industry level as above.
11	14	11	Lieu bonus	Factory level. Negotiated between management and shop stewards.
30	19	2	Total Gross Pay	

It can be seen from these examples that the pay packet of a worker can be made up in a variety of different ways and based on a variety of negotiating levels. The Donovan Report (para 1010) stated that it has become evident that with full employment the bargaining on wages at the work place and company level are coming more and more important in *determining the wages of labour*. The Report pointed out that "The bargaining which takes place within factories

1. Para 139.
2. A report on Wage Councils can be found in April 1974 issueof Department of Employment Gazette, page 311.
3. Decimal currency equivalents of above, in order appearing: £11·083, £4·433, £3·693, £11·746 and £30·96.

is largely outside the control of employers' associations and trade unions. It usually takes place piece-meal and results in competitive sectional wage adjustments and chaotic pay structures. Unwritten understandings and 'customs and practice' predominate".

On occasion the wage structure for a group of workers may be based upon a *Committee of Inquiry*. An example of this was the inquiry into the pay and conditions of service of nurses and midwives.[1] The report was considered favourably by the Whitley Council for Nurses and Midwives (the negotiating machinery) and the increases awarded affected approximately 340,000 nurses and midwives.[2]

Changes in the formal negotiating machinery do take place. At the present time it is envisaged that a new body, the statutory Joint Industrial Council[3], replace Wages Councils.[4] Basically, this change is expected to ease the transition from statutory regulations to voluntary agreements – a development towards free collective bargaining.

Sometimes is is not possible for the two sides at the bargaining table to reach a settlement. The government, through the relevant Department[5], attempts to support the system of agreements by offering services of advice, conciliation, arbitration and inquiry. All these methods have the one aim of helping the two sides to reach a settlement. The organisation set up to provide these services is the new independent Conciliation and Arbitration Service.[6]

Advice given is basically to improve efficiency within firms. Information on manpower and productivity, procedures for arranging agreements, systems of payment. Also included are advice about job evaluation, work study and ways of reducing high labour turnover.

Conciliation, said the Donovan Report (para 434) "makes a very considerable contribution to good industrial relations". Conciliation officers during the latter 1960s handled 300 to 400 differences a year. In the early 1970s they handled more than 800. Pay is one of the major causes of disputes. These officers can intervene in a dispute on their own initiative or they may be asked to intervene at the request of one party to the dispute or both parties. The aim of conciliation is to find the right path to an agreement. On occasions they act as mediators by making suggestions. However, once conciliation fails the problem will probably go to arbitration.

Arbitration is a service provided by the Conciliation and Arbitration Service when the parties to a dispute ask for assistance. CAS will provide assistance

1. Set up by the Secretary of State in May 1974 – known as the Halsbury report.
2. It is suggested that students consult Incomes Data Report, twice monthly publication, for up to date details of settlements in all industries. The Nurses and Midwives settlement is shown on pages 15 and 16 of Report 194, October 1974.
3. JIC was the invention of the Commission on Industrial Relations and noted in its report on the Clothing Wages Council.
   The Commission on Industrial Relations was founded in 1969 and terminated on 16 September 1974.
4. Expected to take effect when the Employee Rights Bill becomes an Act in 1975.
5. At present time, March 1975, the Department of Employment.
6. This new organisation came into operation 2 September 1974. It replaced the Conciliation and Advisory Service. The major difference between these two organisations is that *now* reports are submitted to a 'council of 10' (no longer through senior Civil Servants to a Cabinet minister). The 'council of 10' is responsible for the management and development of the four services: advice, conciliation, arbitration and inquiry. The 'council of 10' has an independent chairman, 3 independent members, 3 members nominated by the T.U.C. and 3 members nominated by the C.B.I.

only after all methods of agreed negotiations within the industry have been exhausted. The problems to be decided may be referred to a single arbitrator or a board of arbitrators. Arbitrators are not full time members of staff; they are people who have had experience in industrial relations.

Inquiry refers to a Court of Inquiry. On the other hand a less formal Committee of Investigation may be constituted. The source of authority for establishing an inquiry is still under the Conciliation Act 1896 or the Industrial Courts Act 1919. Inquiries can be appointed without the consent of the parties involved in the dispute.

If all fails, the dispute may erupt into a *strike* or *lock-out*. These ultimate weapons need to be contained. It is possible to include in a collective agreement the procedures for settling disputes before the ultimate weapons are used. The 'First Oil Rig Agreement'[1] signed in July 1974, stated that the parties to the agreement should not resort to strike, work stoppage, go-slow, mass resignation, lock-out or any other industrial remedy until all procedures for achieving agreement, including the conciliation and arbitration services set up by the government have failed.

All disputes do not end up in peaceful settlement. Strikes, stoppages and the other weapons mentioned above do take place. In 1972 nearly 24,000,000 working days were lost through stoppages. There were 2,530 (33 started in 1971) stoppages in progress *during* 1972 which directly involved 1,453,000 workers and indirectly involved 281,000 other workers. Of the 2,497 stoppages starting in 1972 the number of disputes relating to wages totalled 1,477.[2]

It can be seen that what goes into the pay packet (earnings) is determined by hard bargaining and long negotiations between employees (suppliers of labour) and employers (demanders of labour).

Elements Making up the Earnings

Now that we have learned something about the machinery which is involved in wage negotiations it is important that we return to the contents of the pay packet. We have already noted that there are additions to the basic pay which, when totalled, equals earnings. We have also seen that the earnings of one worker is not made up in the same way as that of another worker. We will view these additions using a general approach, not to any specific pay packet, by stating and discussing the elements any pay packet *may* contain.

Earnings can be broken down into four basic elements, namely:
1. Basic rates.[3]
2. Incentive earnings or Piecework.
3. Special payments.
4. Personal payments.

All packets will include one or more of these elements. There is a fifth element which should be taken into consideration even though it is not included in the pay packet, namely:
5. Fringe benefits.

The '*wage drift*', as noted in Exhibit 7·8, using these elements would be:

1. The basic points of this agreement can be found in IDS Brief 44, September 1974, pages 19–20, published by Incomes Data Services Ltd.
2. "Stoppage of work due to industrial disputes in 1972" in Department of Employment Gazette, June 1973 pages 554–565.
3. May relate to piecework for basic output.

Wage Drift = Elements 1 to 4   less Element 1, or to put it another way,
Wage Drift = Earnings   less Basic rates.

In the following pages we will consider not only the forces that determine the basic rates of pay but the other forces operating in the other elements.

FIRST ELEMENT – BASIC RATES

Industry-wide agreements normally state the minimum level of pay workers in that industry should have. It is true that the minimum in one industry is not the same as in other industries, and it is also true that the basic rate paid to one group of workers in one industry are not the same as the basic rate paid to a second group in the same industry. There are wage rate differences.

Wage rate differences[1]

These differences in basic rates are related to several forces.

1. *Scarcity value of employees in each category.* Either workers are limited in supply or employers are willing to pay more for a special group of workers whose contribution to extra output (marginal product) is high. This concept of supply and demand, the elements of which have already been noted earlier in this part of the book, must play an important role in determining these basic rates.

2. *Workers with a high degree of skill.* Craftsmen may obtain higher rates because it is not possible to pay them through 'payment by results' methods. The higher rate would tend to compensate them for this.

3. *Restriction of supply.* Craftsmen can restrict supply simply by restricting membership – apprentices. By not allowing supply to exceed demand they are able to maintain or raise their wage rates.

4. *Workers are not homogeneous.* Workers have differences in intelligence, physical strength and specially developed skills, for example, craftsmen. Some occupations requiring certain abilities (physical strength) may find an abundant supply of workers whereas other occupations requiring in-born or natural talents (top quality singers) will be short in supply.

5. *Work conditions differ.* Some jobs are more dangerous and unpleasant than others. When such jobs also require special skills the wage rates tend to be high because supply is short. However, when jobs have these qualities but require no special skills (unskilled) then there is likely to be an abundant supply. Wage rates will differ depending upon these factors.

6. *Education and Training* enables individuals to develop special skills. One only needs to compare the training of an accountant and a refuse collector.

7. *Trade union power.* Not all workers are highly organised. The bargaining power of trade unions depends on whether they are highly organized or not. Those that are highly organised will be able to bargain more forcefully for higher wage rates.

8. *Demand changes.* Changed circumstances will affect the demand for an occupation. The demand for bus drivers will increase because of the high price of petrol or petrol rationing. Less passenger vehicles on the road but more buses; thus the need for more bus drivers. Higher rates will probably have to be paid to attract workers into this occupation. On the other hand a new industry may come into existence which require skills which are virtually non-existent, for example when computers first came onto the scene. In such cases demand

1. Briefly discussed earlier in this chapter. Some statements here may duplicate previous considerations but the approach is more detailed. Suggest students read previous notes on this subject before reading this section.

exceeds supply and this will have an effect on wage rates – pushing them upwards.

For these reasons, and others already considered, there will be differences in wage rates.

Rates – Various types

There are different types of wage rates, for example time rates or standard rates. Each will be discussed separately.

Time Rates

Basic rates are normally related to time. The expectation of management is that the worker completes a certain minimum output during that time. Normally we would expect to find time rates prevailing in those occupations that do *not* fit into mass production lines or where output is standardised or where machines operated are standardised. It is not normally considered to be practicable to use piece rates in these situations.

Time rates are considered to be at an advantage when:

1. workers are required to produce precision goods (highly skilled occupations),
2. workers are learning (apprentices or others undergoing training),
3. workers are occupied in supervisory or managerial positions,
4. workers provide an indirect service (maintenance men, cleaners, etc.),
5. work is non-standardised.
6. accuracy of work is more important than speed,
7. spoilage would result as the production line is speeded up. Savings will be less than the value of increased output,
8. the production unit is small and supervision is close,
9. other incentives (financial and non-financial) secure cooperation and desired output, and
10. it is the simplest scheme to operate – it is the easiest to understand.

The disadvantages associated with this method occurs when:

1. workers lack personal incentive to increase output beyond a certain level. This is considered to be the main disadvantage.
2. even the best workers tend to produce less than they are capable of producing, and
3. close supervision of workers is usually considered necessary.

Standard rates

These rates are established by job evaluation. The standard wage rate is a basic rate for a given job and is received by an employee for satisfactory performance on that job.

Job evaluation

Job evaluation is a method of assessing a job, one job in relation to another, and *not* the personal qualities of individuals doing the job. There are different systems of job evaluation that can be applied but basically they can be divided into 'analytical' and 'non-analytical'. Those that are non-analytical tend to consider jobs as a whole; they do not break the jobs down into their various parts. Jobs that are standardised (or almost standardised) are evaluated in this way, for example engineering jobs and many salaried jobs. The analytical methods consider the 'factors' (skill, responsibility, mental, physical, etc.) required for the job and the various degrees of each factor relevant to each job being evaluated.

For example 'education' may be a factor for two jobs in an office. The importance of education for the job of office boy is low compared to the educational requirements of the statistician. Other factors are considered in this way. Certain jobs are picked as 'key jobs' (often called bench marks). The importance of each factor required for these jobs are totalled and a wage assigned (50 points = £25). Other jobs (not key jobs) are evaluated by calculating points against each factor for each job – the points are totalled and these are then related to the key job(s). Let us say that the points of the second job evaluated totalled 80 points; thus the standard wage rate for this job would be

$$\frac{80 \text{ points for second job}}{50 \text{ points for key job}} \times £25 \text{ for key job} = £40 \text{ for second job.}$$

The above notes are highly simplified.

Each method has its special set of advantages and disadvantages. When similar methods are used it is possible that they differ for different work places, companies and industries. As hinted before, the system is used quite often for white-collar workers but not to any appreciable extent for manual workers, at least in Great Britain.

Some principal advantages of fixing standard wage rates by job evaluation are as follows:

1. a systematic wage rate structure is established for one job relative to another,
2. helps to maintain wage differences,
3. enables new jobs to be slotted into the existing wage structure,
4. determines wage rates objectively and thus removes personal and accidental factors often associated with other methods, and
5. enables wage differences to be explained and justified.

Some major drawbacks are:

1. the difficulty of explaining how wage rates are determined (especially analytical method),
2. relative earnings are difficult to maintain when incentive workers form a large part of all workers,
3. does not take into account temporary fluctuations in the market value of occupations (supply and demand), and
4. trade unions often regard wage rates calculated by job evaluation methods with suspicion.

The International Labour Office[1] as part of its conclusion stated that "Job evaluation seeks to give practical expression to two principles of fairness that are so widely recognised that they cannot be regarded as mere subjective assertions inspired by group interests: that of equal pay for equal work and that of differential reward in accordance with discernible differences in the sacrifices that the performance of productive work requires in terms of education, training, personal application and the endurance of adverse conditions. This objective of job evaluation gives the method a broader interest than it would have as a mere wage-fixing device.".

SECOND ELEMENT – INCENTIVE EARNINGS or PIECEWORK

Whereas the first element considers the basic rates which are applied widely, the second element (which is added to these basics) is associated with individual or group performance on the job. The basic rates are normally arranged by agreements industry-wide, but incentive earnings are usually arranged within the workplace.

1. "Job Evaluation" I.L.O., 1960 p.112.

The methods vary from simple payment by result schemes within one workplace to complicated arrangements within a company for several workplaces. Basically there are two major types:

1. Straight piece work. Here the rate paid for the 50th or 100th unit of output is the same as that paid for the first. Extra effort in producing beyond a recognised limit is not rewarded.

2. Differential piece work. Here the same job has at least two rates. The first rate for a specified output and a higher rate for output beyond the standard.

Sometimes workers are not able to reach the standard output for the day; in such cases the worker may be given a guaranteed sum of money.

Piece rates in one workplace may create problems because certain workers may not have the opportunity to earn these rates. In lieu of these payments they are given special payments (third element type payment) which are called *lieu payments*'. Here again job evaluation may be employed.

Piecework (payment by results) schemes expect a certain amount of work (Basic output) to be completed within a specified period of time, like time rates. But, unlike time rates, piece rates tend to encourage increased output and thus enable the workplace to spread overhead costs over a larger output.

This method was possible when engineering and other industries introduced mass production of standardised products on standardised machines. As more and more industries entered the mass production field this method increased in importance. Opposed to the benefits associated with payment by result schemes, the Donovan Report (para 87) stated that these schemes, more than any other method of wage payments, "have obstructed the development of orderly company and factory pay structures."

Piece work rates are usually determined by work study. The findings of the work study section are often modified when discussing jobs with individual. workers or their shop steward.

Some of the advantages and disadvantages, briefly stated, associated with piece work rates are as follows:

Advantages.

1. Suitable where work is measurable.
2. Suitable where work is standardised.
3. Effort is stimulated to increase output because the worker is paid according to his output.
4. Greater efficiency is rewarded.
5. Need of supervision is minimised.
6. Where there is a group product, group output is developed.
7. Interest may be added to dull work.
8. More goods produced in a given period of time has the effect of lowering overhead expenses (rates, rent, etc.).

Disadvantages.

1. Can create over exertion.
2. Forward planning is hindered because of variations in output.
3. Interruption in output, by situations not in control of worker, is detrimental to worker's earnings. Thus the need for some guarantees.
4. Workers might resist being switched from one job to another – from high piece rate earnings to low piece rate earnings.
5. Piece rates need continuous assessment because of increased output by as they become accustomed to repetitive work.
6. Workers' earnings often vary week by week through no fault of their own

7. Inequalities of earnings can arise when two similar products are produced but one requires more operations than the other.
8. Some workers will tend to slow down, especially under straight piece work, once they reach what they consider to be adequate earnings. This can cause 'flow of work' problems and increase overhead cost per unit of output.
9. Conflicts with factory organisation.
10. Obstructs the development of orderly company pay structures.

One major problem associated with piece work is the establishment of the rate. Is the worker being studied working at the correct speed? Does he represent the average ability of workers doing that type of work?

Output Bonuses
Some bonuses are not related to output – our concern is with those that are. *The Concise Oxford Dictionary* says a bonus is something to the good, into the bargain, especially a gratuity to workmen beyond their wages. An output bonus relates to a scheme, like the others listed in this element, in which payments vary according to output. There are many types of bonus methods, but basically they all relate to time saved compared to a predetermined standard time in performing a job. The differences in these schemes result from the variety of ways calculation are made in establishing the bonus. Bonuses may be geared to an individual and his output or to a group of workers and their mass output.

Others
There are other incentive methods: measured day work, high day rate, etc ...

Overall
There is no one best method. Each must be considered and structured to meet the present and future needs of each company and its employees. The application and thus the effect it will have on wages is determined by agreement between employers and employees (or their representatives).

THIRD ELEMENT – SPECIAL PAYMENTS
Special payments are related to social inconveniences at work. These, like incentive payments, are added to the basic rates and would normally include payments for the following:
Overtime work.
Shift work.
Night work.
Week-end work.
Special work conditions ('danger money' for working at heights or 'danger money' for coal miners working at the coal face).

All the above vary the size of the pay packet for many workers, but perhaps the biggest contribution to wages is overtime. Not all workers benefit from overtime as noted previously (retailing: drapery, outfitting and footwear) compared to the overtime worked by road haulage drivers.

Overtime
Overtime in most industries in 1938 related to work hours beyond the standard working week of 48 hours. In comparison the latter 1960s and early 1970s it usually refers to hours for a standard week of more than 40 hours. This is a sign that the number of hours constituting the standard week is on a downward trend. Overtime is expected to fluctuate about a rising trend.

It was noted by the Donovan Report that overtime for men, in 1967, was more than 6 hours a week and that in certain industries (cement and road haulage) at approximately 15 hours. The Report (para 92) stated that "The notion that labour shortage requires these levels of overtime is refuted by comparison with countries abroad." They went on to say that "The only simple explanation which fits the facts is that overtime is widely used in Britain to give adult males levels of pay which they and those who arrange the overtime regard as acceptable." However some situation may require overtime such as rush orders, repairs to machinery, etc.

The rates for overtime can vary from one industry to another. They are determined formally by collective agreement or informally by managers and individual workers (or their representatives). Details can be found in settlements which are reported by the Incomes Data Services Ltd. in their Incomes Data Reports.

FOURTH ELEMENT – PERSONAL PAYMENTS
Personal payments, like special payments, are not related to output. They are related to the individual and would include such things as:
Bonuses for good time keeping.
Cost of living payments (threshold payments)
Long service payments.
Living in London allowances.
Etc.
Of the above only two will be briefly discussed, namely, cost of living payments and London allowances.

Cost of living payments
Normally changes in the cost of living, as indicated by changes in the index of retail prices, are brought into negotiations when determining wage rates. When considered in this light, this topic rightfully should be discussed under the first element. Consideration here relates to additions that are made to wage rates as a result of changes in the index of retail prices *after* wage rates have been determined. The best example of this was the introduction of 'threshold payments' by the Chancellor of the Exchequer in October 1973. [1] This stated that "The government propose that the draft Code should provide for the negotiation of threshold agreements to help safeguard employees' standard of living against the possibility of an exceptionally high rate of price increases during Stage 3." (Para 51).

"The base date for the purpose of these agreements would be the date of publication of the Retail Price Index (RPI) figure for October 1973 and the agreements would run for up to 12 months from that date. They would allow a payment of up to 40p per week to be made if the RPI reached 7 per cent above the base figure and a further payment of up to 40p for every percentage point rise in the RPI above that during the currency of the agreement." (Para 52)

The contribution of the above added to each worker's pay packet in the last week of October 1974 the sum of £4·40 (17 per cent rise in the RPI).

These increases have now stopped, but agreements towards the end of the Stage 3 agreement, for example Kodak workers and staff, have consolidated Stage 3 threshold payments and agreed for threshold payments to be made when the RPI rises. Kodak employees arranged for threshold payments when the RPI

1. "The Price and Pay Code for Stage 3" 'A Consultative Document' Cmnd 5444, HMSO, October 1973.

rises above the figure for May 1974. They agreed a one per cent increase in base rate for each one per cent rise in the RPI beginning for senior staff when the RPI rises by 11 per cent and 12 per cent for junior staff and manual workers.

Other companies are adopting similar arrangements.

London Allowances

Many workers working in the London area receive additions to their basic wages as a result of working in a 'high cost' area. For example in November 1974 Civil Service staff working within a five-mile radius of Charing Cross get £410 per annum whereas Civil Service industrial workers get £1·96 per week for males and £1·86 per week for females. Other organisations will inevitably increase their London allowances.

These allowances are normally determined through collective bargaining.

FIFTH ELEMENT – FRINGE BENEFITS

These benefits are important to workers for they are, in all respects, an addition to their direct wage payments. They *should*[1] be considered as part of the

1. Personal Opinion. Statement may not agree with earlier statements.

pay packet. Most of them are tax free.

The firm considers them to be important because they assist in attracting and keeping its labour force. On the other hand they are important in as much as they are 'costly', but are a cost that can be offset against taxation.

The following are some of many fringe benefits.

Holidays with pay.

Use of company car.

Living in company house.

Life insurance.

Pensions (contributory and non-contributory).

Sickness benefits.

Etc.

It is envisaged that *these benefits are likely to increase in the future*. Workers seek to improve their standards of living by having additions to their overall earnings without them being indicated on their pay slip. In addition, workers are very likely to compare the benefits received by their counterparts in the European Economic Community and, where possible, obtain those fringe benefits which they judge themselves to be behind or which at present do not exist.

THE FIVE ELEMENTS

The first element in the pay packet is the one upon which the other elements are added. The difference between the additions made to the first element and total earnings constitutes the *'wage drift'*.

It should be remembered that the earnings of one worker are not always the same as other workers. One worker may have earnings based on the first element whereas another worker's earnings come from elements 1 and 2, another maybe from all 5, etc.

In most cases these elements are determined by hard bargaining.

Part Two

RETURNS TO THE FACTORS OF PRODUCTION

Chapter Nine

Wages and Productivity

Industrial production (output) and productivity (output per person) are two terms which often cause confusion. The second term refers to the relationship for any sector of industry in its output *to* the efforts involved in obtaining that output (A ratio). The ways to achieve an increase in output are as follows:
1. Increase the numbers of inputs. In other words provide more of each of the factors of production. This increases production but productivity is not increased For example:

	Industrial production	
	Before increasing units of input	*After increasing units of input*
number of units of input	10	12
output per unit of input	× 6	× 6
Total output	60	72

Industrial production has been increased as a result of increasing the number of inputs. There has been no change in the number of units produced per unit of input – it remained at 6.
2. Increase the efforts of the existing inputs in a given period of time. In other words be more efficient in the use of each unit of existing input.
This increases production by increasing productivity. For example:

	Industrial production	
	Before increasing efforts of each unit of input	*After increasing efforts of each unit of input*
number of units of input	10	10
output per units of input	× 6	×10
Total output	60	100

Industrial production has been increased as a result of increasing productivity – output per unit input has increased but there has been no change in the number of inputs.
The second situation indicates that when a factory or an economy has not the opportunity to increase its factors of production producing goods and services it can still obtain an increase in output by making better use of its existing labour, management, raw materials and machines.
In September 1965 the Government produced a National Plan – the plan being a guide to action concerned with all aspects of this country's economic development for the following five years. The important point to be noted here were two statements referring to situations one and two noted above.

With regard to situation one it stated that "Over the last decade the labour force has been increasing by about 0·6 per cent a year. But from now on this growth is likely to be much less."[1] This statement was quite true. The actual
1. "The National Plan" Cmnd. 2764, Sept. 1965, HMSO, Chapter I paragraph 7.
increase in the economic active population between 1961 and 1971 was approximately 1,186,000 (4 per cent increase) which showed the increase per year to be about 0·4 per cent. Between 1971 and the forecast for 1991 the increase is expected to approximate 2,025,400 which represents approximately 0·4 per cent per year. In other words this country can not expect more production simply by injecting more units of labour into the production lines. As the National Plan said ". . . by far the greater part of the increase in output will have to come from an increase in output per head. . . ."[2] In other words, from productivity.
2. "The National Plan" paragraph 7.

PRODUCTIVITY EXPLAINED

Productivity expresses the relationship between goals to be achieved by a firm or the economy (output) to the resources expended (input). The word used to describe this relationship in everday speech is 'efficiency'. The term refers to the amount of goods produced by each worker in a given period of time and is usually referred to as *'output per head'* or *'output per man hour'* (it could be a week, month or year). Increasing productivity simply means getting more output from the existing factors of production.

Productivity, as defined, *is* simply *a ratio* of:

$$\frac{\text{Output}}{\text{Input}} \times 100\%.$$

Inputs

The inputs relate to the factors of production. It is possible to discuss the productivity of capital or the productivity of labour, or land or enterprise. The problem becomes involved because the factors have different measurements, such as tons of coal, machine hours, etc. Land is considered to be of little importance in increasing output. Enterprise is too difficult to measure. Labour is a simpler yardstick to use and it has been found that it is quite a reliable indicator in noting relative degrees of progress. This is why we normally consider productivity as being 'output per head' or 'output per man hour'. It should be remembered that we should note the contribution made by the other factors.

Measuring

Output per head can be obtained by: $\dfrac{\text{Output}}{\text{Number of workers}}$

This is the most widely used measure of productivity. On the other hand:

$$\text{Output per man hour} = \frac{\text{Output}}{\text{Number of man-hours}}$$

These measurements are not useful by themselves. They should be used for making comparisons, for example:
1. compared to the firm's previous productivity measurement,
2. compared to the firm's competitor in the same industry, and
3. compared to a competitive firm in the same industry in another country.

A simple example may clear up the use of each method previously noted. Let us assume that Firm X's two workers produce 1,000 pins a day whereas Firm

Y's six workers have an output of 3,600 pins. The output per head for each firm is as follows:

$$\text{Firm X} \quad \frac{1,200 \text{ units of output}}{2 \text{ workers}} = 600 \text{ units per worker}$$

$$\text{Firm Y} \quad \frac{3,600 \text{ units of output}}{6 \text{ workers}} = 600 \text{ units per worker}$$

The result is that productivity, measured in this way, is the same in both firms. However, when looking at the hours worked by the workers we find that the workers in Firm X work 8 hours a day whereas those in Firm Y work 6. Using the output per man-hour measurement we find productivity to be:

$$\text{Firm X} \quad \frac{1,200 \text{ units of output}}{2 \text{ workers} \times 8 \text{ hours}} = 75 \text{ units per man-hour}$$

$$\text{Firm Y} \quad \frac{3,600 \text{ units of output}}{6 \text{ workers} \times 6 \text{ hours}} = 100 \text{ units per man-hour}$$

Thus, Firm Y has a much higher labour productivity (output per man-hour) compared to each worker (per man hour) in Firm X.

The second ratio eliminates the problem of differences in hours worked. It does not remove differences that exist in the quality of labour nor the amount and quality of the other factors of production used as inputs.

What Affects Productivity?
This question is very simply answered by saying that virtually everything affects productivity; from the smile of a foreman or the feeling generated by management that the workers matter (evidenced by the famous Hawthorne experiments) to the use of the most sophisticated machinery. Everything matters but some considerations are deemed to be more important than others. For example:
1. Transferring workers from old to new machines with the latest technical changes is considered to be one of the most, if not the most, important primary requirement for raising productivity.
2. Increase the skills of workers and management.
3. Improve the health, discipline and patriotism of workers.
4. Remove restrictive labour practices.
   Etc.

There are many ways of improving productivity; some may be outside the sphere of industry, for example trade union attitudes, but others are within the province of firms to obtain more efficient operations in production.

Basically, the forces that operate to increase productivity are those which create greater efficiency in the use of the existing factors of production. To put it another way, productivity can be enhanced by removing waste (waste of time, waste of effort) of all the factors operating in the production field.

One author[1] states quite definitely that there are several general methods of increasing the productivity of labour in promoting economic growth. The effectiveness of these, however, are limited in any given technology:

1. "Understanding Economic Growth" by Robert S. Schultz, Nov/Dec. 1966 issue of Harvard Business Review.

1. Increasing investment in plant and equipment.
2. Rationalisation of operations (efficiency studies, operational research, etc.).
3. Education (work methods, technology, leadership, etc.).

On the other hand the effectiveness of "technological change" (*new* or *improved* products and *new* and *improved* production processes) is rapid and continuing.

RETURNS TO FACTORS, PRICES AND PRODUCTIVITY

The above heading is more commonly referred to as incomes, prices and productivity. Why are they usually linked together? What is the link between these three factors? Basically they are linked together when there is a need to improve output, not by increasing the units of input but by increasing output per man-hour. The assumption is that the units of inputs available for injection into the factory (or economy) are limited; in other words a state of full employment exists. Also it is assumed that the output from these inputs are, so to speak, fixed; the aggregate supply curve is as shown in the following exhibit.

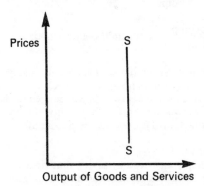

Aggregate Supply Situation in a Period
of Full Employment of Inputs

EXHIBIT 9.1

Exhibit 9.1 shows a situation where there can be no change in supply because there are no additional inputs that can be introduced into the economy. In such a situation a change in demand will push up the general price level (demand pull inflation). On the other hand, an increase in wages and/or other incomes will push up the cost of production and thus increase the general price level (cost push inflation).

The exhibit links:
1. returns to factors (wages and other incomes),
2. prices, and
3. output.

It establishes that without any increase in output (supply of goods and services) there will be no economic growth. For growth to take place and the serious threat of inflation to be curtailed in the face of increased returns to the factors there must be an increase in output. This is where "productivity" comes into the picture.

Because output can not be increased by injecting more of each factor into the

production process (first situation shown at beginning of this chapter) it is necessary to increase the output from each factor already used – productivity (second situation at chapter beginning).

An increase in productivity – increase of output per man – will increase output of goods and services made available to the community. It will tend to offset increases in incomes (returns to factors) with the increased output and so remove õr reduce the level of inflation. Further, it will enable firms and governments to achieve the economic objectives of price stability and raising living standards.[1]

This is why incomes, prices and productivity are linked.

Incomes, prices and productivity must be considered as part of one single policy in a period when factors are fully employed. Inflation must be avoided. Thus, returns to the factors of production, whether they be rent, wages, interest or profits, must be related to their productivities.

PRODUCTIVITY AGREEMENTS

The returns to labour (wages) normally forms a considerable part of a firm's total cost. For this reason considerable emphasis has been placed on firms and trade unions to reach agreements related to productivity.

What is a productivity agreement? It is "a means of offering rewards to workers for their co-operation in the more effective use of resources".[2] The object is to remove the inefficiencies in the use of manpower, raw materials, fuel and capital equipment. Often this requires the introduction of new methods of control to ensure new standards of work measurement are adhered to, and this implies the need to offer workers inducements to compensate for changed working situations. *Remove waste and become more efficient.*

Firms need increased productivity because it helps solve the problem of a firm to survive under modern conditions – increased output at lower unit cost of production and keeping prices lower than competitors.

The idea of improving productivity is not new; at the Annual General Meeting of the Lever and Unilever organisation on 27 July 1950 Sir Geoffrey Heyworth chose the subject for his talk. However, it was the Fawley agreements which covered Esso's main refinery, near Southampton, that first drew British attention to productivity bargaining. These agreements were concluded in July 1960 between the management and trade unions (mainly the Transport and General Workers' Union and seven craft unions).[3] Many other organisations followed this lead.

The Fawley agreements required considerable changes in work practices as a result of introducing new methods. To obtain more efficient methods of working, according to the Donovan Report (para 319), the following were required:

1. Workers were to perform tasks they had previously regarded as being outside their jobs.

2. Workers were to allow others to perform part of their work.

3. Limitations on output were to be terminated or modified.

1. Students are encouraged to link the above with 'money wages' and 'real wages' noted at the beginning of Chapter 8. What will be the effect of increased productivity on money wages and real wages?
2. DEA Progress Report No. 24, January 1967 pages 1 and 2.
3. For full details read "The Fawley Productivity Agreements – a case study of management and collective bargaining" by Allan Flanders. Publishers: Faber and Faber Ltd., 1964.

4. Tea breaks and other interruptions of work were to end.
5. Manning scales were to be revised – in some instances on the basis of work study.
6. Workers to be released from some jobs and other jobs ended.

The above enabled the refinery to reduce or put an end to overtime. The firm was able to meet demands for services at unusual times and make fuller use of equipment. Naturally, this required considerable bargaining over a long period of time and compensation to the Trade Unions members. At Fawley the company increased rates of pay – of the order of 40 per cent. The firm and workers benefited.

Managers benefited because it solved many of the typical problems of industrial relations. The Donovan Report (para 525) claimed that productivity bargaining:
1. raised the standard of supervision and of managerial planning and control,
2. closed the gap between rates of pay and actual earnings (wage drift),
3. permitted negotiations on performance,
4. enabled demarcation difficulties to be eliminated or reduced,
5. concentrated decisions at lower levels (company or factory), and
6. formalised and regulated the position of the shop steward.

Who benefits from productivity agreements? Who benefits from increased productivity? We have already seen that employers and employees benefit directly. Indirectly the community benefits because resources are being used more efficiently, more goods are being made available without using more of the factors and price increases are minimised.

Productivity and productivity agreements are linked with wages – they help in determining the earnings of labour.

Part Two

RETURNS TO THE FACTORS OF PRODUCTION

Chapter Ten

Role of Trade Unions

The Trade Union and Labour Relations Act 1974, which became an Act on July 31st, 1974, repealed the Industrial Relations Act of 1971.[1] The 1974 Act became fully operational on September 16th, 1974.

The 1974 Act defined a trade union in Section 28. The following is an abbreviated definition: a trade union is a temporary or permanent organisation consisting wholly or mainly of workers those principal purposes include the regulations of relation between those workers and employers.

Under the new Act, trade unions must be registered with the Registrar of Friendly Societies[2]. The Registrar decides whether an organisation does or does not satisfy the definition. If accepted the organisation becomes known as a trade union; if not, it is not a trade union.

TRADE UNIONS – GENERAL

Trade unions are workers' societies. They originated at various times throughout the 19th and 20th centuries. Over a span of time the number of trade unions in existence has declined whereas the number of members has increased. These trends continue and are shown in Exhibit 10.1.

Exhibit 10.1 shows a downward trend in the number of trade unions for the period 1962 to 1972 but an upward trend in membership. Over this span of 11 years the number of unions had declined by 183 whereas the increase in membership was approximately 1,301,000.

If we were to consider these trends over a longer period of time we would find that the period 1962–1972 is a continuation of what was occurring between 1932 and 1962. Exhibit 10.2 shows the absolute changes.

This exhibit shows that the number of trade unions declined by 615 over the period 1932 to 1972 whereas membership increased by 6,691,000. At this rate of growth in membership trade unions could expect 100 per cent trade union membership of total labour force by the year 2022. There would be need to recruit over 7,000,000 non-member males and more than 6,000,000 non-member females. This is one of the roles of trade unions.

A comparison of trade union membership at the end of 1971 (11,109,000) with that of the population that were economically active (25,002,600) we find that unions represent approximately 44·4 per cent of the economically active.

1. The re-election of Labour – Oct. 10, 1974 – should ensure the continuance of this Act for several more years. Also, the Government can now carry out two other Acts on industrial relations, namely, Employment Protection Act and Employee Participation Act.
2. (a) Registration under 1971 Act's system of registration was abolished.
   (b) First Friendly Societies Act was in 1793. The Chief Registrar of Friendly Societies was first appointed in 1846.

RELATIONSHIP BETWEEN NUMBER OF TRADE UNIONS AND
MEMBERSHIP FOR PERIOD 1962-1972

YEAR	NUMBER OF UNIONS AT END OF YEAR	MEMBERSHIP*			PERCENTAGE INCREASE (+) OR DECREASE(−) OF PREVIOUS YEAR
		MALES	FEMALES	TOTAL	
		000's	000's	000's	
1962	649	7,960	2,054	10,014	+1·0
1963	630	7,961	2,102	10,063	+0·5
1964	621	8,040	2,171	10,211	+1·5
1965	608	8,080	2,238	10,318	+1·0
1966	600	8,002	2,252	10,254	−0·6
1967	581	7,901	2,281	10,182	−0·7
1968	561	7,831	2,356	10,187	0·0
1969	538	7,963	2,499	10,462	+2·7
1970	513	8,434	2,734	11,168	+6·7
1971	489	8,366	2,742	11,109	−0·5
1972	466	8,426	2,889	11,315	+1·9

Note: * Figures have been rounded to the nearest 1,000. The sums of the constituent items may not, therefore, agree with the totals shown.

Source: "Membership of trade unions in 1972" Department of Employment Gazette, November 1973, Table 2 page 1147.

EXHIBIT 10.1

NUMBER OF TRADE UNIONS AND THEIR MEMBERSHIP
1932-1972

YEAR	NUMBER OF TRADE UNIONS AT END OF YEAR	MEMBERSHIP		
		MALES	FEMALES	TOTAL
1932	1,081	3,859,000	765,000	4,624,000
1942	991	6,151,000	1,716,000	7,867,000
1952	692	7,749,000	1,775,000	9,524,000
1962	649	7,960,000	2,054,000	10,014,000
1972	466	8,426,000	2,889,000	11,315,000

Source: Ministry of Labour Gazette November 1947 and 1954 and Department of Employment Gazette November 1972.

EXHIBIT 10.2

Trade unionism has still a long way to go to achieve total representation of the labour force. To put it another way, there were approximately 13,646,400[1] economically active persons who were not members of trade unions.

Another noticeable feature about trade unions is that there are a large number of small unions having a small proportion of total union membership, and a small number of large unions having a large part of total membership. Exhibit 10.3 substantiates this statement.

1. This figure excludes members of the Armed Forces.

SIZE OF TRADE UNIONS AND MEMBERSHIP
AT THE END OF 1972

NUMBER OF MEMBERS	NUMBER OF UNIONS	TOTAL MEMBER- SHIP*	PERCENTAGES TOTAL NUMBER OF ALL UNIONS	TOTAL MEMBER- SHIP OF ALL UNIONS
Under 100	74	3,000	15·9	0·0
100 and under 500	118	31,000	25·3	0·3
500 and under 1,000	40	28,000	8·6	0·3
1,000 and under 2,500	62	92,000	13·3	0·8
2,500 and under 5,000	53	174,000	11·3	1·5
5,000 and under 10,000	32	214,000	6·9	1·9
10,000 and under 15,000	13	150,000	2·8	2·3
15,000 and under 25,000	18	333,000	3·9	2·9
25,000 and under 50,000	18	609,000	3·9	5·4
50,000 and under 100,000	13	901,000	2·8	8·0
100,000 and under 250,000	14	1,879,000	3·0	16·6
250,000 and more	11	6,901,000	2·3	61·0
TOTALS	466	11,315,000	100·0	100·0

Note * Figures have been rounded to the nearest 1,000 members.
Source: "Membership of trade unions in 1972" Department of Employment Gazette, November 1973, Table 1 page 1147.

EXHIBIT 10.3

Over time society changes and with it circumstances change; thus unions "have had their origins in diverse circumstances and for this reason vary considerably as to size, structure and constitution, though all have the fundamental purpose of improving the status and conditions of their members and are collectively concerned with all matters by which workers are affected".[1]

The size, structure and their constitutions differ because:

1. of their historical development. Some were formed in the 19th century and basically have not changed whilst others formed in the 19th century have amalgamated with other unions. Others were formed in the 20th century,
2. they tend to represent different industries, and
3. They represent different crafts and occupations.

In other words, there are different types of trade unions. Normally, they are classified as:

1. Craft.
2. Industrial.
3. General.
4. Occupational.

Craft unions, generally speaking, are the oldest type of trade union. They, broadly speaking, believe that the "tool operated by the worker" is the base for their organisation. Members are skilled and undergo a system of apprenticeship. Their area of operation is clearly demarcated from other crafts. They are

1. "Industrial Relations handbook", Ministry of Labour, HMSO, 1961 page 9.

highly interested in preserving their technical standards, but, on the other hand, their attitudes tend to be that of not favouring amalgamations with other unions.

Some employers, who use different crafts, find themselves dealing with a special problem of demarcation. For example, when the employer wishes to introduce new techniques into the production line they may find themselves overlapping several craft boundaries. This could trigger-off inter-union and demarcation disputes.

Industrial unions, usually formed by amalgamations, accept all workers (skilled and unskilled) in a given industry. Thus, membership is usually large. The immediate problem that springs to mind with this type of union is the difficulty of creating harmony between skilled and unskilled workers; each has their own special interests. It has been noted that the skilled workers tend to dominate the unskilled in union affairs. The advantage associated with this form of union is that all workers working for one employer in one industry are united.

General unions originated in the 1890s when the intention was to organise unskilled workers without regard to the industry. Thus, members consist of unskilled workers in many industries plus some semi-skilled workers (workers whose work involves some basic training).

These unions have workers in many industries and thus tend to operate across the structure of industrial unions. They have often been criticised on the grounds that they are too large and therefore undemocratic. A prime example of this form of union is the "Transport and General Workers' Union".

Occupational unions organise workers in a well defined occupation; a non-craft activity such as clerical workers. Like general unions they too have their origin in the 1890s. Normally, members are from a given industry.

These four trade union types are organised differently but they often find it worthwhile, when seeking advantages common to their members, to join together in industry by industry negotiations.

ROLE OF TRADE UNIONS

Although trade unions may be of different types and size it is agreed that they have a common role. Role, according to the Concise Oxford dictionary, refers to one's function or to what one is appointed or expected or has undertaken to do. In other words, we must look at the functions of trade unions noting what they expect to achieve.

It should be noted that the role (aims and functions) of trade unions are not necessarily static; the role of yesteryear need not be the same nor have the same emphasis as its role today or in the future. Over time change takes place in the economic (including industrial structure) and social environment which require trade unions to reconsider their functions. George Woodcock[1] stated that "structure, particularly in the trade union movement, is a function of purpose." He also noted that the difficulties in union structure and organisation arose because they grew up to serve functions which are now outdated.

Over time we have witnessed an increase in the size and operation of plants and companies, the introduction of new machinery and new trades and, at the same time, the removal (completely or partially) of old trades and machines. The make-up of the labour force has changed with women and white collar workers forming a larger part of the total. These are only a few of the many changes. All have helped to change the industrial relations scene. All must

1. Speaking at the Annual Trades Union Congress 3 September 1962.

affect trade unions and force them to change their size and role. On the other hand the role of trade unions is of particular importance in the sphere of change. They exert a powerful influence in supporting or not supporting new developments in industry.

What, basically, is the role of trade unions?

Trade unions have many roles.

The Donovan Report noted the role of trade unions under 3 major headings, namely:

1. promoting the interests of their members,   (page 309 of Report)
2. accelerating the economic advance of the nation, and (pages 303/304)
3. accelerating the social advance of the nation.   (pages 303/304)

The items included in each area included:

1. (a) wages and conditions of work,
   (b) effective consultation with managements at national, district, and shop level,
   (c) 100 per cent trade union membership,
   (d) participation in the conduct of union's affairs at all levels,
   (e) fidelity to union rules and decisions,
   (f) help in personal problems,
   (g) help in dealing with grievances,
   (h) help in legal matters,
   (i) maintenance of full employment, and
   (j) maintenance of the real value of wages.
2. (a) increase in the national wealth, in real terms,
   (b) increase in the citizens' standard of living, and
   (c) adoption of new and more efficient methods of production and distribution.
3. (a) improvements in the standard and extent of education,
   (b) greater liberty and opportunity for the individual to lead a fuller life,
   (c) more adequate leisure and the proper use of it,
   (d) diminuation of class distinction,
   (e) willingness on the part of the citizen to take his share in civic duties,
   (f) reform of oppressive laws, and
   (g) the awakening of the public conscience in relation to wrongs suffered by any section of it.

Economics students must be concerned more with the economic role but be aware of the social role (3rd role area).

This is one way of looking at the role of trade unions. It is possible to consider these under the following headings:

1. traditional,
2. at the work place, and
3. outside the work place.

The Traditional Role
The traditional role of unions, and this role continues today and into the future, is to bring all workers into an organisation whereby certain persons (similar to firm's managers on behalf of shareholders) could represent them to better their welfare. These officials must be given the authority to act on the behalf of the workers – they are to provide the unity which is essential if workers are to prosper. The trade union would enable workers to enjoy 'unity of action' by giving offi-

cials 'unity of authority' when acting on the behalf of its members. The success of the other roles will depend upon this major role.

Perhaps under this heading one could include those given by the Donovan Report and noted previously as 1c, 1e, 1i and 1j.

At the Work Place

At the work place the role of the unions can be listed as bargaining, communications, consultation and settling disputes.

Bargaining is normally referred to as 'collective bargaining'. This means that union officials will bargain with employers on the behalf of their members to influence their remunerations (and working conditions). It is this function, more than the others, which concerns us when considering 'wages'.

Britain is, so it has been claimed, the home of collective bargaining. The term seems first to have been used by Beatrice Webb in 1891. Today, this form of bargaining is the foremost concern of British trade unions and their members.

In the early days of collective bargaining negotiations were generally carried out locally, but today negotiations are primarily carried out at the national level and supplemented at lower levels between trade union officials and employers or their representative body. When negotiations have been settled at national level it does not mean that all wage rates and all working conditions will be uniform at all factories, mines or firms. Settlements here are basically about basic wages and conditions of work for an industry or an occupation nationally. Adjustments take place at lower levels, but the adjustments must remain within the framework laid down at the national level.

The object of collective bargaining is to reach a voluntary agreement about the terms and conditions of employment. It is at the bargaining table that wages and conditions of work, such as hours, safety, health, etc. are settled.

It might be worth noting at this point that under the new 1974 Act collective agreements will not be legally binding unless they say so and are in writing.

Is collective bargaining an effective method in achieving agreements?

The Donovan Report (para 212) stated that "Properly conducted, collective bargaining is the most effective means of giving workers the right to representation in decisions affecting their working lives, a right which is or should be the prerogative of every worker in a democratic society. While therefore the first task in the reform of British industrial relations is to bring greater order into collective bargaining in the company and plant, the second is to extend the coverage of collective bargaining and the organisation of workers on which it depends".

It would appear that this method is effective but there are reservations. The central defect, so it is claimed, is the disorder in factory and workshop relations and pay structures. The reason for this being that there is a conflict between bargaining carried out at the top of the hierarchy and that carried out at the lower levels, for example, at work places. The conflict could be resolved and collective bargaining become more effective by separating those conditions that could satisfactorily be bargained for at the higher level from those conditions that cannot. These other conditions would be those associated with company and work place levels, for example regulation of hours actually worked, the use of job evaluation, facilities for shop stewards, etc.

Greater order could be brought to collective bargaining by getting more workers covered by collective bargaining.

Perhaps under this heading, one could include those given by the Donovan Report and noted previously as 1a, 1c, 1e, 1j and 3e.

Communications refers to the line of communications from head offices to branches to factory shop stewards and ultimately to union members. This is a vital function of trade unions for it is necessary to provide orders and information downwards enabling shop stewards and workers to have regular contact with officials at the top. If communications are poor it is possible that top officials will establish industry-wide agreements which are not acceptable to a large group of union members. Good communications would ensure top officials and workers are in agreement.

Perhaps under this heading one could include those given by the Donovan Report and noted previously as 1b, 1d, 1e and 1g.

Consultation refers to joint consultation between management and employees. This function must take place between union officials and members and then with employers especially at work place level; each work place will have its own peculiarities affecting the daily life of its workers. The committees established should be concerned with the day-to-day decisions that affect workers at the place of work such as safety, comfort, time study, etc. and not with wages and hours of work. The object being that of achieving success for the business and its employees. Productivity bargaining requires close consultation.

Perhaps under this heading, one could include those given by the Donovan Report and noted previously as 1a, 1b, 1g, 1i and 2c.

Settling disputes requires action by trade unions (and employers). There is a need to establish orderly procedures and clear rules which are acceptable by all for hearing complaints and settling disputes at the firm and industrial level. The Donovan Report (para 400) said that most unofficial strikes arise at plant level and that they concern issues "which are not dealt with at all in agreements negotiated by union leaders, such as rates of pay or piece-rates settled at work-place level, dismissals or working arrangements". If the machinery for settling disputes at the work place is correct it would be possible to settle disputes before a strike is called.

Perhaps under this heading one could include those given by the Donovan Report and noted previously as 1a, 1d, 1e, 1g and 1i.

Outside the Work Place

Outside the work place the roles of trade unions can be listed as benefits, education and training, and economic policy.

Benefits refer to the type of benefits provided by friendly societies to their members. The type of benefits given would include giving some aid to needy workers, providing free legal advice, provide small pensions, provide sick pay, etc. These have long been performed by the trade unions and some of them still provide them. The coming of the 'Welfare State' has reduced the need for unions to carry out this role on the same scale as they did before.

Perhaps under this heading one could include those given by the Donovan Report and noted previously as 1f, 1h, 2b and 3g.

Education and training is largely a post war development of the unions. "The main emphasis is clearly on relatively short courses aimed at equipping lay members, especially branch officers and shop stewards, with information and techniques that will make them more effective. But there have been significant developments outside this range, as well as experiment within it."[1]

1. "Change in the Trade Unions" by John Hughes, Fabian Society publication, page 30.

Donovan Report roles listed as 3a, 3b and 3c would probably be included in this section.

Economic policy refers to the relationship between trade unions and the government. Because trade unions are spokesmen for a very large part of the working community it is only right that one of their roles is that of persuading the government to pass legislation which is favourable to workers, such as safety, health, social security, etc.

Another relationship with the government occurs when the government ask trade unions to help the government to achieve its economic policy. Under the present (1974–1975) government's 'social contract' trade union members of the Trade Union Congress are encouraged not to breach the contract. Unions should not use excessive pressures (work to rule, go-slow, etc.) nor ask for excessive wage agreements. The result may force the firm or firms to close thus creating unemployment. Also, trade unions must help the government to raise living standards and keep inflation in check.

The roles noted by the Donovan Reports and previously listed as 1i, 1j, 2a, 2b and 3f would probably be listed under this heading.

The trade unions have many roles but the most important are those that affect the interest of their members.

THE TRADES UNION CONGRESS

At the top of the trade union movement stands the Trades Union Congress (TUC). It was founded in 1868 and in its early days "it was little more than an annual demonstration of trade union strength and solidarity, and an opportunity for union leaders to discuss their common problems; but there was no executive machinery or authority to decide policy and it remained at most a demonstrative and consultative assembly".[1]

Over time, as changes occurred, it was found that the TUC was needed to provide unity of command for its members (trade unions) and to act as the central organisation for centralizing trade union effort. The TUC, today, speaks on behalf of the majority of trade unions and union members; not all trade unions are affiliated to the TUC.

In very recent years the tendency has been to give more authority to the TUC. At very high level discussions between the government and unions it has been the TUC that has been called to the table. The recent social contract was, in the first instance, a contract between the government and the TUC.

SOME CRITICISMS OF TRADE UNIONS

It has been stated that "it is well known that the union structure and organisation is riddled with inefficiencies, anomalies and built-in obstacles to change".[2] Also, as noted before, trade unions grew up to serve functions which are outdated. The unions are wide open to criticism. Some criticisms, briefly stated, are that they should:

1. *Change* the outdated apprenticeship and craft system. The Donovan Report (para 338) stated that "In the context of technological change the drawbacks of the craft system become even more marked". Also, that "If the only normal method of entry into the craft is via an apprenticeship, supply will respond slowly and inadequately to demand".

1. "British Trade Unionism" Political and Economic Planning (PEP) publication, March 1955 page 129.
2. "Trade Unions in a Changing Society" No. 472, PEP, 10 June 1963 page 217.

2. *Eliminate* rigid boundaries of skill demarcations. The boundaries, stated the Donovan Report (para 337), are "a fruitful source of dispute especially where new work is introduced which does not conform to established limits".

3. *Regulate* the activities of shop stewards. Handbooks for shop stewards exist but not all unions provide them. Those that do exist do not normally tell shop stewards the issues they can satisfactorily handle and the procedure for raising them.

4. *Modernise* dispute procedures and ensure they are always used.

5. *Reduce* multi-unionism. The basic idea is to reduce the number of trade unions in existence; mergers should take place. This would help some demarcation disputes.

6. *Attract* more females into union activities.

7. *Improve* the educational facilities offered by unions to their members.

8. *Increase* contact between work place union members and their officials, and do it on a more regular basis.

9. *Reform* existing procedures in arranging collective agreements – work them through work place and company agreements.

10. *Strengthen* the authority of the TUC as head of the union movement.

Other criticisms do exist. The above are only some of the criticisms that have been levied at trade unions during the 1960s and early 1970s.

Employers' Associations[1]
It is first necessary to distinguish between the terms 'employers' association' and 'trade association'. Employers' associations are directly and indirectly concerned with the negotiation of wages and working conditions whereas trade associations are concerned with trade (contract forms, standardisation of products, etc.). Associations that operate in both areas exist as both an employers' association and trade association combined.

Employers' associations are often on the other side of the wage and work condition bargaining table. Their central responsibility is, according to the Donovan Report (para 729), "to promote and support effective and comprehensive agreements in the company and in the factory". However, it was also pointed out (para 1013) that "The authority of employers' associations has declined". Also, that "from 1914 until very recently nearly ever important innovation in industrial relations which was not the work of the unions came from the Government or from individual companies".

Bargaining Table
The bargaining table which considers wages, hours of work and other conditions relating to work and the worker, is not a one-sided affair. Trade unions are on one side of the table and employers on the other. Each side is out to achieve the best results for those they represent. The rest of the community await anxiously for the contents of the agreements wondering how it will affect them. Will more goods and services be provided? Will wage increases push up prices and push inflation? Will wages force up prices and price those goods out of the export market? These and many other questions are answered by what goes on at all the bargaining tables in Britain.

1. Not required for ONC/ONDBS syllabus.

Part Two

RETURNS TO THE FACTORS OF PRODUCTION

Chapter Eleven

Role of Interest Rates

The return to the factor of production called capital is *interest*, and interest is the price paid for the *use* of borrowed money capital.

THEORY
The theories associated with interest rates are:
1. Classical, and
2. Monetarist.[1]

The *classical theory* states that the rate of interest is determined by the supply of savings which are available for lending and the demand for these funds for the purchase of real capital. The price (interest rate) level is established when there is equilibrium between supply and demand.

The *monetarist theory* states that the rate of interest is reached when equilibrium has been reached between the supply of actual money[2] and the demand for holding it. Interest in this case is the reward for parting with liquidity (cash) or as Keynes stated it, it is the reward for not hoarding.[3]

Equilibrium, in both theories, implies a state of affairs which remain at rest. In other words it implies the economy is static. Because the economy moves from one situation to another (dynamic) we must move ourselves away from pure theory and how interest is determined and consider the role of interest rates. However, before we do this, it is important to consider, briefly, the marginal product theory.

The *marginal product theory*[4] relating to capital considers the relationship between the injection of an extra £1 worth of real capital[5] and the expected net yield (measured as a percentage over a time of one year) from that injection.

Keynes made note of this relationship and called it the '*marginal efficiency of capital*'. Keynes stated that the marginal efficiency of capital in conjunction with the rate of interest determines the amount of new investment in real capital.[6] This is the key to one of the major roles of interest rates. Before discussing this major role we will need to clear up a few basics about interest.

1. This distinction places Keynes as being a monetarist and yet his views are often contrasted with the 'Friedman' monetarists.
2. What constitutes the stock of money has been under considerable investigation throughout the 1970s.
3. For a lucid insight into the differences between classical and monetarist theories read Chapter 5 'The Issues between Keynes and the Classics' in the Pelican publication "Keynes and After" by Michael Stewart.
4. Refer to Chapter 5 this book.
5. Real capital can not be divided into units of £1.
6. He also said that it was the total of this new investment which would determine the level of employment given the propensity to consume.

MONEY AND REAL CAPITAL
Capital can be considered as 'money (or financial) capital' and 'real (or physical) capital'.[1] Money capital refers to sums of money required by businesses to carry out business operations. Real capital refers to assets needed by the business to carry out its production operations. Basically the need of businessmen is that of borrowing money capital before purchasing real capital, and a price has to be paid for borrowing money capital, namely, interest.

DEFINITIONS – PURE AND GROSS INTEREST
Interest is the price paid for the *use* of borrowed money capital. Some say that it is perhaps the most important price of all prices; perhaps because it is related to investment in real capital which most advanced countries have found to be the key to economic growth in a period of full employment and because it is considered to be one remedy to a deficit in the balance of payments. The price is usually expressed as a specified rate *per year* calculated on the amount borrowed. For example, if I lend £100 and expect £110 back at the end of the year, the interest is £10 (£110 less £100) and the interest rate is 10 per cent per annum $\frac{£10}{£100} \times 100\%$).

It is important to note the time element because basically interest is the price paid for borrowing money capital for a specified period of time; in other words *interest places a time value upon the money being borrowed*. This type of interest is known as *'pure interest'*. When other considerations are taken into account, such as inflation, risk and administration costs, in fixing the price to be paid for borrowing money we use the term *'gross interest'*.

VARIATIONS IN INTEREST RATES
The term interest is often used casually as though there is only one rate at which interest is paid, but we have seen that there are rates which vary according to time, risk, administration costs, inflation or a combination of these situations.

Some simple illustrations might help to show the reasons for there being different interest rates.

Time can be considered as short or long. For example, a loan made for 30 days is short compared to a loan for 5 years. Both periods of time simply state the length of time the lender remains without his money – liquidity. The interest paid compensates the lender for the time he does not have the use of his cash. Thus, a person lending his money for 30 days would expect to get less compensation (a lower rate of interest) than he would expect had he loaned the money for 5 years. We might look at it in the following manner:

LOW	INTEREST RATE	HIGH

← ————————————————————————————————————— →

SHORT   LENGTH OF TIME BEING WITHOUT CASH   LONG

Sometimes it is possible for a person to sell the paper representing his loan, for example a debenture.[2] This affects the time the lender would remain illiquid. Thus, the interest rate on this type of loan would be less than that the lender would expect for a similar time period where it is impossible for him to become liquid before the stated time.

Risk is normally associated with uncertainty; the greater the uncertainty the

1. Refer to Volume I page 59.
2. Refer Volume I pages 70–71.

greater the risk. Thus, the standing (government compared to a business organisation) and reputation (ICI as compared to relatively unknown company) of the borrower creates various degrees of uncertainty to the lender. The more uncertain the standing and reputation of the borrower the higher the risk. The higher the risk the higher the rate of interest required to induce the lender to part with his money. Governments are less likely to default paying back the loan than business organisations, and ICI is more certain to make its payments relative to some obscure business organisation. In other words the lender would expect a lower rate of interest when lending to the government and a higher rate if the loan was made to a small size firm. We might view this situation as follows:

LOW	INTEREST RATE	HIGH
←		→
LOW	DEGREE OF RISK	HIGH

Sometimes the degree of risk can be made less of a risk by asking the borrower for security. For example, a company may have to pledge some asset as security should an uncertain event hinder them from paying back the loan. When this situation occurs it has the effect of lessening the degree of risk and therefore we would normally expect the rate of interest to be lower relative to the situation where security is not available.

Administrative costs are often taken into consideration when lending money. It is often necessary to include in the rate the cost of collecting money from the borrower, keeping accounts, sending out statements, writing letters, etc. This cost becomes part of the interest charged. Usually, the shorter the period of time the less the administrative costs, and vice versa. A simple diagram depicting this situation is as follows:

LOW	INTEREST RATE	HIGH
←		→
LOW	COST OF ADMINISTERING THE LOAN	HIGH

Inflation refers to the general rise in the level of prices and thus reflects a loss of purchasing power of money loaned. During a period of rising prices lenders would expect some compensation for their lost purchasing power; in other words they would expect the rate of interest to be such that they can buy just as many goods and services as they could have done at the time the loan was made. This situation can be visualised as follows:

LOW	INTEREST RATE	HIGH
←		→
LOW	RATE OF INFLATION	HIGH

From the foregoing it can be seen that interest rates will tend to reflect a combination of these factors. Low rates and high rates of interest could be expected when the following situations exist.

LOW	INTEREST RATE	HIGH
←		→
SHORT	LENGTH OF TIME BEING WITHOUT CASH	LONG
LOW	DEGREE OF RISK	HIGH
LOW	COST OF ADMINISTERING THE LOAN	HIGH
LOW	RATE OF INFLATION	HIGH

The above illustration indicates that a person or company lending money to the government (low risk) for a short period of time where virtually negligible administrative costs are incurred during a period when there is negligible

inflation would expect the rate of interest to be low relative to the situation of lending money to a speculative firm (high risk) for a long period of time during a period of high inflation and where considerable administrative costs exist. Then, there are other interest rates determined by various combinations of the above mentioned situations.

Usually rates of interest tend to follow the lead laid down by the government's *'minimum lending rate'*. This rate *reflects* the supply and demand for short dated securities (Treasury Bills) and, *more or less*, fits the low rate of interest situation. All other borrowers invariably have situations that are not as acceptable (except inflation). In other words their situations lie to the right of low interest rates as shown in the illustration; some being very close to low and other situations nearer to high interest rates.

The various rates of interest noted in the money and capital market can normally be explained by referring to the situations noted.

ROLE OF INTEREST RATES

The role of interest rates requires an investigation of what interest rates are expected to achieve. Interest rates have a role to play in many areas of economic life (national debt, purchase of house, purchase of car, etc.) but the most outstanding of its roles is that associated with rectifying a deficit in the balance of payments and *regulating the demand for real capital*. From the businessman's point of view it is the latter role that interests him for he is concerned with making a decision whether to invest in real capital. On the one hand the businessman views interest as being an obstacle to investment and on the other hand he views his investment in terms of profit. If he expects total revenue (after paying all other costs) to exceed the sum borrowed plus interest then he probably will invest. If, however, the expected revenue (after paying all other costs) does not exceed the sum borrowed plus interest the investment is not attractive and money capital will not be borrowed; in this case the interest rate is too high relative to the return from the investment. This is the way the businessman (the borrower) views the situation.

Lenders[1] are on the other side of the market. We have already seen how they view lending their money (time, risk, etc.) and noted that interest is their reward; the reward for lending (not saving)[2]. The rate of interest will influence the *way* people save their money (in deposit accounts, with building societies, etc.). Some people have savings in current accounts where no interest, normally, is given. Total savings will depend on how much of income is used for consumption.

Business borrowing

Firms that do not have sufficient retained profits to purchase the necessary capital to carry out production will be forced, if they wish their company to grow or maintain their present position, to go to the 'money and/or capital market' to obtain loans. Their intention is to borrow money today to buy capital goods tomorrow which they expect will bring in revenue months or years later. These returns will be, more or less, continuous over a certain span of time into the future. Thus the decision to invest in real capital will depend upon the sum

1. Refer Volume I Chapters 8, 9 and 10. Relevant pages listing 'sources' providing finance to firms.
2. Lending and saving are two different events. (1) A person may place his money with a bank and thus saves. (2) the bank takes these savings and lends them to others.

borrowed plus the rate of interest that has to be paid during the present time compared to the expected (future) cash flows that are generated by the real capital. The time for which the money is to be borrowed may be certain but the activities within this time period are uncertain. The businessman must calculate the returns that are expected from the investment and then subtract from this total the sum borrowed plus interest. If total revenue is greater than total cost the firms has a profit and will, perhaps, borrow the money and purchase the real capital (building, new machine, etc.). If total revenue is less than total cost the firm would have a loss from that investment and would not borrow. This investment might take place at some future date should interest rates fall; this will lower total cost and may result in the investment being profitable.

It can be seen that the expected returns from the investment will depend upon the demand for goods (or services) produced by the firm. *The demand for real capital is a dervived demand.*

First, it is important to note that some investments made by firms are not affected by the rate of interest. A machine may be worn-out: investment must be made to replace the machine if production is to continue. The decision can not be postponed; the decision does not consider the cost of finance. Some investments may be required by law. Again, the investment must take place and the cost of finance does not enter the decision. Perhaps an insurance company demands that the firm purchase some item (fire engine). Here again the cost of finance is not taken into consideration. Even the returns can not be calculated satisfactorily because some returns can not be put into terms of money (intangible returns).

Investments, other than the above mentioned, whose returns can be measured (tangible returns) and are vital to the operation of the firm (lower costs of production, increase earnings) must consider the cost of capital. Keynes' marginal efficiency of capital was compared to the rate of interest to determine whether an investment was or was not worthwhile. As long as the marginal efficiency of capital exceeded the rate of interest the investment would take place.

Today, this basic idea of Keynes continues but it is known as *'discounted cash flow'* analysis; more commonly referred to as DCF. This term recognises the difference between the future and present value of money. The method is generally used to adjust expected cash flows in the future to the value they would have at the present time. In other words it considers the time value of money. For example, if someone offered you £100 now or a year from now and you know there will be no inflation (prices of goods and services will remain the same) which would you prefer? Naturally you would prefer the £100 now because you know you could lend it to someone else at 10 per cent (rate of interest) and collect £110 a year from now. The £100 today is worth more than that of a year in the future. The reverse of this is simple: the £110 a year from today is only worth £100 now.

It can be seen that to calculate the value of £100 today one year hence we add the interest to the £100 and ended up with £110. To bring this £110 one year hence back to the present value (£100) we discount the £110.

To obtain the future value we use the compound interest formula.

$$A = P (1 \text{ plus } i)^n$$

A ...... refers to the amount received in the future (cash flow) (future value).

P ...... refers to the principal or sum of money loaned (present value).

i ...... is the abbreviation for 'rate of interest'.

n ...... refers to the number of years the sum of money is loaned.

Fitting our previous example to this:

$$\begin{aligned}
A &= \quad P \quad (1 \text{ plus } i)^n \\
&= £100\,(1 \text{ plus } 10\%)^1 \\
&= £100\,(1 \text{ plus } 0.1)^1 \\
&= £100\,(1{\cdot}1)^1 \\
&= £100 \times 1{\cdot}1 \\
A &= £110
\end{aligned}$$

We can note that 'n' is not needed when only one year is considered, but it is vital to include 'n' when considering more than one year as we shall see shortly.

To obtain the present value (P) from a future sum of money (A) we must use the discount formula.

$$P = \frac{A}{(1 \text{ plus } i)^n}$$

It can be noted that this formula is very similar to the above formula. The discount aspect is really $\dfrac{1}{(1 \text{ plus } i)^n}$ but multiplying A to the numerator 1 we get

$\dfrac{A}{(1 \text{ plus } i)^n}$. This has the effect of reducing the future value to the present value: it is like calculating interest backwards.

Fitting our previous example to this:

$$\begin{aligned}
P &= \frac{A}{(1 \text{ plus } i)^n} \\[2mm]
&= \frac{£110}{(1 \text{ plus } 10\%)^1} \\[2mm]
&= \frac{£110}{(1 \text{ plus } 0{\cdot}1)^1} \\[2mm]
&= \frac{£110}{(1{\cdot}1)^1} \\[2mm]
&= \frac{£110}{1{\cdot}1} \\[2mm]
P &= £100
\end{aligned}$$

For clarification purposes we shall consider the previous two formulas for a period of 2 years.

Compounding the present value (P) forward for 2 years we obtain:

$$A = P(1 + i)^n = £100\,(1 + 10\%)^2 = £100\,(1 + 0{\cdot}1)^2 = £100\,(1{\cdot}1)^2$$
$$= £100\,(1{\cdot}1 \times 1{\cdot}1) = £100 \times 1{\cdot}21$$
$$A = £121$$

Discounting the future value (A = £121) over a 2 year period we obtain:

$$P = \frac{A}{(1+i)^n} = \frac{£121}{(1+10\%)^2} = \frac{£121}{(1+0{\cdot}1)^2} = \frac{£121}{(1{\cdot}1)^2} = \frac{£121}{(1{\cdot}1 \times 1{\cdot}1)}$$
$$= \frac{£121}{1{\cdot}21}$$
$$P = £100$$

These examples show how interest and discount calculations are made. The businessman knows, with a great degree of reliability and certainty, what his cost of capital will be when he borrows money today at a specific rate of interest. His cash flows from his investment are uncertain because he is looking into the uncertain future. Nevertheless he must estimate what returns are expected in the future; carried out on a year to year cash flow analysis. He must then compare the sum of the discounted cash flows with the initial cost of capital. If the present values of the cash flows exceed the initial cost the investment project is worth undertaking.

Usually businessmen have several needs for the money that is available. The DCF method will enable him to decide which investment is more worthwhile relative to the others. Two points to note here are that investments have different lengths of life and that future expectations are based upon the state of the economy. Thus, investments that bring returns over a short period of time are more likely to be accurate than those that bring returns over a much longer period of time.

The role of interest rates when considering the factor of production capital is the effect it has upon the decisions of businessmen in making investment decisions. DCF[1] is a method that helps businessmen to make the correct investment decision.

In conclusion, the variables that affect 'real capital' investment decisions are:
1. interest . . . . present time,
2. state of the economy . . . . . . future time, and
3. technological advance . . . . future time.
The last two variables affect the cash flows arising from an investment whereas interest is the price paid for the use of borrowing money capital (cost of capital).

1. The author decided not to get too deeply involved in DCF analysis (calculations, various methods, advantages and disadvantages associated with each method, over-all value in its usage, etc.) because, at this stage, it is too complex for most students to understand.

Part Two
RETURNS TO THE FACTORS OF PRODUCTION

Chapter Twelve

Profit

Profit is the return to the factor of production called enterprise. This return is usually considered to be the ultimate test of a firm's success. Businesses produce goods and services in their search for this return. Thus, in our capitalist type of society, profits has the special function of steering resources into those production processes (supply) that are demanded by ultimate users. If the fourth factor makes the wrong decision the firm will make a loss and resources will be shifted into another supply situation where profits are available, and vice versa.

There are many types of profits: some have already been noted in Volume I.[1] On the other hand, gross profit, pure profit, and accountants profit have not been discussed. This chapter attempts to throw light on these various terms.

Economic profit[2] (or surplus) is the necessary payments to the fourth factor for the services performed in steering resources (other factors of production) into the correct area of production.

FUNCTIONS OF ENTREPRENEUR

The functions[3] of the entrepreneur can normally be broken down into two types:
1. organisation function, and
2. risk-bearing function.

Organisation is a term often used to describe the fourth factor of production because someone is required to organise the other factors, controlling and co-ordinating their activities, in achieving output. The organiser may be an individual called the entrepreneur or several persons (Board of Directors or managers acting on behalf of shareholders).

There is a second part to this function and that is to reduce those risks faced by a firm that can be avoided by expert knowledge (purchasing expert buying best raw materials at lowest cost or market researcher seeking information to remove some uncertainties about the market). Some risks can be insured against (fire insurance) and others can be calculated. These risks can be reduced by the entrepreneur and rightfully must be considered under this function.

Risk-bearing is the prime function of the entrepreneur. These are the risks that cannot be avoided nor insured nor calculated. They are unique and are bound up in changes in society which are not known with certainty. In other words the entrepreneur must make decisions today based upon estimates relating to the uncertain future. What does the entrepreneur risk? He risks the money invested in the firm.

---

1. Refer to page 201 Vol 1 normal profit, abnormal profit, monopoly profit, etc.
2. Refer to section 'Reward for Entrepreneurial Functions' — 'Normal Profit' page no. 126.
3. Refer to Vol. I pages 24–26 for discussion on 'enterprise' and 'fucntions of entrepreneur'.

Reward for Entrepreneurial Functions

In discussing profit as being the reward to the entrepreneurial function we are concerned with these two functions. The return to the 'organisation function' is usually referred to as 'normal profit'. The reward for risk-bearing is called 'pure profit'; this is the function and reward we are most concerned with.

Normal Profit. The entrepreneur, according to classical theory, received a reward (*economic profit*) for the services he performed organising the other factors of production. If he fulfilled these functions properly he received profit; if not, he was penalised and received a loss.

This form of profit was acceptable in the early 19th century when most businesses were owned and controlled by one person – the entrepreneur. He did not receive wages but received what was left after all other costs had been met. Later on in time it was recognised that some part of total profit was compensation for his labour efforts in organising the business and should more rightfully be termed 'wages of management' – not profit.

Today there are still many small firms that are owned and controlled by individuals; they are entrepreneurs in most respects and so this type of profit (if they do not pay themselves wages) still exists. 'Wages of management' appears to be a more acceptable term – after all wages are a cost that can be offset against tax.

On the other hand there are many businesses operating today that are not owned and controlled by entrepreneurs; the joint stock companies. They usually employ managers who perform the organisation function and in return receive wages (salaries) for their efforts. Thus, their reward is considered as a cost and deducted before profits are arrived at. Their reward is truly 'wages of management' and not profit.

In conclusion, the entrepreneur does receive a reward to compensate him for his efforts in organising the other factors of production. The reward should be called 'wages of management' but it is still quite normal to say that the reward is part of his total profit.

Risk-bearing. The other part of total profit is called 'pure profit'. This is a reward to the entrepreneur for carrying out the second function.

The entrepreneur makes decisions about future cost and revenue in the face of uncertainty. Each decision made by the entrepreneur is *an attempt* to maximise his profits at the point where MC = MR.[1] The word attempt has been underlined to note that the entrepreneur can not calculate accurately the costs of using the factors of production nor the revenue he will receive from the sale of his output. He can try to achieve the position where MC = MR, but if he succeeds it will be purely by luck. He must make decisions about future production (and costs) and future sales (and revenues). He can not know these with certainty so he must *estimate*, to the best of his ability, his costs *in advance* and *estimate* the revenues *expected* from his sales. These future considerations require the entrepreneur to make decisions *in advance*. Calculations can only take place when a period in the future has been reached – in some cases this is several years forward.

The entrepreneur accepts risks in deciding forward what his costs and revenues will be. The future will involve many changes (changes in taxes, changes in prices of factors, changes in prices of other goods, etc.) that can not be accurately forecasted at the time the decision must be taken. The risks are the result of these uncertainties. His decision about how much should be produced and what price to sell them at must be made *before* his goods get to the market and are sold.

1. Refer to Vol. I pages 204–205 for details on MC and MR.

For taking these 'risky' decisions the entrepreneur receives a reward called 'pure profits'. If his decisions are correct he benefits by receiving pure profits. Society, too, benefits because his decisions enable goods and services to be produced which otherwise would not be made available.

Thus, the total profits rewarded to the entrepreneur for his success in carrying out his functions are:
1. profits for organising (usually referred to as 'normal profit' or 'wages of management') and
2. profits for risk-bearing (usually referred to as 'pure profit').

At this stage it should be noted that in perfect competition the entrepreneur's total profit is equal to normal profit (wages of management) because 'pure profit' would not exist, especially in the long run. In the long run firms *seeking* maximum profit would move from one type of production to another (one industry to another). They soon eliminate any abnormal profit that might exist thus bringing profits into a state of equilibrium.

In the long run the total profit rewarded to the entrepreneur for his success in carrying out his functions are:
1. normal profit for organising ('wages of management').

DISTINCTION BETWEEN INTEREST AND PROFIT

The first statement made about interest was that it was the price paid for the use of borrowed money. To the business this interest is a cost which must be deducted from earnings to determine profit. More precisely the borrowed money will be used for investment in real capital (machinery etc.). If the revenue (cash flows) from the investment is equal to the amount borrowed plus interest then there is neither a profit nor a loss. In this case the businessman's decision was such that he was neither compensated nor penalised. On the other hand, had he shown more enterprise in *estimating* the returns from the investment, correctly estimating tangible returns and evaluating future changes in society which can not be calculated (intangibles such as change in demand) and judged these to be greater than the cost of borrowing money then the surplus over and above the cost of the financial capital is a profit.

The problem of distinguishing between interest and profit arises when the entrepreneur 'borrows' money from himself to purchase real capital. He feels that he does not have to pay interest on his money so that any revenue greater than the sum borrowed is profit. It can be seen that he forgot to note that money borrowed from himself has an interest element. In such a situation he is earning interest on his own financial capital *plus* a surplus (profit) for his enterprise.

Classical theory did not take this interest element into account when entrepreneurs supplied their own money. This created confusion when firms grew from an entrepreneur to a shareholder (many owners) type business.

Money borrowed whether it be from the individual owner or owners or from debenture holders has a cost. If there is no actual interest to be paid it must be remembered that there is the opportunity of investing that money somewhere else and receiving interest. It is this 'opportunity rate of interest return' which must be deducted from the revenue received from the investment to determine profit. For example the business might lend its money to someone else (another firm, local authority, central government, etc.) and receive interest. This is one way to consider the cost of capital when the firm uses its own financial capital to invest in real capital.

It is not always easy to sort out the reward of financial capital (interest) from

the reward of enterprise (profit). The previous statements should make it clear that there is a distinction – the distinction must be made.

DISTINCTION BETWEEN ACCOUNTANTS AND ECONOMISTS PROFIT

Economists profit is based upon the *expectation* of the business before the business actually commences operation. Commencing operation can refer to the time before a business begins producing goods or can refer to a specific operation (new machine) before it begins producing goods.

Accountants profit is based on *historical* fact. It can not be calculated until all the past transactions (for the year) have been completed. The records used by the accountant are the 'trading account' and the 'profit and loss account'. The trading account starts off by considering the value of the company's sales. From this figure the cost of production (raw materials, fuel or power, wages, etc.) is deducted to arrive at a figure called 'gross profit'. The profit and loss account starts with the gross profit figure shown in the trading account and then deducts those expenses that are not directly associated with the production line (salaries, overhead expenses such as rates and rents, etc.) to obtain 'net profit'.

The accountants calculations indicate that the accountants profit is the surplus of revenue over expenditure. The economists profit agrees with this surplus of revenue over expenditure concept. *But* they do differ:

1. Economic profit is an *estimate* based upon *future* expectations of revenues and expenditures.

2. Accounting profit is an *actual* figure based upon *past* transactions covering both revenue and expenditure.

Another major difference arises from the time concept – economist future and accountant past. Future considerations enables the economist to consider 'opportunity cost'.[1] Here profit is seen as a surplus in excess of opportunity costs; these costs can only be significant *before* operations commence. Accountants, on the other hand, do not consider opportunity costs because they work on past data. Such costs could become partly significant when costs are allocated (or reallocated) in the light of current facts at the end of each year.

PROFIT IN A CAPITALISTIC ECONOMY – IMPORTANCE OF

In an economy where no changes take place place there can be no pure profits; there will be normal profits (wages of management). In such an economy there is no uncertainty about the future, no risk and no pure profit. In an economy where changes take place but these can be foreseen with certainty there are no risk and again no pure profit. In a planned economy many uncertainties are removed, thus approaching the last situation. However in any economy where the state does not interfere or interferes only slightly we find that uncertainties tend to increase and with it risks increase: this we can call a capitalist economy.[2] In this dynamic economy long run profits (pure plus normal profits) are available because of the uncertainties that always exist in the future.

The details required to show the importance of profit in a capitalist economy has already been provided in Volume I[3] and the first page of this chapter. Briefly stated, the importance of profit in a capitalistic economy is that this return to the factor called enterprise is necessary for steering resources into those goods and services that are demanded by society.

1. Refer to Volume I page 8.
2. Refer to Vol. I Chapter 3 for details on 'Economic Systems'.
3. Refer to Chapter 3 pages 27 to 31.

Part Three

MONEY AND CREDIT AND THE BANKING SYSTEM

Chapter Thirteen

Basics of Money and Credit

In a primitive society, with its small population existing in virtual isolation, demand is mainly for biological goods (food, drink and clothing). The exchange system would be something like the following: one person (A) had more wool than he needed but was short of wheat, another person (B) had excess wheat but required meat, and a third person (C) had more meat than he needed but not enough wool. All would be satisfied by bartering. A would barter with B (wool for wheat), B with C (wheat for meat), and C with A (meat for wool). Their needs would be met by the system of bartering but it was a slow and painful process. However, in our primitive society it proved to be a satisfactory method of arranging exchanges.

In our modern society, large population and virtually no isolation, demands for biological needs accelerated and there were new and accelerated demands for psychological and social goods and services (washing machines, deep freezers, swim pools, boats, plumbing, electrical repairs, etc.). Bartering could not satisfy the vast number of transactions that were required to meet the needs of all persons. So, to make it easier for exchange to take place society invented two tools, namely, money and credit.

MONEY

Money is an important section in the study of economics. The importance lies not in money itself but in the goods and services which can be purchased with it. Even when looking at the national income the economist is concerned with the flow of *real* goods and services made available to the community; money is important in *measuring* this flow.

When looking at wages it was noted that employees exchange their efforts for 'money wages'. The employee does not want money for its own sake but having it enables him to purchase real goods and services. It is important to realise the difference between 'money wage' and '*real* wage.'

What is Money?

Economists are always careful in defining money. Some go to great lengths in noting many details usually associated with money and then perhaps they will define it, but follow up with a warning that it is not easy to decide a demarcating line that claims everything this side of the line is money and the other side is not, for example, arranging all assets alongside a liquidity line according to the length of time it takes to make them liquid. Most economists would agree that coins and notes are money. Some would say that money in current account is money whereas others might say it is not. Some include deposit accounts (banks may request you to wait 7 days for withdrawals) and others would not. There is no general agreement on what money is.

Money can be defined as anything which is generally accepted in the payment

for goods and services. In other words it can be notes and coins or tobacco or cattle or beads or diamonds, etc., which is widely accepted by the general public as a medium of exchange. Our employee above provides his labour to buy food, drink, tobacco and other goods. He is paid in notes and coins which he accepts because others accept these in payment for the goods mentioned. Notes and coins (money) become the medium between his efforts in producing good A and his purchases of goods B, C, D, etc.

If notes and coins are widely accepted they become money. On the other hand if some other commodity becomes more widely accepted then that commodity becomes money and notes and coins simply remain notes and coins and cease to be money. This latter situation occurred in Germany after the first world war.

For the time being, money can be defined as anything which is generally accepted as a medium of exchange.

Nature of Money

Nature, according to *The Concise Oxford Dictionary*, is a noun and is defined as 'thing's essential qualities'. In *The New Century Dictionary* it is defined as 'the particular combination of qualities belonging to a thing by birth or constitution.' Thus, when considering the nature of money we should discuss the special qualities of money which make them acceptable.

Qualities of Money

The qualities of money should be considered to determine which material is best to serve as money. It is possible to consider a variety of commodities such as gold, silver, diamonds, other precious gems, beads, cattle, etc., against the following qualities grading each from good to bad. That which has the best grading would normally be selected to act as money.

Acceptability. As already noted it is important that anything that is to act as money must be widely accepted as a medium of exchange.

Divisibility. Anything that is to be used as money must be easily divided into smaller units and at the same time the smaller units should be able to be brought together to form larger units.

Durability. If that which is to act as money is to last a long time it should not be a substance that will perish, nor as a result of frequent handling should it deteriorate through wear and tear.

Homogeneity. It is important that any commodity used as money should be similar, especially in quality. It should not be possible to distinguish one unit from another.

Malleability. Money normally requires identification and any material that is to be used as money should be able to withstand stamping, printing or moulding.

Portability. Money is usually transferred from one person to another. Any substance acting as money must not create difficulty nor inconvenience to anyone *carrying it about*.

Recognisability. If a material is to be used as money it must easily and instantly be recognised by the various senses (sight, touch, and often by hearing).

Stability. This quality refers to the value associated with the commodity. The standard of value must be stable in order to value the other commodities.

Transportability. It is important that the material acting as money can be transported over *long distances* without deteriorating. Also, it should not be

expensive to transport from one place to another. The usual statement here is that it must have high value for its bulk.

The importance of these qualities can be judged when considering an economy as it changes over time. For example, Britain during the 14th century with its manors[1] and isolated pockets of population. Most of the needs of these isolated communities came from the land and the method of exchanging one good for another was by bartering. Money, as we know it today, had only a small role to play. However, as markets and fairs grew in importance so did the need for some commodity to satisfy the qualities mentioned. Today, with national and international markets and isolated communities being a rarity and the tremendous increase in demand for many types of goods which the land cannot directly supply there was need for some commodity to act as a medium that was acceptable to buyers and sellers in the variety of exchanges they were involved in. Bartering, acceptable in primitive societies, became impossible in our modern society. Notes and coins ultimately became the commodities that satisfied the requirements of our modern exchange system.

Functions of Money

The commodity chosen to act as money must, if it is to fulfil its purpose, be capable of acting as:

1. a medium of exchange,
2. a measure of value,
3. a store of value, and
4. a standard of deferred payment.[2]

Medium of exchange. This is considered to be the primary or root function. It does away with bartering by facilitating exchange, but in order to do this it must be widely accepted in exchange for all other goods and services. The possessor of money must be satisfied that his wants can be obtained without difficulty. This becomes possible when money intervenes between one good and another in an exchange. By intervening (acting as a medium) it fixes the terms between the goods to be exchanged. Because it is accepted as a medium it facilitates the settlement of business transactions.

Measure of value. Quite often this is referred to as a 'unit of account'. In other words the value of any good or service to be exchanged can be measured by reference to a standard unit of the commodity serving as money. Having such a standard it becomes easier to measure the value of all goods and thus facilitates exchange. It assists businessmen to calculate gains and losses and it enables society to establish a more accurate pricing system.

Store of value. A person who holds money often wishes to store it away in a safe place and bring it out for exchange at some future time. In the process of storing it this person would not want it to deteriorate; he should not suffer any loss. This can only be done if the commodity accepted is durable and at the same time its own value remains stable.

Standard of deferred payment. In Britain much business is conducted on the basis of credit.[3] Credit refers to an extension of time to pay for goods and services; briefly referred to as 'deferred payment'. Persons who arrange to

1. Manors varied in size with 100 to 200 inhabitants. These pockets of population, so it has been said, considered other pockets of population living, say, 18 miles away as foreigners.
2. These four functions might be remembered by the following rhyming mnemonic:
    Money's a matter of functions four,
    A measure, a medium, a standard, a store.
3. Refer Vol. I pages 139–140 'Provision of credit'.

receive payment at a future date must be assured that money received later will approximate the purchsse of the same quantity of goods and services the money could have bought on the date the transaction was made. To ensure this the money in use must be sufficiently stable (can change with small changes in supply and demand but not big changes). In other words the standard value of today should have almost the same standard in the future.

The Functions and Inflation – Brief Consideration
The word 'standard' has been used frequently when discussing these functions. Standards must be maintained or if changed must not be allowed to change by big amounts. Perhaps the one force that tends to erode standards is the considerable change that takes place in the purchasing power of money (high rate of inflation). Normally, we consider the effect that inflation has on goods and services but all too often we tend to ignore the effect it has on the functions of money.

Briefly, a high level of inflation may lead towards the rejection of one form of money (notes) and acceptance of another form which is considered to be the better medium; Germany after the first world war. Also, inflation would create chaos to those who use it as a unit of account because it makes it difficult to calculate gains and losses (inflationary accounting problem). Who wants to store money today knowing it will not have the same value one, two or three years in the future? A similar picture can be painted for those who were once willing to wait for payment, but inflation would make them less willing to act in the 'deferred payment' field because future money would not have the same purchasing power as now.

High rates of inflation tends to erode standards and thus erode these functions.

CREDIT
Some aspects of credit have already been discussed.[1]

What is Credit?
Credit was previously defined as an extension of time to pay for goods and services – deferred payment. This can now be broadened to consider acknowledgement of debt for goods and services and also money debt. Thus, credit refers to a transfer of goods or money from one person or business to another person or busines with a promise from the debtor that the debt will be repaid at some future date.[2] In both cases the creditor faces the risk of not being repaid; the debtor has possession of the goods or money *now*.

TYPES OF CREDIT

ASSOCIATED WITH GOODS	ASSOCIATED WITH MONEY
Sales credit	Bank overdraft
Trade credit	Bank loan
Trade bill	Bank bill
Hire purchase	Cheque
Etc.	Etc.

EXHIBIT 13.1

1. Refer Vol. I pages 139–143 'credit' and 'provision of credit', relevant pages in chapter 10 for hire purchase, trade credit, sales credit, bank credit, etc.
2. Previous definition given in Vol. I page 139.

Credit arrangements can thus be broken down into two distinct areas, namely goods and money, as shown in the following exhibit.

Two basic elements in any credit transaction are:

1. the amount of credit to be provided, and
2. the length of time credit is given.

Qualities associated with Credit

Confidence. This is perhaps the most important quality associated with credit. No creditor is willing to extend credit to anyone in whom they do not have confidence. Thus, the qualities associated with credit should be mainly considered from the point of view of the creditor. If the qualities do not exist then no credit will be given. It appears to follow that all other qualities listed are really principles associated with the giving of credit to determine the level of confidence the lender has in the borrower.

Safety. A loan must, above all, be safe. The creditor must make certain that the borrower is reliable and that he can repay within the period given. Further, because of the unforeseen events that might take place in the future that might prohibit repayment the credit can be made safer by having the borrower deposit some security as insurance.

Suitability. The giving of credit is often established on the suitability of the asset or the purpose for which the credit is extended. A banker would consider gambling and speculation as not being suitable. Hire purchase may not be given if the life of the asset is less than the period of time covered by the agreement.[1] The less suitable the asset or purpose for which credit is to be used the less confidence the creditor will have.

There are other factors that are taken into consideration in the credit field but the above listed are most important. All factors are considered to determine whether the creditor should or should not have confidence in extending credit.

Banker and Credit

The following will be a simple exposition. Basically the banker will require knowledge about the borrower. If the credit to be given is small and for a very short period of time the knowledge required is little compared to the depth of knowledge for a large amount of credit for a long period of time. The knowledge required can be broken down into two time periods:

1. Past and present, and
2. Future.

At the *present* time is the borrower creditworthy? Here the banker tries to establish the financial strength of the borrower. In other words are the borrower's liabilities greater than his assets? What are these liabilities? these assets? These are the type of questions that must be asked. If the borrower is not deemed to be creditworthy the bank will not give credit. If the borrower is considered to be creditworthy the bank may give credit but only if the risks associated with the future are not excessive.

The *future* involves the banker in establishing the risk that he will face in giving credit. The worst possible risk a company can face is liquidation; for an individual it would be bankruptcy. Thus, the banker would estimate the greatest possible risk associated with the repayment. If the risk is too great and there is no possibility of reducing it the banker would probably not give credit even though

1. For rules followed by hire purchase organisations to determine the suitability of an asset refer to Vol. 1 page 76.

the borrower is at present creditworthy. On the other hand if the risk is not too great the banker would probably give credit.

Both considerations are based upon confidence; confidence at the present time and in the future. Both periods of time must give the banker confidence in the borrower if he is to give credit.

Functions of Credit

When considering the functions of credit we are concerned with the action by which it fulfils its purpose. Sometimes it is easier to see these functions if we assume there is no such thing as credit. Considering it this way we would find:

1. There would be greater need for more notes and coins for all payments would have to be in cash. Cheques, it should be remembered, reduce the need for notes and coins in circulation. Also cheques are a form of credit because you pay by cheque today but it is not debited from your account until it has been cleared through the banks – deferred payment for hours or days. Thus, one of the functions of credit is to reduce the use of notes and coins.

2. That all debts would have to be settled in cash immediately. This may create considerable inconveniences. Thus, another function of credit is to make it convenient for borrowers to settle their debts.

3. That it is not possible for certain trading activities to be carried out in anticipation of demand. Farmers wishing to purchase seeds for sowing in anticipation of demand for their crops at harvest time would face great difficulties. Thus a function of credit is to enable purchasers to buy raw materials now in anticipating the demand for the finished goods in the future.

4. There would be difficulty in channelling savings into investment. Production would probably not be on as large a scale as it is with credit. Thus, a function of credit is establishing a link between savings and purchasing materials needed in the production process. Normally the big creditors (banks, finance houses, etc.) act as mediators in this channelling process, and through their credit policies they minimise the idleness of large sums of money capital.

5. It would not be possible for financial firms with excellent reputations to transfer the use of their firm's name to another firm for trade. Credit, functioning as it does, enables the reverse of this situation to take place.

Inflation and Credit

Rapid inflation tends to disturb the area of credit. Creditors tend to lose in such an inflation because the payments in the future are reduced in value in terms of goods and services they can buy. During inflation at such a high level creditors are reluctant to give more credit and on the other hand they urge debtors to pay their debts sooner. Debtors, on the other hand, gain from rapid inflation. The real value of their debts is reduced; they make payments in depreciated pounds. On the other hand, if they are businessmen they stand to gain because they buy raw materials now (when credit is first given) at lower cost and sell at a future date when prices are higher. In an inflationary period debtors are reluctant to pay sooner, in fact they tend to take a longer period of time before repaying their debts.

METHODS OF PAYMENT

There are a number of different methods by which one person in this country can make payment to another. Some of these are as follows:

Cash – coins and notes.

Cheque.

Promissory note.
Postal order.
Money order.
Bank draft.
Credit transfer.
Direct debit.
Bill of exchange.
Travellers cheques.

Some of these will be discussed at length; the others will be noted.

Cash. A person can make a payment to someone else by paying in coins and notes. In making the payment there is a restriction on the amount that is handed over the counter; often referred to as 'legal tender'. This term simply states that there is a restriction on the currency a debtor can legally compel his creditor to accept. The figures are:

up to 20p in bronze coins,
up to £5 worth of silver (cupro-nickel), and
any amount in notes.

Cash is the normal method by which people pay for their purchases when shopping for everyday needs especially when total outlay is reasonable.

Cheque. A cheque is not legal tender. Nevertheless, it is the method that is most commonly used in paying a debt. Usually anyone using cheques has a current account with a bank, What is a cheque? It is an instrument used to transfer a sum of money from the banking account of one person to that of another. As such it is not money – it is a means of transferring money.

The procedure used in clearing cheques will be discussed later in this chapter.

Promissory note. This is simply a promise made by one person to another to pay a certain sum of money at some agreed date in the future. The debtor draws the note – unlike a bill of exchange.

Postal order. The Post Office provides this method of payment. These are most useful to persons without bank accounts. Payments can be transmitted by post with relative safety; the amounts however are only for a few pounds.

Money order. The Post Office also provides this method of payment when payments are for much larger sums of money. Money orders can be transmitted by post of if speed is essential in making the payment they can be transmitted by telegraph (known as 'telegraphic money order').

Bank draft. This is nothing more than a cheque but the cheque is drawn on a bank. This ensures the cheque will be honoured and there is virtually no risk that the wrong person will be paid. It is quite useful in sending reasonable (say £10 or more) sums of money to persons in other countries.

Credit transfer. Usually the gas, electricity and telephone bills have a section which can be detached which enables the debtor to pay a bill at any bank branch. Non bank customers can also complete a credit transfer slip in the same way. The bank then transfers the sum of money to the creditor's account at the bank where the creditor has his account.[1]

Direct debit. This method of payment requires a bank's customer to authorise his bank to pay his creditors on sight of an invoice which the creditor will send directly to the bank. The bank simply debits the customer's account.[2]

1. The Midland Bank provides useful information about credit transfers in a folded two page notice.
2. Refer Vol. I page 81 for previous mention of this method. Paragraph, at top of page 81 commences "It may be possible. . . ."

Bill of exchange. This instrument is drawn by the creditor – unlike the cheque or promissory note. This method of payment is very useful in exporting and importing.[1]

Travellers cheques. These are a special form of cheque issued by banks or specialised organisations for the convenience of customers who purchase goods and services in foreign countries. Most overseas businesses are often unwilling to accept a personal cheque but quite willing to accept a travellers cheque.

CHEQUE CLEARANCE

Banks are constantly receiving from their customers cheques to be paid into their accounts. Some of these may be from one customer at a branch bank to another customer at the same branch. These cheques are cleared by the branch bank itself. On the other hand a large number of cheques submitted to branch banks are drawn on other banking firms. They are cleared by a system, evolved by the banks, called the *Clearing House system.*

The system involves the 'clearing banks' (such as Barclays, Midland, Lloyds and National-Westminster) and the Bank of England. Each clearing bank has an account at the Bank of England.

Each day the branches of each bank send to their Head Offices all cheques that have to be cleared. Each Head Office sorts the cheques drawn on each of the other banks and totals are calculated. For example, the cheques held by bank A which were drawn on bank B may, when totalled, be greater than the claim that bank B has on bank A. Thus, B owes A money. B pays A by having their account at the Bank of England debited and the sum is credited to A's account at the Bank of England. The cheques have been cleared. The same procedure is carried out by all other member banks of the 'clearing house system'.

Now, each Head Office has its own cheques (drawn by its customers). These are sorted and delivered to their branch banks where each customer's account can be debited.

This completes the 'clearing' system.[2]

1. Refer Vol. I pages 83–84 and 94 for further details on 'bill finance'.
2. It should be noted that banks that are non-members of the Clearing House System must clear their cheques through one of the clearing banks.

Part Three

MONEY AND CREDIT AND THE BANKING SYSTEM

Chapter Fourteen

The Banking System and Credit Creation

The bulk of Britain's commercial banking business is in the hands of the London clearing banks.[1] These include Barclays, Lloyds, Midland, National Westminster (the "Big Four") together with two smaller members . . . Coutts & Co. and Williams & Glyns.

The remainder of commercial banking is carried out by the C.W.S. bank, the Scottish banks and a number of British based foreign banks (e.g. The Bank of America).

All these banks concentrate on "deposit banking" as opposed to industrial banking . . . the latter being the province of the merchant banks (discussed in Vol I Chapter 12). "Deposit" banks are those which accept sums on deposit and current account and use those deposits to provide the base for short and medium term finance for customers. "Merchant" bank lending by contrast, tends to be much longer term with greater concentration upon industrial lending rather than lending to the small private customer.

THE FUNCTIONS OF THE COMMERCIAL BANK

The chief function of the commercial bank is the provision of the country's main payment mechanism which involves the receipt, transfer and encashment of deposits.

1. *Current Account Facilities:* Deposits on current account make up approximately 55% of all deposits. This type of account provides the customer not only with safe keeping facilities but also with a facility for transferring balances from his current account by cheque, banker's order or credit transfer, without notice. Only rarely is interest paid on this type of account and normally some form of bank charge is made. Ready encashment of such deposits can be effected without notice.

2. *Loans and Overdrafts:* The holder of a current account can, in most cases, avail himself of overdraft or loan facilities. In the case of a loan the bank simply credits the customer's account with an entry which can be drawn upon by cheque. In the case of an overdraft, the bank will agree to allow the customer to overdraw his account up to an agreed maximum limit. Interest on loans is normally charged on the whole sum for the duration of the loan, whilst interest on the overdraft is charged only on the amount overdrawn and is calculated daily.

3. *Deposit Account Facilities (Time Deposits):* About 45% of bank deposits are held in this form. These accounts carry interest payments to the depositor but theoretically require notice before withdrawal can be made (many banks in

1. A "clearing bank" refers to a bank which is a member of the London Bankers' Clearing House . . . an institution through which inter-bank indebtedness is settled.

practice waive this demand on small withdrawals). Cheques cannot be used and withdrawals are made with the presentation of a pass book at the bank. Whilst the interest earned on such accounts is not attractive when compared with some alternative employment of funds, the holder of the account probably has greater liquidity and convenience than the other similar investments (e.g. Building Societies).

4. *Ancillary Services:* With the expansion of world trade the commercial bank has continued to develop highly remunerative foreign exchange services for its customers. This involves the provision of foreign currencies to pay for imports, the conversion of foreign currency earnings from exports, and provision of facilities for the speedy transfer of monies. Many banks are now also valuable sources of information for exporters . . . providing up-to-the-minute information on exchange rates, tariffs, documentation requirements and, in some cases, market reports.

In the late 1960s the commercial banks were faced with severe restraints upon their lending activities and this led to the majority of the banks developing new sources of income by the provision of specialist services for customers. Though many of these were in existence well before the great restraints on lending their expansion was most marked in the post 1970 period. A summary of the "service banking" facilities follows:—

1. *Standing Order Services:* Customers' payments which fall due at regular intervals can be made from the customer's account by the bank . . .without further action by the customer. These might include mortgage, insurance, hire purchase payments etc. A small service charge is made for a service which relieves the customer of a memory problem.

2. *Banker's Cards:* These are of two types; (a) the Credit Card (b) the Banker's Guarantee Card.

Credit cards, which include "ACCESS" operated by the National Westminster Midland, Lloyds and Williams and Glyns, and the BARCLAYCARD operated by Barclays, provide the holder with instantaneous credit facilities. A customer possessing such a card simply shows it to the retailer who then invoices the bank directly for the goods sold. The bank then charges the invoices against its customer's account on a monthly basis. In this case no cheque book is necessary for effecting payment.

The Banker's Guarantee card, on the other hand, is not a credit card service but simply a card which helps make cheques more widely accepted. The card simply indicates to the payee that the bank will guarantee to pay up to £30 should the drawee of the cheque default.

3. *Automatic Cash Dispensing:* As banks are generally only open for a few hours each day some of the larger branch banks have installed automatic cash dispensing machines which supply £10 cash by the insertion of a specially coded card. The customer's account is debited with £10 the next day.

4. *Night Safe Facilities:* Night safe facilities also help traders deposit their takings outside bank hours. Cash is deposited by the customer in lockable wallets and posted into the bank's night safe aperture. The next day the customer visits the bank and collects his wallet and banks the takings.

5. *Specialist services:* Most banks also offer their customers a whole range of specialist technical services. These include the handling of investment portfolios, the giving of investment advice, acting as executors to wills, trustees to estates and the provision of insurance broking services.

6. *Safe keeping facilities:* One of the original functions of the bank was to provide

safe keeping facilities for valuables. Today customers continue to use the bank's strong room for the deposit of deeds to property, jewellery, share certificates etc.

THE ROLE OF FOREIGN BANKS IN THE U.K.

Over the past 15 years foreign owned banks in the U.K. have shown remarkable growth rates . . . not only in the volume of business but also in their numbers. In 1960 there were only 77 such banks in the U.K. but today the number is nearer 200. Most of these banks are subsidiaries of large parents based overseas and for whom they conduct foreign business. Although many have now developed normal commercial banking services (including the acceptance of deposits and the provision of loans) in competition with the clearing banks, most still specialise in foreign exchange services. These would include the provision of finance for international trade and the effecting of international payments. The growth of of these banks has undoubtedly been due to the growth of Eurodollars[1] in the finance of international trade and the emergence of London as the chief centre of the market in Eurodollars. These foreign banks have recently been joined by a number of banks formed as consortiums by overseas and British banks . . . their main function has been to conduct the international business of multinational companies[2].

A NOTE ON OTHER BANKS OR "NEAR" BANKS

The Merchant Bank: These are not retail banks offering cheque clearing services but banks which specialise in longer term lending to industry. Many are old-established family companies Rothschilds, Hambros etc . . . but recently they have been joined by newer merchant banks operated as sideshoots of the commercial banks. The functions of the merchant bank are varied. Many help finance international trade, give investment advice, float new issues of shares for companies, arrange takeover bids and mergers and provide status enquiry services.

Building Societies: These are non-profit making institutions which offer deposit facilities to savers, giving the latter tax-free interest payments on deposits. Whilst such deposits are often less liquid than deposits made with the commercial bank they usually offer a better return to the investor.

The funds invested are mainly used to provide loans for the purchase of houses and property. These loans (mortgages) are normally repayable over periods of 10, 20, 25 or sometimes 30 years . . . repayments usually made in monthly instalments which include interest charges.

Hire Purchase Companies: These are industrial bankers which provide hire-purchase finance for private individuals and firms for the purchase of consumer goods, plant and machinery, motor vehicles, agricultural machinery etc. The funds to provide such finance come from deposits made by the public, borrowing from a variety of sources including commercial banks (note many commercial banks own hire-purchase companies and channel their customers' deposits in this direction) and from share capital.

Savings Banks: In the U.K. two types of saving bank exist. The National Savings Bank is government owned and operates through Post Office branches. This bank accepts deposits on which low rates of interest are paid but does not make advances in the same way as the commercial banks . . . the invested funds going to provide finance for Government.

1. See Page 256.
2. See Vol. I Chapter 26.

The Trustees Savings Bank provides similar deposit facilities but rates of interest paid vary according to the type of deposit account opened. Special long term deposits (which cannot be drawn upon for long periods) pay higher interest returns. Depositors' money can also be invested in some form of unit trust organised by the bank and often produces a good return. Current account facilities are also available with the Trustee Savings Bank.

THE CREATION OF CREDIT

One of the most important and interesting features in the development of commercial banking has been the power of the commercial bank to "create credit". This broadly refers to the ability of the bank to create new money beyond that which exists as note or coin, and which is brought into being as bank deposits created by pen entries made in the accounts of the bank's customers. The mechanics of this operation are perhaps best understood by looking back through the history of banking to the period when the goldsmiths were carrying out some of the earliest banking functions in Britain.

Creation of Credit and the early Goldsmiths

With the rapid expansion of trade in the 16th and 17th centuries considerable fortunes were being ammassed by inland and overseas traders. These were frequently deposited with local goldsmiths who were amongst the few people having safe keeping facilities. Small charges were made for such services and receipts, carrying an undertaking to return the valuables[1] on presentation were issued.

The receipts would normally be presented when the depositor needed his gold, silver or other precious metals to settle a debt with a third party and might involve the minting of gold plate into coin. This latter practice tended to be rather inconvenient and it soon became acceptable for a debtor to simply hand over one of his receipts to a creditor in settlement of the debt. The transfer of the receipt meant a transfer of title to the deposit of valuables, which could now be reclaimed by the new receipt holder. As this practice developed the receipts issued by the goldsmiths rapidly became early forms of bank note. The degree however to which such receipts were accepted as currency depended much upon the confidence people had in the goldsmith being able to meet the claims on that receipt. Some goldsmiths therefore tended to have receipts carrying their name in wide circulation whilst others had only a limited acceptability.

As the receipts became more acceptable as currency the goldsmiths faced fewer claims on the valuables deposited with them. Many realised that large parts of these deposits would remain unclaimed and could now be quite safely lent to reliable borrowers . . . providing that sufficient amounts were always kept ready to meet likely withdrawals. The goldsmiths thus developed the two functions of modern banking (1) the acceptance of deposits (2) the making of advances.

The lending activities were developed further when the goldsmiths, instead of lending out customers' gold and other deposits, discovered that they could make loans to reliable borrowers by simply drawing up and issuing new receipts (which had now become acceptable currency). These would technically give the holder a claim on valuables held in the vaults of the goldsmith but were in fact issued without any increase in the goldsmith's holdings of such valuables. Whilst the total receipts held would now exceed the valuables backing them, there would be little danger of the goldsmith finding himself unable to meet claims on those

1. These might include gold bullion, silver plate or other valuables.

valuables since so few receipts were ever presented for the return of the valuables. The goldsmiths therefore were able to create new money (in the form of receipts unbacked by valuables) and providing this was not done to any excessive degree, they could retain the confidence of the holders of the receipts by showing themselves able to meet any of their claims on valuables.

Creation of credit and the Modern Commercial Bank

The commercial banks of today find that, like the goldsmiths, only a small percentage of the deposits they accept are ever demanded in cash. From long experience the banks have found that when cash is deposited with them the customers making such deposits will, on average, rarely demand more than 8% in cash.

Let us assume that a customer deposits £100 cash with his bank. His account will be credited with a "£100 entry" and £100 cash will be available to meet any withdrawals from that "£100 account". However, we have seen that £8 (8% of the deposit) kept in the till would be sufficient to meet any cash claims on the deposit and should the remaining £92 be destroyed the bank would still operate without being embarrassed by cash claims it could not meet. This situation has been made possible by the fact that (1) customers rarely have a need for all their money at any one time and that (2) most transactions today are paid for by cheque, standing order or bank credit card. Payments are made by making adjustments to customers' bank balances rather than by a movement of cash. If, for example, I pay a petrol bill by cheque, my bank simply reduces my bank balance and increases the balance of my garage's account . . . there being no need for cash to cross the bank's counter.

The question now arises as to what the bank will do with the remainder of cash not needed to meet "over the counter" demands (the £92). We established that the bank could destroy the money and still meet normal cash demands. Only the insane bank manager would contemplate this suggestion; the prudent manager would realise that if he put the whole £100 cash deposit in his till he would have sufficient money (cash) to meet any claims from deposit holders with accounts far in excess of £100 value. If £8 cash is sufficient to meet demands from a deposit of value £100 (8% of the value of every deposit may be demanded over the counter in cash) then £100 cash will be sufficient to meet "over the counter" demands on deposits of $12\frac{1}{2}$ times that £100 i.e. £1,250 (8% of £1,250 being the £100 cash). The bank, therefore, by keeping £100 worth of cash in the till can not only meet the cash demands from the initial depositor of the £100 but also from other depositors (to a total of £1,250). The bank therefore could create additional deposits to the value of £1,150 ($11\frac{1}{2}$ times the initial cash deposit) by, for example, crediting a customer's account with a loan created by a pen entry. Total deposits would then stand at £1,250 (Note that the crediting of the customer's account with a loan increases that customer's deposit . . . "every loan creates a deposit"). A £100 cash asset therefore can support a banker's liability of £1,250. If however for any reason, the bank's holding of cash falls below £100 whilst its deposits are still £1,250 the bank could find itself being faced with demands it could not meet. Any such happening would create such a loss of confidence that the banker would undoubtedly be forced to suspend operations. The golden rule therefore is that if a bank can maintain deposits to the value of $12\frac{1}{2}$ times its holding of cash, then should its cash levels fall it must reduce its deposits by $12\frac{1}{2}$ times the fall in cash in order to maintain the safe 8% cash to deposits ratio. i.e.:

If £100 cash will support deposits of £1,250
then £50 cash will support deposits of only £625.
. . . a fall in cash of £50 means a reduction of deposits of £625 ($50 \times 12\frac{1}{2}$) if the 8% cash to deposits is to be maintained. The reader may now like to consider the above in terms of what happens in the commercial bank's balance sheet when credit is created and should refer to Exhibit 14.1.

STAGES IN CREDIT CREATION

BALANCE SHEET POSITION   COMMENTARY

STAGE I

Liabilities	Assets	
Deposit £100		Bank accepts £100 cash deposit from customer. This is a liability to bank since it has an obligation to repay the deposit.

STAGE II

		BUT
Deposit £100	Cash £100	The cash received by the bank will be an asset from which the bank can repay that deposit.

STAGE III

Deposit £100	Cash £100	The bank, however, knows that £100 cash (assets) in the till will meet demands from depositors with accounts far in excess of £100. Thus, bank can create new deposits by giving loans to customers – this brings deposits, in this example, to $12\frac{1}{2}$ times the value of cash held.
Deposits (Loan accounts, etc.) £1,150		
£1,250		

STAGE IV

		BUT
Deposit £100	Cash £100	The bank has now acquired additional claims against people who have received those loans. These, therefore, will be entered in the balance sheet as an asset – i.e. Advances £1,150.
	Advances	
Deposits £1,150	£1,150	
£1,250	£1,250	

EXHIBIT 14.1

So far we have limited the discussion of credit creation to a system in which there is only one bank. Under this system a customer that has had his account credited with a loan (which increases deposits in the bank) will draw cheques on that account making payments to his creditors. If these creditors also bank at his bank, the bank's liabilities (to meet cash demands) will still remain to its

own customers . . . the money merely being transferred from one account to another. Thus cash kept in this bank's till will be there to meet all its liabilities.

Now let us assume that we have a system comprising more than one bank. If our customer now makes a payment from his loan account to a creditor who banks elsewhere this will create a deposit in another bank and on which the recipient is likely to want to draw some cash. The second bank will now require cash from the first bank. The first bank must therefore be careful when creating credit that it does not find itself with too little cash. However, it must be noted that the second bank will also be creating credit using its own cash and some of this credit will be paid to payees who are customers of the first bank. Cash transfers will therefore be required the other way and tend to offset the latter's initial loss of cash. Therefore the final amount of cash transfer necessary may be quite small and should not interfere unduly with the individual bank's liquidity position.

One practical problem, however, remains unanswered. How does one bank make its cash transfers to another? All the big clearing banks keep part of their cash holdings in accounts at the Bank of England . . . this cash being available to the banker on demand. If one bank owes another cash, it is a simple matter for it to draw a cheque on its account at the Bank of England and make it payable to the account of the other, in the same institution . . . the settlement being effected by adjustment of the balances.

The Importance of the Liquidity Ratio in Credit Creation

Even though most commercial banks have found that a ratio of £8 cash to £100 worth of deposits is more than adequate to meet "over the counter" claims against these deposits, they have developed a secondary line of defence to cater for excessive cash claims. Each bank ensures that a large part of its lending is arranged in such a way that it is capable of being turned into cash quickly. This will therefore help to supplement cash in the till when the latter comes under excessive pressure. Instead of all bank lending taking the form of advances to customers (such advances are normally difficult to recall) a large part will therefore take the form of extremely short term loans and investments which can be quickly realisable in cash.

Until quite recently[1] banks were expected by the Bank of England to keep between 28% and 30% of their lending in a highly liquid form. This was for two reasons; (1) to make the banks more liquid and help maintain customers' confidence (2) to provide a fulcrum against which the Bank of England controls could operate . . . this will be dealt with later.

Banks in practice therefore cannot risk making all their lending by way of "advances" credited to customers' accounts as these are very often very illiquid. A high proportion of newly created deposits are therefore used by the bank to purchase assets which can be quickly turned into cash (Treasury Bills etc.) and for making very short term loans to the Discount Market (the latter being subject to recall in cash in one day).

How then does this liquidity requirement alter the power of the bank to create deposits? We saw earlier that £100 was sufficient to sustain any "over the counter" cash demands on deposits of £1,250 . . . a deposit of £100 cash enabling £1,150 worth of additional deposits to be created. However if the bank is expected to keep 28% of its deposits in a liquid form (and not just 8% as above) then a £100 cash deposit would be sufficient now to support deposits of only approx-

1. Competition and Credit Control 1971.

imately 3½ times that deposit (£100 providing the 28% liquidity requirement for £350 worth of deposits).

Banks are now more concerned about maintaining their liquidity ratios than their cash ratios, since deposits used to purchase assets such as Treasury Bills can be considered almost as good as cash . . . the 8% cash requirement therefore losing much individual significance to "general liquidity". This is reflected in the latest Bank of England policy[1] which relieves the commercial banks of their obligation to maintain the 8% cash ratio. The Bank now demands the maintenance of a new reserve-assets ratio of 12½% of the value of deposits (the old 28% liquidity ratio having been removed). This means that 12½% of the bank's deposits must be held in specially nominated investments which are highly liquid (this excludes cash in the till). Most banks now keep about 4½% of their assets in cash thus their total assets held in a liquid form will amount to about 17% of the value of deposits (liabilities) (See Exhibit 14.2). Thus if £17 out of every £100 of deposits has to be held in this way, £100 worth of cash would sustain new deposits of approximately £600 (£17 is sufficient to meet cash claims on deposits of £100 (6 × £17), therefore £100 cash is sufficient to meet claims on deposits of 6 × £100 = £600) As this £600 will include the claims on the initial deposit of £100 cash the bank will be in a position to create a new deposit of £500.

Credit created will therefore be 5 times the initial deposit . . . a far cry from the original credit multiplier based solely on 8% cash (see page 141).

LIQUIDITY v. PROFITABILITY

The need for commercial banks to arrange their lending in such a way as to ensure that some of their loans can be converted into cash when "till money" comes under pressure has a marked effect upon the revenue earning powers of such banks. The most profitable form of lending has always been the longer term loan to the businessman or private customer. However, such loans do not fit in the high liquidity category and so must not dominate lending policy. Loans and other investments with a higher degree of liquidity (those which can be turned into cash quickly) whilst essential to supplement cash, are low interest earners. This is because lending risks tend to be lower and the borrower is often under obligation to repay the loan quickly. The banker therefore, when deciding on a lending policy must try to achieve compromise between profitability and liquidity. This can be seen most clearly by examining the balance sheet of a commercial bank shown in Exhibit 14.2.

The Asset Structure (Refer Exhibit 14.2)

Cash in Till: This is the bank's most liquid asset and is readily available to meet cash demands from depositors. Holdings of cash will of course be kept to a minimum in order to free resources for interest earning purposes. Today, there is no minimum requirement demanded by the Bank of England thus the banks keep an amount just sufficient for their needs.

Cash at the Bank of England: These are cash deposits held at the Bank of England essentially to facilitate the settlement of inter-bank indebtedness. These funds carry no interest but can be considered as liquid as cash in the till. The clearing banks have agreed to keep these deposits at 1½% of their eligible liabilities.

Money at Call: These are investments which take the form of loans to the London Money Market and other firms carrying on a similar business. As these are to be repaid on the day on which notice to return the loan is given they carry

1. Competition and Credit Control 1971.

POST 1971 BALANCE SHEET
OF
TYPICAL COMMERCIAL BANK

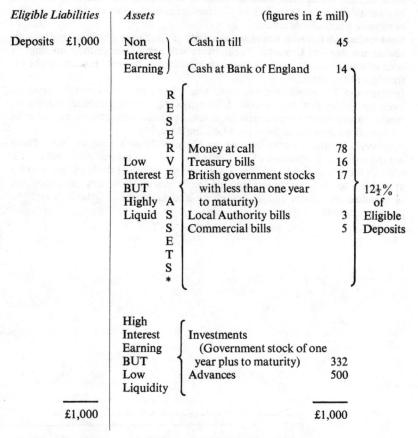

Eligible Liabilities	Assets	(figures in £ mill)
Deposits £1,000	Non Interest Earning { Cash in till	45
	Cash at Bank of England	14
	RESERV Low Interest EAS BUT Highly Liquid SE TS * { Money at call	78
	Treasury bills	16
	British government stocks with less than one year to maturity)	17
	Local Authority bills	3
	Commercial bills	5
		12½% of Eligible Deposits
	High Interest Earning BUT Low Liquidity { Investments (Government stock of one year plus to maturity)	332
	Advances	500
£1,000		£1,000

Note: *Reserve assets specially nominated by the Bank of England.

EXHIBIT 14.2

a low rate of interest. Money at call is the commercial banks' most liquid investment.

Treasury Bills: Banks purchase Treasury Bills from the Money market when the bills have already been held for some time by the institutions in this market. Purchases are arranged at regular intervals so that the portfolios of bills held by the bank always contains some bills which are maturing and ready to provide cash to supplement "till money". These are of course safe investments but do not yield great returns.

British Government Stocks: These include investments in government securities and in the stocks of nationalised industries. Such investments must have one year

or less to run before maturity. If they are to be considered as part of the Reserve Asset ratio.

Local Authority Bills: These are loans to local authorities in return for which, securities are issued. The securities must be eligible for rediscount by the Bank of England. This means the Bank will accept them for cash should the commercial bank have a liquidity problem.

Commercial Bills: These are essentially Bills of Exchange which are rediscountable at the Bank of England . . . the banks will again arrange their holdings of such bills so that there will always be some maturing to provide cash for the till should it be required.

Investments: These will include purchases of longer term government stock (with up to 10 years to run before maturity). Again the purchases will be arranged to provide a regular maturing quantity. These investments will bring in returns about the same as Minimum Lending Rate.

Advances: Advances normally take up about 50% of a bank's assets. These are the real money spinners of the banking world with returns well above bank rate . . . the actual rate being dependent upon the length of the loan, the security available and the credit-worthiness of the borrower. Advances take the form of loans or overdrafts and go to private and nationalised industries and the private customer.

MONEY AND CREDIT AND THE BANKING SYSTEM

Chapter Fifteen

Bank of England and Credit Control

THE BANK OF ENGLAND

The origins of banking in England are obscured by the mists of time but certainly banking as we recognise it today developed at a greater pace in the seventeenth century. However public confidence in the system was often shaken by failures as when the goldsmith-bankers over-reached themselves or when the Government borrowed and failed to repay. There was the need for a strong central bank on the lines of those that already existed at Amsterdam and Stockholm . . . consequently in 1694 the Bank of England came into being. It was established as the result of:

1. William III's need for cash to carry on his war against Louis XIV of France.
2. The public's refusal to trust the Government with a loan because of complete lack of faith in the Government's ability to repay.
3. A scheme put forward by Thomas Paterson to lend to the Government the sum of £1,200,000 in return for a Royal Charter of Incorporation.

Thus began the Bank of England and the National Debt.

This Royal Charter, reinforced in 1697 and 1708, gave to the Bank:

1. The right to issue notes to the extent of the sum lent to the Government.
2. The privilege of limited liability (which was very rare).
3. The monopoly of joint stock banking . . . with the following results:

(a) It forced all future development in English banking with the exception of the Bank of England to be carried on by private banks . . . this accounts for the late appearance of English joint-stock banks which were formed only after the monopoly was withdrawn in 1826 and 1833.

(b) The activities of those banks were localised in the areas where the owners were personally known.

(c) The private banks which had the right of note issue tended to over issue and so considerable numbers of them failed because of their inability to meet cash demands on these notes (100 failures in 1793, 600 between 1810–17 and 104 in 1825–26).

These frequent failures gave rise to two schools of thought concerning the correct method of note issue:

1. *The Banking School* believed that the size of the note issue should be left to the discretion of the bankers; that a 100% gold backing was not necessary. The size of the note issue would therefore be dictated by the needs of industry and commerce.

2. *The Currency School* believed that the only safe method was if the amount of notes issued was completely backed by gold bullion held by the bank.

The controversy raged until a compromise was reached by the Bank Charter Act 1844 which aimed at reducing outstanding private note issue and concentrating it in the hands of the Bank of England. This was achieved by:

1. Prohibiting the right of note issue to any new bank.
2. Limiting the note issue of existing banks to their average circulation over the previous twelve weeks.
3. Any bank would lose its right if:
    (a) it became bankrupt.
    (b) amalgamated with another.
    (c) opened a branch within a 65 mile radius of London, (thus most of the important banks were deprived of the right).
4. Allowing the Bank of England to take over two-thirds of any lapsed issue.
    Control over the Bank of England's issue was to be secured by:
1. Allowing the Bank to issue notes against the deposit of securities up to £14 million. This was the beginning of the Fiduciary Issue.
2. Permitting excess issue over £14 million only against the deposit of equal amounts of gold coin or bullion.
3. Separating the functions of the Bank by establishing:
    (a) *The Banking Department* to conduct normal banking business.
    (b) *The Issue Department* whose sole function was to issue notes up to £14 million against securities and beyond that only on deposit of gold.
4. Making a weekly return which would explain the activities of both departments and make public the level of the note issue.
    The 1844 Act was subsequently amended by later Acts, e.g.:
1. In 1928 the Bank took over the wartime issue of Treasury notes thereby increasing the fiduciary issue and furthermore it was empowered to increase the fiduciary issue for limited periods to meet seasonal demand.
2. In 1931 the Bank was freed from the obligation to exchange notes for gold.
3. In 1939 the gold reserves were transferred to the Exchequer Equalisation Account and in effect the whole of the note issue became fiduciary.
4. In 1946 the Bank of England was nationalised.

PRESENT DAY FUNCTIONS OF THE BANK OF ENGLAND

1. *Issue of notes.* In England and Wales it is the only note issuing authority; the banks in Scotland and N. Ireland still have the right of note issue but most of their issue is backed by Bank of England notes.
2. *Public Deposits.* The Bank of England is banker to the Government and is therefore continuously involved in monitoring the financial and economic climate and taking whatever action is necessary in the Money and Capital Markets and in the Foreign Exchange Markets in response to current developments. It is therefore the Government's adviser on monetary policy (though ultimately the responsibility rests with the Treasury) and its chief instrument in executing such policy. As the Government's banker it holds the central accounts, the Public Deposits which includes the Exchequer, National Loans Fund, National Debt Commissioners and Dividend Accounts. All receipts and disbursements of Government departments go through the Bank of England which will make funds available by means of Ways and Means Advances to departments which are temporarily short of funds.
3. *Management of the National Debt.* All the borrowing made by the Government comprises the National Debt. The administration of this is the responsibility of the Bank of England by maintaining a register of the holders of all Government securities and ensures that the payments are made on maturity. Week by week it arranges the issue of Treasury Bills and bonds and buys back those which have reached maturity, it arranges the issue of securities for the Nationalised In-

dustries, Local Authorities and Public Corporations and through the Government Broker it arranges the Open Market Operations. In managing the debt the Bank clearly wants to be able to obtain funds as cheaply as possible for the Government which means that it would aim to keep interest rates down. This presents the Bank with two problems:

(a) the Government may be pursuing an anti-inflationary policy and needs to use higher interest rates as one of its weapons.

(b) the Government may be dealing with a drain on the Balance of Payments and needs higher interest rates to keep (or attract) foreign reserves and capital in London in order that the value of Sterling will not suffer on international currency markets.

4. *Operation of the Exchange Equalisation Account.* The main purpose of this account is to protect the value of Sterling on foreign exchange markets. If the U.K.'s Balance of Payments is in deficit it means that there is an excess supply of Sterling on the world's money markets and so the exchange rate falls. Holders of Sterling fearing that the fall will continue will start to sell it and so aggravate the fall. To prevent this the Bank steps in with 'support operations' using the reserves held in the Exchange Equalisation Account to buy Sterling on the market and so stabilize exchange rates. If the loss of confidence in Sterling is prolonged for any reason then the sale of Sterling on the foreign exchange market will be on a scale too large for the Bank of England to go on buying pounds indefinitely in order to support the price. This is because the total gold and foreign currency reserves of the Bank are small in relation to the total supply of Sterling in circulation, consequently the Government may have to borrow foreign currency from external sources in order that the Bank can continue to buy up surplus pounds and prevent the exchange rate falling still further It is when the Government can no longer borrow sufficient funds to enable support operations to continue that it may have to resort to devaluation of the exchange rate.

The external value of Sterling is not only important for the U.K., the Bank also has an obligation to maintain its value for the members of the Sterling Area who keep part of their reserves in London.

5. *Banker to the Commercial Banks.* After the Government the most important customers are the joint stock banks which hold part of their cash reserves at the Bank of England. The commercial banks draw cash from these reserves as required, they settle net payments with each other after the day's clearing through the Bank and they follow the general advice given by the Bank.

6. *Lender of last resort to the Money Market.* The London Discount Houses are a most important part of the entire financial mechanism in that they are the prime borrowers and lenders of short term money. The Discount Houses are the main traders in the securities which form the bulk of the eligible liabilities of the Minimum Reserve Ratio and it is through these activities that the Bank can influence interest rates in the Money Market. If the Bank wants to reduce the supply of funds in order to push up interest rates it sells more Treasury Bills which causes a drain on the cash reserves of the banks as funds are then transferred and so to restore the cash position the banks call in the overnight loans made to the discount houses. The latter might then have difficulty in finding sufficient funds to balance their own books (because open market operations are keeping money short in the money market) and so they will be 'forced into the Bank' i.e. they will sell Treasury Bills back to the Bank or borrow against the

security of first class bills. The Bank will help as *lender of last resort* but the rate it charges for re-discounting, the Minimum Lending Rate, is set by the Bank of England. This has the effect of making money borrowed by the discount houses dearer, consequently they lower their bid price for the next issue of Treasury Bills in order to increase their yield. Treasury Bills do not carry a guaranteed rate of interest, instead purchasers make a profit by bidding for them at a discount. Thus by lowering their bid price the yield on the Bills will rise and because of the importance of the Treasury Bill Rate in the money market there will be an upward movement of other interest rates.

7. *International dealings.* The Bank acts as the Government's agent in dealings with other central banks (e.g. in negotiating credit facilities to give temporary assistance in Balance of Payments difficulties) and in the work of such international organizations as the International Monetary Fund, the Bank for International Settlements, and the International Bank for Reconstruction and Development.

8. *Regulation of the credit policies of the commercial banks.* Until the changes suggested by the consultative document 'Competition and Credit Control' (May 1971) the Bank relied primarily on maintenance of the cash ratio of 8%, the further liquidity ratio of 20% (28% in all), movements in Bank Rate, Open Market Operations, Special Deposits and Directives (both Quantitative and Qualitative).

CREDIT CONTROL
Pre-1971

It may be said that the prime function of the Bank of England is to control the amount of money in the country. In the main the level of deposits was determined by the commercial banks themselves, thus if they increased their lending their total deposits would increase and if they cut back on lending their total deposits fall. To meet demands for cash against such deposits the banks kept a cash ratio of 8% . . . experience having shown that this amount was sufficient . . . but since they kept about half of this cash reserve at the Bank of England they had to be prepared for changes of policy by the Bank which would affect their balances which in turn would affect their lending policy and so ultimately the level of bank deposits.

Until 1945 the Bank relied upon the two traditional weapons of monetary policy to control the activities of the commercial banks:—

1. Open Market Operations.
2. Bank Rate.

but in the 1950's other instruments were developed, namely:—

1. Treasury Directives.
2. Funding.
3. Special Deposits.

Open Market Operations

Although a large proportion of money in circulation consists of bank deposits there is a close connection between the amount of cash and these deposits . . . thus any increase of decrease in the amount of cash held by the banks will be matched by a multiplied increase or decrease in the level of bank deposits (see page 141 on credit creation). Although approximately three quarters of the money in the U.K. is in the form of bank deposits there is a very close connection between these and the amount of cash in existence so that any increase or decrease in

the latter will cause roughly three times as much increase or decrease in the quantity of bank deposits. Therefore under the old system any action by the Bank of England to reduce the amount of cash available meant that for every £1 it was reduced a further £3 of bank deposits disappeared so that in total the money supply was reduced by £4. It is through this multiplier effect that the Bank has power to influence the amount of cash in circulation and the traditional method of doing this was by open market operations. If the Government wishes to reduce the total amount it instructs the Government Broker to sell Government securities (including Treasury Bills) on the market; these will be paid for with cheques drawn on the commercial banks and so subsequently their balances at the Bank of England are reduced. Since the balances of the commercial banks are regarded as part of their cash holding it follows that any reduction in the balances is automatically a reduction in their cash base and because of the need to restore this they will call in loans. Similarly if the Government wishes to increase the money supply it can buy back securities . . . or sell fewer . . . thus leaving the banks with more cash and the ability to create further credit.

Bank Rate

The rate at which the Bank would lend short-term as lender of last resort to the discount market was known as Bank Rate. This facility was . . . and still is . . . only available to the Discount Houses and it is because the commercial banks know that the Bank will always lend to the Discount Houses that they themselves can operate with only a small cash base i.e. if the banks need a sudden inflow of cash they can call back the overnight money from the Discount Houses knowing that the latter can always turn to the Bank of England in the last resort. The importance of the Bank Rate was that it was the focal point of all interest rates e.g. the commercial banks usually paid 2% less than Bank Rate on deposit accounts and charged between 1–2% above to borrowers.

From 1932 up to 1951 Bank Rate was both static and low but it was subsequently used as one of the principal weapons of monetary policy. However there was considerable criticism of the effectiveness of using Bank Rate to control the economy. Not only did the Radcliffe Report conclude that changes in Bank Rate have very little effect on long term interest rates but in general Bank Rate was a rather crude and indiscriminate weapon.

Changes in Bank Rate have been used on many occasions as one of the weapons to deflate or reflate the economy through control of aggregate demand. It affects aggregate demand by varying the cost of borrowing and by shifting the relative attractiveness of saving to spending; the change in the Bank Rate affects the interest rate structure and therefore the demand for loans. However changes in interest rates alone are not very effective in controlling aggregate demand. For entrepreneurs the decision to invest depends much more on their expectations of the future and the net marginal productivity of capital than simply the cost of borrowing . . . consequently a high Bank Rate may not deter them from borrowing anymore than a low one will necessarily overcome their pessimism. For consumers the situation is similar in that they are not necessarily put off from entering into a Hire Purchase contract when interest rates rise because:—

a) there may be no other method available for them.

b) the marginal utility of the commodity is greater than that of the extra interest charges.

However if a rise in interest rates plus other measures does have an effect on the

level of demand then the Government must be prepared for the effects of reduced economic activity e.g. unemployment . . . and similarly a fall in interest rates etc., ultimately creating more activity producing inflationary pressures.

Bank Rate has also been used as a weapon to help the Balance of Payments and protect the exchange value of Sterling. An increase in Bank Rate (backed up by other measures) is intended to dampen the effective quantity of money and the general level of prices. This should make goods available for export more competitive while stimulating saving and reducing the demand for imports. The combined result should have a favourable effect on the Balance of Payments however no reliance can be placed on the effectiveness of Bank Rate policy unless reinforced by other measures to stimulate exports and reduce demand for imports.

Externally, the flow of international funds should be affected by movements in Bank Rate . . . a rise will attract foreign funds seeking higher interest rates so improving the balance of payments position in the short run (even though the increase in Bank Rate means that the yearly interest paid abroad is increased), and a fall in the Rate will cause 'hot money'to leave the country to more attractive centres and so will adversely affect the balance. These movements of funds are however of secondary importance to the impact changes in Bank Rate have on the internal economy because ultimately foreigners' confidence in Sterling depends on whether they believe domestic costs and prices are sufficiently under control for Sterling to hold its position and not to be devalued.

Treasury directives

Under Section 4 (3) of the Bank of England Act 1946 the Bank has had the power to legally enforce its wishes on the commercial banks . . . it has not been necessary to resort to this power because as the clearing banks said to the Radcliffe Committee, ". . . we listen with great care to what the Governor says to us at any time. He might give us a hint and we should not be likely to ignore it." These official requests and suggestions have taken two forms:—

a) *Quantitative Directives* . . . which in effect placed a ceiling on bank credit. For example when they were directed to reduce their advances by March 1969 to 98% of the November 1967 level . . . later when monetary restrictions were relaxed in mid 1970 they were firmly recommended not to increase their deposits too rapidly.

b) *Qualitative Directives* . . . which are really recommendations that preferential treatment should be given to certain borrowers and discrimination against others. For example, favourable consideration should be given to provide credit finance for exporters and for firms producing import substitutes and for firms in Development Areas; in 1972 it was suggested that lending to property speculators should be discouraged.

Funding

This is an additional method of affecting the liquidity position of the commercial banks, it is, briefly, the conversion of short term into long term securities. If the Bank issues fewer Treasury Bills or replaces them with a greater issue of Government bonds it can change the asset structure of the clearing banks by increasing their investments and reducing their reserve assets, consequently to restore their reserve ratio the banks have to reduce their advances and so funds become more difficult to obtain. The reverse action by the Bank of course ultimately makes funds easier to obtain.

Special Deposits

The weakness of Open Market Operations is that they are voluntary . . . there is no guarantee that the institutions will buy . . . except the assurance of the discount houses to take up unsold Treasury Bills. Funding creates the following difficulties:—

a) it adds to the cost of borrowing by the Government.

b) it raises long term interest rates.

After the war the Government increased its borrowing through Treasury Bills (because of the relative attractiveness of short term borrowing) so that ultimately the banks' holding of Treasury Bills formed a large proportion of their liquid assets. If funding was to be a successful method of controlling the activities of the banks there had to be considerable reduction of the short term debt which would have required a considerable increase in long term interest rates to hedge against the possible depreciation of the value of money in the long term.

Since 1958 the Bank has had the power to call for Special Deposits which in effect are forced loans. They are paid into a special account at the Bank of England and are 'frozen' . . . they cannot be included in either the cash reserve or liquid reserves (reserve asset ratio) of the banks but they are paid a rate of interest approximately equal to the Treasury Bill rate of the preceeding week. Special Deposits have certain definite advantages:—

a) The banks must deposit them with the Bank of England thus their liquidity is immediately reduced and to restore this they must curtail their advances (note the multiplier effect on the supply of money).

b) This reduction in liquidity is achieved without any large scale funding.

c) The consequent tightening of their credit creating ability makes open market funding operations more effective.

Special Deposits were first called in 1960 (1% of total deposits rising to $3\frac{1}{2}$%). These were released in 1962 but were re-imposed in 1964 and in 1969 stood at 2%. In spite of their unpopularity with the banks and speculation that they might be discontinued it was clear in 1969 that the Government intended to make further use of them. In that year the rate of interest on them was reduced until such time that the banks complied with the earlier Directive to reduce their advances to 98% of the November 1967 level. Thus the reduction in interest was being used as a fine on banks which stepped out of line with the Directive. In May 1970 Special Deposits were increased to $2\frac{1}{2}$% and in October to $3\frac{1}{2}$%.

CREDIT CONTROL SINCE SEPTEMBER 1971

Since the introduction of the new measures in September 1971 the Bank has relied less on particular methods of influencing the creation of credit and more on changes in interest rates backed up by calls for Special Deposits on the basis of a Minimum Reserve Ratio of $12\frac{1}{2}$% applied to all 'listed banks' i.e. the London and Scottish clearing banks and their subsidiaries, merchant banks, London based consortia, Commonwealth banks, foreign banks and a number of smaller U.K. banks. Finance houses and discount houses are subject to similar controls

The main changes introduced in September 1971 can be summarised as:—

1. The minimum liquidity ratio of 28% including the cash ratio of 8% of gross deposits kept by the London clearing banks has been terminated.

2. All banks are now obliged to maintain a minimum ratio of $12\frac{1}{2}$% of eligible reserve assets to eligible liabilities.

3. Special Deposits are no longer to apply just to the London and Scottish clearing banks but to the finance and discount houses also.

4. Restrictions on bank lending have been removed and in future control will be by Special Deposits and through interest rates.
5. The English and Scottish clearing banks have ended their collective agreements on interest rates.

The two concepts of eligible liabilities and eligible reserve assets are new and require further clarification. .

Eligible liabilities
These include:—
1. All sterling deposits from U.K. residents or overseas residents, excluding those deposits originally made for more than two years (these could not really be regarded as short term bank deposits).
2. Funds held temporarily on suspense accounts (i.e. amounts due to customers).
3. All sterling deposits from U.K. banks less sterling claims on U.K. banks.
4. All sterling Certificates of Deposit issued less holdings of certificates of Deposit (these are certificates which acknowledge the deposit of large sums of money, they can be readily bought and sold in a special market).
5. The net liabilities in sterling to its overseas branches and the net liability in other currencies.
6. 60% of the net value of items in transit.

Reserve Assets
These include:—
1. Balances at the Bank of England other than Special Deposits.
2. Treasury Bills.
3. Company tax reserve certificates.
4. Money at call to the London Discount Houses and to others, such as brokers involved with the overnight finance of the gilt-edged market.
5. British Government and Nationalised Industry stocks with one year or less to run to final maturity.
6. Local authority Bills eligible for rediscount at the Bank of England.
7. Commercial bills eligible for rediscount at the Bank of England (up to a maximum of 2% of total eligible liabilities) generally speaking these are Bills payable in the U.K., accepted by certain British and Commonwealth banks.

These new concepts involve the following changes compared with the previous system.
1. Notes and coin held in the till are excluded whereas previously the London Clearing banks included such holdings in their 8% and 28% liquidity ratios. With regard to balances maintained with the Bank of England the clearing banks have agreed to maintain these at a level equal to $1\frac{1}{2}\%$ of eligible liabilities and although they will be regarded as a reserve asset they will not earn interest.
2. Money at short notice is excluded, funds must be at call for the Money Market.
3. The inclusion of British Government stocks with one year or less to run whereas previously all gilt edged securities were regarded as earning assets rather than liquid assets.
4. The new regulations apply to all banks not just the London clearing banks.
5. The new system means a much more flexible role for Special Deposits and in future the call can be related to domestic deposits or overseas deposits. This is because it was felt that there might be occasions when the Government wanted to increase Special Deposits but did not want to affect the banks' overseas

deposits or other occasions when the Bank wanted to limit the effect of overseas deposits with the banks on the supply of domestic credit.

6. The Minimum Lending Rate which has replaced Bank Rate is linked to market rates and therefore reacts automatically to market trends. The Minimum Lending Rate is based on the average Treasury Bill Rate at the weekly tender plus $\frac{1}{2}\%$ and rounded up to the nearest $\frac{1}{4}\%$ above. Changes are announced each Friday afternoon though the Bank reserves the right to fix a rate independent of the new formula if it is felt there is a need to give a lead to interest rates in general.

7. The new Credit Control measures also affect the arrangements for the weekly Treasury Bill issue in that although the Discount Houses continue to underwrite the issue in return for which they retain the right to turn to the Bank as lender of last resort, they no longer make a syndicated tender, in future each House will make an individual bid.

From the banks' point of view they have:—

1. Abandoned their collective agreements on interest rates by which uniform deposit rates were linked with Bank Rate and lending rates were also related to Bank Rate. For many years the deposit rate was fixed at 2% below the current Bank Rate . . . under the new system each bank decides its own 'base rate' for advances and its rates for deposit accounts. For certain large customers the banks are relating their lending rates to money market rates in order to prevent corporate customers from using their bank facilities simply to place funds at a higher rate on the money market and not for the commercial purposes originally intended.

2. Agreed to keep cash amounting to $1\frac{1}{2}\%$ of their eligible liabilities with the Bank of England to help the Bank's money market operations . . . this amount is included in the $12\frac{1}{2}\%$ ratio.

The measure outlined in the previous section represent far reaching changes in the relationship between the Bank, the Commercial Banks and the Finance Houses but since all the institutions are unhappy with bank lending restricted by ceiling levels and official priorities they believed that the changes were necessary.

The Supplementary Credit Control Scheme.

Following the changes in September 1971 there was a rapid increase in the money supply in the U.K. and because of the growing pace of inflation, not all of which could be blamed on wage settlements and the cost of imports, further measures were introduced to control the activities of the commercial banks. The scheme introduced in December 1973 is a major supplement to the Competition and Credit Control arrangements implemented just two years earlier. Basically the new measures are to assist the monetary policy of the authorities . . . they are new in that they will operate on the liabilities of the banks rather than on their assets. The control is not on the total amount of liabilities but only on those which earn interest; these have now become known as IBELs (interest bearing eligible liabilities) as distinct from NIBELs (non-interest bearing eligible liabilities).

The new regulations state the maximum rate at which IBELs can grow over a stated period and the penalty which must be paid if an institution exceeds this amount. The penalty is a Supplementary Special Deposit which will not bear interest and will operate thus:— if the excess of IBELs is 1% or less the supplementary special deposit will be 5% of the excess; between 1 and 3% the call will be 25% of the excess and thereafter 50%. It is therefore intended to be a very

real penalty and the banks were instructed not to increase their general lending
rates in order to offset the penalty with increased earnings.

The authorities say that the supplementary scheme is intended to improve the
Bank of England's control over both the money supply and bank lending. Clearly
there are some points which will need to be watched, for example, the banks are
still free to arrange their portfolio of assets and therefore there is nothing to stop
them moving into the "penalty area" if they can find areas of lending which
would still be profitable even after the payment of the penalty. The Bank has
noted that rates of interest offered by the banks affect the growth of IBELs but
also points out that, "the authorities will continue to use their previously established monetary instruments to influence the general level of money market
rates notably by daily operations, supported as necessary by general calls or
repayment of Special Deposits." It would seem therefore that the new scheme
is designed to control not only the money supply and bank lending but also
interest rates.

In the past the Bank has regulated the activities of the commercial banks
through the Assets by means of reserve ratios thus ultimately controlling the
level of deposits; the new scheme shifts the emphasis. It is presumed that the
banks will keep within the set limits because by convention they have always
concurred with the Bank of England in its implementation of monetary policy
but there is now a very good reason why they should comply, namely the penalty
they will incur if they exceed the prescribed limits. It is therefore hoped that the
banks will now have reason to work actively to control the money supply rather
than to resist or at the best simply acquiesce to limitation of the money supply.

The banks were liable to place their first supplementary deposits with the Bank
of England on 15 July 1974 if the level of their interest bearing eligible liabilities
in the three months up to June exceeded by more than 8% the level of the October-
December 1973 base period. The average increase in IBELs for all banks was in
fact 2·3% and for the clearing banks alone 4·4% which was well inside the 8%

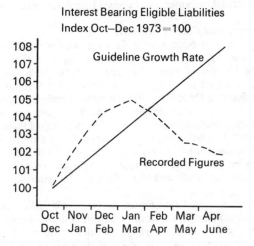

Interest Bearing Eligible Liabilities
Index Oct–Dec 1973 = 100

Source: Treasury Information Division

EXHIBIT 15.1

guideline . . . although 14 of the smaller banks did have to place supplementary deposits of £6 million. Exhibit 15.1 shows the position for all banks at that time. However not too much should be read into the above, it may well be that the slackening off in the expansion of the money supply was not due entirely to the introduction of the scheme but to other factors also, such as the fact that industrial companies had built up substantial borrowing positions with the banks in 1973 to take advantage of prevailing interest rates and so did not need to turn to the banks to the same degree.

In the three months to October 1974 the growth of IBELs was well within the guideline. The Budget of November 1974 announced that the scheme was to be extended to June 1975, the guideline rate of growth for IBELs being 1½% per month; however in case any of the banks should have any inhibitions about increasing IBELs at a rate close to the guideline, the first 'penalty area' above the guideline has been widened.

Part Four

THE GOVERNMENT AND THE ECONOMY

Chapter Sixteen

Major Objectives of Government Policy

Since World War II successive governments have all pursued the following economic goals:
1. To improve the standard of living.
2. The maintenance of full employment.
3. Stability of prices.
4. A Balance of Payments equilibrium.

The rank order of these objectives has of course changed from time to time. Before the war the fear of a return to the depression of the 1930s made full employment the major objective of policy. However, the postwar period brought with it a greater understanding of the causes of unemployment and more effective techniques of controlling it. As a result, governments were able to concentrate their efforts on creating policies for the improvement of the standard of life.

Unfortunately, the fully employed post-war economy has been very prone to inflation and this in turn has had serious effects upon the balance of payments. This has meant that the longer term objectives of increasing the standard of living and maintaining a high level of employment have frequently had to be shelved whilst the more immediate problems of inflation and the balance of payments are given priority.

THE STANDARD OF LIVING

This can probably be best described as the "well being" of an individual or nation. In its simplest terms one tends to think of the standard of living as a reflection of the availability of material wealth. If an individual is in a position whereby he can purchase 10% more goods than he did last year we might say he is "better off". By the same token a nation may be described as having improved living standards if more goods and services are available than in previous years.

There are however, important qualifications to the above statements. Firstly an individual may be able to acquire more goods and services but only at the expense of a fellow citizen going without. For example, if z million goods were available in the U.K. last year and there is no change this year, any increase in consumption by one citizen this year over last must be accompanied by a decrease in consumption by another.

If, however, there is say a 10% increase in the availability of goods and all citizens share in that increase, then not only will we be better off as a nation but also as individuals.

The Quality of Life

The standard of living, however, involves much more than just the possession and acquisition of material wealth. In recent years people have become in-

creasingly conscious of the society and environment in which they live. They have become concerned about the degree of pollution and congestion, the stresses of industrial society, the length of the working week and the availability of leisure time; all of which will seriously affect their "wellbeing" or living standards. Whilst, therefore, longer working hours may provide the individual with the means to acquire more material wealth the lack of leisure time, as a result of these longer working hours, may prevent him from enjoying that wealth. Thus, in this instance, the well being of the individual may not improve. Often the drive for increased production to satisfy the material demands of society will lead to a reduction in the quality of other goods. Water, for example, has a multiple role to play in society. Not only is it important for sustaining life and servicing industry in a variety of ways but also provides recreation in the form of fishing, boating, swimming and the enhancement of scenic beauty. Increased industrial use of water may result in pollution which reduces its value to society as a recreational good. Thus a 10% increase in the material well being may not mean a 10% increase in the standard of living since in the process of achieving this 10% increase there may be a 10% deterioration in the quality of life in some other direction.

From the above argument the student will have grasped that the standard of living is a measure of "well being" which embraces both "materialism" and the "quality of life". However, as the wider social benefits that one associates with the quality of life are difficult to quantify and are valued in the widest sense differently by most people, the standard of living will mean different things to different people.

In practice, therefore, perhaps the most convenient measure of the standard of living is still national income per head of population. Although the quality of life aspect is becoming increasingly important to the individual, particularly in the highly industrialised economy, the individual is still obsessed with material acquisition of wealth. As this aspect of the standard of living is more readily understood and has this high appeal to the individual, governments tend to use National Income figures as the yardstick.

Economic Growth[1]

Economic growth in its simplest terms means the growth in national output or production. If the nation produces 5% more goods and services this year than last then we could say we have had a 5% growth rate. However, some increases in national output are simply the result of employing some of the spare productive capacity of the economy (e.g. the unemployed) and strictly speaking, output from this source cannot be considered as growth. Growth is more accurately an increase in national output which is achieved over a period in which the economy is fully employed. In other words it is output which is the result of an increase in the productive capacity of the economy. One could therefore define growth as simply the increase in the productive capacity of the economy.

THE GOVERNMENT AND ECONOMIC GROWTH

As we have seen above, there is a strong connection between the availability of goods and services and the standard of living. National "Growth" policies could therefore, be said to be designed to increase the standard of living.

1. The theoretical approach to growth is considered in Chapter 4.

How can growth be increased?

"Growth" refers to the growth of national production. To find the forces which generate growth we must look to the basic factors of production . . . land, labour, capital and enterprise. It is the fusion of these factors which results in production. Thus forces influencing the growth of production must lie within these factors of production or be associated with the way in which they are organised or utilised. In the U.K. the availability of the factors of production is probably more limited than in many developed nations. Domestic raw materials have, to a large extent, been exhausted as a result of an early industrial development and a high population/land ratio. Industry is also often short of skilled labour, and there are considerable pressures upon the supply of capital and managerial talent.

Increases in output in the U.K. will thus be achieved more from intensive development of the existing factors available within the economy rather than from acquiring new resources. Growth of output achieved by more intensive use of one's factors of production is normally referred to as "productivity".

THE SOURCES OF GROWTH

1. Capital Investment

Capital investment is considered by most economists to be a major force influencing economic growth. Lord George Brown in the National Planning Document 1965–70 dubbed investment as . . . "The Engine of Economic Growth." The principle expounded in this document is based on the idea that the more horsepower behind each worker's elbow the greater his output. Evidence to support this can be clearly seen in statistics which compare national growth rates with rates of investment. Such a table is shown in Exhibit 16.1.

To claim unreservedly that there is a causal relationship between one set of statistics and another is dangerous. There is, for example, a close correlation between the change in the stork population of Norway and Norway's birth-rate though, not surprisingly, few actually believe that one causes the other. However, as far as the relationship between investment and growth is concerned, a great number of countries with statistics showing high degrees of correlation between investment rates and growth indicates a link much greater than one of co-incidence. Sir Frederick Catherwood as Director General of the National Economic Development Countil (NEDC) summed up the relationship in this way:[1]

. . . "I have a natural suspicion of graphs which purport to show the relationship between one set of circumstances and another completely dissimilar set of circumstances. But there are some correlations which are so dramatic that cause and effect are clear as can be. And the correlation between investment and economic growth are so clear that one must cause the other." (In this statement investment is considered the causal factor).

The Quality of Investment

Increasing investment levels are not the complete answer to higher rates of growth. The quality of that investment is equally important. Investment in modern machinery will yield better results than simply adding to the stock of machinery of the older type. The British approach to investment has often been described as a "glue and string" approach where valuable investment funds have been used for "repair" rather than "replacement". In contrast nations like

1. Production Engineer 1968.

COUNTRY	Annual Increase in Output Per Man-hour 1965-70	Capital Investment as % of G.N.P. 1960-69
JAPAN	14·2%	27
NETHERLANDS	8·5%	20
SWEDEN	7·9%	18
FRANCE	6·6%	18
GERMANY	5·3%	20
ITALY	5·1%	14
U.K.	3·6%	14
U.S.A.	2·1%	13

TABLE SHOWING A RELATIONSHIP BETWEEN IN-VESTMENT AND INCREASES IN OUTPUT PER MAN-HOUR.

EXHIBIT 16.1

Germany and Japan, have learned the value of new and advanced investment, having had to rebuild their industries after World War II. Their miraculous economic recoveries have made them constantly conscious of the value of modernisation and replacement. Exhibit 16.2 might serve to illustrate the value of the quality of investment.

	The Increase in Investment	Increase in Output (Tons)	Output per £1,000 mill of Inv. (Tons)
JAPAN	$7,500	71 mill	9·4 mill
U.K.	$2,500	4 mill	1·6 mill

Japanese investment yielded almost 10 mill tons more per $1,000 mill than U.K. investment.

EXHIBIT 16.2

COMPARISON OF THE QUALITY OF INVESTMENT IN THE JAPANESE AND BRITISH STEEL INDUSTRIES.

What action can be taken by government to help investment?
There are two broad fields of action.
1. To provide industry with the financial incentives to invest.
2. To create an economic climate which is conducive to investment.
Financial Incentives. These might include cash grants to provide part of the cash for the investment, special tax free allowances (where expenditure on plant and machinery could be set off against any profits thus reducing the tax liability of the firm) and the provision of loans by the government at concessionary rates of interest.
Stable Economic Climate; No matter how much a government may create financial incentives for investment, no rational entrepreneur in the private sector will invest when the future prospects for demand look uncertain. Constant credit squeezing to control inflation will have an adverse effect on consumer demand and reduce the prospects of a good return to new investment. This might cause the entrepreneur to delay his investment decision and so slow the modernisation of industry. Where a country can avoid the problem of serious inflation and so maintain a steadily growing level of demand then business confidence will be generated and investment will expand.

2. Labour and Growth
One of the simplest ways of increasing the productive capacity of the economy is to increase the labour supply. This could be done by relaxing immigration laws or, as in very sparsely populated countries, simply encouraging an increase in the natural population growth. Both of these methods however are likely to have little effect upon the standard of living since although output will increase there will be an additional population to consume that output.
Education and training; One could however eliminate these problems and achieve growth by increasing the productive capacity of the existing labour force. This might be attained by investing in human capital i.e. by spending cash training the individual, so making him more productive. Many countries claim great results from such investment. The U.S.A. for example, claims that up to one-third of the annual increases in her national output are attributable to education and training.

Education and training as a force influencing growth is naturally closely associated with investment in plant, equipment and machinery. As the country employs more advanced machinery and greater quantities of capital per worker it is important that training programmes within industry run parallel with these increases in investment. It would be foolish for a nation to spend great sums in computerising its industry when its labour force was not equipped with the skills necessary for the operation of those computers.

The Government and Education & Training
Whilst Government is usually convinced of the value of education and training it is often difficult to persuade the entrepreneur that this investment in human capital is worthwhile. The problem stems largely from the fact that the return from investment in education and training is often long term, (especially so with management training) ... and shareholders are naturally eager to see quick returns from investments. To this one must add the problem of a firm losing the labour it has trained to other firms which do no training.

The Government's role here would be, assuming it thought education and training worthwhile, to create the incentives to invest in education and training. The introduction of the Industrial Training Act 1965 did precisely this. Firms were charged a levy by the Government on labour employed . . . this levy being refundable on completion of approved training of that work force. Firms that did no training therefore lost the chance of reclaiming their levy.

There are, however, serious limitations to the effectiveness of education and training as a source of growth.

Firstly, there is a great danger of training beyond the needs of the economy. Producing more workers than the economy needs is just as wasteful as buying a machine and leaving it in the factory yard.

This leads us to the second problem which concerns the need for adequate and effective manpower forecasting. We have already seen that training takes time and that some training might not show itself to be fully effective for a number of years from commencement of the training programme (the training of a doctor might fit into this category). Thus the training programmes starting today are often for the manpower needs of many years hence. Accurate forecasts of one's labour requirements are essential to avoid future surpluses or shortages of qualified manpower.

More Effective Use of the Existing Labour Force.
Many people in employment – are, for various reasons, not developing their full productive potential. Some workers are employed in situations where their talents far exceed the demands of the job. A male worker from the service trades for example, might be considerably more productive if employed in manufacturing whilst an intelligent road sweeper might be more valuable to the community if employed in some other capacity. This waste of potential productive capacity may be the result of the individual's own choosing or of circumstances beyond his control. Whilst few people would want to interfere with the freedom of choice of the individual there would be many cases where an employee would like to take a job more commensurate with his ability. In such circumstances government action to improve the mobility of labour and capital might go some way to ensure the availability of talents and job requirements are more effectively matched.

To take this argument a little farther, we might find that the economy has a high percentage of its population making little or no contribution to national output and yet are large consumers of that output. Many of these people would welcome the chance to make a contribution to expansion. Some pensioners, for example, might be happier doing a light job of work rather than sitting in their garden but would only do so if taxation were not such a disincentive. More married women with families might return to work if working hours could be adjusted to fit in with their children's schooling.

It must be noted however, that efforts to raise national output in the ways described above are essentially "one shot" techniques and once fully exhausted offer no possibility of further improvements. Some of these methods, whilst increasing output and hence national wealth, are also likely to have a deleterious effect upon the quality of life of the individual. He may suffer, for example, from increased strain, loss of leisure time and loss of freedom.

3. Technology and growth
Technology, in its simplest terms, is the state of technical knowledge or technical capability that exists at any one time. The availability of this knowledge is usually

the result of investment in research and involves contributions from all the factors of production. Technology has two important effects:

1. It provides the ideas for improving the production process by developing more advanced machinery and equipment and by developing newer and more efficient methods of production.

2. It provides the consumer with products of superior design, quality and capability ... factors likely to expand the market for the product and so make possible economies of scale.

The state of technical knowledge is probably the most important single factor influencing a nation's growth, since all other factors which influence growth are geared to technology and limited in their effectiveness by it. Let us assume that investment in Research and Development results in a capability of building an advanced machine. The development of this machine increases the growth potential of the economy and this will be realised when the money is invested in building the machine, and in training the labour force to use it. Once, therefore, a nation is using its technology to the full the scope for growth is limited until the frontiers of knowledge are again pushed forward by further investment in technology. Once this is done the new technology can then be translated into investment in new and more advanced machinery etc. and the labour force retrained to use that technology. Technology, might therefore be seen as dictating the tempo of economic growth.

The role of the government in technology

The development of technology involves the investment of large sums of money in projects which will tend to put those funds at considerable risk. Two types of uncertainty arise and make the raising of research and development capital difficult (and often impossible).

1. Uncertainty as to whether the project will be technically feasible.

2. Should the idea be technically successful, will it have commercial viability ... i.e. will it sell?

Since the funds needed for research and development are often large and the risks great, many firms are unable to develop technology; and the ones that do, have to rely largely on the ploughing back of profits. The government, therefore, has an important role to play in providing financial assistance to help develop the knowledge so important to national growth.

4. Management and Growth

Since output and growth are associated with the availability and utilization of the nation's stock of factors of production and since such resources are generally limited in supply, it is important that these resources are used in such a way as to get the greatest output[1] at the least resource cost. A major function of management is the organisation of these resources ... it decides on what quantities and combinations will be used and when and how the resources will be deployed.

As the size of the business unit increases, the difficulty of organizing the factors efficiently increases.[2] Management is therefore becoming a matter for experts who need to be equipped with the tools of modern management. The provision (possibly by government) of training schemes in the fields of investment appraisal, manpower planning, work-study, and so on, undoubtedly has a beneficial effect upon the nation's growth rate.

1. Taking into account the need for quality.
2. See diseconomies of large scale production Book One page 219.

THE LIMITS OF GROWTH

Having now examined the major forces which influence growth we must now turn out attention to a question which is now being asked with increasing frequency . . . is there a limit to growth? The simple answer to this is, yes. Production consumes resources and as these are finite they must eventually disappear, unless recycling is employed. The more difficult question is how soon will we reach the limit of growth. Some of the following considerations may shed light on the question:

1. If we assume that the world economy will expand at say 5% p.a. over the next 10 years, each year's growth will be at a compound rate so that the actual increase in output each year will rise markedly. The increase, for example this year will be 5% of last year's total output but the increase next year will be 5% of the total of this year's figure and the 5% increase. At this rate of increase the total volume of annual production would be astronomic and this is where the problem of the steady depletion of the earth's resources puts a black cloud on the horizon of growth. The disturbing thing is that many of our most important and valuable resources are already showing signs of depletion, with the turn of the century being forecasted as the crisis point for the world's supply of crude oil.

Out of this gloom, however, comes a little light. Technology can in many cases produce substitutes to ease the shortage of natural resources. Nuclear energy could ease the strain on coal and oil, whilst plastics might be substituted at a faster rate for some – metals. However, these themselves have their origins in the world's finite natural resources and production could never be limitless. However perhaps the greatest problem is that the world's natural resources are being consumed at such a pace that technology is not developing fast enough to provide the substitutes, which themselves are often costly to produce. Measures taken to ease the resource shortage problem through reclamation and re-cycling of materials may raise the limits to growth but again, whilst not to be condemned, are temporary solutions which only delay the real problem.

2. The pace of growth of many of the developed economies puts great strain on the infra-structure of those economies. When an economy has reached a high stage of development the natural benefits from industrial expansion often start to be outweighed by the environmental costs of that expansion. Expansion of the nation's output is usually accompanied by pollution, congestion and general deterioration of environmental conditions and the faster the growth the greater the problems.

Growth produces serious side effects, such as the problem of coping with the waste produced, the problems of pollution and the pressures on the infra-structure to handle the increased wealth. The increased production of the motor car provides a good example of this point. With the growth of motor car production comes the intensification of carbon monoxide pollution of the urban regions, the increased congestion of the available road space and a rising cost of accidents etc. The economy will also experience the problem of the scrap motor car . . . its effects as an eye-sore and the problem of its disposal. One can see from this illustration that a society can benefit materially from growth but that the cost to society can sometimes outweigh the material advantages. The more intensively the economy is developed the greater and the more apparent this problem. In an economy where there is little industrialisation the disposal of effluent in rivers may be adequately handled by the natural biological action of the river, but as this effluent increases the problem may become too great for the natural cleansing

operation, and as a result the river as a natural asset is seriously devalued i.e. the recreation and pleasure value will disappear. Again, the atmosphere can only absorb pollution of a certain degree and beyond that the pollution becomes harmful to both human life and vegetation.

Some of these costs can be avoided by society ensuring that the polluters pay for the costs they inflict upon society . . . unfortunately the market mechanism is not usually sophisticated enough to entrap them. Some economists argue that an economy can, to a high degree, overcome the above problems providing that it is willing to devote some of its new found production to coping with the increasing social costs brought about by that production. The problem, however, in many economies is that "growth is to be achieved at all costs" and that expansion is so rapid that they have little time to equip and condition their society to counter the adverse side effects. Japan's remarkable growth rate of 10%+ has largely been achieved at the cost of grossly polluted coastal and inland waters and atmospheric pollution the latter being responsible for a high death rate through respiratory diseases. Obsession with growth has led to the channelling of investment funds into areas which solely produce material wealth, thus leaving the economy with inadequate housing conditions, unbelievably congested public transport systems and serious problems of waste disposal.

THE GOVERNMENT AND FULL EMPLOYMENT

To understand how Government can pursue a policy of full employment it is first necessary to understand how unemployment arises and to note that for the economist it is not simply a case of men out-of-work. Economists . . . and politicians, have needed to know the causes and possible duration of unemployment in order to devise plans to maintain a satisfactory level of employment. Over the years the problem has been examined in great depth in order to diagnose the causes of the various types of unemployment.

UNEMPLOYMENT

Economists have often been criticised for being out of touch with reality. This may be so or it may be that somewhere along the way they lost their sense of direction and became too involved with theory than reality. Ironically it was at the very time when this gap seemed to be at its widest that the work was being done that gave us a better understanding of the problem which had bedevilled the capitalist countries since the advent of modern industrialisation. In the early 1930s most economists were concentrating their study on the problems arising from scarcity of resources yet in the real world the fact was that resources were anything but scarce . . . land, capital and above all labour were lying idle, neglected and wasted. The problem of unemployment was not new but in the early '30s it reached such proportions that a whole new approach to it was necessary. Whatever criticisms have been levelled at economists and Government policies since then the fact remains that the situation has changed markedly. In the U.K. between 1919–39 the average level of unemployment was 14%, since the war for most of the time it has been between 1 and 2%; even the figure of nearly a million jobless in the period around 1970 was still less than 4% of the labour force.

The classical economists of the 1920s stuck to their guns; they knew that the market system produced full employment . . . there was nothing wrong with the system that a few adjustments would not correct. If only this view had remained as theory the situation might not have worsened but the ideas appealed to right

wing politicians who duly acted upon the recommendations. Amongst other measures Government expenditure was heavily reduced in order to liberate factors of production for the private sector, but if private firms had wanted to expand there were factors available. The truth is that firms did not want to expand, knowing that they could not sell their products in a market whose purchasing power had been reduced by nearly 3 million jobless.

The new approach to the problem of unemployment came from John Maynard Keynes, but before examining the Keynsian approach it will be useful to see that unemployment is not a simple single problem. There are different types of unemployment stemming from different causes and a diagnosis of these will help us to understand the intensity of the problem.

SEASONAL UNEMPLOYMENT

Employment in some occupations is seasonal by nature. Agriculture is an obvious example in that although there will be an all-round-the-year demand for a nucleus of labour capable of performing a variety of tasks there are times of the year when farmers require additional labour for the picking and packing of the various crops whose harvesting times are staggered. Farmers have tended to rely on local female labour and casual student labour to do this work but clearly the competition from other forms of work offering higher rates of pay (and/or better conditions) plus the increased marketing costs have created employment problems for farmers. The holiday and tourist industry also creates an increased demand for labour in the better weather months while in retailing there is a short lived demand for extra labour in the weeks around Christmas and the January Sales.

The building trade is another which is susceptible to weather conditions . . . although something can be done to mitigate this where it is possible to plan the work on a long-term basis e.g. outside work, taking advantage of the drier weather and longer hours of daylight and interior finishing in the poorer months. Local authorities invariably follow this pattern with their painting and decorating teams as part of planned maintenance programmes.

This type of unemployment does not present a serious problem except for those people living in areas particularly affected who would like more permanent employment . . . on the other hand the erratic demand suits those people who cannot take paid employment on a permanent basis or those who periodically wish to supplement the family income.[1]

FRICTIONAL UNEMPLOYMENT

There are many 'frictions' in industry which cause short-duration unemployment. It may be that workers are laid off because of an industrial dispute either within the same firm or in another firm in the same industry on which the firm is dependent for continuous supplies (the motor car industry being a good example of this). It may be that workers have become unemployed in one area and are unaware of job opportunities.

STRUCTURAL UNEMPLOYMENT

This type is brought about as the name suggests by changes in either the structure of the economy or the structure of the industry. The demand for labour is derived

1. The numbers of people affected may however be greater than we know of statistically, simply because some of this casual labour may not bother to register at the Employment Exchange if the periods between jobs are likely to be short or they do not want to be offered regular employment but want to be free to work for short stretches when it suits them.

from the demand for the product, consequently if there is a change in demand for the latter there will be for the former. Note the effect of this on the cotton industry of Lancashire when customers could substitute and buy either the cheaper products of other manufacturers or man-made fibres. Similarly the reduction in world trade in the 'thirties meant less demand for shipping space so ships were laid-up and there was less demand for the repair services of the yards on Tyneside.

Sometimes the technological structure of the industry changes; new inventions, new techniques create a demand for capital rather than labour. Sometimes an industry finds that it is necessary to change its location e.g. supplies of raw materials become exhausted, subsequently new plants are established but labour being more immobile is left behind. This is what happened as the iron and steel trades moved out of the South Welsh valleys towards the coast or when the pits closed down in the western part of County Durham.

Structural unemployment tends to be hard-core unemployment since its solution lies in either creating a fresh demand for labour in the affected area or in encouraging workers to move to regions where comparable vacancies exist. The problem is clearly most severe in those areas where a much concentrated industry has declined e.g. in the late 1960s when national unemployment was around 2·2%, the level for the North East was some 4·3% despite the various forms of Government aid available for a Development Area.

TRANSITIONAL AND RESIDUAL UNEMPLOYMENT

There is always a number of workers who are temporarily out of work because they have decided to change their form of occupation or part of the country in which they live and are looking for a new job, or they are workers who are engaged for a specific contract which has been completed and are waiting for similar work.

Similarly there will always be some people who are technically unemployed but do not really want to work. Some people would have us believe that this is the result of unemployment insurance, the facts are that the percentage is small and for the numbers to grow significantly workers would have to be considerably better off unemployed than in receipt of wages.

CYCLICAL UNEMPLOYMENT

This is the type associated with the alternating booms and slumps of industrial and commercial activity known as the trade cycle. It was primarily the cause of the persistent unemployment of the '20s and '30s and therefore at the centre of Keynes' examination of the general problem. Since the end of World War II we have not suffered from depressions on the scale of earlier times and much of the credit for this must go to Keynes who showed Governments the importance of maintaining the levels of incomes in order to maintain the demand for labour. The student should note carefully this theme of aggregate demand management in the whole of this section on government economic objectives.

The level of employment is largely determined by the level of aggregate demand; one man's income and job being the result of another's expenditure. A sudden reduction in national spending is, therefore, likely to have a serious effect upon the demand for the nation's production of goods and services and thus upon the job prospects within that nation.

On the other hand an increase in aggregate demand (national spending levels) could have the reverse effect. For any economy therefore, to be experiencing full

employment of its productive resources there must be a certain level of expenditure to generate the employment. (See Exhibit 16.3)

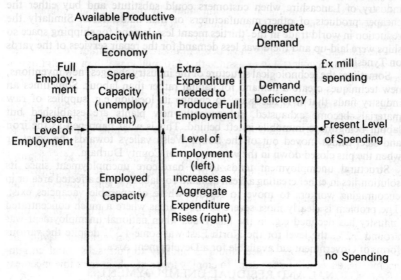

A barometer diagram showing a level of
aggregate demand insufficient to employ
all the nation's productive capacity.

EXHIBIT 16.3

In Exhibit 16.3 £x million of spending would be necessary to ensure full employment. Expenditure above £x million could not possibly push employment any higher since the economy would already be operating at full capacity (using all the resources available in the short run). The effect in this instance would be to

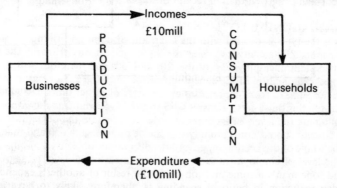

A highly simplified
model of the economy (1)

EXHIBIT 16.4

generate inflation rather than employment . . . this will be discussed towards the end of this section.

In practice the economy does not automatically move to, and maintain, the full employment position. In fact the tendency in an affluent society is very much the reverse. As we have seen, incomes (and employment) are the result of expenditure and these incomes must be spent in order to maintain future income levels (and employment). Let us assume that £10 million worth of expenditure is necessary to create work to fully employ the economy. Exhibit 16·4 shows the effect of this expenditure in a highly simplified model of the economy.

All money spent produces incomes in the form of wages and profits, interest and dividends . . . these being rewards to the factors of production employed in the business. These incomes will be received into the household and then spent to generate further work and employment. In this economy, providing *all* incomes were spent, £10 million worth of employment (and income) would constantly be available and since we assumed £10 million would generate full employment the economy would continue to operate at full employment. However in an economy experiencing high levels of income it is unlikely that all income will be spent. Savings will be possible and more and more people will be putting money aside for some future event. Savings will reduce demand and as there will now be less cash flowing into the firm, the latter will be unable to continue paying the same incomes as before. Since labour is unlikely to take substantial cuts in income, the effect will be for firms to employ fewer people at the same incomes; savings therefore tend to produce unemployment. The more affluent the society the greater will be the possibility of savings and the greater the problem of maintaining full employment.
(See Exhibit 16.5)

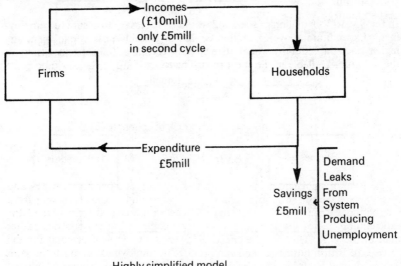

Highly simplified model
of the economy (2)

EXHIBIT 16.5

If the role of the government is to maintain aggregate demand in order to preserve employment levels, then it must ensure that demand leaking away via savings is re-injected into the economy. This could be achieved by ensuring that savings are spent (i.e. INVESTED)[1]. However matching savings by investment is not an easy task. For example, when a person decides to save and place these savings in a bank, there is no guarantee that businessmen or other persons will come along and borrow all or any of that money for investment or other purposes. There is nothing, therefore, to suggest that saving will automatically be matched by investment. If we have a situation where savings are in excess of investment and where the level of aggregate demand is insufficient to maintain full employment, then the government's role should be to encourage investment by creating a climate conducive to investment. It might for example attempt to lower interest rates to make borrowing cheaper or give banks active encouragement to lend. (See exhibit 16.6).

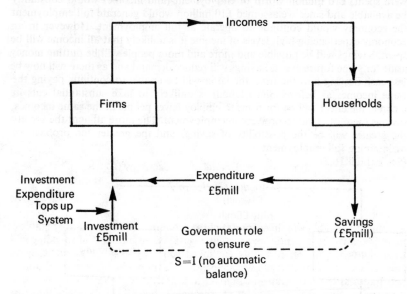

Highly simplified model of economy (3)

EXHIBIT 16.6

The level of aggregate demand is affected by factors other than savings and investment. One of the most important is receipts and payments arising from international trade. When goods and services are purchased from abroad the expenditure creates incomes and work for people in other countries rather than in the U.K. This has the effect of lowering the level of demand for the services of British businesses and can produce unemployment in much the same way as savings. However when British based firms sell abroad incomes are created from the money flowing into the U.K. Thus when imports start to run higher than exports and produce falling incomes the Government could attempt to

1. Money spent on investment will create jobs in the capital goods industries.

change the position by pursuing export promotion policies and discouraging imports.[1]

Exhibit 16.7 summarises the position so far.

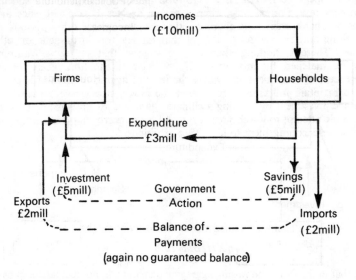

Highly simplified model of the economy (4)

EXHIBIT 16.7

Through this highly simplified model of the economy we have seen that employment is created by expenditure and that a certain constant level of spending will be necessary to maintain a fully employed economy. Since it is not easy to balance leaks from the system with injections (Savings and Investment: Imports and Exports) the Government can make adjustments to demand levels by using the national Budget as a regulator of economic activity.[2] Taxation has the same effect on national demand as imports and savings. Taxation reduces consumer incomes and will therefore have an important effect upon levels of expenditure and employment prospects. On the other hand public expenditure creates work and employment. Let us assume the government decides to build a motorway extension costing £20 million. The public money spent on this will create work for civil engineering and other associated firms. Thus if the economy is experiencing unemployment the government, by spending more than it raises in revenue can stimulate the level of demand to correct the problem – in effect, the government will be injecting new money into the economy. (See Exhibit 16.8).

So far our discussion has been centred on the problem of maintaining a sufficiently high enough level of demand to ensure full employment and we are left begging the question . . . "What happens if we raise the level of demand to a higher level than is necessary to maintain full employment?" One thing is

1. See Chapter 21, page 259.
2. For full details see Chapter 17.

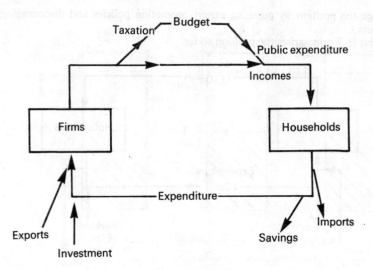

Highly simplified model of the economy (5)

EXHIBIT 16.8

certain; that in the short run raising aggregate demand will not increase employment since we would already be using all available resources to the full. Secondly because the economy would already be working at full capacity, it is unlikely that there would be any significant increases in output to match the increase in aggregate demand. The total effect, therefore, would be too much demand in relation to the availability of goods and services, or in short . . . inflation. Exhibit 16·9 shows the effect of an increase in aggregate demand when the economy has (a) spare capacity, (b) when it is fully employed.

The Government and Inflation

Having considered the anatomy of inflation in Chapter 3 we can now examine the role of the government in its control. Our discussion here will be concerned with the major policy options open to government and the relative merits and limitations of each option. The two major options open to Government are.
1. Demand Management policies.
2. Incomes policies.
There are of course a string of other minor anti-inflationary devices which include such measures as savings campaigns and productivity drives. Our discussion will be concerned with the two major options:

1. DEMAND MANAGEMENT POLICIES
Inflation is a situation in which aggregate demand exceeds the supply of goods and services and results in rising prices. The simple answer to this problem might therefore, be to "cream off" the excess demand using *Fiscal* and *Monetary* techniques.

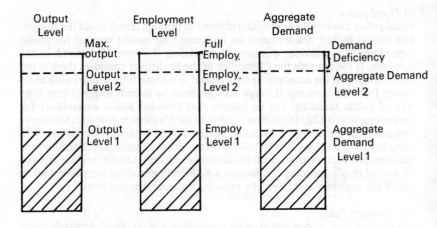

A barometer diagram showing an increase
in aggregate demand raising the level of
employment and output.

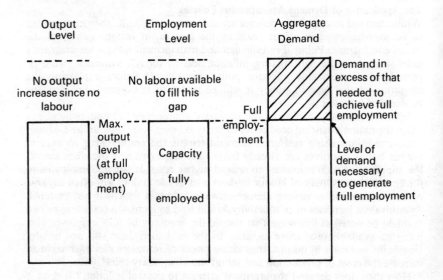

A barometer diagram showing how an
increase in aggregate demand at full
employment has little effect on output.

EXHIBIT 16.9

(i) *Fiscal policy*

Fiscal policy involves the controlling of demand through taxation and the Budget. The annual Budget besides being an instrument for raising revenue for public expenditure[1] also provides a means of regulating the level of demand in the economy. If for example the Chancellor of the Exchequer considers there is too much demand in the economy he may decide to remove it by withdrawing more money from the economy through taxation than he intends to inject into it by way of public spending. Let us assume that intended public expenditure for the coming year is £20,000 million . . . should the Chancellor now wish to remove demand from the economy he could budget for a surplus by levying taxes to bring in a revenue of say £20,200 million. Thus in this example £20,200 million of spending power is removed from the economy and only £20,000 million injected by way of public spending . . . leaving a £200 million surplus to remain locked out of the economy and hopefully reducing national demand levels.

(ii) *Monetary Policy*

Monetary policy is concerned with controlling the national demand levels through the banking system. The lending activities of the commercial banks are responsible for the generation of a considerable volume of demand in the economy (See Creation of Credit Chapter 14) and the Bank of England attempts to regulate these lending activities through control of interest rates, directives, calls for special deposits and open-market operations . . . all of which are covered in Chapter 15.

The Application of Demand Management Policies

Whilst demand management policies are still used in the U.K. they have tended to be overshadowed in recent years by the growth, in various guises, of the Prices and Incomes Policy. Pre 1966 demand management was the government's chief weapon in the fight against inflation and by today's standards could be considered a reasonably effective policy instrument. Before explaining the operation of this type of policy it will be useful to re-examine, broadly, the problem of inflation.

Inflation normally occurs as the economy approaches full employment . . . when the nation's existing productive capacity is being fairly fully utilised. Under these conditions rising consumer demand tempts the entrepreneur to expand output but as resources are already fairly fully employed and therefore scarce, the suppliers of such resources command higher rewards. At full employment, for example, the supply of labour is short and Trade Unions are often capable of negotiating and achieving abnormal wage increases which, if not matched by equivalent increases in productivity, could lead to increased costs and prices. It might be noted at this stage that should the economy be fully employed (i.e. using its available productive capacity to the full) then there will not be any significant increases in output, thus rising prices of resources can only serve to increase the costs of production and set off the inflationary spiral.

How then does demand management attempt to control inflation? It does it by deliberately lowering consumer demand levels through fiscal and monetary techniques. The pressure of demand for productive resources (labour etc.) is cut back and spare capacity is created within the economy (labour lying idle, machinery under-utilised etc.). The effect of this can again be seen clearly in the market for labour . . . there will now be more labour available for employment

1. See Page 187.

than job vacancies. As labour is no longer a scarce commodity, wages are more likely to keep in line with productivity, so helping stabilise costs.[1]

It appears therefore that the more fully employed the economy the greater is the danger of inflation (as a result of competition for limited productive resources). A policy therefore of deliberately reducing the level of economic activity and creating a margin of spare capacity in the economy seems a logical way to keep down costs and prices Exhibit 16.6 shows the operation of a demand management policy (see page 177).

Effect of demand management on the firm

High and steadily rising levels of consumer demand are generally conducive to business expansion since they augur well for returns to capital investment. Providing output and the supply of goods can keep pace with that demand, prices and costs should remain fairly stable. However, as we have seen in Chapter 3 when the economy is operating at full capacity, inflation is likely and may upset the Balance of Payments.

The efforts to correct the situation by removing the excess demand from the economy often has a damaging effect upon industrial growth. Substantial removal of demand is likely to kill business confidence to such an extent that expansion plans are abandoned and production trimmed back. In a squeeze the "cut back" will obviously be most strongly felt in the capital goods industries.

If the inflation is later brought under control and the balance of payments begins to show improvement, the government may then decide to reflate the economy to achieve a higher level of economic activity (i.e. take up the slack produced by the squeezing of demand). This would be achieved by attempting to inject new demand into the economy through measures such as reducing taxation and making credit easier and cheaper. Unfortunately such measures are often slow to work. When an economy has passed through a recession . . . whether this is artificially induced or not . . . the consumer and particularly the businessman will remain cautious for fear that new restrictions may still be introduced. Thus the recovery phase tends to be slow until such time as it becomes really obvious that demand is to remain buoyant. The recovery itself often has to be induced by big injections into the economy of government expenditure. Thus industries in the public sector and those that supply the public sector tend to be first to expand in the 'recovery phase.' As consumer demand builds up and creates greater confidence in industry new investment in plant and machinery will take place to meet the rising consumer demand . . . the capital goods industry therefore being the first to suffer in a squeeze and the last to recover.

The lesson for industry might therefore be:—

1. To hold back new investment and particularly the launching of new products when the balance of payments shows signs of deterioration and requires corrective measures.
2. To try to predict the point of recovery so that investment can be made when there is still idle capacity in the capital goods industry. Delay may mean paying over the odds or delays in supply when all firms will be in the market for capital goods.
3. Note also that raw material prices tend to escalate during a boom thus a

1. Note, if wages rise by 10% and output rises by 10% costs should remain stable. However if wages rise by 10% and output by only 5% then costs will normally rise.

firm may be wise to increase stocks early in the recovery period. (See Exhibit 16·10).

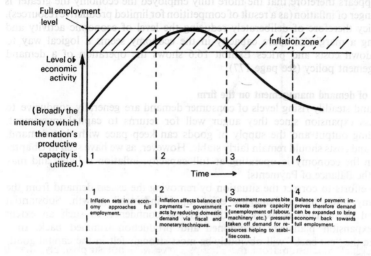

Control of inflation using a demand
management policy

EXHIBIT 16.10

THE RELATIONSHIP BETWEEN UNEMPLOYMENT AND INFLATION

The relationship between the degree of unemployment and the rate of inflation has been researched by many economists but perhaps the most well known work in this field is that of Prof. A. W. Phillips (published in Economica Nov, 1958). Phillips collected unemployment and wage rates statistics between 1863–1914 and from these produced a prediction table from which one might forecast the rate of inflation, given the level of unemployment. (See Exhibit 16.11 below).

The Phillips Prediction Table

Unemployment rate	1·0	1·5	2·0	2·5	3·0
Percentage change in wage rates	8·7	4·6	2·8	1·8	1·2

EXHIBIT 16.11

This table simply showed that the higher the rate of unemployment the lower would be the wage rate change. These predictions were tested and found to be surprisingly accurate.

Exhibit 16.12 shows the relationship graphically.

The Phillips curve relates to unemployment and wage rates and not unemployment and inflation directly. However, any wage increases above say 5% in the U.K. economy are unlikely to be matched by equivalent increases in output and hence are almost certainly inflationary. Thus operating the economy at 1% unemployment would produce wage increases of around 8% whilst increases in output would rarely be expected to approach this level.

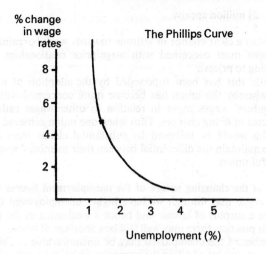

EXHIBIT 16.12

The chief conclusion from the Phillips curve was, not surprisingly, that if inflation was to be controlled demand levels should be held down to create a margin of spare capacity in the economy. Phillips actually claimed that at 5.5% unemployment, wages should keep in line with productivity and help stabilise costs (note, however, he did not advocate running the economy at this level of unemployment)

Does the Phillips Curve hold true today?
Since 1966 there appears to have been a serious breakdown in the Phillips relationship. Statistics indicate now that if the economy is run with say 4% unemployment, wages are likely to increase far in excess of the Phillips' predictions. In 1970, for example, the U.K. experienced 4% unemployment together with wage increases in excess of 12% . . . this was well above the Phillips' predicted figure for this level of employment.

Why has the relationship broken down ?
Numerous reasons have been put forward, some of the more important ones are listed below.
1. The problem seems to have started immediately after the 1966 statutory wage freeze (June 1966 – Jan 1967) when unions, having been straight-jacketed on wage negotiations for six months, suddenly burst forth with a back-log of claims which were generally met. At this time there was 2·4% unemployment (considered a high level at that time) and the trade unions discovered their bargaining power stronger than they originally thought under such conditions, i.e. when there was so much unemployed labour about.
2. Social Security benefits increased markedly around this time. This meant that families of strikers were no longer totally dependent upon union strike funds. Strike funds were invariably very limited and thus strikers were likely to return to work as the funds ran down. The increasing militancy of unions from 1966 onwards is well illustrated by comparing the number of strike days lost in the 1964–66 period with the 1967–69 period.

1964–66   2½ million approx.
1967–69   5   „   „

3. There was also a clear change in attitude towards wage bargaining. Pre 1966 unions had been most concerned with wage/price relationships (how wages moved in relation to prices).

More recently this has been superseded by the adoption of a "wage/wage psychology" whereby the union has become more concerned with the way in which its members' wages move in relation to other wages rather than just in relation to cost of living changes. Thus when one union achieved a substantial wage award this would be followed by substantial claims from other unions who wished to maintain the differential between their members' wages and those of the successful union.

Consideration of the changing nature of the unemployment figures since 1966
Some writers argue that, though we have higher unemployment figures which should indicate a surplus of labour and hence a weakening of the power of the trade unions, in practice, there may well still be a shortage of labour.
1. A large number of the unemployed may be unemployable . . . registered unemployed but not capable of filling the vacancies which exist, either because they have different skills from the ones required, or that the job opportunities are in different places to the available work force. (Government policy to improve the mobility of labour may help here).
2. A substantial amount of unemployment in the late '60s was caused by the reorganisation of British industry . . . particularly as a result of mergers and rationalisation programmes. Many of the unemployed tended to be in the higher average age group and as such were often considered unsuitable for re-training. Thus part of the pool of unemployed may consist of technically unemployables and hence will not swell the supply side of the labour market.
3. The unemployment figures may also be higher than normal because the unemployed are taking longer to find new jobs (possibly due to higher unemployment benefits). Again, these unemployed would not constitute "slack" in the labour market and so despite a high unemployment figure labour could still be in short supply.

If these factors discussed above are an explanation of the apparent breakdown of the Phillips' relationship it is possible that all that has happened has been a movement bodily to the right of the Phillips curve. The relationship therefore may still exist but at much higher levels of unemployment (See Exhibit 16.13).

Objections to Using Unemployment as a Means of Controlling Inflation
1. For reasons discussed above this policy appears to have lost much o˘ its effectiveness. However, with unemployment levels of much greater magnitude than envisaged by Phillips (say 6–8%) it may have a controlling effect, though this would undoubtedly be politically and socially unacceptable.
2. The deliberate creation of unemployment wastes valuable productive resources. For an economy as desperately short of resources as the U.K., this would seem a rather clumsy way of tackling inflation.
3. Using unemployment as a means of controlling inflation means the abandonment of one of the objectives of economic policy ("full employment") in order to achieve another.
4. Deliberate attacks on consumer demand usually have the effect of destroying business confidence. Falling demand levels may serve to postpone investment

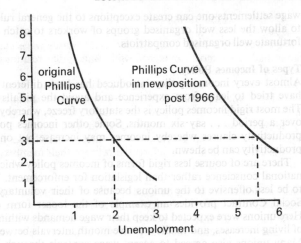

The possible movement to the right of the
Phillips Curve

EXHIBIT 16.13

programmes and hence have an adverse effect upon future economic growth and
efficiency.

THE INCOMES POLICY ALTERNATIVE

The inadequacy of demand management policies has led to efforts to find a
policy alternative . . . the incomes policy in its various guises is seen by many
to be the most effective alternative.

An incomes policy is an attempt to control inflation by attacking one of its
major root causes. Incomes . . . both profits and wages . . . make up a significant
part of production costs and hence increases in incomes which are not matched by
equivalent increases in output are likely to lead to higher costs and eventually
higher final prices. The incomes policy attempts to keep incomes in line with
increases in output in order to stabilise costs. In short it is a "prevention is better
than cure" policy.

Apart from simply being an anti-inflationary device the incomes policy
has the advantage that it can restrain inflation without the serious side effects of
the demand management policies described earlier. We saw that with the latter
policy excess demand was allowed to develop and was then syphoned off by
fiscal and monetary techniques. This demand squeezing tended to hold back
investment decisions, slow economic growth and produce unemployment.
The incomes policy, however, theoretically avoids these problems since demand
levels are kept down by income control, thus avoiding the need for deflationary
policies. In practice, of course, keeping incomes in line with output is extremely
difficult but if the incomes policy can reduce the rate of inflation it will reduce
the severity to which demand management policies have to be applied, so
reducing the adverse effects associated with the latter type of policy.

Incomes policies have one further advantage in that they provide a weapon for
achieving social justice in wage settlements. Once one is able to control national

wage settlements one can create exceptions to the general rules of settlement . . . to allow the less well organised groups of workers to catch up with their more fortunate well organised compatriots.

Types of Incomes Policy

Almost every incomes policy introduced has been different since governments have tried to learn from experience and avoid the pitfalls of earlier polic'es. The most rigid incomes policy is the statutory freeze, whereby incomes are frozen over a period . . . say six months. Some other incomes policies have in-built productivity clauses whereby incomes may increase but only where increased productivity can be shewn.

There are of course less rigid forms of incomes policy which tend to rely upon national conscience rather than legislation for enforcement. These policies tend to be less offensive to the unions because of their voluntary nature. The 1974 Social Contract provides an example of the looser form of incomes policy. Here unions were expected to keep their wage demands within the bounds of cost of living increases, and to allow twelve month intervals between major increases. Many unions also agreed to accept wage controls through "threshold" agreements. Under this system wage adjustments would be allowed only when the cost of living index rose above a certain level. When this happened there would be an automatic triggering off of special wage supplements.

It might be noted that the latter type of agreement could be inflationary since it does not relate directly to productivity. However, when it is difficult to get wage restraint accepted, tying incomes to something is likely to be less inflationary than letting them float freely.

Problems of Implementing Incomes Policies

Whilst the incomes policy appears a logical development in the control of inflation there have been few really successful incomes policies in the Western World. Some of the major difficulties of implementing the policies are examined below:
1. The incomes policy must be accepted by both unions and employers. Where the policy is based on a NORM, the norm level for future wage increases is usually disputed by both parties . . . the unions claiming it should be higher and the employers naturally wanting as low a norm as possible.
2. However, once the norm is accepted (assuming it is not a "nil norm") then there may be disputes as to how it should be distributed. If, say, 6% is chosen as the national norm, workers in industries where productivity is increasing faster than 6% may well be disatisfied with wage increases of that magnitude. On the other hand if all wage increases were limited to individual plant productivity, then discontent is likely to emerge from the workers engaged in the low productivity industries, particularly where the low productivity is due to the nature of the industry and not the fault of the workers.
3. Perhaps the biggest obstacle to the implementation of an incomes policy is the reluctance of the trade unions to give up their long won right to free collective bargaining. Membership is often determined by success in wage negotiations thus any form of "tying the unions' hands" in wage negotiations is at the best only likely to be tolerated for a limited period.
4. Once a period of wage restraint is over there is always the danger of the flood gates opening and wage claims proceeding at an abnormal rate, quickly wiping out the benefits of the policy. This was the experience after the six months freeze in 1966.

5. Incomes policies often fail because they appear inequitable. Firstly they tend to freeze the existing wage structure so if there is some unjust differential between the payment for one job and another, that injustice will continue during the period of the incomes policy. Secondly, to ensure complete co-operation on wage restraint, unions expect that there should be some control on prices. Prices, however, have proved more difficult to control due to the immense number of pricing points that have to be policed. In addition there is the problem of import prices over which we have little control. Thirdly, it is unreasonable to expect unions to accept wage restraint when profits are left uncontrolled. Whilst it may be possible to control the *distribution* of profits, the shareholder can still gain the benefits from undistributed profits in the form of capital appreciation of his shares, which might result from those profits being ploughed back into the company.

6. An incomes policy is likely to be difficult to implement in a slow growing economy where the norm for wage increases would, of necessity, have to be low. In a faster growing economy, such as that of Japan, high rates of growth would allow much greater increases in incomes, making the policy more palatable to the unions. Unfortunately the U.K. economy is one characterised by slow growth which, therefore, reduces the chances of achieving a workable policy.

INTER-RELATIONSHIPS BETWEEN THE OBJECTIVES OF ECONOMIC POLICY

Having now examined the chief objectives of government policy[1] and methods by which they can be attained, we must now consider the implementation of those objectives.

The most striking feature about these objectives is that no government will find it easy to attain all of them simultaneously. Let us assume that the government agrees to tackle unemployment as a priority. Presumably, this will be largely achieved through raising the level of aggregate demand. This will create a shortening of supply in the market for materials, labour and other resources. As the slack is taken up in the economy, the suppliers of the factors of production will take advantage of their scarcity and put up resource prices (Wages, material prices etc.); as a result costs are likely to rise, pushing up the rate of inflation. The inflation is then liable to affect the balance of payments by making imports more attractive than domestic products and also spoiling export sales (as a result of higher costs of production). The problem does not stop there; Britain is dependent upon imports for the expansion of production and hence a reduction in the availability of foreign currencies could seriously affect her rate of growth.

There appears little answer to the problem of reconciling these objectives and thus Government has to steer us as close as possible to the achievement of all objectives without the achievement of one objective having too serious effect upon the others.

1. Note Govt. policy measures on the balance of payments can be seen in Chapter 21.

Part Four

THE GOVERNMENT AND THE ECONOMY

Chapter Seventeen

INSTRUMENTS OF GOVERNMENT ECONOMIC POLICY

Fiscal and Monetary Policy

THE BUDGET: Nature & Purposes

In Book One, Chapter One it was stated that the word Economics was derived from the Greek word meaning 'the management of the household' and that the only difference between the housewife and the Chancellor was the complexity and scale of the operation of managing the national household.

The purpose of early budgetary policy was simply to raise sufficient money to cover essential government activities, primarily the maintenance of law and order and 'defence against the King's enemies'. When the philosophy of laissez-faire held sway any intrusion by the State into other aspects of our affairs was looked upon with great suspicion.

However if the Government is to carry out its proper role it must do more than just provide for defence against the King's enemies in a military sense ... it must maintain the level of general prosperity and take whatever steps are necessary for our economic survival.

Before the Second World War the annual Budget was an exercise in orthodox book-keeping in which the task of the Government was to try to balance income and expenditure; the idea of accepting, let alone deliberately creating an unbalanced Budget, would have been regarded by many as an act of certainly political and perhaps even criminal negligence.

In the late nineteenth century the State became involved in greater expenditure e.g. when it took responsibility for elementary education. In the early years of this century it began to make the first welfare provisions e.g. old-age pensions and in the '20s and '30s it was forced to intervene much more in the economic affairs of the country. Indeed in the 30s a great deal of economic thought was stood on its head as the result of the work of J. M. Keynes and gradually it began to be realized that the level of Government spending and the level of taxation could exert considerable influence on aggregate consumer demand and thus on output and employment. The White Paper on Employment 1944 said that "there was no merit in a rigid policy of balancing the Budget each year, regardless of the state of trade" and since then every Chancellor has used the Budget as a major instrument of regulating the economy by deliberately budgeting for a surplus or deficit.

Essentially the Budget is the opportunity for examining the Exchequer's accounts and dealing with the estimated revenue from taxation and other sources and the estimates of Government spending on its various services in the financial year to come. Thus it is a statement of the policies by which the Government will attempt to regulate the national economy in the light of the prevailing

and anticipated conditions and how the revenue will be raised to give effect to such policies. Any proposals concerning taxation will be designed not simply to raise the necessary revenue but for the burden to fall on those sectors of the economy where the Chancellor wants the effects to be felt.

The Chancellor's principal task is therefore to survey the whole economic situation and to decide whether the economy is in need of stimulation or restraint and if so what degree is necessary. If the survey shows that unemployment is higher than the normal level, that the retail trades are stagnant, that order books are depressed and businessmen are waiting for some sign before going ahead with investment projects then the Chancellor will budget for a deficit i.e. he will make plans to spend more in the coming financial year than he takes out of the economy by way of taxation. By so doing he releases more purchasing power which would raise the level of aggregate demand and the economy should respond . . . if it does not then the Chancellor could increase welfare payments to increase the purchasing power of the lowest income sector and speed up those items of public expenditure which through the multiplier effect will increase purchasing power.

Conversely if his examination of the national scene shows that we are suffering from inflationary pressures he will budget for a surplus i.e. he will take steps to reduce aggregate demand.

As the major instrument in regulating the economy the Budget has been used in six main ways.

1. *To counter inflation.* By increasing the levels of taxation it is possible to bring considerable influence to bear on overall demand. A higher level of income tax will reduce the level of take-home pay and so reduce the volume of purchasing power; similarly higher levels of indirect taxation when passed on in the form of higher prices will also affect the overall level of demand (note the effect of different elasticities of demand of different commodities). Fiscal policy is therefore used to soak up surplus purchasing power thereby reducing the amount of money chasing too few goods. This action of neutralising a certain amount of purchasing power is sometimes called "forced saving".

2. *To counter a recession.* When the economy is in a state of stagnation the Budget can be used to stimulate economic activity. The Chancellor can reduce the levels of taxation and increase the level of public expenditure thus increasing the amount of purchasing power. He can assist recovery by giving tax incentives for investment and by varying the levels of assistance i.e. higher rates of relief to the Assisted Areas he can give greater relief to those regions of the country most badly affected. Other devices which the Chancellor can use include the Hire Purchase regulations e.g. in 1967 he relaxed the restrictions on motor-cycles in order to stimulate demand and to encourage the industry to expand in order to be more competitive both at home and overseas.

3. *To reduce the inequality of incomes.* The Budget is the principal instrument by which the pattern of personal taxes and social security benefits can be readjusted. These decisions affect the distribution of wealth within the community and so reduce the inequality of incomes.

4. *To assist the Balance of Payments.* If the country is experiencing a continuing balance of payments deficit then the Budget is an opportunity to introduce corrective measures. Higher taxation could be imposed on consumer goods which would reduce demand in general and so not only lower the demand for imports but also liberate more of our own production for export and so bring an improvement in our trade figures. Excise duties in general can be used to regulate

the volume of imports or specific measures can be introduced to affect the balance. Because of the severe imbalance in 1964 the Import Levy of 15% was imposed and then gradually phased out as the worst of the crisis passed. However because the situation again worsened further measures had to be introduced and in the mini-budget of November 1968 an Import Deposit Scheme was launched whereby importers had to deposit 50% of the value of the imported goods with Customs in order to obtain clearance of the goods. The deposit carried no interest and was repaid after six months.

5. *To influence the level and location of employment.* During a period of inflation or shortage of labour, a policy of higher taxation could be introduced to depress the level of demand and consequently the demand for labour, perhaps even causing some unemployment. Conversely, in a period of recession, taxation rates could be reduced in order to stimulate demand for goods and so reduce the level of unemployment.

The Selective Employment Tax introduced in the Budget of 1966 was not a measure designed primarily to raise revenue but to bring about what the Prime Minister described as a "shake-out of labour". By penalizing the service industries for their use of labour it was hoped that some of this scarce factor of production would be liberated for employment in the manufacturing sector particularly in export industries.

When cash grants were introduced in place of investment allowances for firms engaged in modernisation schemes, they were made selective by area. Thus though in general they encouraged investment in new buildings and equipment they were also intended to encourage industry in certain areas.

6. *To encourage saving.* Increased saving not only reduces current consumption but also provides the funds for investment which is vital to modernisation schemes in British industry. Emphasis in saving was given by the 1969 Budget which introduced the Save-as-you-earn scheme, a new 7% British Savings Bond and raised the limits on holdings of Savings Certificates and deposits in Trustee Savings Banks and the National Savings Bank.

The level of expenditure in the public sector, by central and local government, has increased enormously over the years and currently accounts for approximately half of the Gross National Product. Much of this expenditure is either committed years in advance as with investment projects or is of a recurring nature e.g. pensions, and though modifications can be made, variation in the level and pattern of government expenditure is not an ideal instrument for budgetary policy. For these reasons some critics argue that the Budget is no longer the main instrument of economic policy . . . but this is to view the Budget only from the revenue it raises rather than the ways by which it is raised. Since the Budget determines the level and pattern of taxes and what part of public expenditure is to be financed by borrowing it remains the principal weapon in the arsenal of economic regulators even though in recent years we have seen the emergence of other important weapons such as the introduction of mini-budgets, various prices and incomes policies and the continuous use of the various monetary measures available through the banking system

The Budgets of March and November 1974 present a good example of the use of budgetary measures to regulate the economy. The broad objectives of the March Budget were to make the greatest possible use of our resources, to improve the Balance of Payments, to check the rate of inflation and to establish a greater degree of social justice by a more equitable spread of the tax burden. Amongst the measures announced was a considerable reduction in

public sector borrowing and in the light of this priority was to be given to pensions, food subsidies and housing. The nationalised industries were to be allowed to increase their prices substantially, not only to reduce their deficits and the level of government support, but also, as the effects of the increased price of oil imports began to work through, to prevent excessive demand for their products. The effect of the changes in taxation on revenue was estimated at £1,378 million in a full year. The effect of the proposals would limit the net increase in public expenditure to just over £700 million, consequently public sector borrowing in 1974–5 would be £2,700 million which was £1,500 million less than in 1973–4. Finally it was stated that a later Budget would be introduced to make any further necessary adjustments.

By November the Chancellor was faced with a worsening balance of payments situation a continuing high rate of inflation, a stagnant economy with many firms experiencing cash-flow difficulties and low levels of investment. The Budget of November 12th was designed to prevent mass unemployment developing by relieving industry of some of its financial pressures and by diverting resources away from private and public expenditure into investment and exports. The Chancellor proposed three main methods of achieving this:

1. By relaxations in the Prices Code the effect of which should increase the profitability of firms by some £800 million.
2. By relaxations in Corporation Tax, principally by granting relief for stock appreciation in 1973–4 thereby reducing the tax liability. The net effect of tax changes would be to release some £790 million in 1974–5.
3. Measures were introduced to give firms access to greater credit and capital funds by:

  a) the finance houses and banks were to give top priority to industrial borrowers.

  b) the payment of interest on the banks' Special Deposits was modified in order to increase their capital base and therefore their ability to create credit.

  c) the clearing banks, supported by the financial institutions, were to make up to £1,000 million available over the next two years to Finance for Industry.

These measures, it was estimated, would stimulate demand sufficiently to contain unemployment below the one million mark.

On the public expenditure side it was announced that:

  a) over the next four years the growth of total public expenditure should not exceed 2½% in demand terms per year on average.

  b) the revenue support, currently £1,000 million p.a., payable to the nationalised industries in order that they can restrain prices, is to be phased out.

By raising the rate of V.A.T. on petrol from 8% to 25%, it was hoped to reduce the demand and so aid the balance of payments.

In order to lessen the impact of inflation on the less fortunate sectors of the community, improvements in a range of State benefits were made amounting to £1,130 million.

FISCAL POLICY

The fiscus was the privy purse of a Roman Emperor; fiscal policies may therefore be crudely described as government measures which affect peoples' pockets. Clearly Government exercises its gretest influence over the economy by its 'fiscal' or 'budgetary' policies, indeed since 1945 all governments have used fiscal rather than monetary policy as the main tool of financial planning. This is not to say that monetary measures have not been used because obviously all governments have manipulated Bank Rate, tightened and relaxed bank

credit and altered hire purchase regulations in their efforts to deal with inflation or recession. The emphasis on fiscal policy has probably been due to the fact that changes in taxation have a more obvious effect on the pattern of consumer spending and the effects are easier to predict than those which would result from changes in the supply of money. It may be that at the moment we are at a point of change partly as a result of the renewal of interest in monetarist theories highlighted by the work of Milton Friedman at Chicago University and certainly because, apart from external factors, there would seem to be a connection between the large increase in the money supply in the U.K. during 1973 and the current wave of inflation.

Earlier we saw that the Budget is one of the expressions of Government policy for regulating the economy . . . the Government examines current aggregate demand and tries to forecast its trend in the immediate future and then decides whether it needs to be stimulated or dampened down. If the forecast is that the level of aggregate demand is not going to be sufficient to maintain a satisfactory high level of employment the Government will introduce measures to increase it and conversely if the forecast suggests that there will be excess demand then the Government will try to reduce the level of aggregate demand and so relieve the inflationary pressures.

Aggregate demand (Y) must comprise Consumption by the private sector (C), Investment in the private sector (I) and Government consumption and investment (G); thus

$$Y = C + I + G$$

and the level of Y can be altered by changes in any of the variable components.

C can be increased or decreased by changes in direct taxation which affects the level of disposable income or by changes in indirect taxation which affects the level of real incomes, thus demand for goods and services will be increased or decreased.

I can be changed by the use of various incentives such as the level of tax allowances or actual cash grants. I can also be encouraged or discouraged by pursuing a 'cheap money' or 'dear money' policy though the price of loan capital will not in itself determine the level of investment.

G can be altered by expanding or contracting public expenditure or by changing the levels of various State benefits (an increase in pensions will increase purchasing power just as a reduction in taxation would).

In deciding on its policy-mix the Government has to take care not to pursue measures which will alter the variables in opposite directions i.e. if it is trying to increase the level of aggregate demand in private consumption it should not simultaneously decide to cut back on public expenditure.

Simply knowing that changes in any of the variables will affect aggregate demand is not sufficient in a well planned economy because clearly there are variations of policies which will have different degrees of desirability. For example if the Government decides to reduce taxation in order to increase purchasing power so as to raise the level of employment it will be more effective to put the emphasis on the bottom end of the income scale; exempting the lowest strata of taxpayers will do more to increase demand (because their propensity to consume is high) than reducing the level of tax for the highest strata (who are more likely to save rather than spend the extra income).

If public expenditure is increased to generate more income/expenditure, then Government must also take into consideration the quality of the projects under-

taken. It is easy to think of some countries where public works programmes have for example produced magnificent roads and yet the volume of traffic does not warrant such highways. If authorities in the U.K. at the present moment needed to undertake public works programmes which would have a lasting value they need look no further than reclamation of derelict land in the old industrial areas. Land is one of the scarcest resources in the U.K. and will become increasingly more valuable in the future with the increased demand for it. It is encouraging to see the large metropolitan authorities using their powers to recover vast tracts of land previously laid waste by industrial pollution so that it can be used for housing or industry or simply left as public open spaces and so improve the environment in the conurbations.

Government too must be mindful of the speed with which the proposals will take effect. Changing the levels of indirect tax will affect the level of demand sooner than changes in direct tax because they can be implemented much quicker. Similarly changes in all kinds of tax will work quicker than changes in the G factor because clearly there will be a timelag in between the Government placing its contracts, the work being started and the multiplier effects of increased income working through the economy.

Budgetary policies can obviously be used on a selective basis. If for example the problem of unemployment is concentrated in certain areas, the Government does not take measures which will have a nation-wide effect on demand but introduces steps whose greatest impact will be in the problem areas (see Chapter 19 on regional planning).

Lastly any item of fiscal policy has to be reviewed against the background of Government objectives in toto, e.g.:

1.) The Government may wish to produce a greater degree of social equality by reducing the disparity of incomes and this it may do by reducing the burden of taxation at the bottom end of the scale. The subsequent increase in C may be good for employment levels but may produce inflationary pressures.

2.) If the Government's primary aim is to achieve economic growth rather than to deal with some short-run situation the emphasis would be on investment rather than on consumption and thus there would be presumably measures to encourage savings.

3.) A general increase in C must have an effect on the level of our imports and possibly make less of the goods we produce available for export and so there would be an undesirable effect on our balance of payments position.

The ways in which Government can manage the level of demand have been explained primarily with the level of employment in mind, but governments have also used budgetary policies to deal with other major problems. In the whole of the postwar period Britain has suffered from a series of balance of payments crises and often these have been the result of inflation. Both problems have necessitated government action, thus the pattern of the whole period has been one of bursts of growth with the accompanying demand for labour, the ensuing price rises and balance of payments deficits followed by measures to dampen the inflationary pressure, to correct the deficit and consequently to reduce the demand for labour. It has been a bumpy and at times rough journey but at least we have avoided the miserable depths of the pre-war trade cycle, the level of economic activity has been greater and the level of employment has been consequently higher.

Because of the 'stop-go' nature of the policies followed there have been critics of them. J. C. R. Dow said, " . . . budgetary and monetary policy failed to

be stabilising."[1] Other economists have taken a similar line. What must be said in defence is that whereas the Keynsian approach to fiscal policy was primarily to eradicate the cancer of mass unemployment, successive post-war governments have had as their objectives not only full employment but also the achievement of steady economic growth with stable prices and a satisfactory balance of payments. What experience has now shown us is that the four objectives are not necessarily compatible and that fiscal and monetary policies alone may not be sufficiently adequate to deal with the problems. The unemployment of pre-war days was mainly cyclical and the Keynsian method of increasing Y was the appropriate counter-measure but in the post-war period when there has been unemployment of any consequence it has not been caused by deficiency in aggregate demand and fiscal measures in themselves cannot correct structural unemployment. Similarly in tackling inflation a policy of reducing the level of aggregate demand would be appropriate if the prime cause were demand – pull; however in the last twenty years much of the pressure has been cost–push. Very often this type of inflation is imported and obviously the U.K. government has no control and little influence over such costs. Furthermore if fiscal measures were taken to reduce the level of demand for such imports it must ultimately lead to short-time working and then to unemployment.

Assuming that Government really knows its objectives and there is no swing in the political pendulum to upset the emphasis, there are still very real obstacles in the path of effective fiscal and monetary policy. Firstly any forecasting must be based on adequate and relevant information, unfortunately even with the most sophisticated methods available it takes a long time to collect the necessary economic data and thus there is always the possibility that it is already out of date by the time it is used and so the forecast is made on a faulty base. Secondly to predict with any accuracy the effect of the changes it is necessary to know 'the multiplier' and even then there are untold external factors which can upset the calculations.

It is easy to see the short-comings of fiscal policy in the post-war period, it is a much more difficult task to make the decisions and to 'walk the plank' knowing that excess demand will lead to inflation and insufficient demand to unemployment. In criticising fiscal policy we should remember that it is implemented by politicians and so not all the measures introduced have been taken with solely economic aims but with political ones also. If the student wants to play an even more difficult game than deciding where fiscal policy has gone wrong he should try to visualize what the position might have been if we had not attempted those policies. Finally we should note that the Republican party in the U.S.A., for so long the advocate of a balanced budget, has at the beginning of 1975 seen the necessity for deficit budgeting when faced with the spectre of a severe recession ... no doubt the Democrats of the New Deal would have found this U-turn very interesting.

MONETARY POLICY

A considerable volume of demand is generated by the banking system making available to its customers spending power in the form of loans and overdrafts. The degree to which these facilities are made available and the degree to which they are taken up is thus likely to have a significant effect upon aggregate demand levels. The regulation of the lending activities of the banking system is referred to as *monetary policy*. Such policy is normally formulated by the Treasury (usually

1. J. C. R. DOW, "the Management of the British Economy, 1945–60".

in conjunction with the Bank of England) and implemented by and through the Bank of England using a number of techniques described in Chapter 15, page 150. These measures are broadly concerned with controlling the level of demand in two ways:

1. By bringing about a change in interest rates the monetary authorities can induce a change in the incentive to invest . . . the cost of borrowing having some effect upon the purchases of plant, equipment, machinery and the resources which go to produce them.[1]

2. The monetary authorities can control *the availability* of funds making them, as the situation may demand, either easier or more difficult to obtain. The Radcliffe Report[2] refers to this as the 'Liquidity effect'.

Public Expenditure

"In the English language there is no couple of words whose effect is as sleep inducing as the soporific phrase "public expenditure". (Frances Cairncross . . . The Guardian 15.7.74) Most students of economics would echo these sentiments yet public expenditure is becoming an increasingly important part of our life . . . accounting now for nearly half of the U.K.'s G.N.P. . . . and deserves at least a little consideration.

Public expenditure includes all spending by government departments, local authorities and the investment expenditure of our nationalised industries. About 60% of public expenditure is "direct" in that the government itself makes the expenditure so making direct calls upon the nation's resources to produce the goods and services considered desirable for the social and economic well-being of the nation. The other 40% of Government expenditure consists of "transfer" payments (pensions, social security payments, grants to universities etc.) which are not direct calls upon resources but simply a re-distribution of spending power from one part of the economy to another. (e.g. reduction of spending power of one person by taxation and giving it to another by subsidy). In this case the recipients and not the government make the expenditure and the calls upon national resources.

PURPOSE OF PUBLIC EXPENDITURE

The purpose of public expenditure is four fold:

1. To provide collectively, rather than as individuals, certain products and services which are thought by government to be essential to the well-being of the society in which we live. Such expenditure might include sums devoted to education, health, social services, defence etc.

2. To provide the nation with those products and services which, whilst important to society, may not normally figure (through ignorance of their value and importance or simply through lack of the private individual's cash resources) in some families' shopping baskets.

3. To provide a vehicle with which the government can influence the level of aggregate demand and so eliminate some of the problems of unemployment and inflation (See page 187 for details of this).

1. Note views as to the effectiveness of interest rates on the decisions to borrow are a point of great debate.
2. Committee on the Working of the Monetary System. Cmnd. 827. 1959.

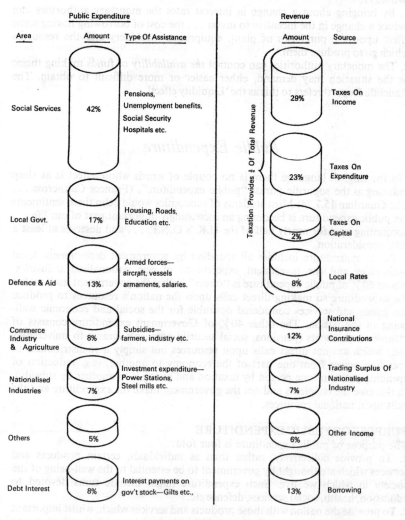

Public Expenditure

Area	Amount	Type Of Assistance
Social Services	42%	Pensions, Unemployment benefits, Social Security Hospitals etc.
Local Govt.	17%	Housing, Roads, Education etc.
Defence & Aid	13%	Armed forces— aircraft, vessels armaments, salaries.
Commerce Industry & Agriculture	8%	Subsidies— farmers, industry etc.
Nationalised Industries	7%	Investment expenditure— Power Stations, Steel mills etc.
Others	5%	
Debt Interest	8%	Interest payments on gov't stock—Gilts etc.,

Revenue

Amount	Source
29%	Taxes On Income
23%	Taxes On Expenditure
2%	Taxes On Capital
8%	Local Rates
12%	National Insurance Contributions
7%	Trading Surplus Of Nationalised Industry
6%	Other Income
13%	Borrowing

Taxation Provides ¾ Of Total Revenue

Public Revenue & Expenditure 1973-4

(Adapted from Treasury Broadsheet No 1 Sept 1973)

EXHIBIT 17.1

4. To provide a means of redistributing income by taxing the higher income groups and giving the revenue to the poorer sectors of society.

A simple breakdown of the government's expenditure and the sources of revenue for that expenditure is shewn in Exhibit 17.1.

Growth of Public Expenditure

There are many techniques for measuring the growth of public expenditure but perhaps the most useful and meaningful is to examine its growth in relation to the growth of the G.N.P. Using these methods we can see from Exhibit 17.2 that not only has public expenditure grown more quickly than the G.N.P. but the rate of increase has also increased.

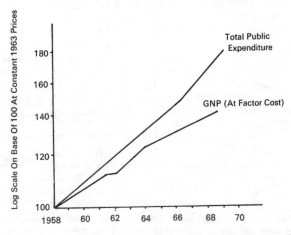

Relative Rates Of Growth Of G.N.P. And Total Public Expenditure In Real Terms
(Adapted From "The Banker" April 1970)

EXHIBIT 17.2

In 1958 total public expenditure equalled 38% of G.N.P. but by 1968 it had reached nearly 47%.

Why Has it Grown so Quickly?

The growth in public expenditure cannot be put down to any one reason but a combination of factors which might include some of the following:

1. It has been noted that the fast growing rich economies whilst having considerable private affluence, are often bugged by public squalor. Thus, to avoid falling into this trap many governments consider public expenditure a priority and allow it to grow at a faster rate than private consumption.

2. In the post war period the increasing acceptance of Keynsian economics placed great emphasis on public expenditure as a means of influencing aggregate demand and the level of economic activity. The use and acceptance of the "unbalanced budget" gave the government greater freedom and made the control of public spending seemingly less important.

3. The more affluent Britain becomes the greater is the desire for certain social

goods such as health and education. These tend to be higher in our individual priorities than many private goods.

4. Local government spending, particularly in the area of education, has increased markedly. As the expenditure increases and puts a greater strain on the Rates, the central government has helped out with grants so removing the deterrent to excessive spending.

On December 19th 1973 the Chancellor made a statement in the House concerning the National economy and subsequently Circular 156/73 was issued indicating the nature and extent of the reductions which were to be made in public expenditure 1974/75. There was to be a general reduction of 20% in Capital expenditure and 10% in Procurements (i.e. revenue expenditure on goods and services including pay and debt charges). In making these reductions local authorities were to have regard for the following:

a) the necessity of maintaining essential services.

b) the exceptional personal needs of the community which could arise due to adverse economic conditions.

c) the desirability of minimising disruption by concentrating reductions in activities where fuel shortages are likely to affect the supply of materials.

The Chancellor also indicated that the cuts must be "such as to avoid reduction in employment in the public sector. It is consumption of fuel and power by the public sector that has to be reduced, not its employment of people."

Almost one year later in the Budget of November 1974 the new Chancellor announced that it was the government's intention that growth in the level of public expenditure, over the next four years, should not rise by more than $2\frac{3}{4}\%$ in demand terms per year on average. There was to be a re-assessment of spending between programmes with priority given to housing and social services.

Further in the Budget statement of November the Chancellor said that the need to give priority to investment and the balance of payments had very important implications for public expenditure. It was essential that firm control was established over the demand for resources of the public sector as a whole so as to ensure that public expenditure did not increase in demand terms by more than the figure of $2\frac{3}{4}\%$ on average over the next four years. Expenditure by local authorities accounted for about 30% of the total and therefore presented a special problem. In the three years from 1971–2 current expenditure by local authorities had been rising by 7%–8% in real terms (i.e. excluding inflation). The Chancellor noted that it was very desirable that there should be further development of standards and services afforded by local authorities but a rate of growth which far outstripped the growth of national resources could not go on indefinitely. Local authorities were therefore instructed to play their part in the achievement of national objectives by limiting the rise in expenditure, other than that due to inflation, to what was absolutely inescapable . . . with the further cautionary note that the planned rate of growth of local authority expenditure in 1976–77 to 1978–79 will need to be further reduced. The Government's views on the future of local authority expenditure were set out in a Joint Circular issued December 1974.[1]

5. It has been further argued that attempts to control the growth of public expenditure have actually led paradoxically to relaxation of control on public expenditure. The Plowden Report . . . a committee on the Control of Public Expenditure set up in 1961 . . . recommended that public expenditure should be planned long term and not subject to frustrating chopping and changing.

1. Joint Circular. D.O.E. 171/74; Home Office 233/74: Dept. of Employment 1/74.

Short term economic management should be left to taxation and monetary policy rather than changes in public expenditure.

The Problem of Public Expenditure

As public expenditure makes up such a large part of the G.N.P. changes in its levels will have a significant effect upon level of economic activity. Direct government spending is likely to have a more immediate effect upon output than public expenditure through transfer payments. The effect of transfer payments will depend much upon what the recipients do with them. Thus should the recipient save an income received in the form of a transfer payment (a pension say) nothing would be done to increase the level of demand and therefore, economic activity.

We have already noted in Chapter 16 that the government has a responsibility of ensuring that the level of aggregate demand matches the total resource capacity it expects to be available at any one time. In other words, if there are resources capable of producing output which are lying idle then the government should see demand is sufficient to bring those resources into production and ensure a fully employed economy. By the same token the government must ensure that the economy does not become too overheated with a level of demand likely to cause inflation. Since public expenditure is responsible for a significant and substantial part of this aggregate demand, should this be allowed to rise more quickly than the available resource capacity, inflation is likely.

Much of course will depend upon the source of revenue for financing the expenditure. Taxation may, for example, reduce consumer demand and so offset any increase in aggregate demand generated from the government spending of that revenue. However, if the revenue through taxation came from the more well-off section of society and was channelled back through public expenditure into the pockets of the poor, then money which might normally have been saved would suddenly be responsible for generating new demand.

The recent rise in public expenditure has thus created the following problems for government.

1. To control and keep public expenditure in line with the expected growth of the nation's productive capacity.
2. To avoid upsetting the electorate which may prefer to make its own expenditure decisions rather than allow the government to take an increasing role in such decisions.
3. Where necessary to be able to justify increases in public expenditure at the expense of a fall in private consumption.
4. The problem of defending rising public expenditure at a time when restraint in consumer spending is being demanded.
5. The problem of deciding in which directions public expenditure should be channelled. How much, for example, should be devoted to defence, economic aid, pensions etc.?

Part Four

THE GOVERNMENT AND THE ECONOMY

Chapter Eighteen

INSTRUMENTS OF GOVERNMENT ECONOMIC POLICY

Taxation

This is a subject which has been of great concern to governments for many centuries if only for the reason that no-one likes paying taxes even though we all recognise that everyone who is capable of contributing to State revenue should do so in order that collectively we can achieve ends which would be impossible if we acted independently. Taxmen have always been unpopular figures both before and since St. Matthew sat at the receipt of custom and unfair or heavy taxation has been so often the cause of political upheaval. It is interesting to note that at the very time when the American colonists were voicing their objections to being taxed without being represented and the French their dissatisfaction with l'ancien regime (which involved so much objection to their iniquitous tax system), that in Britain, Adam Smith was formulating the principles of what he considered to be the basis of a just system of taxation.

ADAM SMITH'S CANONS OF TAXATION
Smith maintained that there were four basic tenets which a government should observe: Certainty, Equality, Convenience and Economy.

1. *Certainty* . . . by which he meant that the taxpayer should know how much tax he has to pay, why he is liable and when the tax has to be paid. Taxation should not be the subject of arbitrary decisions made by tax gatherers.
2. *Equality* . . . there are several ways of interpreting this but what Smith implied was that the tax should be proportional to the taxpayers' incomes.
3. *Convenience* . . . collection should be so arranged that the convenience of the taxpayer is taken into account.
4. *Economy* . . . the administration of the system should be devised to ensure that the yield from taxation should be always greater than the cost of collection.

At this stage it is worthwhile examining how Smith's four basic principles have developed in the U.K. On the first point it can be certainly said that with regard to taxes on income the British system satisfies the requirement. The majority of taxpayers do know in advance the approximate amount they will have to pay in income tax once they have received their notice of coding under the Pay-as-you-earn scheme. The system of allowances is complicated and it could be said that this is the area where uncertainty remains . . . but it is the uncertainty which arises from not understanding fully the regulations rather than arbitrary decisions made by the authorities. Certainly it is not possible for the Inland Revenue to discriminate against one and in favour of another. In the field of indirect taxation it is again complexity rather than arbitrariness which creates uncertainty. The different levels of Purchase Tax could be confusing and similarly with Value Added Tax although the majority of people know that the

rate is 8% they do not necessarily know which goods and services are taxed, which are zero-rated and which are exempted.

As said earlier there are several ways of interpreting Equality. It may be said that a per capita tax is equal i.e. the sum paid by each person is equal. Smith's interpretation was that the tax should be proportional to income e.g. everyone paying 10% of his income. A third and more modern approach is that the burden of the tax should be equal. Under Smith's system every taxpayer would pay say £10 out of every £100 of income therefore the burden of £50 for a man with £500 is much greater than the £500 for the man with £5000 (the latter is still left with nine times the former's gross income). . . . thus although the rich would pay more in cash the system is unfair because the burden is less. The progressive system which has evolved tries to remedy this by relating the burden to taxable capacity i.e. increasing the rate at which tax is paid as the ability to pay increases; this is demonstrated in Exhibit 18.01.

Progressive Taxation Rates

Income tax at the basic and higher rates is chargeable on taxable income i.e. that part of income remaining after all allowable deductions including personal reliefs have been made. Comparison of the tables for 1973/4/5 and 1975/6 will also show how the Chancellor has used Income Tax in the current situation.

1973/4	1974/5
Basic rate 30% on first £5000 taxable income	Basic rate 33% on first £4500 taxable income
Higher rate 40% on next 1000 ,, ,,	Higher rate 38% on next 500 ,, ,,
,, ,, 45% ,, ,, 1000 ,, ,,	,, ,, 43% ,, ,, 1000 ,, ,,
50% ,, ,, 1000 ,, ,,	48% ,, ,, 1000 ,, ,,
55% ,, ,, 2000 ,, ,,	53% ,, ,, 1000 ,, ,,
60% ,, ,, 2000 ,, ,,	58% ,, ,, 2000 ,, ,,
65% ,, ,, 3000 ,, ,,	63% ,, ,, 2000 ,, ,,
70% ,, ,, 5000 ,, ,,	68% ,, ,, 3000 ,, ,,
75% on the remainder	73% ,, ,, 5000 ,, ,,
	83% on the remainder

EXHIBIT 18.01

The progressive system being the fairest has been adopted by most countries and is justified by the fact that the law of diminishing marginal utility applies to income in every additional pound of income will give less satisfaction to the rich man than to the poor.

The actual payment of tax is never wholly convenient to the taxpayer therefore a system has been devised to create the least inconvenience. Before the introduction of P.A.Y.E. tax was payable in two lump sums in January and June and this was clearly even more inconvenient for small income earners than it was for those who still pay by this method. It meant that people had to assess how much they would need for tax purposes and put part of current income aside in order to meet their later liabilities. The P.A.Y.E. system which deducts the tax at source is not only more convenient (and certainly less painful than first receiving the money only to have to part with it) but it also reduces the possibility of running into arrears or actually defaulting. Taxes on goods and services are also made more convenient to pay by including them in the price paid at the time of purchase.

Any tax which costs more to collect than it raises in revenue is clearly a bad tax unless of course it was imposed deliberately to achieve some other purpose e.g. to reduce the consumption of some commodity which was considered to be harmful to the health or the social life of the nation. By the nineteenth century there was a vast range of commodity taxes many of which were barely economic and in the Budget of 1853 Gladstone abolished the duties on some hundred items in order to simplify the system and make it more effective. Today, at first sight, the British system seems to be particularly cost-effective, e.g. in 1969 the cost of collecting each pound of direct tax was only 1·32p while for Customs & Excise it was merely 0·91p; unfortunately this underestimates the true cost. The manner in which P.A.Y.E. operates means that a large proportion of the collection costs are in fact met by the thousands of employers who have to employ additional staff to make the necessary calculations and deduct the tax before forwarding it to the Inland Revenue. Much the same too can be said of the change from Purchase Tax to Value Added Tax which has meant that many more firms need to make returns to Customs & Excise and therefore require more staff. We could go further than this and say that a good tax system should not necessitate expense in complying with the regulations . . . as it is there is considerable expense on all sides of the fence. On one side there are the Treasury experts who devise the taxes, on the other there are the tax accountants who advise individuals and companies (including advice on how to avoid taxation); in the middle are the Inland Revenue officials who administer the whole system and determine appeals . . . naturally they all have supporting secretarial, clerical and technical staff. It is extremely debatable how productive such work is . . . and might not such highly qualified personnel be more gainfully employed in giving advice of greater value to companies particularly at a time when so many are beset with financial difficulties. The real difficulty is that the tax system has developed in a haphazard way and really radical reform would be a daunting task.

ADDITIONAL MODERN PRINCIPLES
In Smith's day almost the entire purpose of taxation was to raise revenue to cover government expenditure thus he was able to confine himself to establishing principles to ensure a fairer system. Today taxation is still primarily for raising revenue but it also has many other objectives and consequently the Chancellor has to be mindful of other principles:

1. Impartiality. The Chancellor should seek to make the system as impartial as possible. This is easier with direct taxation which if also progressive achieves what is called *vertical equity*. To achieve *horizontal equity* i.e. that two persons with similar income and commitments pay the same tax, the Chancellor should again concentrate on direct taxes because to hope to achieve this through indirect tax would mean relying on people having the same range of priorities in their consumption of goods and services.

2. Adjustability. Taxes should be capable of being varied so that they comply with Government policy, but they should not be subject to frequent changes. What the Chancellor has to do is to decide the net gain or loss of altering a particular tax compared with the effect of leaving it at its present level.

3. Tax should not be a disincentive to effort, work or enterprise. At one end of the scale there is what might be called a natural level of taxation i.e. people expect to be taxed . . . what they regard as a desirable level will to some extent depend on their estimate of what they get back from the Government, but there comes a time when the tax level becomes irksome. The Government should avoid levels

of taxation which induce people to work less or shun responsibility otherwise production and therefore prosperity will fall.

THE STRUCTURE OF TAXATION
It should be clear from the previous paragraphs that taxation is imposed for a variety of purposes and so consequently it follows that Government cannot achieve these varied ends by one single tax or even one type of tax. The structure of taxation in any country falls broadly into two categories, Direct and Indirect.

DIRECT TAXATION
Direct taxation includes all those taxes where the payer makes payment directly to the tax authorities.

INCOME TAX
The best known form is of course personal income tax which was first levied as a temporary measure in the U.K. in 1799. It was repealed shortly after the end of the Napoleonic Wars but was re-introduced in 1842 and has continued since then as the main form of taxation, the major change being the development of the progressive principle (as explained earlier).

CORPORATION TAX
.... until 1966 companies were liable to income tax plus a profits tax of 15% ... the system was then replaced by Corporation Tax which is a proportional tax in that all companies pay the same rate irrespective of the size of their profits. Profits distributed to shareholders are then subject to income tax. The April 1974 Budget set the rate for 1973–74 at 52%; the November Budget introduced certain selective changes.

Critics of the system argue that this discriminates in favour of companies retaining their profits and although they concede that retention should stimulate investment they point out that there is no guarantee that companies retaining profits will actually invest. They further argue that it has caused certain inhibitions in the capital market which has been further distorted by the fact that although the tax paid by shareholders on their dividends cannot be offset against the liability of the company, the interest payable on debentures can. The effect has been to encourage firms to raise additional capital by means of debentures rather than new issues of Ordinary shares which has consequently altered the gearing of such firms.

CAPITAL GAINS TAX
In 1962 a tax was introduced on capital gains where the assets were realised within six months of the original purchase. In 1965 the qualifing period was amended to twelve months and measures for long term tax introduced but in 1971 the distinction between long and short period was abolished and in the case of disposals of less than £500 p.a. the gains were exempted from tax. For this purpose an asset is any form of property (other than sterling currency) whether situated in the U.K. or elsewhere. Owner occupied houses, cars and chattels if worth less than £1,000 at the time of the acquisition and the disposal were exempted.

Capital gains had been a controversial subject for a long time and certainly from the viewpoint of equity they should have been taxed. Advocates of the tax argued that if an investment appreciated in value and was subsequently

sold, the gain should be treated as income; opponents argued that if all prices were rising then the purchaser was no better off in real terms and if the tax were then levied the investor could be worse off. The background to the case was that an increasing number of people had made very quick and large profits from sheer speculation particularly in the land and property sector and in view of the anti-social and inflationary consequences of this together with the fact that income tax from the less well-to-do was high it was only right and proper that such gains should be taxed.

ESTATE DUTY

The justification for such a tax is again based on the principle of equity; not only is the inheritance a windfall for the legatee but also the sum involved has been amassed not solely by the deceased but also by the efforts of his workers, tenants, customers who contributed in some way. The popular view is that after due provision has been made for the heirs the estate should be taxed in order that it can in part be returned to those who helped create it. The present system does not wholly answer the principle of Equity and there have been many suggestions that a more comprehensive wealth tax should be introduced in the U.K. Some countries already operate wealth taxes and more than forty have gift taxes e.g. in Belgium there is a stamp duty on the capitalisation and issue of shares; in the Netherlands and Denmark there are annual progressive taxes on the value of all net assets owned by individuals. In the U.K. in 1948 and 1968 a one-time capital levy was imposed.

WEALTH AND CAPITAL TRANSFER TAXES

In the Budget of March 1974 the Chancellor promised that the Government intended to introduce legislation to bring about a more even distribution of wealth and income in the U.K. and this would be done by means of a capital transfer tax and a wealth tax. At the present there is still much inherited wealth whose surface is only scratched by the tax system except where the generated income is taxed. The purpose of the proposed legislation is to tax more effectively at source thus spreading the burden of tax and perhaps making it possible to reduce the level of taxation on earned income.

CAPITAL TRANSFER TAX.

This tax will replace the present Estate Duty and as with that tax the starting point would be on wealth above £15,000. The principal differences are:—
1. Whereas with Estate Duty it is possible to avoid it by transferring the wealth before death or moving it into a Trust, the capital transfer tax will apply to all transfers of personal wealth irrespective of the timing.
2. The rates originally proposed were lower particularly at the lower end e.g.

Estate Duty Rate	*C.T.T. Rate*
£0 – 15,000. . . . . 0%	£0 – 15,000. . . . . 0%
15,000 – 20,000. . . . . 25%	15,000 – 20,000. . . . . 10%
	20,000 – 25,000. . . . . 15%
20,000 – 30,000. . . . . 30%	25,000 – 30,000. . . . . 20%
30,000 – 40,000. . . . . 35%	30,000 – 40,000. . . . . 25%
40,000 – 50,000. . . . . 40%	40,000 – 50,000. . . . . 30%

On Feb. 7th 1975 the Chief Secretary to the Treasury announced that the proposed reduced rates of C.T.T. on life time gifts would be:—

Up to £15,000	nil	£100,000 – 120,000	27½%
£15,000 – 20,000	5%	120,000 – 150,000	35%
20,000 – 25,000	7½%	150,000 – 200,000	42½%
25,000 – 30,000	10%	200,000 – 250,000	50%
30,000 – 40,000	12½%	250,000 – 300,000	55%
40,000 – 50,000	15%	300,000 – 500,000	60%
50,000 – 60,000	17½%	500,000 – 1 million	65%
60,000 – 80,000	20%	1 M. – 2 M.	70%
80,000 – 100,000	22½%		

Where the gift was made within three years of the death of the donor the tax charged would be increased to that appropriate to a transfer on death.
3. Transfers of property between husband and wife (or vice versa) at any time will be exempt. This will relieve the burden particularly on smaller estates because the tax will not now be paid until the surviving partner has also died.

WEALTH TAX

This will be an annual tax and will be novel in that it will include wealth as well as income in the tax structure. The introduction of the tax could be argued on the grounds of equity since it is estimated that in the U.K. between 25 – 30% of all personal wealth is owned by just 1% of the adult population. The Green Paper Cmnd 5704 suggests a starting point of £100,000 and a levy of 1% rising in stages to 2½% on wealth over £5 million or alternatively by stages to 5% at the highest level. This would mean that the annual tax would be:—

Up to £100,000	Nil
£100,000 – 200,000	£1,000
£5 million	£86,500 (or 171,000)

and on each additional £1 M over £5 M .. £25,000 (or £50,000)

Apart from the grounds of equity it can also be argued that if a capital gains tax is justified because the gains are seen merely as deferred income then a wealth tax would overcome the difficulty that a capital gains tax only applies when the asset is realised and so tends to make capital less mobile.

Against the imposition of the tax it might be said that it would be difficult to define and value 'wealth'. The system might be costly to administer and the impact might result in a dis-saving if it led to increased consumption and so added to inflationary pressures. It might discourage enterprise and effort and it could upset the capital market if it meant that illiquid assets had to be realized in order to make tax payments.

OTHER DIRECT TAXES

Stamp duties, motor-vehicle licences and rates levied by District Councils are all further examples of direct taxation.

INDIRECT TAXATION

In general indirect taxes are those paid by the individual but through someone else; the best example of this being commodity taxes such as Purchase Tax which operated from its inception in 1940 until it was replaced by V.A.T. Though at first sight the distinction between the two categories seems to be one

of just administrative convenience there is a deeper economic significance in that indirect taxes can be legally avoided whereas direct cannot.

COMMODITY TAXES.

Such taxes are of two kinds: either specific or ad valorem. As the name suggests the former means that the tax is a fixed amount of money per unit e.g. tobacco, beer, petrol, whereas an ad valorem tax is calculated as a proportion of the value of the good. It is obviously easier to use specific taxes but it does create an inequality of burden when different grades or qualities of the same article exist e.g. if a tax of £100 is imposed on an article which comes in different qualities ranging from £400 to £2,000 it means that the customers most likely to buy at the bottom end of the range will be the lower income groups and they will be carrying a 25% tax whereas the higher income groups most likely to buy from the top end of the range will be paying a tax of 5%. Consequently in such commodity ranges it is better to use ad valorem taxes and so retain the progressive principle and to restrict specific taxes to commodities where the variation in quality and price is small.

The effect of imposing specific commodity taxes can be seen in the following Exhibits. Exhibit 18.02 shows the quantities suppliers are willing to supply at various prices . . . conversely how much customers must pay for particular quantities. The imposition of the tax in effect raises prices to the consumer and though the basic conditions of supply have not changed the supply curve in effect moves upwards and to the left.

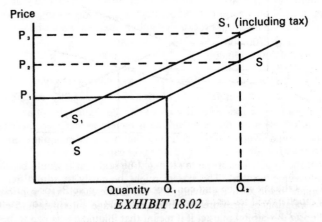

EXHIBIT 18.02

Thus originally consumers paid P_1 for Q_1 and P_2 for Q_2. The imposition of the tax means that customers must now pay P_2 for Q_1 and P_3 for Q_2.

If we now assume the demand curve in Exhibit 18.03 we see the effect of the tax.

Originally the market is in equilibrium at P_1 and Q_1. The imposition of the tax in effect raises the supply curve and the intersection of DD and S_1S_1 shows the reaction of consumers, namely that they will now pay P_2 but will buy only Q_2. Consumers pay a higher price and obtain a smaller quantity while the supplier sells less and obtains a lower price P_3 because the vertical interval P_3P_2 is in fact the tax levy; thus the supplier's revenue is OP_3BQ_2 and the Government's tax is P_3P_2AB.

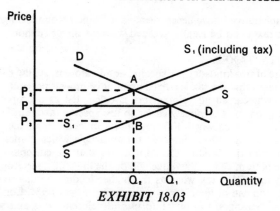

EXHIBIT 18.03

In the case of the ad valorem tax the only difference is that the 'new supply curve' will not be parallel to the old since the tax being a proportion of the price will increase as basic price rises. Exhibit 18.04 shows the effect.

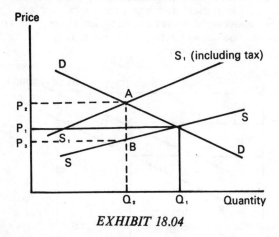

EXHIBIT 18.04

The effect of the tax will be that consumers will pay more P_2 for a smaller quantity Q_2; suppliers will sell less and obtain a lower price P_3. The Government's tax will again by P_3P_2AB.

Commodity taxes and elasticity of demand and supply

When imposing commodity taxes the Chancellor must also bear in mind that different commodities have different elasticities of demand and supply and both will influence the effect of the tax.

Exhibit 18.05 and 18.06 show two commodities with the same supply conditions but with different elasticities of demand.

Where the demand is elastic . . . because consumers can substitute or do without the commodity . . . they contract their demand to Q_2 at the price P_2 and the supplier suffers very much with sales falling off to Q_2 and only obtaining P_3.

Where the demand is inelastic . . . perhaps because the commodity is a necessity

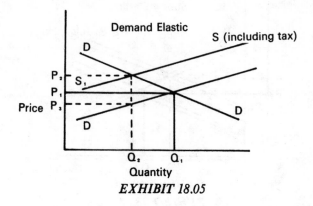

EXHIBIT 18.05

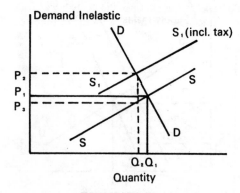

EXHIBITS 18.06

... demand contracts very little ... Q_2 at P_2 while the supplier does not suffer to the same extent his price dropping to only P_3. (The unit profit is the same in both instances but the cut-back in demand is more severe in the case of elastic demand).

Exhibits 18.07 and 18.08 illustrate two commodities having the same elasticity of demand but different elasticities of supply.

Where supply is elastic, consumers will contract demand to Q_2 at P_2 and suppliers will obtain P_3, not a great fall in price ... but where the supply is inelastic the burden really fails on the supplier whose price falls to P_3 as the consumer's price rises to P_2 and demand contracts to Q_2. A large proportion of the supplier's costs may be fixed capital costs which cannot be changed, consequently production cannot be quickly adjusted and the supplier must bear most of the tax.

Until 1973 commodity taxes in the U.K. were levied by means of specific Excise duties and ad valorem Purchase Tax, but in that year one price we paid for admission to the European Economic Community was the introduction of a Value Added Tax in place of Purchase Tax and Selective Employment Tax (five of the six E.E.C. countries had adopted VAT by 1972). Because it is a relatively new form of taxation a closer examination is worthwhile.

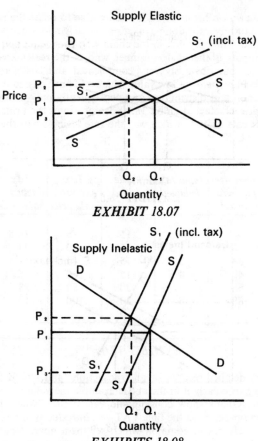

EXHIBIT 18.07

EXHIBITS 18.08

VALUE ADDED TAX

France first introduced Taxe sur la Valeur Ajoutée in 1954; West Germany introduced a form of it a little later and in 1967 the E.E.C. Council of Ministers by means of a Directive approved a recommendation of the Commission that all members should adopt the system. Outside the Community the three Scandinavian countries introduced VAT systems of their own. In general a VAT is a broad indirect tax falling on the generality of goods and services sold to the public, with a number of specified exceptions. It is by its very nature a multi-stage tax levied at every stage of production and distribution on the value added at each point of sale. Value added by a particular trader is the difference between his allowable costs and revenue from sales . . . it is not the same as profit. Each trader at every stage of production and distribution charges VAT on his sale price, at the same time he has already paid tax on his 'inputs' (raw materials, components and services bought in). When he settles his VAT with Customs & Excise he will be liable to tax on his turnover less his 'inputs' . . . the tax which he hands over is therefore the difference between the "output tax" which he has passed on to his customers and the "input tax" which he has already paid on

supplies and is shewn on his invoices. By being able to offset the tax on inputs against the tax on turnover the double taxation which would occur with a general sales tax is avoided. The only link in the chain who cannot pass on the tax nor reclaim tax on inputs is the final consumer who is the real taxpayer. VAT is simple in principle but obviously very complicated and costly to administer because there are many items of low value which will have passed through many stages of production and distribution and consequently only a tiny amount of tax is collected at each stage. Exhibit 18.09 demonstrates the principle of VAT assuming the flat rate of 10% which was the rate levied when the system was introduced in the U.K.

	Tax inclusive purchase price	Input tax deducted	Value Added	Tax exclusive sale price	Tax inclusive sale price	V.A.T. payable to Excise
A sells to B	—	—	15	15	16·5	1·5
B ,, ,, C	16·5	1·5	15	30	33	1·5
C ,, ,, D	33	3	15	45	49·5	1·5
D ,, ,, E	49·5	4·5	15	60	66	1·5
E ,, ,, F	66	6	20	80	88	2
F ,, ,, G	88	8	20	100	110	2
						10

EXHIBIT 18.09

It calls for very detailed records of all transactions and would seem a very costly procedure particularly if in the above example the values are in pence.

The European systems show considerable variations; Exhibit 18·10 shows the regulations in operation at the time VAT was introduced in the U.K.

There are two features in common which set them apart from the system introduced into Britain, namely the Standard Rate is considerably higher and none has the range of zero rated reliefs included in the British system . . . though the terms 'exemption' and 'zero-rated' are not as straight-forward as they appear. There are basically two forms of exemption:—

1. A trader with a turnover of less than £5,000 p.a. is exempt . . . but he is in the same position as a consumer in that VAT has been paid on his own purchases and there is no means of reclaiming the tax paid. There is a provision whereby such traders can voluntarily register to be included in the system because it is not always an advantage to be exempted from VAT.

2. Businesses in a limited range of services including banking and insurance, postal services, rents, betting and gaming and funeral services are not VATable on their own services but of course there is a VAT element in their prices because of the VAT already paid on their outgoings.

Zero-rating is not like exemption in that it does give full relief from the tax; no tax is levied on the goods sold to final customers and any tax charged on any input used in the production of the zero-rated article can be recovered e.g. a retailer can recover the VAT he pays on the packaging of foods because the latter is zero-rated. The main zero-rated categories are;– all exports, all food (except meals eaten on the premises), building and construction, (excluding repairs and

FRANCE	Food	7·5%
	Fuel & some other essentials	17·6
	Standard rate	23
	Luxuries	33·3
W. GERMANY	Food	
	All other items	11
ITALY	Food, fuel, medicines	6
	Standard rate	12
	Luxuries (inc. cars over 2000 c.c.)	18
NETHERLANDS	Food	4
	Standard rate	16
	Cars	32
BELGIUM	Food	6
	Fuel & some other essentials	15
	Standard rate	20
	Luxuries	25
LUXEMBOURG	Food	5
	All other items	10
DENMARK	All items	15
SWEDEN	All items	17·65
NORWAY	All items	20
AUSTRIA	Food, some services & printed publications	8
	All other items	16

EXHIBIT 18.10

maintenance), passenger transport (excluding taxis), fuel and power, approved children's clothing, books, periodicals and newspapers.

The controversy concerning VAT raged throughout the 1960s and it is interesting to see how certain attitudes changed over the period. In 1963 the Government appointed a Committee under the City banker Mr. Gordon Richardson to look at the possibility of a VAT replacing either Purchase Tax or profits tax. The Committee rejected both possibilities . . . "In itself, a VAT does not (any more than P.T.) stimulate exports or promote growth . . . The P.T. system in fact affords a more logical, efficient and economical means of consumer taxation than a value added tax."[1]

Mr. Reginald Maudling said in his Budget speech, ". . . in this country, the purchase tax is superior as a method of taxation to the value added turnover tax,

1. Report of the Committee on Turnover Taxation Cmnd. 2300. 1964.

and . . . there is no advantage either to exports or to the economy generally in switching over from Purchase Tax to VAT."[1]

However by 1971 the attitude of the Conservative politicians had changed and in the Budget of that year the Chancellor, Anthony Barber said, ". . . the replacement of Purchase Tax and Selective Employment Tax by VAT will enable us to remove the whole tax charge from our exports and impose it on imports. . . ."[2]

The Government Green Paper 1971 said, "The existing pattern of indirect taxation in this country is open to the objection that it is selective and is based on too narrow a range of expenditure."[3]

Mr. Barber in the Budget took the strange line of arguing that taxing essential items of household expenditure would be fairer than purchase tax. "The VAT is, by its very nature, a comprehensive tax and its introduction in this country will produce a much fairer system of indirect taxation."[4]

Before summarising the advantages and disadvantages of VAT it is worthwhile noting that the VAT system of high rates in several European countries were necessary because of the weakness of their personal income tax schemes. No other country has a system like our PAYE with its sophisticated system of coding with its week-by-week adjustments, indeed many countries do not have a system at all which deducts the tax at source. In some countries tax evasion is a national disease with which governments have no ability to cope. O.E.C.D. statistics for the period 1968–70 reveal an interesting comparison:—

Taxes on incomes & profits as % of Total Tax Revenue

U.S.A.	48%
U.K.	40%
Italy	18%
France	16%

Mr Oliver Stanley, quoted in The Times, March 1972 said, "In Europe, taxes on sales or turnover, have been widely adopted because of a tendency to evade taxes upon profits. You can readily produce a plausible set of final accounts showing nil profits but it is less easy to produce a set showing nil turnover."

Summary of advantages and disadvantages of V.A.T.

Advantages.

1. It could lead to improved efficiency because of greater use of machinery rather than labour. Investment in plant means that any VAT paid could be offset against VAT chargeable on sales; employment of labour would give no such advantage unless a Regional Employment Premium were paid. Comparison would have to be made between the cost of tax free investment and labour costs . . . it could happen that the cost of labour was still lower than the cost of capital.

2. Less chance of evasion . . . because it would be to every seller's advantage to see that all tax credits to which he is entitled have been received.

3. Aid to Balance of Payments. The price of goods for export would be lower than similar goods for the home market because credit would be allowed for all VAT included in costs. Consequently there could be:—

   a) increased demand for exports.

   b) a lower level of domestic demand (which would be welcome in the fight against inflation)

1. Hansard Col. 249. 14 April 1964.
2. Hansard Col. 1393–4 30 March 1971.
3. Value Added Tax. Cmnd. 4261.
4. Hansard Col. 1394, 30 March 1971.

   c) consequently an inducement for manufacturers to export more rather
   than accept a reduced level of activity.
4. In the U.K. it was claimed that many purchase taxes were reaching saturation
point and though VAT would be smaller percentage levy, the range of items
included in the tax base would be greater.

Disadvantages.
1. Inflationary aspects; VAT is a cost and so would be recovered by higher
prices. There is plenty of evidence to support the view e.g. N.E.D.C. Report
March 1972 showed that in the Netherlands prices rose by 5% in the first three
months of VAT and though perhaps only 1½% was directly attributable it gave
businesses the opportunity to increase their margins. In Denmark the first six
months of VAT saw an increase in the cost of living of 7·9% Apart from the
fact that this could clearly trigger off a price/wage spiral there is also the dis-
quieting fact that the width of the tax base means that many items which are
taxed form a considerable proportion of the lower income group's purchases,
. . . those least able to bear the increased burden.
2. It is costly to the State. Purchase Tax had 75,000 registered businesses and
was collected at a single stage; S.E.T. was collected simply by a surcharge on
the employer's National Insurance contribution. Experience has borne out the
warning of NEDC that a switch to VAT would mean that there would be
between 1½ – 2 million collection points and the employment of an extra 6,000 –
8,000 civil servants.
3. The complicated nature of the tax and extra work involved is a cost to industry
in that:—
   a) the 50,000 or so employees could be used in some more profitable way.
   b) more than a million firms are now involved in expensive paper work (and
   the allied office equipment) who were not previously involved in indirect
   taxation.
   The future of VAT in the U.K. is bound up with the results of Britain's renego-
tiation of membership terms of E.E.C. If Britain withdraws from the Common
Market there will no longer be an obligation to operate the system, if on the
other hand the outcome of the talks were that Britain remained a member then
we should be bound by the 1967 Directive to continue operating the tax.

CUSTOMS AND EXCISE DUTIES
Customs duties are levied on imported goods e.g. taxes on wines and tobacco,
whereas excise duties are levied on home-produced goods and services e.g. the
taxes on beer and spirits and the licences required by gaming establishments.
Both can be used as counter-inflationary measures and similarly they can be
used to deal with Balance of Payments problems.

DIRECT *versus* INDIRECT TAXATION
   In recent years, and particularly when the controversy regarding the introduction of VAT was at its height, there were some economists who said that the
greater proportion of tax revenue should be raised by indirect rather than direct
taxation. Clearly in the countries where the administration of direct taxation
is inefficient as in France and Italy, the Government has very little alternative
but to rely more heavily on indirect taxation. . . . and furthermore the Government knows that the only way to avoid paying such taxes is not to buy the
items taxed (if that is possible!) In countries where the yield from direct taxation

is satisfactory the issue is not clear cut. The student should try to assess the situation in the U.K. bearing in mind the following case for and against each system.

Advantages of Direct Taxation

1. Direct taxes are in general economical to collect, particularly as with PAYE employers act as – unpaid collectors.
2. Direct taxation by incorporating the progressive principle can be made equitable i.e. they can be made to relate to income and commitments. Indirect tax is basically regressive in the commodity taxes are based on consumption not on the ability to pay.
3. The yield from direct taxation can be assessed more accurately whereas that from indirect taxation depends on the elasticity of demand for the goods and services taxed.
4. Direct taxes are not so likely to be inflationary in effect and lead to wage claims. Commodity taxes raise prices immediately and therefore increase the cost of living thus the effect on real incomes is more obvious because it affects all purchasers whereas increased direct tax reduces only the take-home pay of tax-payers.

Disadvantages of direct taxation

1. The impact of direct taxation falls on the taxpayer who cannot pass it on to someone else thus it may act as a deterrent to effort and enterprise, whereas, it can be argued, since indirect taxes raise prices they may encourage people to work harder and earn higher cash incomes so that they can go on buying the goods.
2. Similarly it is argued that high levels of direct tax are a disincentive to saving whereas if prices rise as a result of indirect tax some consumers might prefer not to buy the commodity and consequently save the money.
3. There are more opportunities for avoidance and evasion compared with indirect taxes.
4. Even if direct taxes are economical to collect they are costly to administer because each taxpayer has to have a separate assessment and this calls for a large Inland Revenue Department.
5. Because of the complexities of the system there is a need for experts to advise companies and wealthy individuals as to their best tax position. There are ways which are perfectly legal to avoid payment of some tax . . . but surely the employment of experts to find such loopholes (and further accountants and lawyers employed by Government to plug them) is a mis-use of talents.
6. Direct taxes are not as flexible as indirect ones because it is not just a matter of amending legislation but making the necessary changes in the administration and collection. Consequently there is a time lag in the effect of direct taxes and so they are not an 'instant' method of dampening down or stimulating the economy. Similarly they cannot be used to divert economic resources to or away from particular sectors whereas with selective indirect taxes the Government can by changing the rate of tax on a specific item influence the demand for it.
7. There is a very real difficulty in assessing irregular incomes.

Advantages of Indirect Taxation

1. It has always been claimed that indirect taxes are easy to administer and cheap to collect. This certainly was largely true of Purchase Tax but in the light of the

earlier comments on VAT it is very doubtful if it can be said of that particular form of indirect taxation.

2. They are flexible and so changes in the level of taxes have a more immediate effect upon the consumer. Under the Purchase Tax system the Chancellor had power to change the level of taxation by up to 10% simply by an Order in Council . . . under the VAT system the Chancellor recently changed the standard rate from 10% to 8%.

3. Where the system selects individual items to be taxed rather than a flat rate right-across-the-board levy, the Government can discriminate for or against particular consumption and so can influence definite sectors of the economy.

4. It is often claimed that because the tax is included in the purchase price the purchaser is often not conscious of paying a tax and so is less likely to object to the burden. Furthermore it is argued that it broadens the tax base and thus most people contribute something to Government including those on low incomes whose contribution in relation to the cost of assessment and collection of direct tax would be uneconomic.

5. Indirect taxes avoid the disincentive effects on effort, initiative and saving.

6. They are difficult to avoid.

7. They can be used to achieve ends other than fiscal objectives e.g. they can be used for social reasons, a heavy tobacco tax may be imposed because of the risk of lung cancer, a high rate of duty on alcohol to reduce the possibility of drunkeness and its social consequences, high import duties can be imposed to protect an infant industry behind a tariff wall or lower import duties charged in order to forge trading links with particular countries.

Disadvantages of Indirect Taxation

1. The incidence is uncertain.

2. They are not impartial e.g. the teetotaller and non-smoker avoid a heavy burden of taxation.

3. Indirect taxes are basically regressive in that they are related to consumption and not the ability to pay tax. Rich and poor alike – pay the same tax yet the utility of the sum paid in tax is clearly greater for the latter and thus the burden for him is greater.

4. The economic effects and the yield is uncertain because the final effect depends very much on the elasticity of demand. When considering an increase in indirect tax the Chancellor has to take care that the burden on certain commodities has not reached saturation point otherwise any further increase may result in a loss of revenue. In Exhibit 18.11 the demand curve (average revenue curve) is 'kinked' around point A. At the lower prices demand is inelastic and the Chancellor receives satisfactory revenue PP_1 AC while the industry suffers only a small loss in revenue QQ_1CB. If the price including the tax rises above P the demand becomes elastic, tax revenue falls to P_1P_2GE and the loss to the industry is much greater Q_1Q_2FC.

5. It can be argued that indirect taxes are more inflationary than direct ones in that the effects of increased prices are felt right-across-the-board including those whose incomes are so low that they are excluded from Income Tax. Any rise in prices without a complementary increase in cash wages means that real wages are falling, thus to preserve the standard of living, labour will make claims for increased wages thus raising total costs. If these are passed on in increased prices there is not only further inflationary pressure at home but the Balance of Payments position could also worsen as export prices rise and become less

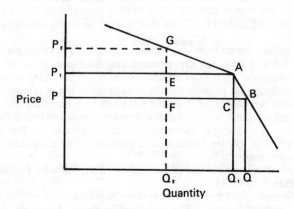

EXHIBIT 18.11

competitive. There are also serious social implications in that somegroups in the community will not be well organised or will be in a weak bargaining position and consequently will be left behind in the upward spiral. This has happened so often to old age pensioners and students on grant and the only way in which Government can remedy their position is by increasing their allowances which subsequently means increased Government expenditure which has to be met either by cuts in other sectors or by increased taxation on those able to pay.

In conclusion it can be seen that both forms of taxation have advantages and disadvantages and it is not surprising therefore that in the U.K. they are used to complement each other almost to an equal extent. The point at which the balance is struck is not arrived at on purely economic grounds for as already explained:
1. taxes are not imposed solely for revenue purposes.
2. there can be far-reaching social as well as economic effects.
so consequently there is a considerable political input in reaching the decision.

Part Four

THE GOVERNMENT AND THE ECONOMY

Chapter Nineteen

GOVERNMENT ECONOMIC POLICY

Location of Industry and Regional Planning

LOCATION OF INDUSTRY

The term location of industry is concerned with the actual geographical location of an entire industry or individual firms comprising that industry. The factors influencing the choice of location have been of interest for a long time and study of these has led some economists to say that there is no general theory of location though there are definite factors which are relevant to the choice of location. In general economists have approached the subject by again assuming rational behaviour; this time by the entrepreneur. They have assumed that in trying to maximise his profits the entrepreneur will choose a site which is not only convenient but where production can be carried out with the lowest avaerage costs per unit of output. In practice such assumptions are frequently not justified; (the student will quickly think of examples of locations not based purely on the concept of the optimum) but just as we were justified in assuming rationality in examining consumer behaviour so are we in establishing a basis for studying the choice of industrial and commercial sites. The rational businessman would want to examine all the factors which influence the costs of production and only when the cost differences between alternative sites was small would he turn to the non-economic factors in making his final choice.

There are several factors to be examined but quite clearly the most important of these must be the costs of transport. Indeed it has been said that if it were not for transport costs there would be no problem of location of industry . . . but that would be looking at the matter from one point of view only.

Transport Costs

Freight costs are incurred at all stages of production, thus in theory the firm will locate where its total transport costs are lowest. It is obvious that if the firm locates near to the source of its raw materials it will minimise the cost of transporting them but conversely will increase its distribution costs if such a move has pulled it away from the market for the ultimate product. Similarly, distribution costs can be minimised by moving nearer to the market but presumably, in most cases, only by increasing the total expense of obtaining its raw materials. Sometimes the entrepreneur does not have a choice as for example in what are sometimes called tied industries, the source of supply is given and will be influenced only by such factors as accessibility, quality and market price; the agricultural industries will be influenced by climatic and geological conditions while for the service industries the market is of paramount importance. However the manufacturing industries are not so tied and so the choice of optimum loca-

tion is not only more complicated but can have a considerable influence on the prosperity of the firm.

In some industries the raw materials used are either bulky or heavy and consequently more expensive to transport whereas by comparison the end product is light and easily handled and so transport costs are less. Clearly the choice of location is near to the source of the raw materials . . . a decision which would be endorsed further if in the reduction of the bulk a considerable amount of waste was created. The choice of location can be complicated further when there are several raw materials involved which are not found together. The location of the iron industry in South Staffordshire and North Worcestershire in the 18th and 19th centuries presented few problems because the three basic ingredients, iron-stone, coal and limestone were all present in the same area, but this was not the case in other parts of the country. Should iron move to coal or vice versa? All other things being equal the choice depended on the relative quantities of the various inputs used in the reduction process (the student should examine the location of the early iron industry in Durham and North East Yorkshire). Technological progress, exhaustion of the old black-band iron ore deposits and the quality of available iron-stone have all influenced the location of new iron-works in the present century both in the U.K. and U.S.A. The location of iron and steel works near the low grade iron-ore fields as at Corby reduces the cost of transporting a large proportion of potential waste (or more accurately a low-value by-product). Similarly the choice of coastal sites such as Margam reduces the costs of handling and transporting inland ores which are now imported.

The opposite of these *material orientated* industries are those where in the process of manufacturing there is an increase in the weight or bulk so that the cost of transporting the final product is relatively more expensive than carrying the ingredients. In such cases it pays the manufacturer to locate near to the ultimate consumer and so we speak of market orientated industries. Examples of such industries are the furniture industry where the assembled items are much greater in volume than the materials from which they are made and (until recent improvements in bulk transport and the desire to concentrate in large units), the brewing industry, where the addition of the water added greatly to the bulk of the barley and sugar.

However the majority of industries are not wholly material or market orientated, most can be termed *footloose industries* where either the material inputs or the final product can be transported. In some industries the components are so easy and cheap to transport and in others the value of the final product to be carried is so valuable that clearly transport costs alone have little influence on where the firm is located. Lastly, as indicated earlier, technological progress can transform an industry over a period of time, e.g. some fifty years ago it was possible only to refine some 30% of crude oil into saleable products consequently there was considerable waste produced during the reduction process and so it made sense to locate the refineries on or very near to the oil-fields. Since then there have been enormous technical advances in the petroleum industry, the range of by-products has increased until some 90% of the crude is made into commercial products and in consequence it is more sensible and safer to transport the crude oil and the refineries have moved nearer to the ultimate markets. Thus an industry which was essentially material orientated has become market orientated.

Power

Until comparatively recently proximity to a source of power was a most important factor in those industries using machinery too big to be driven by human or animal power. The great tilt hammers and the improved spinning machines needed the motive force of the water wheel, the great stones of the corn mills needed wind to drive the sails of the windmills. The steam engines developed in the late eighteenth century liberated industry from being dependent on wind and water but they themselves were wasteful, the input of coal was great in relation to the output of energy and so the new breed of industrialists using steam power found it necessary to locate their works on the coalfields in order to reduce the total cost of the coal they used.

In the last century the development of gas, electric and internal combustion engines together with the construction of the grid systems and the net work of pipelines has made the proximity of the source of power a less important factor than in former times (the student should trace the development of manufacturing industry in say the South East of England). However this is not to say that the source of power is still not an influencing factor. It may be easier to transport energy but it still has to be paid for and everyone is now conscious of the increased cost of energy. The effect of this on total costs and therefore on prices has such far-reaching ramifications that when seen with the need to conserve energy supplies will cause a re-appraisal of the use of power. The cost is not only measured in cash but also in the use of land and it will be interesting to see what effect the exploitation of the oil and gas fields in the North and Celtic Seas has on the location of British industry in the future. Similarly in North America there are tremendous sources of hydro-electric power but to transfer the energy to the present centres of industry would be uneconomic. No doubt in the future these supplies will come into use and unless technology solves the problems of transfer then there will be a re-location of industry and the centres of population.

The Availability of Factors of Production

Land

The influence of this factor will vary from one country to another depending on the total supply relative to the demand for it . . . though there is one aspect common to all namely the immobility of land. It is generally agreed that the high level of rents in urban centres is a deterrent to industrial activity there but this apart the entrepreneur usually has the choice of several alternative sites where the variation in rent (or purchase price) will not have a great impact on the final choice particularly when it is remembered that rent is only a part of total costs and often only a small part. The cost of land to the firm will be decided by the price system. Other firms, perhaps from different industries, will be looking for the same site advantages, thus the price will be fixed as the result of such competition and will settle at the highest price which the firm most determined to secure it will pay . . . the opportunity cost. This firm is the one which regards the advantages as being higher than the advantages of sites elsewhere. In the early days of the Industrial Revolution it seemed that Clydeside might become the centre of the cotton industry; it had all the conditions necessary for the establishment of the industry. However it also had deep-water facilities for which the shipbuilders were prepared to pay more, so for the cotton men the cost of a site on the Clyde was greater than any disadvantage of being in South East Lancashire. Indeed it might be that the latter area had no particular

advantages; the Barlow Report on the Distribution of Industrial Population 1940 quoted a Board of Trade statement that, "the cotton industry first settled in S.E. Lancashire for no particular reason, except perhaps that the woollen industry was already there, foreigners were kindly received and Manchester had no Corporation." Probably much more important than the cost of land is the ability to obtain suitable land with the necessary planning permission.

Capital

Capital does not suffer from the handicap of immobility and neither is there such a geographical variation in interest rates as there is with rents. Nevertheless there are variations in the availability and the price of loan capital for different types of borrowers. One of the obvious advantages of large scale is the greater facility with which the large firm can raise both share and loan capital. Conversely small firms may not have the same access to New Issue markets nor be able to raise loan capital so easily and cheaply and this may lead to some limitation in their freedom of choice i.e. they may be restricted to the area where they are known.

The availability of capital must also be related to the prevailing political climate. The suppliers of capital will obviously be reluctant to invest in a company whose activities are in a country where the profits are likely to be frozen within the territory or where there is a danger of the assets being expropriated. Similarly the borrowers of capital, particularly where plant is very expensive, will be very wary of locating in areas where the political climate is unstable and such equipment could be destroyed. The earlier example of the re-location of oil-refineries can not be explained solely in the terms previously given . . . the political troubles in the Middle Eastern states have re-inforced the decisions to build the expensive refineries in countries with more stable political systems.

Labour

Entrepreneurs will obviously locate near a source of adequate labour wherever possible but again we cannot be dogmatic about this because the supply of labour in an area is affected by the degree of mobility of labour and the demand for labour has to be seen in terms of adequacy of quality as well as adequacy of numbers. Some economists have noted that the one factor of production which can move of its own accord manifests a surprisingly high degree of immobility. However there is historical evidence that there was a considerable degree of geographical mobility of labour in the early days of industrialisation; the rapid growth of towns such as Birmingham, Manchester and Sheffield testifies to the influx of migrant labour rather than just natural growth. Modern economists examining the problems of location, unemployment and the disparities of labour supply in the different regions always comment on the geographical immobility of the factor. We should perhaps examine the problem from two points of view both in time and distance.

In the short run, labour is relatively immobile but Professor A. J. Brown has commented that present day mobility over short distances is quite high and is increasing. In living memory short run mobility was limited to foot transport but improvements in public transport increased the average distance travelled to work. More recently other factors have further increased the daily mobility of many workers; the ownership of more private cars, the development of the motorway network into the conurbations and the difficulty of obtaining and affording accommodation in the urban centres have all contributed to the

growth of dormitory towns and villages. Tens of thousands of workers today cover distances to work which for their grandparents would have been a complete day's outing. Just as improvements in fuel technology have lessened the importance of the proximity of the source of power as a locating factor so too have improvements in the technology of transport modified the immobility of labour in the short run.

When mobility of labour involves actually moving house there is obviously greater immobility; there are economic and social pressures influencing the decision (see Book I page 20). The average frequency in moving home is between 8–10 years and only a small proportion of these moves are from one region to another. The immobility of labour contributes to the regional variations in the supply of labour and therefore to the variations in regional rates of pay.

Businessmen comparing such rates of pay may not necessarily by attracted to low rates areas . . . all other things being equal. Firstly, labour may be available but it may not be the right type of labour with the result that lower wage rates may be offset by higher training costs and lower productivity. Secondly, individual rates of pay are not so important as the proportion of labour cost to total cost and obviously this would be different for a sophisticated technology-based company which is capital-intensive compared with a firm which is labour-intensive.

The supply of labour is an important determinant in the location of industry but the precise strength of its pull depends on the different requirements of individual firms and so it is difficult to make generalisations. The final choice is more difficult for firms requiring considerable numbers of specifically skilled workers than for firms who can quickly train local green labour for the bulk of the work and transfer a nucleus of skilled men. It is rather ironic to hear the comments of training officers of firms which have moved to a Development Area where there is unemployment and therefore no shortage of labour in general that they have encountered serious labour problems because they cannot obtain an adequate supply of certain grades of labour. This problem certainly shows itself where the industry which moves may be said to be alien to the existing 'occupational culture' of the receiving area e.g. when an engineering firm moves to a district with a previously predominantly agricultural background or a locality where at certain times of the year there are more attractive forms of employment than the factory e.g. nearby holiday resorts.

Supply of Components and Access to Ancillary Trades and Services

For some firms their 'raw materials' inputs are the finished products of other firms; these will range from small components to large sub-assemblies. The consideration of transport costs for them is therefore similar to that for the processors of primary products. An early example of this was the establishment of the motor car industry in Coventry and Birmingham. These companies had easy access to the supplying trades of the immediate neighbourhood; the iron and steel trades and foundries of such towns as Wednesbury and Tipton, springs from West Bromwich and Redditch, leather from Walsall, rubber from Birmingham's Fort Dunlop and later from Goodyear's at Wolverhampton, locks from Willenhall, wheel rims, brake drums and metal fabrications from Rubery Owen at Darlaston, the brass industry in Birmingham and later the aluminium industry in Smethwick, the tubes and metal sections of the world-renowned Accles & Pollock of Oldbury and the engineering skills of a host of small companies spread over the entire region.

Improvements in transport have lessened the importance of the proximity of component suppliers but for some firms it is still an important consideration, for example, firms in which are called 'linked industries' i.e. companies engaged in different stages of a process, will find that there are very real economies from proximity to one another, consequently a new comer may well decide to locate where the entire industry is already established. Some firms will be pulled to a particular area because it already has developed financial services, warehousing facilities or public services such as fire brigades and other emergency services.

Waste Disposal

Until we pay more attention to the recovery of waste material and the possibility of re-cycling, the disposal of waste will be an important consideration for companies as well as local authorities. Gone are the days when industrialists could just abandon the waste to mar the landscape, pollute the atmosphere and create the causes of the tragedies like Aberfan. This is not to say that these problems do not still exist, unfortunately they do, but a steady stream of legislation is directed against them. Arrangements for, and the control of, waste disposal is now one of the concerns of the County Councils and no-one is more aware of the magnitude of the problem than the new Metropolitan Counties which control the urban areas such as West Midlands and Greater Manchester. Waste disposal has been described as simply a matter of ' 'eaps and 'oles', unfortunately the majority of holes are now full and the problem is where to put the heaps.

Superficially waste disposal may seem to be just an aspect of social policy, the whim of the conservationists and those who want to improve the 'quality of life'; it is also a question of economics. In the past some local authorities have provided facilities below economic cost, believing that by providing a service to local industry they were contributing to the creation of employment in their areas. With these tipping facilities now under very great strain, costs of disposal will rise and perhaps significantly add to the total costs of firms already in such areas. For firms which create great quantities of waste and are considering re-location the problem of disposal will be of great importance. Likewise Planning Committees in considering applications will need to know how much waste will be created and what burden it will place on disposal services.

Ethos of the Area

This term could be used to describe many influences about which it is difficult to be more specific. A reputation for good craftsmanship or a stable population might attract a firm to a region just as a history of stormy labour relations might cause a firm to look elsewhere when everything else seems favourable. The attitude of the local authority or even the local technical college in providing courses may have a bearing on the final decision.

Industrial Inertia

When we consider the location of many present day plants in the light of the above factors we might wonder if a reasoned decision was ever made. Often there were very strong reasons for the location of firms in particular places but very different reasons which keep them there i.e. to go on doing what they are already doing. The pottery industry of North Staffordshire and the steel makers of the Sheffield area have long since exhausted the local supplies of raw materials and the coalfields no longer exert the same pull but the industries persist in their traditional homes.

Just as there may now seem to be no good reasons for a firm remaining in an area there are also examples where it would seem that there were never particularly strong pulls to a locality other than the entrepreneur's own choice. Cadbury in Birmingham, Rowntree in York. Morris in Cowley and Ford in Detroit are all cases of industrialists establishing their businesses in their home towns but the decisions could not have been based on personal preferences alone, the sites would have needed to have satisfied the other requirements though this is not to say that the decisions were based on adequate information or examined in the manner by which Lever chose Port Sunlight.

CHANGES IN LOCATION
As already intimated there are changes occurring which gradually affect the location of industry. Improvements in transport and fuel technology have reduced the pull of the rivers and the coalfields; as a result of these factors together with the capital intensive nature of many of the new industries, firms have been much more free to choose their location. However this has not led to a wider dispersal of industry, rather it has changed its direction back to the Midlands and the South, particularly the London area where the advantages of concentration and access to large urban markets are so apparent.

In addition to these internal factors there has also, in the last forty years, been the influence of Government policy. In Chapter 15 we saw that some areas of the country have suffered from unemployment which is not only above, sometimes considerably above, the national average but also tends to be long term. At the same time that these older centres of labour intensive industries have been declining, other areas have been developing rapidly and intensifying the urban problems of inadequate housing, school and hospital places, traffic congestion and general inflationary pressures resulting from demand far exceeding the supply of factors of production. Government therefore has been faced with the twin problems of trying to relieve highly localised unemployment, producing a less uneven distribution of industry while at the same time not doing anything to affect the prosperity of the more affluent regions.

REGIONAL PLANNING
Until the present century, industry has very largely chosen its own location in accordance with what might be called 'location theory' without any interference by the State. The late nineteenth and early twentieth centuries saw the State becoming more involved in the economic and industrial life of the country with the passing of regulatory legislation e.g. concerning employment of women and children, hours of work, factory conditions, railway and canal tariffs, the establishment of Labour Exchanges, thus it was not surprising nor unprecedented when the State began to intervene to deal with the problem of mass-unemployment which began to develop in the 1920s. Since those early days Government policy to influence the location of industry has been concentrated in three main categories.
1. Restriction on further expansion and building on the present sites.
2. The provision of new factory premises.
3. Financial incentives (whose form has changed many times over the years).
In implementing these measures to deal with the regional problems of unemployment governments have followed two broad lines of approach:
1. Encouraging people in the areas with unemployment problems to move to areas where there are job opportunities and better prospects.

2. Encouraging firms, both new and established ones wanting to expand, to go to the areas badly affected by unemployment.

In general the first of these policies will have limited effects of a positive nature and at the same time will have negative effects. Some workers will be mobile but others will not (see Book One, pages 20–22) consequently such a policy does nothing for those left behind. If substantial numbers did move away then the area would become even more depressed in many ways. Firstly the social capital of the area would be under-utilised; houses, schools, hospitals etc. are not mobile. Secondly total purchasing power in the district would be reduced and the multiplier in reverse would take effect. Thirdly there would be social implications in that it is more likely that the people who move out would be the younger ones and so the area would be left with an aging population which in time would create even greater demand for social services and be less able to participate in the public, social and cultural life of the district. The net effect of this would be to make the area even more depressed for those there and depressing for any-one contemplating moving in. The effect at the receiving end must also be taken into account; if the influx of workers into the more prosperous regions were considerable there would be increased demand for housing, school places etc i.e. the very social capital left behind, subsequently there would need to be increased expenditure to meet this demand particularly in the public sector. The overall effect of such policy could only be a widening of the gap between the haves and have-nots what Mr Harold Wilson described as "the two nations in one".

The alternative policy of encouraging firms to move to the depressed areas has been the one favoured since 1945, recognising the facts that:
1. resources in those areas were under-utilised.
2. mass movement of population is not only expensive but also helps to build up inflationary pressures in areas such as S.E. England.

The ways in which the policy has been implemented reflects recognition of the main problem . . . namely that although many of the old industrial areas were attractive for the industries which located there in the nineteenth century, they were not attractive to the new industries of the inter-war period (many of which were consumer-durable industries rather than raw materials and capital goods industries and so were differently orientated) nor apparently to the growth industries of the post-war period unless some form of Government aid was given to mitigate the unattractiveness. Generally speaking the depressed areas represent higher costs to firms and though this is not the only cause of un-attractiveness, the main Government encouragement has been directed to over-coming the disadvantage of higher costs. In essence the main post-war policy has been based on holding out in front the carrot of financial incentives while pushing from behind with discriminatory granting of Industrial Development Certificates i.e. making it more difficult to obtain an I.D.C. in the prosperous regions and much easier in the assisted areas. The full effect of the post war measures is difficult to assess for while it is possible to calculate the number of new job opportunities created in the regions it is much more difficult to know what additional demand for labour has been created as the result of increased local purchasing power.

SUMMARY OF STATE INTERVENTION

Pre-War Period

In 1928 the Industrial Transference Board was set up to increase the general mobility of unemployed workers in the regions. The main effect of this was that by the outbreak of war some half million people had migrated to the London area. The student should consider the wisdom of this.

In the following year an attempt was made to reduce the unattractiveness of high Rates in the old industrial areas compared with the more prosperous towns e.g. compare Merthyr Tydfil and Bournemouth. The effect was minimal because Rates paid by industrial companies form only a small percentage of total costs.

The first really positive step was the designation in 1934 of the Special Areas ... Central Scotland, South Wales, the N.E. coastal region and West Cumberland ... together with the provision of £2 million. By the second Special Areas Act in 1937 the Government established trading estates, building factories to let at subsidised rents, making loans available at low interest rates and giving some relief from taxation. Bearing in mind the size of the problem, the prevailing economic situation and the scale of public expenditure needed it is not surprising that progress was slow, indeed at the outbreak of the war only 12,000 new jobs had been created in the Special Areas.

The War Period

The War of course ended the horrors of mass unemployment much more quickly because there was an increased demand for labour ... if only as cannon-fodder or to produce the weapons of destruction. The war period however is important for the publication of two significant documents:

1. The Barlow Report on the Distribution of the Industrial Population which suggested that if industry were left to its own devices the distribution would not be satisfactory and so consequently Government would need to intervene to bring about a better regional balance and greater diversification within each region.

2. In "Full Employment in a Free Society" Lord Beveridge not only laid the foundation for all the Parties accepting responsibility for full employment but called for the planned location of industry in order to achieve it.

Post-War Period

As soon as the war ended the Distribution of Industry Act 1945 enlarged the boundaries of the old Special Areas into four Development Areas in which the Board of Trade could acquire land, build factories and make loans and grants to companies moving into the Areas while requiring all businesses to notify the Board of Trade of any proposed development exceeding 10,000 sq. ft. Consequently in the next two years 50% of all approved new factory premises were built in the Development Areas.

The Town & Country Planning Act 1947 underlined the Government's approach to the problem by making Industrial Development Certificates necessary for any building (or extension) over 5,000 sq. ft. while making the Board of Trade responsible for the distribution of industry in the whole country ... not just the Development Areas.

During the 1950s further financial aid and incentives became available and in the early '60s two important steps were taken when:

1. In 1964 the Government recognised that the solution to localised structural unemployment, in part, lay in re-training. Consequently the Industrial Training Act established Government Training Centres where workers could be re-trained at State expense . . . between 1968–70 it was planned to open 17 (11 in the Development Areas).

2. In 1963 a Cabinet Minister was appointed with Special Responsibility for the North East and in 1964 the Department of Economic Affairs established Regional Economic Planning Areas covering the whole country.

The mid-60s witnessed two more important measures:

1. By the Industrial Development Act 1966 the 165 Development Districts which had replaced the old four Development Areas in 1959 were abolished and five Development Areas were designated in which a range of investment, building and training grants were available.

2. In 1967 a Regional Employment Premium was introduced to offset the cost of labour in the Development Areas.

The 1966 Industrial Development Act was a most important development in many ways best shown in the words of the Board of Trade . . . "the purpose of the Act is to provide a more positive system of investment incentives to improve the efficiency of those parts of the economy which contribute most directly to economic growth and the balance of payments to encourage development in those parts of the country where it is most needed." Not only was the Act comprehensive in that it dealt with investment and training grants and IDCs and the other forms of assistance for the assisted areas but by abolishing the larger number of small Development Districts and reverting to the large Development Areas it was a much wider approach to regional planning . . . indeed the emphasis was very much on the *regional* approach in that it was to be the needs of a region which determined the assistance to be given. The most significant step was that whereas previously assistance in the Development Districts had depended on the level of unemployment, in future other criteria were to be used; changes in the population, net migration and the long-run objectives of regional policy both current and anticipated. It was most encouraging to see that possible future developments were to be taken into consideration; it is a great pity that our economic crystal balls had only a short range.

The late 1960s saw an enquiry into some of the effects of Development Area policy . . . which is again relevant to the present situation. The White Paper of June 1967 which introduced Regional Employment Premium said that the Government intended to study the problems of areas which were intermediate between the Development Areas and the more prosperous regions. The subsequent Committee under Sir Joseph Hunt was given the following terms of reference: "to examine in relation to the economic welfare of the country as a whole and the needs of the Development Areas, the situation in other areas where the rate of economic growth gives cause (or may give cause) for concern, and to suggest whether revised policies to influence economic growth in such areas are desirable and, if so, what measures should be adopted." The Hunt Report of April 1969 concentrated on identifying intermediate areas by indicating the factors which give "cause for concern" and suggesting remedial measures. The criteria for such identification were:

1. Sluggish or falling employment.

2. Slow groth in personal incomes.

3. A slow rate of additional industrial and commercial premises . . . reflecting a low level of investment.

4. Significant unemployment.

5. Low or declining proportion of female workers (particularly important in areas where there was a tradition of female employment).

6. Low earnings.

7. Considerable reliance on industries where the demand for labour was falling (or was likely to fall) or at best was growing slowly.

8. Inadequate communications.

9. Decayed environment including derelict land.

10. Serious net outward migration . . . reflecting attitudes to employment and educational opportunities, social activities and the general environment.

The Government had certain qualifications over the Report and considered that resources should be concentrated in the few areas where the need was greatest; "The Government consider that the selection of areas to be given assistance to industry must be governed strictly by criteria of need, especially the level and character of unemployment and numbers of unemployed, the incidence of high net outward migration and the real scope for industrial growth."[1]

Consequently the Secretary of State for Economic Affairs in June 1969 announced the establishment of the following Intermediate Areas.

1. The Yorkshire Coalfields.

2. The Erewash Valley in Derbyshire.

3. Parts of Humberside.

4. The main industrial areas of N.E. Lancashire.

5. The greater part of S.E. Wales.

6. Leith.

7. Plymouth.

The Government announced that aid would take the form of building grants, Government factories and training facilities, increased expenditure on roads, housing and derelict land clearance but it did not accept the Hunt recommendations that IDCs should be available on the same terms as in the Development Areas but did recognise the need for a more flexible policy. The assistance was estimated to cost £20 million and to finance the programme the premium on Selective Employment Tax refunds which went to manufacturing businesses in the Development Areas was to be withdrawn but the payment of the Regional Employment Premium was not to be affected.

The Secretary of State concluded his statement with these words, "The work of the Hunt Committee and our proposals for the new Intermediate Areas . . . mark an important new stage in the development of regional policy. We are pressing on with the recovery of the Development Areas. We are responding flexibly to the changing needs of the different parts of the country. We will continue to serve the interests of every region and of the whole country".

Following the General Election of June 1970 there were changes in Government aid to the regions. On October 27th it was announced that investment incentives would no longer be paid on new investment projects but instead a new system of depreciation allowances was to be introduced to encourage spending on new plant, there was to be a new first year allowance of 60% of the investment expenditure to be written off for the tax purposes and a standard rate of writing down allowances, allowing 25% of the reducing balance to be written off in succeeding years. Unlike the investment grant system, these investment incentives will only benefit companies making good profits since allowances are

1. Peter Shore, Sec. of State for Economic Affairs. House of Commons. 24.4. 69.

written off against tax liabilities. Critics of the system also point out that it mainly benefits capital intensive industries whereas if a quick solution is sought for localised unemployment then help should be given to labour intensive industries. In defence of the new system it is pointed out that it applies also to the service industries in Development Areas but is intended primarily to encourage investment and modernisation and so raise productivity rather than subsidize labour costs . . . also it aims to develop a better infra-structure in the regions.

In 1972 the Conservative Government published a White Paper on Industrial Regional Development which proposed:

1. Tax allowances on investment previously reserved for the Assisted Areas be extended to the whole country. This extension of free depreciation would mean that the differential incentive in favour of the Development Areas would disappear.

2. High initial allowances for buildings and cash grants in the regions to supercede the building and operational grants under the Local Employment Act 1963.

3. Regional development grants towards new buildings and adaptation of existing ones, 22% in the Special Development Areas, Development Areas and Intermediate Areas and 20% in the derelict land clearance areas for two years.

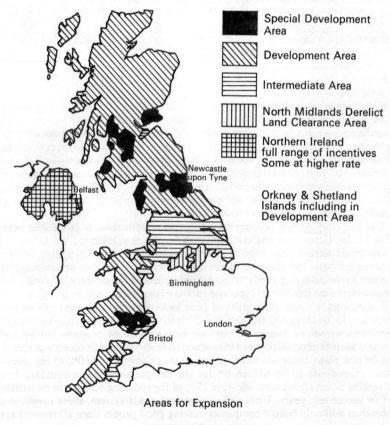

EXHIBIT 19.01

4. Planning applications for industrial development to be considered more quickly.

5. IDCs . . . exemption limit raised to 15,000 sq. ft. in all areas except S.E. Economic Planning Region where it is raised to 10,000 sq. ft. proposed to dispense with IDCs in the Special Development and Development Areas.

6. Office Development Permits . . . no case was made for the removal of these in the South East except that particular account should be taken of the special importance of London as a financial and commercial centre.

The Industry Act (August 1972) gave effect to these proposals and stated that the objectives of the programme for industrial and regional development were to:

1. Promote and sustain faster economic grow.
2. Secure expansion and modernisation of industry.
3. Attack the problem of regional imbalance.
4. Assist Industry to meet the challenge of Europe.

The present designation of the Assisted Areas is shown in Exhibit 19.01 and the present pattern of assistance is summarised in Exhibit 19.02.

Incentives for Industry in the Areas for Expansion

Incentive	Special Development Area	Development Area	Intermediate Area	Northern Ireland
Regional Development Grants				
New machinery, plant and mining works	22%	20%	Nil	}30–40%
Buildings and Works (other than mining)	22%	20%	20%	
Loans	Favourable terms for general capital purposes for projects providing additional employment.			Favourable terms for general purposes
Interest relief grants	Grants towards interest cost for projects providing additional employment (alternative to the above)			As in S.D.As, D.As and I.As
Removal Grants	Up to 80% of certain costs incurred in moving.			Up to 100% of costs
Removal Assistance for Service industries	For offices, research and development, fixed grant of £800 per employee moving up to 50% limit; grants to cover rent of approved premises.			Flexible range of assistance
Govt. factories for rent or sale	Two year rent-free period.			3 year Rent-free plus concessionary rent for further 2 years
Employment Grants	Nil.			Substantial during initial period

Incentive	Special Development Area	Development Area	Intermediate Area	Northern Ireland
Tax Allowances; Machinery and Plant	100% first year allowance on capital expenditure incurred.			
Industrial Buildings	44% of construction costs can be written off in the first year and subsequently 4% p.a. These tax allowances apply to the country as a whole.			
Regional Employment Premiums	Full-time: £3 p.w. for men. £1.50 for women and boys, 95p for girls. Part-time: £1.50 men, 75p women and boys, 47½p girls.		Nil	As in S.D.As and D.As
Training Assistance	Special courses and grants			Free training at G.T.Cs. Grants. of £15 p.w. for men, £12 p.w. for women for training with employers
Help for transferred workers	Free fares, lodging allowances and help with removal expenses.			Full fares, removal costs, lodging allowances for key-workers from outside N. Ireland
Preferential Contracts	Benefits from contracts placed by Government Departments and National Industries.		Nil	As in S.D.As and D.As

Adapted from "Incentives for Industry": Department of Trade and Industry.

EXHIBIT 19.02

EFFECTIVENESS OF REGIONAL POLICY

The previous sections have outlined many of the measures introduced by various Governments over the last 40 years to deal with the problems created by the decline of the old basic industries in the traditional industrial areas and the growth of new industries in different areas . . . too often in the South East quadrant of the country. Critics would say that the policies in general must have failed otherwise we should not still be talking in such forceful terms as the Labour Party's "Labour's Programme for Britain" presented to the 1972 Annual Conference. "We are determined to reduce the unjust and wasteful disparities which exist between different parts of the country . . . and to root out the cancer of regional and structural unemployment, whilst easing the inflationary pressures which result from the present lopsided and unbalanced development." Advocates

226   ECONOMICS FOR BUSINESS STUDIES PART FOUR

of regional planning accept this philosophy in general noting that labour tends to be geographically and occupationally immobile which adds to the problem of regional and structural unemployment. If we were to rely on the normal process of the market mechanism to correct the situation it would take too long and as a nation we cannot allow such resources to remain unemployed for so long. Indeed market forces would tend to accentuate the disparaties between the regions because the pressure would be on labour to move to the more prosperous regions and the subsequent migration would affect service industries and cause further decline making new firms even more reluctant to move in. Macro-policy of aggregate demand management can deal with the problem of mass unemployment but more selective measures have been needed to deal with the localised problem. In brief the objective of regional policy has been to spread the benefits of expansion to all the regions and by removing the constraints on growth to strengthen the national economy.

As said earlier, the emphasis since 1945 has been to move work to the workers; the critics of this kind of location policy say that it pays no attention to the forces which really govern the location of business enterprises. The majority of firms in the U.K. today are not raw material orientated or dependent on a particular power source consequently the chief 'natural' factor would seem to be the availability of external economies. Presumably these are not present in the Development Areas and so Government policy is really asking them to move from lower cost areas of their choice to regions where costs are relatively higher, consequently the Government must offer assistance which is sufficient to offset the disadvantages. The point which some critics now make is that since we are still trying to persuade firms to move to the Assisted Areas, the level of Government assistance has not been sufficient to overcome the loss of the external economies they are enjoying at their present sites.

A further criticism is that the assistance given has not always been based on the creation of new jobs e.g.:
1. The Regional Employment Premium is paid to firms who are already in the Development Areas (not just those moving in) irrespective of whether they increased the number of job opportunities. The critics then re-inforced their arguments by saying that this indiscriminate payment meant that it was also received by employers who are inefficient or who are in declining industries. This amounts to a subsidy for employers who are using too much labour . . . indeed it may cause them to hoard labour particularly skilled labour which generally is in short supply. The R.E.P. is not paid to employers in the service industries which could provide many additional jobs and so reduce the level of localised unemployment. This increased service employment would then as the result of increased purchasing power generate further employment in the area and the consequent uplift of economic activity would make the area generally more attractive to many more firms.
2. One criticism of investment grants . . . as with free depreciation allowances . . . is that they were aimed primarily at helping capital intensive firms. It may be argued that this could be the correct long-term policy in that it encourages efficiency and leads to a better infra-structure in the region but if what is needed is more job opportunities in the short run then aid should be given to labour intensive and service industries. One practical difficulty which has been experienced is that often the new capital intensive industries have not been able to find the right skills in sufficient quantity in the Development Areas, which consequently has had to be imported from other areas. This problem may decline as the

Government Training Centres contribute more to occupational mobility and now that free depreciation allowances have been extended to the service industries.

The Second Report of the Expenditure Committee (Trade & Industry Sub-Committee) on Regional Development Incentives in 1973 commented: "Regional policy has been empiricism run mad, a game of hit and miss, played with more enthusiasm than success. We do not doubt the good intentions, the devotion even, of many who have struggled over the years to relieve the human consequences of regional disparities. We regret that their efforts have not been better sustained by the proper evaluation of the costs and benefits of policies pursued." The emphasis on regional policy has always been on unemployment rates but today a growing number of economists point out that unemployment is not the only barometer of the economic state of a region and are critical of the fact that even recent policies to try to redress the imbalance between the regions are still justified in terms of unemployment rates. It follows therefore that a region must have unemployment rates high enough to attract attention before it qualifies for aid i.e. it must already be depressed; consequently when the assistance is given the recovery is slow.

The Hunt Committee put forward criteria other than unemployment levels in its case for Intermediate Areas; it is now suggested that if the yardsticks of investment, output, incomes, social, educational and environmental conditions were applied then a case could be argued for a new category of assisted area with very real incentives. It must be emphasised that unemployment represents the decline that has taken place . . . there are other indicators which show what is taking place currently in a region and since prevention is better than cure it would seem sense to shift the emphasis of approach to the problem.

The present approach also suffers from the fact that:
1. Economic data takes time to collect and by the time it is analysed current events may have overtaken the analysis.
2. The information is collected on a regional basis which tends to obscure what is happening in sub-regions and in specific industries.

The area of greatest criticism of regional policy has been against the negative policy, the operation of Industrial Development Certificates . . . the means whereby industrialists can be prevented from going where the Board of Trade does not want them to go. That criticism has perhaps been strongest in the West Midlands where if the yardsticks other than unemployment are used it would be seen that it is no longer an area of fast economic growth as stated at the time of the Hunt Report. There is clearly a strong case for an I.D.C. policy to give aid to the less affluent areas, equally clearly help has been given because since 1948 when I.D.C.s were introduced a substantial number of jobs have been transferred to the assisted areas . . . but two questions must now be raised:
1. How long can this transfer of jobs go on without having a deleterious effect on the areas they move from?
2. Considering the help given, why is it that the assisted areas are still problem areas?

Just as we need to consider criteria other than unemployment in assessing the economic health of a region so too I.D.C. policy needs to be more selective. If investment is to be encouraged in areas where the first signs of run-down are apparent . . . and the social structure and environmental decay are good indicators of this . . . then a relaxation of present IDC policy would be an encouraging sign.

In conclusion it must be said that perhaps in the future we should concentrate on a regional policy which gives greater diversity of job opportunities to each region. This is not to ignore the very obvious external economies of scale which result from concentration of an industry but if an area is excessively dependent upon a particular industry, such as motor vehicles or the heavy metal-working trades, and that industry declines then severe localised unemployment will develop and drastic measures will be necessary whereas if present regional planning policies were modified to encourage greater diversification of trades the impact of one industry declining would be lessened.

Part Five
INTERNATIONAL TRADE AND MONETARY ARRANGEMENTS

Chapter Twenty

International Trade and Payments

WHY FOREIGN TRADE TAKES PLACE
International trade which is essentially the exchange of goods and services between individuals and institutions of one country with those of others takes place for a variety of reasons. Mineral resources are not distributed throughout the world in the areas where they are most needed and similarly some countries have been endowed with some resources far in excess of their immediate needs. Likewise variations in climate and geological structure are responsible for either scarcity or plentiful supply of agricultural and animal products. Some goods and services can be obtained from other countries more cheaply than they can be produced at home and such goods will tend to be imported whereas other commodities can be produced cheaper at home than abroad and these will tend to be exported. In addition to this exchange of goods and services, individuals and companies acquire assets in other countries in order to gain some advantage. for example, because they believe their capital will earn a better return or because there are tax advantages. Generally therefore countries import goods in order to supplement home production or because they can be obtained more cheaply elsewhere. Thus even when a country can produce all it needs of a particular product it may still buy from abroad e.g. Britain buys electrical goods from the Netherlands in spite of having a large and varied electrical industry of its own and similarly the Netherlands buys cars and trucks from Britain rather than build up its own reputable vehicle industry. The explanation for this is to be found in the Law of Comparative Costs . . . a theory concerning the advantages of specialisation first developed by David Ricardo from Adam Smith's principles of the international division of labour.

Opportunity Costs and Specialisation
The concept of opportunity cost was discussed in Book One, Page 8; the cost of using time, effort and ability in one particular way is the opportunity foregone of using them in other ways. It is therefore best for the individual to find the highest rewards offered in the labour market to match his abilities and application and to specialise in that pursuit which brings him the best rewards; so it is also for countries. They should employ the factors of production at their disposal in such a way as to obtain the highest returns, bearing in mind the prices ruling in world markets, and be prepared to abandon the production of some commodities if relative prices change, otherwise they will not maximise their welfare.

PRINCIPLE OF COMPARATIVE COSTS
The Law of Comparative Costs may be stated thus: *countries find it profitable to trade with each other when they have different alternative cost ratios and terms of trade are within the limits of their domestic cost ratios.* Thus two countries

having different domestic cost ratios or different relative cost structures with regard to the same two commodities while in a state of pre-trade isolation, can engage in mutually beneficial trade with each other (even if one is more efficient than the other in the production of both commodities). This is achieved by exporting the commodity in which its comparative advantage is greatest or comparative disadvantage is least and importing that in which its comparative advantage is least or comparative disadvantage is greatest. This trade to be mutually beneficial must be conducted on such terms of trade that the ratio of import to export prices is better than the pre-trade domestic cost ratios of either country.

Imagine two countries Alphium and Omegaria each devoting x factors of production to either the production of iron-ore or sugar with the following alternatives. Alphium can produce either 100 units of iron ore or 50 units of sugar while Omegaria can produce 50 units of iron-ore or 100 units of sugar. Without specialisation total production would be as follows if both countries devoted x factors to iron-ore and x factors to sugar production:

	Units of iron-ore	Units of sugar
Alphium	100	50
Omegaria	50	100
	150	150

If each country now specialises i.e. instead of devoting x factors to iron-ore and x factors to sugar it uses $2x$ in the production of the commodity for which it has the comparative advantage, total production will be:

	Units of iron-ore	Units of sugar
Alphium	200	0
Omegaria	0	200
	200	200

By specialisation there is therefore an increased output of 50 units of each commodity. If therefore terms of trade were arranged whereby 60 units of iron-ore were exchanged for 60 units of sugar the position would be:

	Units of iron-ore	Units of sugar
Alphium	140	60
Omegaria	60	140
	200	200

Consequently as a result of the exchange each country will have a bigger supply of each commodity. International trade therefore benefits both countries.

Even if Alphium can produce both commodities more cheaply than Omegaria it could still be advantageous to both countries to specialise. Suppose Alphium, for a given cost of production, can produce 100 units of iron-ore or 100 units

of sugar while Omegaria for the same costs can produce 40 units of iron-ore or 80 units of sugar; then without any specialisation the position would be:

	Units of iron-ore	Units of sugar
Alphium	100	100
Omegaria	40	80
	140	180

If Alphium were to specialise in iron-ore production (in which its comparative advantage is greatest) but continued to produce some sugar while Omegaria specialises in sugar (in which its comparative disadvantage is least), total production would be:

	Units of iron-ore	Units of sugar
Alphium	160	40
Omegaria	0	160
	160	200

As the result of specialisation there is an increase in total production of both commodities, an extra output of 20 units of iron-ore and 20 units of sugar. If terms of trade can now be arranged within the limits of their alternative cost ratios both countries will benefit. Suppose Alphium exchanges 50 units of iron-ore for 70 units of sugar the position will be :

	Units of iron-ore	Units of sugar
Alphium	110	110
Omegaria	50	90
	160	200

Each country will have 10 extra units of each commodity than it would have if there were no specialisation and no international trade.

If the world were as simple and uncomplicated as the previous model then presumably international trade would be based solely on the principles of comparative costs and countries would specialise, however the world is not the simple model and there are many reasons preventing complete specialisation.

1. Firstly there are more than two countries in the world indulging in simply bi-lateral trade. It is true that many countries which could produce a certain commodity prefer to import it from others having a comparative advantage (e.g. Britain could still produce tin but at the moment Malaysia has a comparative advantage . . . but if the price of Malaysian tin were to rise it could well be advantageous to stop importing it and re-open the Cornish tin mines) . . . but equally it is true that many countries will not specialise even when it is economically advantageous to do so. One reason for this is the strategic considerations; the law of comparative costs implies that Britain should have abandoned farming and concentrated on certain manufacturing trades but this would have meant

being totally dependent on foreign supplies of food – and the near disasters Britain faced when the U-boat campaigns were at their height in 1917 and 1942–3 demonstrated the folly of such a policy.[1]

Similarly the developing countries have industries, particularly service industries, solely for prestige reasons, for example they may think that having a National Airways Company will put them into the big league whereas in reality they could obtain all the airline service they need (and better service) from the established international companies.

2. The Law presumes that all factors of production are equally efficient whereas in reality they clearly will not be e.g. some of the men moved from iron-ore production to sugar production may be as efficient as the original sugar workers but as the movement continues the workers will be less efficient and some of them will not want to be sugar workers.

3. Complete specialisation may be prevented by limited market demand. An individual worker may have a particular talent and aptitude for a certain job and would prefer to spend all his time doing it, but if the market demand for his services is insufficient for him to make a satisfactory living he will have to modify his inclination and spend part of his time doing alternative work. E.g. an artist may prefer to spend all his hours "creating masterpieces" but if they do not attract customers he may have to spend some of his time teaching drawing even though he may detest doing so. Similarly there is no point in a country using scarce factors to produce surplus output which no-one wants.

4. The Law does not take into account the additional costs of transport associated with specialisation, thus in reality the limits for establishing the terms of trade are more confined than just the domestic cost ratios. Transport costs must be added to the domestic cost ratios in deciding whether specialisation and trade is to be mutually beneficial.

5. The law assumes that trade takes place without any artificial barriers. In practice there is a jungle of tariffs, quota systems and import levies all impeding the full implementation of the competitive effects of free trade.

Specialisation therefore increases total output, international trade raises the standard of living of countries which engage in it. It has been suggested that if Britain did not participate in world trade the standard of living of its people would fall back to that of early medieval times. (The student should quickly draw up a list of commodities which are entirely imported . . . and contemplate what his standard of living would be like without them.)

TERMS OF TRADE

The second part of the Law of Comparative Costs stated that trade would take place if the terms of trade were within the limits of the domestic cost ratios; it is therefore important to know what is meant by the Terms of Trade and to understand the implications of movements in them. The terms of trade of a country is the relationship between the prices paid for its exports and those paid for its imports; it does not refer to the volume of imports and exports. Unfortunately the commodities traded have different units of measurement; vehicles are single units, sugar is in tons, oil is in barrels thus it is difficult to compare. Even if we

1. Between the wars Britain allowed the watch and clock making trade to run down because it was possible to import cheaper clock movements from Germany and Switzerland, consequently when war broke out in 1939 there was a shortage of skilled micro-precision engineers needed to make bomb sights, navigational aids etc, for the armed forces. After 1945 the Government gave considerable aid to re-establishing the watch making industry.

know the average prices of imports and exports it is difficult to judge the effect on the economy . . . but if we know how these relative prices have moved over a period then we can say whether the terms of trade have improved or deteriorated. If the terms of trade move in favour of a particular country it implies that export prices have become relatively higher compared with import prices. This may be the result of a rise in the prices of the country's exports or because of a fall in the prices of the commodities imported. In either case the effect may be to increase the country's ability to import if more foreign exchange becomes available from export revenue . . . consequently the same volume of imports could be paid for with a smaller volume of exports or the same amount of exports could pay for a larger quantity of imports. In the first case it means that less domestic production will need to be exported and so is available for home consumption and in the second case a greater volume of imports will be available. In both cases the standard of living will rise at least in the short run . . . however there are other considerations. If the export prices of Alphium rise then ultimately fewer of its exports will be purchased because (a) demand for exports tends to be elastic (b) if Omegaria is obtaining lower prices for the goods it produces its earnings are reduced and so its ability to purchase from Alphium. Meanwhile if import prices for Alphium remain the same then a greater volume of imports can result so that although the terms of trade have moved in Alphium's favour it may suffer from an adverse balance of trade which will lead its government to impose restrictions to slow down the rate of consumer spending.

One method to express the terms of trade is to use an index system taking a base year and expressing the average prices of exports and imports as 100. Consequently as prices change so will the index numbers and movements in the terms of trade can be expressed by using the formula:

$$\frac{\text{Index of export prices}}{\text{Index of import prices}} \times 100 = \text{Terms of Trade}$$

Thus if the average price of exports rise by 7% and import prices by 3% then the terms of trade would be:

$$\frac{107}{103} \times 100 = 104$$

This means that the country's exports would exchange for approximately 4% more imports and so the country would be better off. If therefore comparison is made with the base year a figure above 100 means that the terms of trade has improved and if less than 100 they have worsened.

In a previous paragraph it was said that an improvement in the terms of trade could lead to a worsening of the balance of trade eventually but this result is not inevitable. For example the rise in export prices may not be the result of a rise in domestic costs but because the overseas demand for these goods has increased, in which case the country gains in two ways, a greater quantity of exports and at higher prices. This is the way in which the balance of trade of primary producers improves following an increase in world demand for raw materials. Conversely if there is a general depression in world trade the prices of primary products fall rapidly whereas those of the manufactured goods of the secondary producers tend to hold steady. (The reason for this is that the supply of raw materials is basically inelastic and there is little that producers can do to adjust in the short

run whereas the supply of manufactured goods is more elastic and manufacturers can make adjustments i.e. they can cut back on output to meet the new demand situation and so prevent prices from tumbling.) Consequently for a country like the U.K. importing very large quantities of raw materials and exporting manufactured goods, a general falling off in the level of world trade means that the terms of trade will move in its favour but since all economic activity is depressed the volume of U.K. exports will also fall and it is for this reason that the balance of trade will probably worsen . . . it will depend on the degree by which the demand for the manufactured goods declines.

Some countries may be able to improve their terms of trade by deliberate action. If a country is in the position of being a monopoly supplier then clearly like any other monopolist it is in a position to influence price. However the result of this action will undoubtedly spark off the very reactions a monopolist would wish to avoid . . . namely the customers will look for a substitute and/or other producers will enter the market. For example the Brazilian action of restricting the production of coffee (or the deliberate destruction of "surplus" production) undoubtedly improved the terms of trade for Brazil in the short run but it encouraged the growing of coffee in other parts of the world so that world output increased.

For a country like the U.K. which is a very large trading country the terms of trade are extremely important. Over the years the standard of living of the so-called developing countries has been rising . . . even if slowly; this together with the increase in world population and the volume of world trade has resulted in an upward movement of the prices of raw materials imported by the U.K. Simultaneously many countries have increased the level of their industrialisation, not necessarily in the field of sophisticated hardware but certainly in the general run of manufactured goods and consequently there has been more competition for U.K. exports. It is difficult to make accurate forecasts but the implications are obvious if the U.K. found what the general price level of its imports continued to rise and the volume of its exports fell.

Exhibit 20.01 shows the movements in the terms of trade for the U.K. between 1955 and 1963 using the formula already explained. Exhibit 200.2 shows the movements in the terms of trade 1964–73 in graphical form.

U.K. TERMS OF TRADE 1955–63

Year	Index of Exports	Index of Imports	Terms of Trade
1955	92	108	85
1956	95	110	86
1957	100	111	90
1958	99	103	96
1959	98	102	96
1960	100	102	98
1961	100	100	100
1962	101	99	102
1963	104	103	101

EXHIBIT 20.01

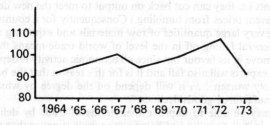

Source : Treasury Information Division

EXHIBIT 20.02

Factors operating against free trade

We have already seen that in theory the whole world would benefit if countries specialised their production in accordance with the law of comparative costs but we have seen also why in practice countries do not specialise completely. Similarly if the full advantages of international trade are to be enjoyed in terms of increased welfare then there should also be free movement of goods between countries. Though the law of comparative costs is still a valid explanation of why international trade takes place its full implementation would create implications which do not fit in with the politics of the twentieth century either nationally or internationally. Consequently the benefits of international trade involving the free movements of goods have had, in part, to be sacrificed to other ends. Economic policies can be recommended by economists but they have to be implemented by politicians who must also be mindful of the political, strategic and social consequences of their actions. The following may be regarded as the main reasons for the existence of import duties and quota systems.

1. To Raise Revenue. An obvious reason for the imposition of a tax is the revenue it brings in for the Government. However if the tax is to yield a worthwhile sum it cannot at the same time be a protectionist duty, i.e. if it were to discourage the flow of imports then the revenue yield would be cut, thus although the tax was imposed primarily for revenue the ultimate higher price would most likely lead to a reduction in demand.[1]

2. Protection of Home Industries.
a) Infant industries. Protection is often sought to protect newly established industries in the early stages of their development from foreign competition. There may be very good reasons why such industries should be protected at their outset, unfortunately there is a tendency that although such firms grow older they do not necessarily mature i.e. there is not the same urgency to be as efficient as possible because the tariff protects them from the cold winds of competition.
b) Established industries. The industry may no longer be in the infant stage and yet the Government regards the industry as being worthy of protection. This may be because the continued existence of the industry is important strategically or it

1. Similarly Governments have to proceed very warily if they contemplate imposing a levy on exports; in the case of Britain the importance of doing nothing to restrict the volume of exports was recognised as early as 1828 when Huskisson abolished duties on exports. Only when the demand for the commodity is extremely inelastic can a country really contemplate an export tax . . . as India did in 1947 with the export of tea.

may be because the workers in that industry form an important political bloc and so expect special treatment as do the French viniculturists.

3. To prevent unfair competition and to protect the standard of living

Goods are sometimes sold abroad at a price lower than on the home market, this may be an instance of discriminating monopoly or because the exporter is being subsidized. It may be that people in the importing country receive some price benefit in the short run as the result of the *dumping* but if eventually the exporter establishes himself in a monopoly position and begins to exploit the situation then obviously the long run result will be detrimental to them.

The argument that the livelihoods of workers in the importing countries must be protected from the competition of cheap foreign goods produced by sweated labour is very involved.

(a) It is understandable why the exporting country is concentrating on the manufacture of a certain product if its greatest comparative advantage is that it has an abundance of cheap labour.

(b) It does not necessarily follow that cheap labour in the sense of low wage rates means low labour costs . . . what has to be examined is the wage cost per unit of output. Thus it can be (indeed is) in one country wage rates can be high but because of efficiency the level of productivity ensures that labour costs per unit is low, whereas in another country although wage rates are low productivity is also low and so labour costs per unit of output are not cheap.

(c) If a tax is levied against the goods of a poor country with low labour rates it restricts the exports of that country and therefore its earnings . . . consequently its ability to buy the products of the richer country. There is another possible consequence namely that the poor country, finding the doors to its exports have been partly closed by the richer country, may make a more determined effort to win other markets (which may be the outlets for the products of the richer country). In other words the country imposing the tariff can only protect its home market against *cheap* labour, its actions will not apply to *third markets*.

(d) If cheap foreign goods do flood into a country and consequently there is such a falling off in demand for home produced goods that factories have to close down then there will be a considerable rise in unemployment. The advocates of free trade say that we should sympathise with those workers who lose their jobs but if an industry is declining and unemployment rising because another country can produce more cheaply, then we should not prop up the lame duck but divert labour and resources to those industries in which the country can compete effectively. Oh that it were so easy! Firstly all political parties have an obligation to maintain a high level of employment, secondly the factors of production tend to be immobile and thirdly what would be the point of having cheap foreign imports if mass unemployment meant that because of reduced income hundred of thousands of workers and their families could not afford them.

At this point the student could well examine the state of the British car industry and market in the light of foreign competition. Many trade union leaders have accused Japanese firms of indiscriminate dumping on the British markets and have warned that unless the Government acts to limit these imports the jobs of many of the million workers in the car industry and component firms would be at risk. Although the Japanese are only part of the overseas challenge to the British industry Exhibit 20.03 shows why they have been singled out for special consideration.

BRITISH NEW CAR MARKET 1969–74

	1969	1970	1971	1972	1973	1974
All new registrations in U.K.	965,410	1,076,865	1,285,661	1,637,866	1,661,639	1,268,655
All imports	100,734	153,801	247,883	385,057	455,802	353,931
Japanese imports	3,867	4,532	13,013	52,484	92,453	84,698
Percentages						
Imports of all new cars	10·0	14·2	19·3	23·5	27·4	27·9
Japanese of all imports	3·8	3·3	8·8	8·1	20·1	24·0
Japanese of all new cars	0·4	0·4	1·0	3·2	5·6	6·9

EXHIBIT 20.03

In the early 1970s the Conservative government relaxed credit restrictions to encourage car sales but nothing was done to ensure that the industry had the capacity to meet the increased home demand as well as maintain the export drive . . . consequently the door was opened wider for foreign manufacturers. Thus while between 1969 and 1973 the market for new cars grew to 1.6 million imports grew at a very much faster rate, rising from a tenth to a quarter of all new car sales. Interest concentrates on the Japanese not only because Japan alone accounts for a quarter of all foreign imported cars but also because the Japanese assault on the British market clearly follows the measures taken by the American Government to limit the sale of Japanese cars in the U.S.A. and the imposition of quota restrictions by the Italian Government to protect their own car industry. Trade must be a two-way arrangement but at the moment it is virtually one-way only . . . in 1974 British manufacturers managed to sell 1,800 cars only in Japan. This was not because of any quotas imposed by the Japanese or even high tariff walls (cf. British tariff on Japanese cars of 11% – Japanese tariff on imported cars 6.4%) . . . there are other ways of giving protection . . . what the Japanese have done is to set up a close knit link-up between manufacturers and distributors supported by the Government which has frozen out the foreign competition.

4. Political reasons. For purely political reasons one country may place a complete embargo on trade with another or may prohibit trade in a particular commodity because of strategic considerations. Consequently trade or more precisely non-trade becomes one of the weapons used in the battle of the ideologies . . . note the American attitude towards trade with mainland China or with Cuba because of its dread of Communism.

5. Balance of Payments. Sometimes it is necessary to resort to import restrictions as one means of correcting an adverse balance of payments and the easiest way to reduce the demand for imported goods is to impose a tariff which will eventually make those commodities more expensive. In the autumn of 1964 such was the severity of the deficit on the U.K. Current Balance that the Government imposed a 15% import surcharge on manufactured goods. The reasons for the imposition were explained to our trading partners particularly the fellow members of E.F.T.A. To be effective such a tax must adversely affect the position of exporters, hence the reason for the explanation and the assurance the the surcharge would be removed as soon as possible . . . indeed the Government did just that, first reducing it to 10% and then in November 1966 it was abolished completely.

Imported raw materials and foodstuffs were not included in the Order because demand for them was obviously inelastic so that not only would domestic consumers have had to pay higher prices but the falling off in demand would have been negligible.

As an alternative to tariffs a quota system can be adopted either in the form of a maximum number or a maximum expenditure. The objection to this form of control is that it is complicated because of the issue and checking of licences and this requires an additional administrative machinery.

Finally the Government can restrict the amount of imports by alterations in the exchange control regulations i.e. restrict the amount of foreign currencies for firms to spend abroad.

Conclusion. To restate the Law of Comparative Costs . . . if countries specialise in producing that in which their comparative advantage is greatest (or comparative disadvantage is least) and then arranging mutually beneficial terms of trade the general standard of living must rise; it therefore follows that if countries cannot so specialise and trade freely then the standard of living must suffer. However, as shown, there are political and social implications as well as other kinds of economic considerations and in the last analysis the politicians must decide on how *free* trade can be and decide on the trade policy which affords the greatest advantages.

EXPANSION OF WORLD TRADE

In spite of all the restrictions placed in the path of international trade the outstanding feature since 1945 has been the rapid growth of world trade, particularly between the industrialised countries. Between 1945–65 world trade grew by $120 billion to $165 billion; between 1955–65 trade in the non-communist world grew at a rate of 7·6% per annum.

The traditional view of trade based on the Law of Comparative Costs was exchange between countries using land and those using labour . . . indeed Ricardo's classic example was Portugal's wine for England's cloth. The argument of the 19th century economists was that labour produced manufactured goods exchanged for food and raw materials but as population grew and land became more scarce the basis for trade would decline. The argument assumed that comparative costs were determined by natural advantages so that countries with few such advantages would concentrate on using their labour to best advantage and differences in comparative costs would be powerful incentives to engage in trade. A great deal of world trade still follows this classical pattern and it is because many of the primary producers believe that the system is not advantageous to them that they wish to end their reliance on the production of such commodities and to become more industrialised. If as world population grows and the demand for food and raw materials increases causing a rise in the price of Britain's primary imports while simultaneously the spread of industrialisation meant a growth in the total output of secondary products so that Britain found it more difficult to sell her manufactured goods then the terms of trade could turn against Britain and the future could be gloomy. It is difficult to forecast with any accuracy what the future holds in store, suffice to say that this situation could happen and then to note that in the last twenty years the terms of trade have in fact improved for the industrial countries rather than worsened. Three contributing factors to this should be noted:—

1. The greatest increase in population has been in the poor countries conse-

quently there has not been a correspondingly large increase in demand for primary products and thus there has been sufficient to meet the needs of the richer countries.

2. Food production in the richer countries has itself increased while their population growth has been slower thus they have not needed to increase their imports significantly.

3. The most significant expansion in world trade has been between the manufacturing countries themselves. In 1928 this type of trade accounted for less than 40% of the world total but by 1966 it had reached almost 60%. Between 1953–64 world exports of manufactured goods rose by 228% compared with only 84% for other products . . . trade in manufactured goods accounted for two-thirds of the total growth in world trade during the period. Indeed the balance was shifting more in favour of the industrial countries since in 1965 the trade between industrial countries made up a larger share of total world trade than it did in 1955 and the exports of the primary producers declined in proportion.

Tariff Policies

The rapid growth of world trade in the post war period is of course closely connected with the growth in output and income levels in the industrial countries . . . but growth in trade in manufactured goods between North America, W. Europe, and Japan is significant because it does not fit the classical explanation of international exchange furthermore there is evidence that the domestic cost structures of the industrial countries are becoming more and more similar so that the reasons for trade between them would seem to be decreasing rather than increasing. Three developments should be noted in this context:

1. Wage levels between different countries still vary but the gap has narrowed in the last twenty years . . . wage levels in low rate countries have increased more rapidly than in high rate ones.

2. Differences in the cost of borrowing international capital have narrowed.

3. Technical skills have been more widely available as labour has become more internationally mobile.

There have however been other developments working contrary to this, the most obvious of which have been:

1. The gradual lowering of the tariff barriers which handicapped world trade during the 1930s.

2. The re-building of the European economies after the war and increase of industrial capacity.

Although immediately after the war there was a need to have direct controls on trade and payments the members of O.E.E.C. (Organisation for European Economic Co-operation established 1948) quickly saw that the restoration of trade and rapid recovery were indisolubly bound together and they agreed to remove quantitative restrictions on at least 50% of trade between members by the end of 1949 rising to 75% by 1951. By 1961 when O.E.E.C. was transformed into O.E.C.D. (Organisation for Economic Co-operation and Development) 94% of intra European trade had been liberated from such restrictions. Similar improvements took place in trade with N. America whereas in 1953 only 11% of total imports for the dollar area were free from restrictions of this kind the figure had risen to 89% by 1961.

While European countries were engaged in their improvements, G.A.T.T. (General Agreement on Tariffs and Trade) was pursuing the liberalisation of world trade and seeking to eliminate quantitative restrictions. From 1947 to the

so-called Kennedy Round there were six international sessions of conferences aimed at reducing tariffs, the first of these secured substantial reductions, the Dillon Round 1961–2 achieved further cuts of 20% on a range of industrial goods, agreed on cuts averaging 30–40% spread over a 5 year period. It was difficult to predict what effects these reductions would have but clearly the lowering of tariff barriers has contributed to the growth of world trade especially among the industrial countries and even the countries which did not take part in the negotiations have benefited under the most favoured nation clause.

Finally, the post war period has seen the creation of a number of trading blocs throughout the world . . . most significant of which for Europe is the European Economic Community (E.E.C.) established in 1957 by the Treaty of Rome and the European Free Trade Association (E.F.T.A.) in 1959 formed by the signatories to the *Convention of Stockholm*. With regard to trade the E.E.C. members were committed to the gradual removal of barriers between members and certainly all orthodox barriers had been removed by mid 1968, similarly the EFTA countries had fully established conditions of free trade in industrial goods by the end of 1966. Trade between members of both groups grew at a rate of about 10% p.a. during the 1960s though imports from non-members grew at a slower rate.

Transport costs

Even more important than tariff barriers for many products are the costs of transport therefore it is equally important to examine what has happened to them in the post-war period. There have been three significant factors regarding freight rates by sea.

1. They have not been affected by inflation to the same degree as other prices.
2. The emphasis of world trade has been moving from low value to high value products (as explained in Chapter 19 transport costs have to be seen in the light of the value of the freight carried).
3. There have been important technical developments . . . bulk carriers, containerisation and better port facilities mean that it is now possible to deal with much greater loads with the resultant economies.

Consequently it can be said that transport costs have fallen relative to the value of the goods carried.

Changes in outlook

It must also be said that businessmen have reacted to changes in tariff policies and transport costs and have become more aggressive in seeking outlets for trade. This has not only been by the large companies, particularly the multinationals, but by smaller ones too who have seized the greater opportunities for international trade.

CHANGES IN THE PATTERN OF U.K. TRADE

Britain has shared in the general expansion of world trade though it has not maintained the proportion of world exports it once enjoyed. A significant development has been the way in which the pattern of trade has changed over the years. Britain has had to deal with many problems concerning international trade and payments and more difficult than the dilemma facing her now of whether or not to accept fully the European idea. At the time the European Economic Community was formed Britain would have joined a free trade area but the Six were not looking for such a loose organisation thus Britain did not

join but became instead a founder member of EFTA. It is interesting to note the effect which membership of EFTA had on Britain's trade. From the beginning the U.K. dominated EFTA and certainly between 1959 and 1968 her exports to the other member countries grew at 7·3% p.a. while her imports from them increased by 8·6% p.a. but even more significant is the simultaneous growth of Britain's trade with the EEC countries. Exports to EEC grew by 8·1 % and imports by 10·1% p.a. Taking W. Europe as a whole it is the biggest customer for British goods and the largest supplier of British imports as the diagrams in Exhibit 20·04 show.

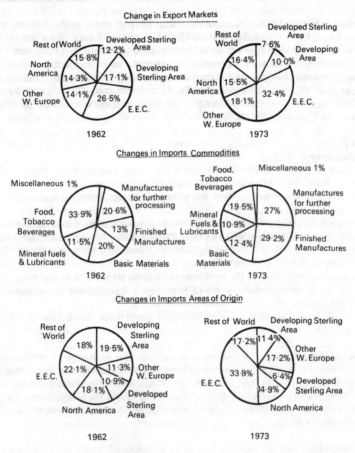

Source : Treasury Information Division

EXHIBIT 20.04

In 1973 more than 50% of all the goods sold by Britain abroad went to W. Europe and though the overall increase of sales of 34% was spread over all the European countries the diagrams show the growing importance of EEC as an outlet for British exports. This growth of sales to Europe has been at the expense of exports

to the Sterling Area outside Europe (even though they increased in 1973 by 18%
over the 1972 level) and it is significant that the N. American share of British
exports rose by only 1·2% over the period 1962–73.

On the import side a similar picture is developing in that the U.K. now takes
50% of all its imports from W. Europe whereas in 1962 the figure was only 33%
and only 28% in 1957. The increase in the share during the period demonstrates
the growing importance of manufactured and semi-manufactured goods in our
import trade. Not only has the percentage of the total increased but the increase
in trade with W. Europe has been at the expense of N. America and the Sterling
Area.

During the period 1962–73 there have also been changes in the type of commodity imported . . . though Exhibit 20.04 does not reflect the effect of the
sudden and dramatic increase in oil prices during 1973–4. The emphasis was
clearly on imports to meet the needs of industry but it is significant that raw
materials, chemicals and semi-finished goods for further processing continued to
increase their share at the expense of foods and tobacco. These latter items in
1973 accounted for slightly under 20% of total imports whereas in 1962 they
had been 34% and in 1957 36%.

Over the period there has been therefore a move away from import of primary
goods to finished and semi-finished products which is an interesting development
in our economic growth.

BALANCE OF PAYMENTS STATEMENT

All exchange of goods and services has to be paid for . . . international trade is no
exception it is simply that trading by a country is obviously more complex than
that by an individual company and payment is more complicated because many
different currencies are involved and not all of them are acceptable internationally
(i.e. there is no demand for them outside their own frontiers). How these difficulties are overcome and how a country finally balances the inflow and outflow
of payments is dealt with in the next chapter, at this stage we shall simply look at
the constituent parts of the Balance of Payments statement and the implications
of any imbalance.

In simple terms the trading accounts of any country are divided into a Current
Account which deals with items settled in the current accounting period and the
Capital Account which includes those items of revenue and expenditure payable
over a period of years. Current trading includes the exchange of merchandise
and also services and so that we can judge the trends and relative importance of
each it is customary to divide the Current Account into *visible* and *invisible*
items. The former comprises the *Balance of Trade* which together with the
invisibles makes up the Current Account or Current Balance. We could therefore
devise a simple Balance of Payments Statement for Alphium as shown on page
243.

On this statement Alphium would have a deficit of 300M on its·balance of
trade but a surplus of 400M on its invisible trade, thus on current account it
would have a surplus of 100M. On the capital account foreign investment exceeded investment by Alphians abroad by 200M thus its overall balance of
payments (total receipts from exports of goods and services and investment all
net of payments) would be 300M. Consequently although Alphium had an
adverse *balance of trade* she would have a favourable overall balance of payments.

It is most important to realize that the balance of trade is only part of the story
and it is quite possible for a country to have a persistently adverse balance of

trade without running into any difficulties provided the surplus on "invisibles" is more than sufficient to cover the "visible "deficit. This is most important in the case of the U.K.; in the twenty five years 1946–70 the balance of trade was in deficit for 22 of those years and yet because of the invisible earnings the Current Balance was in deficit only 11 times and two of those years, 1946 and 1947 were exceptional years in the immediate post war period.

VISIBLE ACCOUNT

The visible items which make up the Balance of Trade are self explanatory, a country such as Britain must import a very large proportion of the food and raw materials it consumes and consequently must export manufactured goods to help to pay for them. Visible trade forms the largest part of the U.K.'s current transactions with the rest of the world. Historically there has usually been a deficit on this trade . . . the only surplus in recent years was in 1971. The figures for this trade are published monthly in detail in the *Overseas Trade Statistics of the U.K.* compiled from returns made to H.M. Customs and Excise by importers and exporters.

The figures published are calculated on:

    a) recorded value or overseas trade statistics basis.

BALANCE OF PAYMENTS FOR ALPHIUM

CURRENT ACCOUNT

Balance of Trade

Receipts		Payments	
Exports & re-export of goods	1000M	Import of goods	1300M

Invisibles

Shipping & Aviation		Shipping & Aviation	
Banking		Banking	
Insurance & financial services	900M	Insurance & financial services	500M
Interest ,Dividends, Profits		Interest, Dividends, Profits	
Travel & Tourism		Travel & Tourism	
	1900M		1800M

CAPITAL ACCOUNT

Investment by foreign		Investment by Alphian	
Companies and individuals		Companies and individuals	
in Alphium	500M	overseas	300M
		Inflow of Gold and Foreign	
		Currencies to finance the	
		imbalance on:	300M
		Current A/C 100M	
		Capital A/C 200M	
	2400M		2400M

b) overseas trade statistics seasonally adjusted.

c) balance of payments basis seasonally adjused.

The latter indicates to the Government whether action is needed to correct the balance.

U.K. VISIBLE & INVISIBLE TRADE 1945–70 (£M)

	1946	1947	1948	1949	1950	1951	1952	1953
Visible Trade	−103	−361	−151	−137	−51	−689	−279	−244
Invisible Trade	−127	−20	+177	+136	+358	+320	+442	+389
Current Balance	−230	−381	+26	−1	+307	−369	+163	+145

	1954	1955	1956	1957	1958	1959	1960	1961
Visible Trade	−204	−313	+53	−29	+29	−117	−406	−152
Invisible Trade	+321	+158	+155	+262	+315	+260	+141	+148
Current Balance	+117	−155	+208	+233	+344	+143	−265	−4

	1962	1963	1964	1965	1966	1967	1968	1969	1970
Visible Trade	−102	−80	−519	−237	−73	−552	−643	−141	+3
Invisible Trade	+214	+194	+124	+160	+116	+240	+324	+557	+576
Current Balance	+112	+114	−395	−77	+43	−312	−319	+416	+579

EXHIBIT 20.05

Overseas Trade statistics basis

The monthly figures relate to documents received during the calendar month to which they refer; export documents are presented to Customs & Excise after shipment and then there is a period of grace of 14 days which can be extended whereas importers must present their papers before they receive customs clearance to remove the goods. Because of this whereas the figures for imports correspond closely with those goods actually passing through during the period, the export goods covered are those passing through in the month ending halfway through the calendar month.

Overseas statistics basis seasonally adjusted

The quantities and values involved are those declared by exporters and importers; the export values are declared f.o.b. (free on board) i.e. they represent all the costs involved for the foreign buyer right up to the arrival on board the ship carrying the goods overseas . . . however imports are declared on a c.i.f. basis (i.e. cost, insurance, freight). Consequently by including c.i.f. in the entry-to-

Britain price the value of imports is inflated in comparison to exports and this is why the recorded values are later adjusted to obtain figures on which a better assessment of the balance of payments position can be made. Seasonal adjustments are made to level out the fluctuations in trade resulting from climatic factors, effects of industrial disputes or the effects of holidays. Thus at the same time that it publishes the monthly figures the Department of Trade also shows the trend by averaging the figures over the last three months.

Balance of Payments basis seasonally adjusted

As already shewn, adjustments are necessary to convert the trade statistics to a balance of payments basis . . . principally this is the removal of the insurance and freight element from import values which in 1973 for example accounted for a monthly deduction of £114M from the £1,321M recorded value. Similar adjustments have to be made for exports, Exhibit 20.06 shows the comparison of the recorded value of exports 1972 to mid 1974 with the balance of payments seasonally adjusted figures.

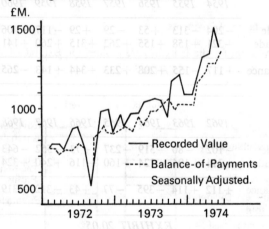

Source : Treasury Information Division.

Comparison of Recorded Value &
Balance-of-Payments
Seasonally Adjusted Exports
EXHIBIT 20.06

INVISIBLE ACCOUNT

Exhibit 20.04 showed the importance of the changing pattern of the visible trade over the period 1962–73. What must now be examined in more detail is the importance and composition of the invisible trade. Exhibit 20.05 demonstrated the importance of the total invisible trade in relation to the visible trade in arriving at the Current Balance; Exhibit 20.07 shows the relative importance of the different invisible items 1959–70.

U.K. INVISIBLE TRADE 1959–1970 (£m)

	1959			1970		
	Credit	Debit	Net	Credit	Debit	Net
Govt. Services	43	270	−227	51	537	−486
Shipping	620	606	+ 14	1,371	1,466	− 95
Civil Aviation	82	64	+ 8	316	279	+ 37
Travel & Tourism	143	164	− 21	433	385	+ 48
Financial & other services	440	224	+216	1,126	521	+605
Interest, Dividends, Profits	656	396	+260	1,381	869	+512
Private Transfers	100	100	—	182	227	− 45
	2,084	1,824	+260	4,860	4,284	+576

Source: U.K. Balance of Payments.

The Invisible Account for the U.K. in 1973 is shown in Exhibit 20.08.

EXHIBIT 20.07

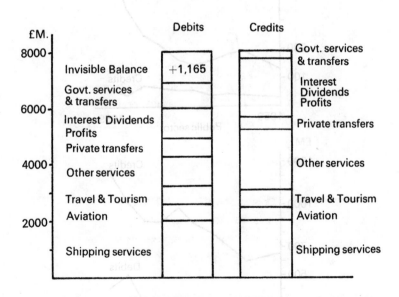

U.K. Invisible Account 1973

EXHIBIT 20.08

Examination of the constituent items show that there have been interesting developments over the years.

Shipping

Gone are the days when Britain had the world's largest mercantile marine which made very large contributions to our total earnings. Even in the inter-war period when trade was depressed this income was still a significant one but in the post-war period other countries have developed merchant fleets, very often heavily subsidized, which together with the growth of fleets sailing under flags of convenience means that the share of world trade carried in British vessels has declined. The net position has fluctuated throughout the '60s from a deficit of £39 to a surplus of £60M and as seen in Exhibit 20·07 the deficit in 1970 was £95M.

Aviation

This is becoming an increasingly more important contributor to the U.K. invisible earnings particularly as specialist aircraft and handling equipment are

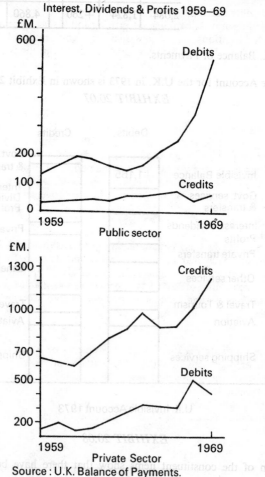

Interest, Dividends & Profits 1959–69

Public sector

Private Sector

Source : U.K. Balance of Payments.

EXHIBIT 20.09

commissioned to deal with freight. The initial cost of air transport appears great but when it is compared with costs saved then the total cost is more attractive. Thus whereas we are not likely to see substantial improvement in earnings from sea transport we can be more optimistic about future earnings from civil aviation.

Travel and Tourism

Generally speaking the net position represents on the one hand the attractiveness of a country to foreigners and on the other the ability of its own nationals to afford holidays in other countries. For some countries, e.g. Spain, tourism is an invaluable earner of foreign currency . . . for the U.K. the balance on tourism is usually adverse but in recent years very determined efforts haae been made to "sell" Britain as a holiday centre and the number of foreign visitors has increased tremendously. In 1970 there was a small surplus on this account.

Financial and Other Services

The activities of insurance, banking, advertising and the licensing of foreign firms to use British inventions etc. always make a significant contribution to the economy . . . indeed the City is always quick to point out the per capita foreign currency earnings of these institutions compared with those of manufacturing industry.

Interest, Dividends and Profits

It must be clearly understood that these are receipts/payments which arise as the result of investment in previous years. They are not movements of fresh capital otherwise they would be included in the Capital Account. To examine them in their true perspective this item should be divided into the Public and Private Sectors in which case if we view them over the period 1959–69 we see that in the former case there was a marked deterioration consequently it was even more important that the latter section showed a distinct improvement.

Government Services

These include:

(a) *Military expenditure* such as maintaining garrisons overseas. This represents a considerable loss each year because against payments made by the U.K. there is only a small income from foreigners using bases here. This defence expenditure is a burden on the balance of payments of between £400–£500M p.a.

(b) *Civil expenditure* abroad such as the maintenance and servicing of embassies and consulates.

Private Transfers

There are many private reasons for the movements of funds which are either to the benefit or detriment of a country's balance of payments. A significant development since the 1960s has been the remittances made by immigrant workers to their countries of origin.

As explained earlier the Current Balance is the result of aggregating all Visible and Invisible Trade. The Current Balance for the U.K. in 1973 is shewn in Exhibit 20.10.

THE CAPITAL ACCOUNT

The Current Balance shows whether we are currently earning more than we are spending overseas but to complete the overall picture of our Balance of Payments

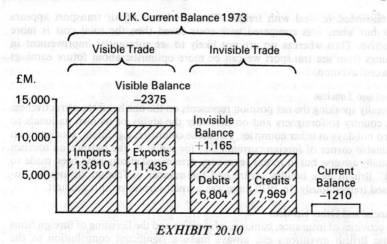

EXHIBIT 20.10

we must now include the flow of investment capital. This may take the form of *direct* investment i.e. the expansion or establishment of British owned companies overseas or *portfolio* investment in stocks and shares. The volume and direction of these capital flows varies from year to year e.g. the surplus inflow of £1,071M in 1973 contrasts markedly with the net outflow of £707M in 1972 . . . usually the most important factor determining this is the inflow of foreign money into investment in the British private sector.

Other items in the capital flow include loans between governments, trade credit for the financing of imports and exports, borrowing in overseas currencies by such bodies as the nationalised industries and changes in the exchange reserves held by other countries in Sterling.

Exhibit 20.11 shows the Investment and other Capital Flows for the U.K. in 1973.

U.K. Investment and Other Capital Flows 1973 – £M.

Inward		Outward	
Overseas Investment:		Official long-term capital (net)	252
Public sector	312	U.K. private investment	
Private sector	1,440	overseas	1,382
Borrowing by U.K. banks in		Export credit	232
overseas currencies:		Other flows (net)	440
To finance U.K. investment			
overseas	515		
To finance lending to U.K.			
public sector	831		
Increase in other countries'			
sterling reserves	151		
Import credit	128		
	3,377		2,306
		Net Balance	+1,071

EXHIBIT 20.11

THE BALANCE OF PAYMENTS MUST ULTIMATELY BALANCE

To the Current Account and flows of investment and other capital are added the Capital Transfers paid to certain foreign holders of sterling under guarantees given under Sterling Agreements (in 1973 these amounted to £59m but in the Budget of November 1974 the Government decided that this arrangement had been overtaken by events and consequently the guarantees were not to be renewed.) The estimates on these various accounts never exactly match the amount of foreign exchange gained or lost by the country during the year because very few of the transactions can be recorded accurately and because of the considerable differences of timing between transactions and payments. This discrepancy between the total value of recorded transactions and the actual flow of money into or out from the country is covered by an entry in the accounts known as the *Balancing Item* . . . the total of errors and omissions. If this item is positive then more money has flowed into the country than the estimated value of transactions show and conversely if the item is negative then less money has been received. In 1973 the Balancing Item was + £408M.

Adding together the Current Balance, the Capital Transfers, the Capital Flows balance and the Balancing Item gives the Total Currency Flow. If this flow is positive it means that there are funds available to repay debts to IMF, to central banks and other bodies; if the flow is negative then this is the amount which has to be borrowed in order to balance the account unless the Reserves are to be run down. Exhibit 20.12 showing the U.K. Balance of Payments for 1972 and 1973 demonstrates that when in 1973 there was a net currency inflow of £210M which was all transferred to the Official Gold and Foreign Currency Reserves whereas in 1972 there was a net outflow of £1,141 which was financed by drawing from the Reserves and by borrowing from various overseas bodies.

U.K. BALANCE OF PAYMENTS £M

	1972	1973
Visible balance	− 677	−2,375
Invisible balance	+ 791	+1,165
Current Balance	+ 114	−1,210
Capital Transfers	—	+ 59
Investment and other capital flows	− 707	+1,071
Balancing Item	− 672	+ 408
Total Currency Flow	−1,265	+ 210
Allocation of Special Drawing Rights	+ 124	—
Gold subscription to I.M.F.	—	—
Total	−1,141	+ 210
Total official financing	+1,141	− 210

EXHIBIT 20.12

The presentation of the U.K. Balance of Payments was changed in 1970; until then the Current Balance was combined with the Official long-term capital, Overseas investment in the U.K. and private investment overseas by U.K. nationals to give what was known as the basic balance. All other capital

prices. Examination of the non-oil section of the accounts would indicate that the worst is over . . . in the last three months of 1973 the monthly deficit averaged £234M while in the first six months of 1974 its averaged £113M. Though there has been an improvement on the non-oil account, the oil still has to be paid for and the overall deficit has to be reduced. This really means that Britain will have to reduce the extent to which it lives off its Reserves and foreign loans.

There is some small comfort for Britain in that she and the other oil importers should not try to correct their deficits too quickly for if they did it would surely lead to a world slump. However there is the deficit on the non-oil trade which has to be dealt with and although there is the prospect of having our own oil from the North Sea to meet some of our requirements by 1978 it is quite clear that Britain cannot run a balance of payments deficit of 1974 proportions until then.

PROBLEMS OF A BALANCE OF PAYMENTS SURPLUS

A hard currency is one for which demand exceeds supply at the present exchange value. Under the system of fixed exchange rates the central bank of that country would have to buy foreign currency on the market in order to hold the exchange rate within the permitted limits above parity. The balance of payments of such a country will be in surplus and the central bank will be increasing its reserves. This has been the case with W. Germany for over 20 years and indeed the strength of the Deutschmark has been a dominant feature in world finance since 1968. This surplus has arisen because of a large excess of visible exports over imports which has been only partially offset by a deficit on invisible trade . . . even though that deficit has been increasing.[1] However taking visible and invisible trade together W. Germany averaged a balance of payments surplus on current account of DM 3,000m (S750m) in the late '60s . . . a surplus which was strengthened by a net inflow of private long term capital.

In the light of this it is not surprising why many people in the U.K. faced with a recurring balance of payments deficit problem have asked . . . how has Germany achieved this position? Much more important is the question, what are the implications of this surplus for Germany's trading partners and the rest of the world? Some people have pointed out the rapid recovery of the German economy and said that the tremendous growth of the economy . . . particularly real output per man . . . has enabled her to achieve her present balance of payments position. Against this it must be noted that other countries e.g. Japan, have achieved a similar rate of growth in the post-war period but not the same balance of payments story. It is quite true that German exports have been large but so too has her savings and a great deal of that has been invested at home in industrial capital and social capital such as housing. Thus what needs explaining is why savings have been so large and why exports have exceeded imports even after satisfying the demand for investment at home. Clearly the decision on how savings should be used and how the balance of payments should be managed are matters of political policy. Thus the simple reason for the continued existence of the surplus is that the German Government has not wished to eliminate it even if at times they have introduced measures to reduce the size of it. A large surplus could cause inflationary pressures and we should remember that Germany's experiences in the '20s have created an almost pathological fear

1. Mainly transfer payments. Up to 1962 there were war reparations to pay; since then there has been the large outflow of remittances by immigrant workers, the growth of foreign travel by Germans and the earnings paid to foreign investment in W. Germany.

of inflation. The implications for the world monetary system are clear enough. If there is to be equilibrium internationally then there has to be a regular inflow of fresh reserves, thus if some countries want their reserves to be rising constantly then there cannot be equilibrium for all countries if the total reserves remain constant . . . obviously a rise in the reserves of some countries must mean a fall in those of others consequently they are in deficit and may ultimately face a balance of payments crisis. It follows therefore that when apportioning blame for the world's monetary problems we should examine the actions of those countries with surpluses as well as those in deficit.

Part Five
INTERNATIONAL TRADE AND MONETARY ARRANGEMENTS

Chapter Twenty-one
Solutions to Balance of Payments Deficits

We saw earlier in this part of the book that all balance of payments accounts are expected to balance; the balancing procedure being carried out in the monetary movements account (short term capital account).

A balance of payments problem occurs when the total receipts of foreign currency from trade and capital flows have been insufficient to meet total expenditure overseas. If this balance of payments situation is considered to be temporary, and surpluses are likely in the near future, then these future surpluses could be used to meet the deficit. However, in the meantime there will be a need to find some form of interim financing to plug the gap before surpluses become available.

Short Term Solutions

1. *Run down the nation's gold and foreign currency reserves.* Every nation maintains reserves of gold and foreign currencies in order to help finance future deficits. These reserves are often built up from the surpluses of previous years in anticipation of future deficits. As Britain's gold and foreign currency reserves are nearly always slender and are used for purposes other than financing deficits,[1] we can often only make relatively small payments without endangering the stability of the pound. This leads us to a second possibility.

2. *Raise the Minimum Lending Rate* (old Bank Rate). This should have the effect of raising short term interest rates throughout the U.K. and thereby making investment in Britain more attractive. If overseas investors respond and increase their investments in the U.K. we should acquire more foreign currencies as they sell their dollars, etc. to buy pounds. These newly acquired dollars might then be used to finance our deficit. It must be noted, however, that such action can often have serious consequences in the longer term. If U.K. interest rates fall, or interest rates in other financial centres of the world rise these foreign currencies are likely to flow out of the U.K. to the more remunerative centres. These volatile funds are usually referred to as "*hot money*" and have a serious effect upon the level of a country's reserves.

3. *Borrowings from the IMF.* Most western nations are members of the IMF[2] whose major functions is to provide a pool of gold and foreign currencies which can be borrowed by any member who experiences balance of payments difficulties. There are, of course, limitations on the amounts nations may borrow and these are discussed further in another chapter.[3]

4. *Borrowing from central banks.* Most central banks have arrangements such that when short of foreign currencies they can borrow from other central banks. The arrangements are referred to as "*swap agreements*". One of the

1. Used as backing for our sterling liabilities. See Chapter 26 page 293.
2. Discussed in detail pages 283 to 289.
3. Refer to chapter 25.

earliest of these dates back to the turn of the century when the Bank of France, the Bank of England and the Federal Reserve Bank of the U.S. signed the Tripartite agreement under which the parties to the agreement pledged to supply gold to any signatory experiencing balance of payments difficulties.

5. *Borrowing from private banks.* Most nations prefer not to rely upon any one source for a temporary solution to a balance of payments problem. Thus, many will borrow currencies from private overseas banks in much the same way as a U.K. citizen might borrow from his own bank.

6. *Borrowing in the Euro-dollar market.* The Euro-dollar market is a market in the borrowing and lending of dollars which have accumulated ouside the U.S.A. (mainly held in Europe – hence, "Euro-dollar"). The holders of such dollars (essentially balances held in U.S. banks) often have little immediate need for the dollars and so lend their holdings to banks for short periods. These banks then relend the balances to governments, firms and individuals for financial, trading and other purposes. In recent years many governments have made a practice of borrowing dollars from this market to finance their balance of payment deficits (France and Italy being some of the biggest borrowers).

7. *Gifts and grants.* These are sometimes given by large industrial nations to less developed economies as a form of aid to ease their balance of payments difficulties.

8. *Exchange control measures.* An adverse balance of payments position may often be the result of a nation indulging in excessive investment overseas. Such investment often produces a great outflow of foreign currency as money is spent acquiring overseas assets. If these outflows are not matched by inflows of foreign currency produced by people from overseas acquiring assets in the U.K., the balance of payments could swing adversely. Some nations have, therefore, found a remedy in restricting the availability of foreign currencies for investment purposes. These measures are usually implemented by the central bank and are referred to as "*exchange control regulations*'. In Britain we control the availability of foreign currency for investment overseas by having a separate market for currencies required for such purposes. Since the supply of currencies to this market is restricted the exchange rate normally yields less foreign currency per £1 than for other purposes (that is to say, foreign currency will be more expensive) and thus deters the investor. Some nations will also take active measures to encourage foreign investment into their economies and so provide an enlarged foreign currency inflow. This might be achieved by removing restrictions on foreign (inward) investments and offering investors tax concessions on those investments.

Medium Term Solutions

The use of tariffs. We saw in a previous chapter[1] that the use of tariffs would militate against the principles of free trade laid down in the law of comparative costs. However, when a nation has a balance of payments deficit which has failed to respond to normal measures it may be forced to reduce its imports by tariff policies. This situation was faced by the U.K. in 1965 when an import surcharge of 15 per cent was placed on imported goods. Technically such a move would offend the basic principles of the General Agreement on Tariffs and Trade (an international agreement to remove restrictions to trade). However, GATT does have a provision for the use of tariffs when all other measures have failed, but even then the tariff must be of a temporary nature and removed when the

1. Refer to chapter 20.

situation begins to ease. There is, of course, also another major deterrent to the use of tariffs and that is the possibility of retaliation from other nations who might feel that their exports are being unjustly penalised.

In view of the above difficulties many nations, who feel the need to protect their domestic market from imports, have cunningly devised other restraints to trade.

The use of non-tariff methods. Though these might offend the general principles of GATT they are difficult to detect and even more difficult to prove. Space precludes a detailed examination but the following are two well practised examples of non-tariff distortions used to restrict imports:
(a) the imposition of standards, and
(b) public procurement policies.

The imposition of standards. If a nation wishes to control the import of certain products it might insist that they meet certain minimum quality standards before they are allowed in. The manufacturer might find such standards too bothersome to meet, particularly when the nation to which he is selling is continually changing the standard requirements. He will, therefore, eventually withdraw from that market and concentrate on others. The exacting safety standards and pollution laws relating to motor cars in the U.S.A. has deterred some exporters of motor cars from exporting to that country.

Public procurement policies. Certain governments insist that their department buy only products manufactured in the home economy. Hence, in the case of computers, European governments following such policies have seriously damaged the U.S. computer exporting industry.

A Note on the General Agreement on Tariff and Trade

The General Agreement on Tariff and Trade (GATT) arose out of the failure of the Bretton Woods conference of 1944 to establish an organisation to promote free trade. Out of this failure came a substitute – GATT. This was an informal association of countries whose basic objective was the ambitious task of removing the restrictions to trade that had grown up since the 1930s. The agreement was signed in 1947 and although it contained no elaborate set of rules, all members agreed in principle to pursue inter-nation bargaining sessions whereby mutual agreements to reduce barriers to trade could be negotiated. These sessions have, so far, taken the form of a series of annual meetings and special tariff conferences.

Perhaps the most important principle of GATT is the "most favoured nation" clause. This is to be applied to all rounds of tariff negotiations and states that where country A grants country B a concession (allows B's goods into its country at new lower rate of tariff) then concessions must be extended to all other members. Thus, all concessions successfully negotiated bilaterally are extended multilaterally so that *all* the signatories to GATT gain *all* the benefits that are negotiated at the conference.[1]

The Kennedy Round. This has, perhaps, been the most successful of the tariff conferences to date – the round of negotiations lasting 5 years from 1962 to 1967 and achieving average reductions in tariffs of some 35 per cent. At this conference the method of tariff negotiation was changed. Instead of agreements being struck on tariff reductions for particular products, members agreed to "across the board" cuts on all goods (with a few exceptions). The aim was a 50 per cent across the board cuts on tariffs relating to industrial products. Whilst

1. There are a number of exceptions to this rule but a special GATT waiver is necessary.

each country would reduce its tariff by 50 per cent each would still maintain roughly the same degree of protection relative to the other. If, for example, Spain had a 50 per cent tariff on imported cars and the U.K. a 20 per cent tariff then a 50 per cent across the board cut would leave Spain with a 25 per cent tariff and the U.K. with a 10 per cent tariff. Thus, Spain would still be better protected than the U.K. but there would be an overall reduction in tariffs.

Apart from being concerned with tariffs GATT also outlaws the use of other non-tariff means of protection. Some of these distortions have, however, been difficult to detect, let alone remove, and hence GATT has taken on the role of researcher collecting and collating information.

Finally, GATT has also taken on the role of arbiter in disputes over tariffs. When a nation feels that someone is unfairly discriminating against its exports GATT will normally intervene. It will ask the offender (if breaking the rules) to stop the discrimination or allow a bending of the rules of GATT to allow limited retaliation by the aggrieved.

Longer Term Measures

If the balance of payments problem is not resolved in one or two years then the continuing deficit indicates that something is fundamentally wrong with the economy. Action, therefore, is required to establish the root cause of the problem and for the appropriate treatment to be applied. If the problem is largely attributed to inflationary pressures at home then excess demand may be removed by deflationary policies. Note that most of the long term measures to ease balance of payments difficulties have been dealt with elsewhere in this volume and thus the following is only a cursory examination of these measures.

1. *Deflationary policy.* The national government of a country suffering continuous balance of payments deficit may attempt to stabilise its domestic costs and prices by removing excess demand from the economy through the fiscal and monetary techniques.[1] By slowing down the rate of inflation and hoping that competitors abroad inflate more rapidly the country's balance of payments should show improvement. Many economies now also use some form of incomes policy[2] in order to try to keep wages in line with productivity and thereby help stabilise costs and prices.

2. *Use of the Exchange Rate.* The above remedies are aimed at attacking the problem from within the domestic economy by reducing costs and prices. However, a similar effect may be achieved by a simple exchange rate adjustment. If, for example, British goods are becoming too expensive for the overseas buyer a lowering of the foreign exchange value of the pound will counter this problem. There are two possibilities of achieving this:

(a) allowing the exchange rate to float downwards.

(b) devaluation of the exchange rate.

Allowing the exchange rate to float. If a country has a balance of payments problem its currency is unlikely to be in great demand. By the same token that country's demand for imports and therefore foreign currency will probably be high (domestic goods being expensive). This high demand for foreign currencies will increase the flow of the country's own currency into the foreign exchange market and as there will be little demand for it, its price will fall (assuming the central bank does not interfere with the mechanism). If, for example, the price of the pound fell from £1 = $3 to £1 = $2 imports into the U.K. would become

1. These are described in Chapter 16.
2. See Chapter 16 page 180.

more expensive and presumably fall whilst exports would become less expensive and presumably increase. The total effect therefore would be for the balance of payments to swing back towards equilibrium.[1]

Devaluation of the exchange rate. When the price of a currency has been pinned at some specific level rather than left to float the government may decide the foreign exchange value of that currency is too high and announce a new lower exchange value (at which it will agree to maintain the currency). This will have much the same effect as allowing the rate to float downwards in that exports will become less expensive in terms of foreign currency and imports into the country will cost more.[2]

3. *Export incentives.* A nation could also, in the longer term, take measures to make it easier and more attractive for its firms to export. Such measures might include tax allowances on export profits and the provision of financial assistance to bridge the gap between receipts of orders and the customer's final payment (many foreign orders are accompanied by demands for credit and many sales are lost because firms fail to offer such facilities to their overseas customers).

Many firms, though capable of exporting, are deterred by the risks of the overseas creditor failing to pay. Thus, guarantees of compensatory payments to such exporters may help improve the country's export trade.

Finally, many firms fail to export simply because of lack of knowledge of exporting and export practices; thus provision of information services may encourage more firms into this field.

Whilst exports may be encouraged through the incentives described above there are limitations to the extent these can be used. A nation has to be careful that the assistance offered does not infringe international trading agreements, for example, EEC rules. Some subsidies, for example, tend to distort trade and give unfair advantage, and as such will probably conflict with the articles of GATT.[3] Nevertheless, the British Department of Trade and Industry, through the British Overseas Trade Board, offers considerable assistance to the exporter. Some of the major services include:

(a) Export Credit Guarantee service,
(b) Information, and
(c) Technical assistance.

Export credit guarantee service. For a small premium this service guarantees the exporter payment should his overseas debtor fail to make settlement within a certain time period. This guarantee will also act as a form of security on which the exporter may be able to raise finance to support his business operations between the receipt of the order and the final payment by the debtor.

Information. The British Overseas Trade Board offers a comprehensive system of export information services available through "Export intelligence". These are available mostly free of charge. The service has close links with major export markets. These are through the "commercial attachees" resident in most British embassies. The attachees monitor markets abroad and channel the information back to the U.K. Though much of this information concerns general market conditions exporters can get, on request, reliable information on prospects for their products in particular markets, the degree of competition in those markets and details of tariffs and standards to which products must conform.

1. This topic has been dealt with in more detail in Chapter 22 page 265.
2. Further details on this can be found in Chapter 22 page 266.
3. For details on GATT refer to page 257.

Technical assistance. Many firms, particularly small ones, do not export because they lack the "know how". Problems of documentation, tariffs and foreign exchange requirements frequently confuse and deter the would-be exporter. To overcome such problems the British Overseas Trade Board will now offer the firm specialist help which sometimes includes the personal services of a Board official to help the firm over those initial hurdles.

Part Five

INTERNATIONAL TRADE AND MONETARY ARRANGEMENTS

Chapter Twenty-Two

The Mechanics of Foreign Exchange

The process of making international payments is complicated by the fact that most countries have their own individual currencies which differ considerably in type, value and denomination. Whilst a country's currency will normally have unlimited acceptability within that country's national boundaries only a few such national currencies possess the qualities which allow them to be used as a direct means of making world wide payments. If, for example, the British motor car manufacturer received all the payments for his exports to India in rupees it is most unlikely that his shareholders, suppliers of materials, and his work force would relish the thought of receiving their share of payment in that currency!

As a result, it is normal practice for an importer to take steps to acquire supplies of the national currencies of his suppliers. This is done through the foreign exchange market which comprises a set of institutions specialising in the provision of foreign currencies.

The Foreign Exchange Market
The key institution in this market is the foreign exchange department of the commercial bank – this is in effect the market's retailer of foreign currency. These departments are supported by other banks which operate as foreign exchange brokers carrying out a "wholesaling function" in foreign exchange. Finally, the central banks of the world operate within the foreign exchange market buying and selling their own country's currencies when this is considered politic.

In the U.K. the foreign exchange market is centred on the City of London. It comprises nearly 200 dealers made up of the foreign exchange departments of banks authorised by the Bank of England to buy and sell foreign currencies. In addition there are 10 or so firms which act as foreign exchange brokers to the dealers, and finally the whole operation is overseen by the Bank of England.

The Operation of the Market
The operation of the market is an extremely complicated business involving numerous methods of transacting international payments. The following, therefore, is a highly simplified version of its operation.

A U.K. importer requiring foreign currency will normally approach his commercial bank and request the supply of foreign currencies in exchange for sterling. As most commercial banks are faced with numerous requests of this nature they find it convenient to hold overseas bank accounts in which they hold deposits of foreign currency. A U.K. bank, for example, will probably have a permanent account with a French commercial bank (usually referred to as its "correspondent bank") in which it holds 'francs'. When the U.K. bank's customer requires 'francs' he will make a sterling payment to his bank which in return

will transfer part of its holding of 'francs' to a separate account from which the customer can make payment to the French supplier. It might be noted at this stage that the French commercial bank will have similar arrangements with a U.K. bank through which it can supply sterling for the use of its French customers.

In some cases foreign exchange is arranged through simple bi-lateral arrangements. A U.K. bank, for example, might put some of its sterling resources at the disposal of its French correspondent bank. These resources could then be transferred to the French bank's customers for paying their U.K. creditors. In return, similar facilities would be provided by the French correspondent bank for the U.K. bank and its customers. If, in practice, the two banks use each others facilities to an equal extent their indebtedness to one another is cancelled out. However, if the U.K. bank uses the French bank's facilities to a greater extent than the latter uses the U.K. facility then the U.K. bank will find itself owing its French correspondent 'francs'.

This is the point at which the foreign exchange broker enters the scene. The broker's chief function is to iron out the surpluses and shortages of currencies in the foreign exchange market. A bank that needs a particular currency will be able to purchase this from the broker who will have bought the currency from another bank whose receipts of that currency are in excess of the immediate needs of its customers.

The latter situation may occur where a bank's customers may be selling more foreign exchange earnings to the bank than the bank can find customers.

The Exchange Rate
The exchange rate is simply the price of a currency measured in terms of other currencies – usually dollars. If the current exchange rate for the pound is £1 = $2·40 this means that a British resident needing dollars for the purchase of U.S. goods will get $2·40 for each of his pounds. The U.S. resident will in turn get one pound's worth of sterling for each payment of $2·40 (two dollars and forty cents).

What then determines the exchange rate or price of a currency? The answer to this depends upon the type of exchange rate system adopted by a country. This may be a freely floating system, a rigid or fixed exchange rate system or a system lying somewhere between these two extremes.

It is now proposed to examine the operation of some of the more important systems.

FREELY FLOATING EXCHANGE RATE SYSTEMS
Under this system the exchange rate is determined solely by the interaction of free market forces. In other words, the price of the currency will be determined by the laws of supply and demand – totally free from any interference by government. Let us consider the £ and the $ under a floating system. As British importers purchase goods from the United States the British commercial banks will be faced with customers demanding dollars in exchange for pounds. The higher the demand for U.S. goods the higher will be the demand for the dollar. On the other side of the Atlantic our American cousins may be directing their banks to sell their dollars to purchase pounds in order that they could buy British goods. This latter operation will obviously increase the supply of dollars on the foreign exchange markets. If the demand for the dollar (or U.S. goods) is exactly matched by the supply of dollars put onto the foreign exchange

Reserves of foreign currencies kept for this operation come from the Bank of England's 'Exchange Equalisation Account'.

If the pound is in great demand on the foreign exchange market and supply is limited the exchange rate for the pound will tend to move outside the upper limits of the band. Under these conditions the Bank of England will sell £'s to increase supplies on the market and to push the price down towards the central rate. See Exhibit 22.2.

$2.42

If price rises into this area the Bank of England will be selling £'s

————————— £1 = $2.40 —————————

$2.38

If price falls into this area the Bank of England will be buying £'s

OPERATION OF FIXED EXCHANGE RATE

EXHIBIT 22.2

Exchange rates of this nature, however, suffer from one major problem. Countries that experience a continuously adverse balance of payments will find their central banks constantly having to defend their currencies. This means heavy drains on their limited resources of foreign currencies and this may, in turn, force them to resort to international borrowing to supplement reserves.

To avoid this, and many other problems associated with a fixed exchange rate, the latter has now largely been replaced by more flexible exchange rate systems. In 1970 the agreements made at Bretton Woods (to fix exchange rates) were broken by many nations who went on to what they called a 'temporary float'. Most were persuaded to go back to fixing their rates in 1971[1] but this time a wider band of fluctuations was allowed (2¼ per cent either side of parity rather than the previous 1 per cent). However, this agreement was quickly abandoned with Britain refloating the pound in June 1972, only to be followed by most other major trading nations.

THE MERITS OF A FLOATING RATE

Perhaps the chief attraction of the adoption of a floating or highly flexible system of exchange rates is the claim that balance of payments problems will be automatically countered by movements in the exchange rate.

Suppose, for example, that the U.K. economy is experiencing severe problems of inflation. The effect might be a reduction in the competitiveness of our exports and tendency for U.K. residents to replace higher priced domestically produced products and services by cheaper imports. Under such conditions the balance of payments would be likely to swing into deficit. The fall off in the demand for U.K. exports would, in practice, mean a fall off in demand for the pound in the foreign exchange markets of the world. By the same token the

1. The Smithsonian Agreement – December 1971.

increase in demand for imported goods by U.K. residents would mean an increase in the supply of pounds as the British importer sold his pounds to purchase foreign currencies. As the exchange rate under a floating system is determined by the free operation of the laws of supply and demand a fall in the demand for the pound accompanied by an increase in its supply would produce a fall in the price of the pound. Let us now assume that the price falls from £1 = $3 to £1 = $2. U.K. exports would now become cheaper to overseas buyers. A U.K. product selling at £1 sterling could now be acquired with $2 instead of $3. Thus, such a movement would give a boost to the export trade pulling the balance of payments back towards equilibrium.

As the price of our currency depreciates in the foreign exchange markets, further help is given to the balance of payments by a tendency for imports to fall. The falling exchange value of the pound pushes up the costs of the foreign currency necessary to purchase them. In our example we assumed the price of the pound moved down from £1 = $3 to £1 = $2. This being so, one pound would have originally bought $3 worth of imports but the same pound would now only purchase $2 worth of imports. The operation of this mechanism is shown below. However, it must be noted that the effect of an exchange rate change on the demand for imports and exports will depend upon the elasticities of demand for the products or services being traded.

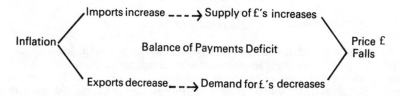

continuing from above

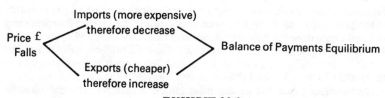

EXHIBIT 22.3

A country with a balance of payments surplus creates as much an economic problem as one with a deficit, since the surplus will be the product of less fortunate nation's deficit. As Keynes pointed out "the existence within any payments system of a chronic surplus country is a maladjustment. If allowed to continue it leads to the piling up of reserves by the surplus country and to measures of self defence by neighbours, which have service effects on the volume of trade."

The floating exchange rate will tend to pull the surplus country's balance of payments back into equilibrium by reducing the competitiveness of its exports.

A country experiencing a high demand for its exports will naturally find the demand for its currency rising but if its products are so competitive there will be little demand by that country's residents for imports (domestic products will probably be cheaper than imports). This will produce a shortening of the supply of the country's currency on the foreign exchange market and this, together with the high demand for that currency, will simply push up the price of the currency. If the U.K. had a balance of payments surplus the price of the pound would rise, say from £1 = $2 to £1 = $4. U.K. exports would thus become much more expensive to overseas buyers whilst the U.K. importer would get more foreign currency, and therefore imports. for his pound. The final result would be a deterioration of the balance of payments and a movement back towards equilibrium. The process is summarised below:

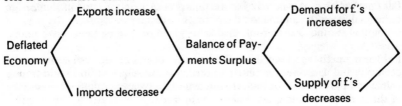

EXHIBIT 22.4

2. Since the floating exchange rate looks after the balance of payments problem, this should theoretically reduce the need to pursue stringent internal deflationary policies to improve our international payments position.

Under a fixed exchange rate system rising domestic prices are not countered by a fall in the value of the exchange rate and hence price competitiveness can only be restored by removing excess demand levels in the domestic economy. However, any such demand management policy[1] is likely to destroy business confidence thereby retarding investment and the rate of economic growth.

3. Floating exchange rates may also ease the problem of a shortage of world liquidity. Nations need to keep reserves of gold and foreign currencies to meet their indebtedness to other countries when exports are insufficient to pay for imports. However, since floating exchange rates work towards eliminating deficits and surpluses the need for reserves is reduced.

4. A floating exchange rate enables a government to pursue full employment policies without the fear of upsetting the balance of payments position. One of the major objectives of economic policy is the maintenance of full employ-

1. Refer to Chapter 16 page 176.

ment. A fully employed economy, however, has a great tendency towards inflation[1] and hence governments will often run their economies with a margin of spare capacity (unemployment) to ease this problem. A floating exchange rate, however, theoretically enables a government to pursue policies of full employment without the fear of inflation upsetting the balance of payments – the automatic depreciation of the exchange rate offsetting the effects of inflation.

Case against floating Exchange Rates

Not all economists are convinced of the argument that floating rates are the complete answer to balance of payments difficulties. Many such arguments are purely theoretical and when seen in practice are subject to serious limitation. However, the floating rate has only recently been given a serious trial and until this time has been considered by most countries[2] as merely a "stop gap" measure to be used when the international payments system breaks down.[3]

Some of the major arguments against a system of floating rates now follow:

1. Floating exchange rates create uncertainty as to international receipts and payments and as a result are likely to restrict the development of world trade.

It is usual practice for an exporter to invoice his overseas sales in the currency of the nation to whom he is selling. Thus, if a U.K. exporter agrees to sell a motor car to a U.S. importer for $2,000 when the exchange rate is £1 = $2 his receipts in sterling will be £1,000. However, if in the period between making the sale and the receipt of the payment, the exchange rate moves to £1 = $4 the British importer will only receive £500. Although it is unlikely that there will be such a great exchange rate fluctuation over such a short time period, even a small movement in the exchange rate could mean the difference between profit and loss – especially when the exporter is having to work on fine profit margins because of the intensity of international competition. It could be argued, however, that the exporter also has an equal chance of gain through exchange rate movements. If in the above example the exchange rate moves from £1 = $2 to £1 = $1 the $2,000 payment made by the U.S. importer will produce £2,000 on conversion. It might be further noted that there are many banks and other institutions which will agree (for a fee) to convert future receipts of foreign exchange at today's exchange rate hence eliminating risk of loss on conversion.

2. One of the strongest arguments against floating exchange rates is that they perpetuate inflation. The degree to which this is likely will depend upon the economy's dependence upon imports and the import content of its exports.

Let us assume that the U.K. is experiencing inflation and that as a result our balance of payments position deteriorates. Falling demand for the pound will produce a depreciation in the exchange rate – say from £1 = $3 to £1 = $2. Whilst our exports will become cheaper in terms of foreign currencies, imports will become more expensive. If imports make up a significant part of the costs of production in the U.K. the rise in import prices will affect final prices, including our export prices. This may lead to a further deterioration in the demand for U.K. goods and cause the exchange rate to depreciate even further. There would, therefore, appear to be no guarantee that the depreciating exchange rate would

1. A fully employed economy is one where demand levels are such that all the available productive capacity (labour, machinery, materials, etc.) is being fully utilised. Shortages of these resources will mean they can command higher prices (higher wages, higher material costs, etc). Thus pushing up costs and prices, so making our exports less competitive.
2. With the exception of Canada.
3. Example: Used in 1931 on the failure of the 'gold standard'.

Part Twelve

INTERNATIONAL TRADE AND MONETARY ARRANGEMENTS

Chapter Twenty-Four

INTERNATIONAL MONETARY PROBLEMS

International Liquidity

International liquidity can be defined as the availability of internationally acceptable currencies used to settle debts between nations incurred as a result of international trade and capital movements.

At present there is no one currency which is universally considered as capable of financing the whole of world trade. In practice, world liquidity is provided by an amalgam of currencies made up largely of gold, but supplemented by national currencies like the U.S. dollar and the pound sterling. Deutsch marks, francs and the Japanese yen also play some part in the supply of international liquidity but tend to be more restricted in their use.

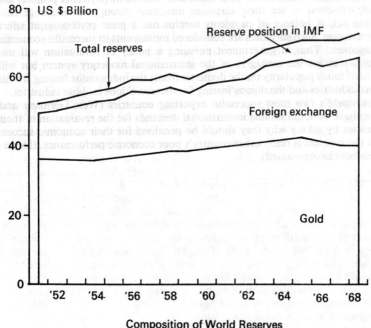

Composition of World Reserves

1951 – 1968

EXHIBIT 24.1

Exhibit 24.1 gives a graphical picture of the composition of world liquidity from 1951 to 1968. Here, it will be noticed that some part of the world's liquidity is provided by the International Monetary Fund. This is an international institution whose major objective is to provide its members with currencies when they experience liquidity problems.[1]

So far we have only discussed general world liquidity. However, equally important is the liquidity position of an individual nation. This will consist of that nation's stock of gold and foreign currencies held in reserves, plus its ability to raise currencies from institutions such as the IMF and the central banks of the world. In short, the liquidity position of a nation is a measure of its ability to get hold of the means of settling a balance of payments debt quickly.

Before proceeding to deal with the problem of international liquidity it will, at this stage, be useful to outline some of the more important terminology used in the discussion of international monetary problems:

Trading currency. This is a currency which private and other traders regularly conduct their international payments. Such currencies would include the U.S. dollar and the pound sterling, and to a lesser extent the Deutsch mark, yen and franc.

Reserve currency. This is a national currency which is held by other countries as part of their reserves of gold and foreign currencies and naturally as such will be accepted in settlement of international debts.

Key currency. This is basically a reserve currency but one which commands wide acceptance. Thus, the U.S. dollar and pound sterling are not only reserve currencies but also key currencies; that is to say, "key reserve currencies". The Deutsch mark and yen would not, of course, fall into this latter category since, though they are well accepted, they are not widely used. The yen, for example, will make up an important part of the reserves of many countries in south-east Asia because of their strong trading relationships with Japan.

The Need for International Liquidity

Nations need to keep reserves of readily acceptable currencies for the purpose of settling balance of payments debts. Thus, if all trade were to balance or all trade was conducted by barter then the need for liquidity would be limited.

In practice, however, demands for international liquidity have increased sharply whilst the availability of international reserves have grown only slowly. Since 1950 world trade has increased over 5 times faster than the supply of money available to finance that trade – as shown in Exhibit 24.2.

Although the increases in money need not exactly match the increases in trade there is still obviously a need for significant increases in the availability of international monies. One could imagine the difficulties of financing the number of domestic transactions taking place in the U.K. today with the volume of money that existed in say 1930. The problem in the domestic economy is alleviated by the central bank ensuring that the money supply is expanded at a rate suitable to the needs of the economy. However, in the international payment system, there is no institution providing a service similar to that of the central bank. The nearest the international payments system has to this is the IMF with its issue of "Special Drawing Rights".[2]

In recent years the size of balance of payments deficits has increased markedly. A £200,000,000–£300,000,000 deficit in Britain's balance of payments in the

1. Refer to pages 283–289 for further details on the operation of the IMF.
2. Refer to page 287.

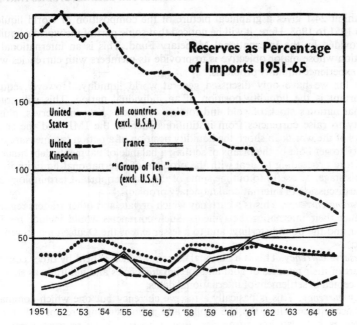

Reserves as Percentage
of Imports 1951-65

United States — · —
All countries •••••• (excl. U.S.A.)
United Kingdom — ■ —
France ▬▬▬▬▬
"Group of Ten" ▬▬ (excl. U.S.A.)

1951 '52 '53 '54 '55 '56 '57 '58 '60 '61 '62 '63 '64 '65

The Liquidity Gap

EXHIBIT 24.2A

late 1960s was considered a serious problem for the U.K. economy. However, in the 1970s deficits of well over £1,000,000,000 have not been uncommon.[1] As deficits have also tended to become longer lived many nations have found their reserves inadequate to cope with the problem. This has resulted in the need to take stringent domestic measures to bring the balance of payments back into equilibrium. Unfortunately, strong deflationary measures usually lead to loss of business confidence and hence result in slowing of economic growth as investment decisions are held back. When this problem occurs world wide it is a clear indication of the existence of a world liquidity problem.

The Problem of the Supply of Liquidity
As noted earlier the supply of international liquidity is made up of gold supplemented by the international use of certain domestic currencies including the U.S. dollar and the pound sterling.

Gold supplies, particularly for international payments purposes have been slow to increase averaging only 8 per cent per year since 1951.[2] This has largely been the result of the U.S. government holding down the official price of gold (the price at which central banks will buy and sell gold) at $35 an ounce from 1934 to 1971. Because the costs of mining have naturally increased over this period mining has become less profitable and resulted in the closure of all but the really efficient mines.

1. Largely as a result of the increase in oil and commodity prices.
2. Very little newly mined gold has entered the international payments system since 1968.

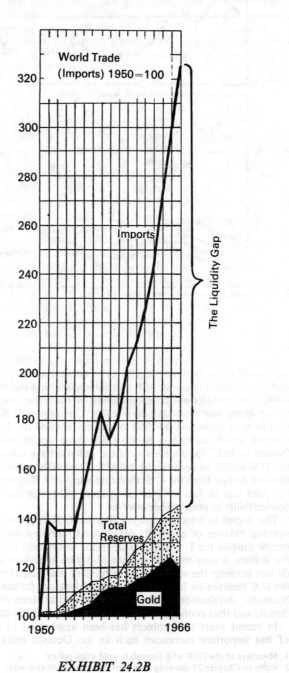

EXHIBIT 24.2B

solve the balance of payments problem and that the depreciation of the exchange rate would appear to be continuous.

This argument, however, could be considered fallacious on the grounds that it would be impossible for the currency to be persistently depreciating against others. If one currency is depreciating another must be appreciating in relation to it, thus countries with depreciating currencies are bound, at some point, to gain at the expense of countries with appreciating currencies.

3. Floating exchange rates may also discourage foreign investment since a movement in the exchange rates between purchase and sale of an investment could produce substantial capital losses for the investor.

If, for example, a U.K. businessman invests £1,000,000 in the U.S. when the exchange rate is £1 = $2 his capital sum would buy a $2,000,000 investment. However, if after say one year, he sells the investment for the same $2,000,000 but in the meantime the exchange rate falls to £1 = $4 the value of his investment in sterling falls to £500,000.

One must, however, bear in mind that we have assumed that no capital appreciation takes place. Very often a small exchange loss will in practice be outweighed by gains from an appreciation in the value of the investment. We have also only considered the fact that the exchange rate appreciates. It is, of course, just as likely to depreciate, making the investment more attractive.

4. A further argument against the floating exchange rate system is that whilst the problem of inflation is taken care of by movements in the exchange rate the monetary authorities (the central bank, etc.) will be left with greater freedom in the management of the domestic economy. Thus, as inflation will cause less concern, the monetary authorities may be tempted to be less strict on controlling the growth of public expenditure, wages and prices. The inflation, therefore, may still produce social injustice as people, such as fixed income earners, fight to maintain their real incomes against a rising tide of inflation.

FIXED EXCHANGE RATES UNDER THE GOLD STANDARD

The 'gold standard' operated in its various forms until the early 1930s (with a break between 1914 and 1925). This was the earliest form of rigid exchange rate system and was based on a series of unwritten rules variously interpreted and followed by members of the system. The chief feature of the system was that exchange rates were stabilised by the linking of national currencies to a specific weight of gold. The U.K. might, for example, declare that £1 sterling was equivalent in value to 1/10th ounce of gold, whilst the U.S.A. might declare her dollar to have the value of $10 to 1/10th ounce. On this basis £1 would be equal in value, through gold, to $10. The rules of the system were essentially that the quantity of money in the economy was to be related to that nation's stock of gold, and currency could be converted into gold on demand through the central bank. The free movement of gold was to be allowed between nations and as gold stocks increased or decreased with international gold movements the nation's money supply was to be adjusted accordingly.

The system had two main advantages:

1. The exchange rate would always remain stable.

2. The balance of payments would always be tending to move towards the equilibrium.

In the first case, if we assume the demand for the dollar is greater than the demand for the pound the effect would normally be for the price of the dollar to rise as more dollars were demanded. However, since all central banks agreed

to buy and sell dollars at a fixed price the U.K. importer would find it cheaper to buy gold from his central bank with pounds and then buy his dollars from the U.S. central bank with gold; such action, therefore, militating against a rise in the price of the dollar. A balance of payments deficit in the U.K. was therefore unlikely to be accompanied by an increase in the price of foreign currencies needed to settle the deficit. Since buying gold in the U.K. and selling it abroad for foreign currencies, provided a cheaper method of obtaining the currency such balance of payments deficits would be financed by gold movements out of the U.K.

If we now invoke the rule that a country experiencing a reduction in its gold stocks should decrease its money supply such action will have the effect of deflating the economy so stabilising prices and helping to improve the country's international competitive position. The balance of payments therefore should move towards a surplus.

If, however, a nation has a balance of payments surplus the reverse situation will apply. The country will be experiencing an inflow of gold and will therefore expand its money supply. This will lead to an expansion of demand, producing inflationary conditions which will eventually spoil the country's superior competitive position and so eliminate the surplus. The effects are summarised below:

The Self Balancing Mechanism of the Gold Standard

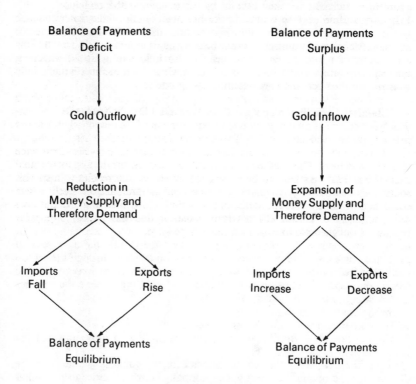

EXHIBIT 22.5

Why did the gold standard fail?

1. The system was based upon a series of unwritten rules which were frequently ignored particularly when their strict implementation was likely to lead to unpopular national policies. For example, a balance of payments deficit would result in an outflow of gold and reduction in domestic money supply. Such deflationary movements produce unemployment and many nations, who were unwilling to see this occur, failed to ensure a reduction in money supply. It is worth noting here that as bank credit became an important form of currency the movement of gold abroad would not necessarily reduce the money supply if the former could be expanded.

Furthermore, many nations with balance of payments surpluses failed to ensure their money supply was expanded in accordance with the increase in their gold stocks. This might again have been due to the fear of inflationary conditions producing unemployment or simply a desire to keep their balance of payments in surplus.

2. Under the gold standard a country's money supply depends upon its holdings of gold. Reductions in gold stocks would mean a reduction in the money supply which would in turn hold back economic growth. Many nations therefore became dissatisfied with such constraints and were tempted to expand their money supply without having the required gold backing. Many, in fact, simply wanted greater freedom in domestic economic policy and were unwilling to allow their external payments position to dictate internal economic policy.

3. It also became easy to upset the normal functioning of the gold standard system whilst still technically following the rules. If a nation had a balance of payments deficit and wanted to expand its money supply all it had to do was increase interest rates. This would produce an inflow of gold on which an expansionary policy could be based at a time when the true functioning of the system should be demanding a deflationary action.

4. A balance of payments deficit meant an outflow of gold and accompanied by a domestic deflationary policy. However, this often had no effect on improving the international payments situation. Instead of the reduction in demand reducing prices the effect was simply to produce unemployment.

5. Many nations adopted unrealistically high exchange rate levels which were difficult to defend. This was Britain's chief problem on her return to the gold standard in 1925. As her currency was too expensive the resultant large and continuous balance of payment deficits produced substantial gold losses which could not be sustained. The deflationary action which followed the outflows was insufficient to correct the payments situation and was grossly unpopular because of the unemployment which came in its wake.

Part Five

INTERNATIONAL TRADE AND MONETARY ARRANGEMENTS

Chapter Twenty-Three

INTERNATIONAL MONETARY PROBLEMS

Revaluation and Devaluation of Currencies

Revaluation and devaluation are techniques used to ease the balance of payments difficulties of countries which subscribe to a system of fixed exchange rates.

In our discussion of a system of floating exchange rates we saw that the price of a currency was determined by the free operation of the forces of supply and demand and was thus likely to fluctuate from hour to hour. However, when a system of rigid exchange rates is in operation a country maintains the price of its currency to some pre-arranged level. If, because of changes in market forces, the value of the currency falls below or rises above this pre-agreed level, the country's central monetary authorities will enter the foreign exchange markets to buy or sell currencies so as to artificially influence those market forces and keep the price of its currency at the agreed level.

In some circumstances a nation may find that the value of its currency has been fixed at an unrealistic level. If, for example, the country has been experiencing a long lived deficit on balance of payments and this has not responded to domestic measures, the falling demand for its exports and therefore its currency may result in a fall in the price of the currency on the foreign exchange market.

In order to get the price (or exchange rate) back to the pre-agreed level that country will have to use up some of its stocks of foreign currency to buy up its own currency on the foreign exchange markets (shortening the supply and artificially stimulating demand) and so forcing the price back up. Such action will often consume large amounts of a country's reserves of foreign currency so that it has to abandon the attempt to maintain the price at that level. The currency, in this case, might, therefore, be considered overvalued and the nation concerned may seek the permission of the International Monetary Fund to adopt a new lower value for its currency (and agree to maintain the value at the new lower level). A deliberate announcement on the part of a government that it is to adopt and maintain a new *lower* value for its currency is referred to as a '*devaluation*'. If, for reasons discussed later in this chapter, a nation decides to *raise* the foreign exchange value of its currency, then this is referred to as a '*revaluation*'.

It must be noted at this stage that frequent adjustments of exchange rates would flout the international agreement, (made at Bretton Woods, 1944,) to operate a policy of fixed exchange rates. Devaluation was, therefore, considered a last resort corrective for balance of payments disequilibrium – only to be used when other measures had failed, and never without the International Monetary Fund's permission.

It is now proposed to look at some of the economic effects of revaluation and devaluation.

Effects of devaluation on the current account of the balance of payments

The devaluation of a country's currency theoretically makes its exports cheaper in terms of foreign currency and thereby helps to expand its overseas sales. At the same time the devaluation will make the devaluing country's imports more expensive and so make some contribution to reducing imports.

A. *Effect on exports*

This can, perhaps, be best explained by taking the 1967 devaluation of the pound as an example. Pre November 1967 £1 = $2·80; this meant that if, say, a resident of the U.S. wished to buy a British long playing record costing £1 he would need $2·80. However, in November 1967 the pound was devalued such that £1 was given a new par value of $2·40 on the foreign exchange markets. In other words, assuming the price of the U.K. record remained at £1 the American buyer would now only need $2·40 to make the purchase (the record being approximately 14·3 per cent cheaper). In fact, the British firm therefore could even increase the sterling price of its product a little and the American buyer would still get the product more cheaply than pre devaluation. However, before we proclaim devaluation as the complete answer to our export difficulties there are several considerations to be borne in mind:
1. One assumes that by lowering the price of an article an increase in sales will automatically ensue. However, much will depend upon the elasticity of demand for the product in its overseas markets. Sales, in practice, may not be particularly responsive to price reductions (tend to show a high degree of inelasticity of demand).

Failure to succeed in export markets may be due to factors other than price. These might include quality, design of product, after sales service, etc. Devaluation therefore would not help directly here.
2. Whilst devaluation may make it possible for the exporter to lower the price of his product in overseas markets, whether a lower price is charged depends much upon the import agent. As we saw earlier devaluation of the pound from £1 = $2·80 to £1 = $2·40 will make it possible for a £1 British good to sell at 40 cents less in overseas markets. However, the overseas selling agent may continue to charge $2·80 for the product, keeping the extra 40 cents to improve his profit margin. This problem was well illustrated in 1967 when many U.S. import agents of British motor cars refused to pass on the price advantage from devaluation.
3. Devaluation may well boost our export sales but the volume of sales is only secondary to the foreign currency revenue from those sales – the balance of payments problem is one of matching expenditure by revenue. When a currency is devalued, the revenue in terms of foreign currency per unit sold abroad will fall, that is to say, in the above example the £1 British record would have netted $2·80 pre devaluation but only $2·40 after devaluation. If, therefore, devaluation is to help the export side of the balance of payments, with less revenue forthcoming from each unit of overseas sales, the volume of sales must be increased. In fact, the 14·3 per cent devaluation of the pound in 1967 would have required more than a 14·3 per cent expansion in the volume of sales to net the same total foreign currency revenue as pre devaluation.
4. If devaluation is to be a success, therefore, it must also be accompanied by a

determined export promotion drive on behalf of both government and business-men. A simple lowering of export prices will not automatically attract buyers. Their attention must be drawn to the product and to the new price situation.

5. Devaluation aims at making a country's exports more competitive by lowering their price in terms of other currencies. However, it must be noted that if our overseas competitors also devalue by the same amount there may be little change in the relative competitiveness of each country's exports.

A Note on Devaluation and Sterling Balances

London is a major international financial centre which offers banking and investment services to overseas customers. Many nations hold balances of sterling in accounts in London[1] as a medium through which they can finance their international payment. The external value of these balances will vary according to the exchange value of sterling and thus a devaluation will have a serious effect upon them. If we assume a U.S.A. trader acquires a £10,000 sterling balance when £1 = $3 then this will be worth $30,000. However, if the exchange rate is devalued to £1 = $2 then this trader's sterling balance, whilst still worth £10,000 sterling will now have a dollar value of $20,000; a loss to the trader of $10,000.

A nation which operates as a world banker, therefore, has to be careful not to destroy the confidence of overseas investors. As a result, devaluation has always been a last resort measure, employed only when all other measures have failed.

This problem was eased to some extent in 1968 when the U.K. agreed to guarantee 90 per cent of the value of official sterling balances against losses through devaluation. The agreement, known as the Basle Agreement, was ended in 1974.[2]

B. *Effect of Devaluation Upon Imports*

Whilst devaluation will make the devaluing country's exports cheaper it will also make its imports more expensive. A fall in the exchange rate from £1 = $2·80 to £1 = $2·40 will mean that an importer will need approximately 14 per cent more pounds to buy the same amount of dollars he could purchase pre devalua-tion (for each pound sold on the foreign exchange market there would be 40 cents less for the importer). The total effect of this would be, in theory, to reduce the nation's desire to import and hopefully its outflow of foreign currency. In practice, however, there is no automatic guarantee that this will happen.

Much depends on the individual country's elasticity of demand for imports. If a large part of the devaluing country's imports are in inelastic demand, then the rising cost of imports through the devaluation may not produce a significant fall in purchases. The U.K., for example, is highly dependent upon imported raw materials and foodstuffs. These must be bought whether they become more expensive or not. Devaluation, therefore, will only be successful when domestic substitutes can be made available. In practice, many economies will not be able to produce substitutes immediately because they lack spare productive capacity in their domestic industry, or because they lack the technical ability to produce a fully competitive alternative.

It might be further noted that when domestic substitutes can be provided, the pressure of demand for them is likely to lead to an escalation of prices

1. Refer Vol. II Chapter 26.
2. Refer page 295.

of such substitutes and this in turn likely to set off inflationary pressures which may eventually reduce the benefit devaluation has on export sales. However, where a nation has the spare capacity (unemployed labour, machinery, etc.) to meet the new demand then the devaluation has a better chance of being successful.

Perhaps the most serious criticism of devaluation is that it can easily sow the seeds of inflation which, if not checked, can quickly whittle away any benefits generated by the devaluation.

An economy which imports a large amount of its raw materials and food-stuffs and is unable to provide domestic substitutes is likely to be most vulnerable to this problem. Devaluation will increase the price of imported raw materals and this will, in turn, push up costs of production based on these raw materials.

The rising cost of importing food may also lead to increases in the cost of living. Wage demands will naturally follow the latter and in turn will add again to the costs of production and final prices.

If costs and prices rise in the way described above, the lower export price advantage from devaluation will soon be lost. Thus, great care has to be taken to ensure that the inflationary tendency of devaluation is checked by effective demand management policies.

Effect of Devaluation on Final Prices in the U.K.

If one examines the cost breakdown of the average British product we might find the following:

AVERAGE U.K. PRODUCT

Cost Breakdown (%)		By Price (Assuming final price £100)	
70	Wages	£70	Wages
5	Profits	£5	Profits
17	Imports	£17	Imports
8	Tax	£8	Tax
100		£100	

If the country makes a devaluation of 10 per cent, this means that price of imports will rise by approximately 10 per cent. Total cost of products should, therefore, rise by a figure about 10 per cent of the price of the import content of the product. Prices should rise, therefore, by 10 per cent of 17 per cent *or* 1·7 per cent. If we assume that the average U.K. product costing £100 has £17 worth of import content, then a 10 per cent rise in import prices would increase the cost of the £100 product by 10 per cent of £17 *or* £1·70. Devaluation in this case would appear to affect final prices little. However, in practice the devaluation may be used as an excuse for raising prices generally, and also as a signal for a surge in wage demands which may lead to futher increases in costs and prices.

Revaluation

Revaluation is the raising of the value of one's currency in terms of other currencies. It is a similar action to devaluation in that the central monetary authorities of the country revaluing agree to defend their currency at a new parity

level. This time, however, the new rate of exchange for the currency will be higher than the previously defended rate.

If the pound was operating at its immediate post November 1967 level of £1 = $2·40, and was subsequently revalued, it might then carry a value of, say, £1 = $3. The effect of this would be to increase the price of British exports and as a result one might expect a poorer export performance. At the same time imports to the U.K. would become cheaper and therefore possibly increase (£1 now buys $3 worth but previously only $2·40). Thus, the balance of payments of a revaluing country will, in theory, tend to swing adversely.

Why Revalue?

A nation whose currency is considered to be undervalued is likely to have a preferential trade advantage. If this nation is accumulating large and continuous balance of payments surpluses it means that some other country is experiencing the more serious problem of a balance of payments deficit. One country's surplus can be said to be the other end of another's deficit. Under a system of rigid exchange rates the surplus country might be expected to revalue to spoil its own international performance in order to give an advantage to less fortunate nations. A surplus, therefore, in many ways is as undesirable as a deficit (particularly when it forces deficit nations to take strong defensive action, using tariffs and other techniques which reduce trade).

Revaluation is far less common than devaluation. This is probably because most nations who have achieved a successful balance of payments position are usually reluctant to see their surpluses disappear through an exchange rate juggling act. A balance of payments surplus has a great psychological affect upon a nation. Such surpluses are considered monuments to successful economic management. Thus, a government pursuing a policy of revaluation will undoubtedly please the managers of the international monetary system but will lose itself much popularity on the domestic front; the industrialist fearing for his export industries and the unions fearing for members' jobs in those industries.

The world's two most successful exporting countries (West Germany and Japan) have both questioned international demands for the revaluation of their currencies by asking why they should be penalised for their economic success when the problem is really other country's poor economic performance. (Nevertheless both have revalued).

market by U.S. importers (demanding U.K. goods), then the exchange rate or price of the currency will tend to stabilise at some level – say £1 = $2·40. It is, however, unlikely in practice that the demand for dollars and the supply of dollars will be exactly balanced. If the U.K.'s demand for U.S. goods rises rapidly so will the demand for the dollar. However, if U.S. demand for U.K. goods falls the demand for the pound (and consequently the supply of dollars) in the foreign exchange markets will decrease. A high demand for dollars accompanied by a shortening of supply means that the dollar (like any other commodity in short supply) will increase in price – say from £1 = $2·40 to £1 = $2·00.[1]

Under a freely floating exchange rate system, therefore, the price of a currency will be determined by the free operation of market forces – there being no interference whatsoever by governments or other institutions with those forces. However, the freely floating system is rarely seen in practice. Most governments are unwilling to allow the price of their currency to fluctuate entirely according to the whims and fancies of the forces operating in a free market. Currencies are much more likely to be allowed to float within some pre-determined limits – these exchange rate systems perhaps being better described as 'flexible' rather than floating systems. Space does not permit the examination of all the variations of exchange rate systems but a summary of some of the major types is given in Exhibit 22.1.[2]

FIXED EXCHANGE RATE SYSTEMS

These lie at the further extreme from the freely floating system and have, until recently, dominated the international payments system. Under a fixed exchange rate system a nation will take steps to ensure that the external value of its currency is maintained at a pre-agreed level, irrespective of the forces of supply and demand operating in the market.

In 1944 the major trading nations of the world agreed, at Bretton Woods, to maintain stable currency exchange rates. Individual countries were expected to fix the price of their currency at some agreed level and their 'central banks' were expected to enter the foreign exchange markets to maintain that price by buying or selling currencies when the price moved away from the agreed parity.

An example may help to make this clear. In November 1967 the British government announced 'that it would fix the value of the pound around a central rate of $2·40 to £1. A one per cent variation in movement was allowed either side the central rate so that in practice the pound, whilst to all intents and purposes was *fixed at* $2·40, would be allowed to vary in price from $2·38 to $2·42. Once the price of the pound moved outside this very narrow band action would be taken to bring it back.

Thus, for example, if the demand for U.K. exports fell the demand for the pound would also fall. Should this movement be accompanied by an increase in U.K. demand for imports the foreign exchange market would experience an increase in the supply of pounds. The combined effect of a fall in the demand for pounds and an increase in supply would therefore tend to lower the price of the pound and possibly pull it outside the narrow band. When this happens the Bank of England will enter the foreign exchange market and buy pounds shortening their supply hence pushing the price back towards the central rate.

1. Note that if the price of a foreign currency increases one gets less of it for the same money.
2. The student is advised to complete the section on exchange rates before referring to the exhibit.

1	2	3	4	5
Absolute Fixed Peg	Fixed Peg with Small Fluctuations	Adjustable Peg	Wider Band Float	Moveable Band
$2.40 — £1		a = old parity b = new parity		
No fluctuations allowed. Price in this case pinned rigidly at $2.40	Rate allowed to move narrowly — 1% either side of parity before monetary authorities intervene to influence the price. E.g. gold standard.	System operated 1944–1971. Rates move 1% either side of parity *but* rate may, under pressure of a disequilibrium in the balance of payments, adopt a new parity by a revaluation or devaluation.	Greater flexibility allowed before intervention by monetary authorities. Adopted Dec. 1971 under Smithsonian agreement.	Simply a more flexible version of the adjustable peg. If the exchange rate becomes jammed against the upper or lower limits of the band, the whole band can be moved

6	7	8		
Crawling Peg (Sliding Peg)	The Free Float	The Managed Float		
Rates are allowed to move with market pressures but only slightly — say no more than 2% per annum or per month.	Opposite extreme to fixed peg — exchange rate left to be determined by free market forces.	Managed floating ("dirty floating") occurs where exchange rate allowed to float but government interferes with free operation of market forces when this is considered politic.		

Note : Adopted from "Do We Need a Hover Pound?" – Wilsher –
Sunday Times 5th October 1969.

EXHIBIT 22.1

flows were recorded in a section called "monetary movements" which dealt with short term as opposed to long term funds. The basic balance excluding short term flows was often regarded as the main indicator of the Balance of Payments position. But what indeed did the basic balance show? If the country had a surplus of £200M in the year but invested abroad long term £300M more then foreigners invested here the balance would have shewn a £100M deficit. This outflow might have been covered by an inflow of funds from abroad which would have appeared in the monetary movements so that the Government would not have had to draw from the Reserves or borrow from abroad. On the other hand there could have been an outflow caused by a large increase in export credit or a decrease in sterling balances held in London in which case the Government would have had to make bigger drawings or borrowings than the £100M shewn in the basic balance. Thus the basic balance was not such an important indicator of the true health of the payments position and one reason for this was the difficulty of distinguishing between the short term and long term flows of capital included in the monetary movements and the basic balance e.g. if an investor had bought shares abroad and held them for only a short time the transaction would have been part of the long term capital movements simply because there is no way of distinguishing.

Under the new presentation all capital flows are grouped together so that when they are added to the Current Balance and Balancing Item they show that in the event of a surplus the amount which the Government has for placing in the Reserves and/or using to repay earlier borrowings . . . or if in deficit the amount which the Government has to find to balance the account. The new form of the statement emphasises the importance of the two balances; the Current Balance gives some sign of our success or failure in paying our way, the Total Currency Flow gives the facts regarding the country's ability to build up reserves and pay off its debts, or vice versa.

PROBLEMS OF A BALANCE OF PAYMENTS DEFICIT

When a country's balance of payments is in deficit because the value of its exports is too low to pay for the volume of imports there is one obvious step to "solve" the situation namely devaluation; by altering the exchange rates it is presumed that imports will fall, exports rise and the account move back into surplus. Every time that the U.K. has moved into heavy deficit there has always been the tendency for foreign holders of sterling to wonder whether Britain would devalue to rectify the situation. They are naturally concerned about the possible reduction in value of their pounds and so take precautions by exchanging their pounds for safer currencies. This creates an additional problem for the U.K. for at the very time it is drawing on Reserves or borrowing to finance the deficit it is faced with a "run on Sterling". The presentation of large amounts at the Bank of England for conversion accelerates both the fall in the Reserves and the need to borrow.

It is not inevitable that the two events should be so linked . . . e.g. there was a run on the pound in 1957 yet at that time the U.K. Current Account was healthy . . . it was not that holders of sterling feared devaluation by which they would lose but they anticipated revaluation of the D. mark by which they might gain. In 1964 there was a very large deficit on the Current Account and yet there was no run on sterling until the end of the year . . . this was because a considerable inflow of foreign funds into London had disguised the position.

Whether an adverse balance of payments should cause alarm depends on:

1. The size of the deficit relative to the size of the Reserves ... if it is relatively small no-one will regard it as serious.

2. All countries cannot be in surplus simultaneously. There are variations causing surpluses and deficits to cancel out over a period, it is for example a recognised feature that traditionally the U.K. moves into deficit in the Autumn but reverses the trend in the Spring.

The methods by which the Government attempts to rectify the imbalance will be dealt with in the next chapter; what needs to be remembered at this stage is that whatever policy is adopted to achieve a satisfactory balance really has to be one which does not abandon other economic goals. Governments also have a responsibility for maintaining employment and the standard of living. Thus any measures taken to reduce the level of demand for imports in general which results in a lower level of economic activity and a considerable rise in unemployment must be regarded as very doubtful "solutions" to a balance of payments deficit.

An additional problem today is that many experts believe that the traditional methods of dealing with a deficit (explained in the next chapter) are now useless. For example, the immediate counter-measure for a deficit was deflation whereas the cure for unemployment or low investment was to reflate the economy, but today we have a balance of payments deficit and rising unemployment and clearly we cannot apply both "solutions". Indeed it may be said that the other cures are also non-starters; import controls are against the spirit of our international agreements; devaluation is a very costly method.

Earlier it was said that in assessing the severity of the situation the size of the deficit would have to be seen in relation to the size of the Reserves; another important comparison which should be introduced is to express the deficit as a percentage of the gross domestic product. The following table shows this for the period 1964-74.

	Deficit/Surplus on Current A/c (£m)	% of G.D.P.
1964	−382	1.3
1965	−49	0.2
1966	+84	0.3
1967	−313	0.9
1968	−280	0.8
1969	+449	1.1
1970	+707	1.6
1971	+1,093	2.3
1972	+114	0.2
1973	−1,200	1.9
1974	−3,730	6.0

What the table shows is that for the first time in its history the U.K. borrowed more than 2% of its gross domestic product from abroad ... and the Chancellor has estimated that it will be as high as 6%. Put more forcibly it meant that in 1974 we spent 106% of what we produced, however if we look at the increase in the deficit from 1973 to 1974 ... £2,500M approx. ... then see that the cost of oil imported into the U.K. rose by about the same amount it means that the deterioration in our balance of payments is accounted for by the rise in oil

CONTENTS

Preface

The impetus for writing this book arose from the introduction of a new syllabus to cover a two-year course in Economics for the Ordinary National Certificate and Diploma in Business Studies. The book is divided into two volumes; book I to be used for the first year of the course and book II for the second year. The contents of book I are related mainly to that part of Economics which is directly related to the firm whereas book II is more concerned with the environment, nationally and internationally, within which the firm operates.

The book should also be extremely useful for students on other courses in the business field where knowledge of basic economics and the role of economics in "real business activities" is required. It should be very useful for students taking ICMA and ACCA examinations in Economics; students taking the new syllabus for the Certificate in Works Management and first year Higher National Certificate and Diploma in Business Studies students.

All business students, whether they be in distribution, marketing, production, purchasing, retailing, storekeeping, etc., should be better informed for having read this book.

The book is non-mathematical in presentation although, on occasion, simple calculations and graphs are employed.

Footnotes have been kept to a minimum and are used to explain a word or state an equation. The attempt is to provide information within the book rather than have students search for information in dictionaries and other sources.

As the book has been written with the new student of Economics in mind, we have, *at times*, felt it necessary to *sacrifice some preciseness* for simplicity of exposition.

In general, the book aims to be sufficiently self-contained, thus lessening the need to study preliminary books in this field. Yet, it sets the scene for grasping the essentials necessary for wider reading in each of the areas covered.

There are many books on Economics, but there are few that relate Economics to reality or bring the reality of business into economic analysis. The Joint Committee for National Awards in Business Studies and the professional bodies have recently changed or are changing their Economic syllabuses requiring this approach. This book is intended to fill in a considerable part of this gap.

We wish to take this opportunity to express our deep appreciation to our colleagues for their friendly encouragement and help. They have been generous with their time in reading the typescript and influencing our thinking. Special mention is made to Mr. D. G. Adams, Mr. N. Grimwade and Mr. B. J. Moore, all lecturers in Economics at the West Bromwich College of Commerce and Technology.

Our appreciation is also extended to Business Studies, Accountancy, Works Managers and other students, both past and present, whose influence on our thinking is reflected in the book.

To those who very kindly gave us permission to reproduce some of their copyrighted material we gratefully acknowledge their co-operation.

To two of our children, Mr. Gerald Paulus, B.A. (Econ.) and Miss Gillian King (presently at University of Hull) we would like to express our appreciation especially for useful comments on the approach that would most likely meet the approval of students.

Finally, we would like to express our gratitude to our wives and children whose patience and sympathy smoothed the way to bringing this book to fulfilment.

| | B. J. E. Jukes | N. L. Paulus |
| | S. King | A. G. Whitehouse |

Staffordshire and West Midlands
July 1975

Part One

NATIONAL INCOME AND EXPENDITURE

Chapter One

National Income Accounting and Income Flows

Introduction

In this first part of the second volume the reader is introduced to that branch of economics known as macroeconomics. Macroeconomics – the Greek word "macro" means big or large – deals with economic aggregates or totals; it is concerned with the functioning of the economy as a whole as opposed to microeconomics which is concerned with the working of the various parts of the economy.

Macroeconomics tries to provide answers to questions such as the following: what determines aggregate demand for an economy's output; why is there a particular level of unemployment; why is it that demand, output and unemployment fluctuate, often significantly, so that at one time there is considerable unutilised industrial capacity and unemployment and at another there is undesirable inflationary pressure on resources; how can such fluctuations be regulated and offset; what causes changes in the general level of prices; what determines an economy's growth rate?

All these are questions of crucial importance. We may at some time or other be out of a job; each one of us will certainly be affected to a greater or lesser degree by inflation; we may become dissatisfied with improvements in our standards of living, and so on. Hopefully, in the study of what follows, at least some of the answers will present themselves. At the same time the reader should gain an understanding of the complex inter-relationships within the economy and of its working. This may lead to a better appreciation of what government intervention in the economy is trying to achieve and an understanding of the effects of such intervention on business in general and on the student's firm in particular.

Measurement of Economic Activity

We can regard economic activity as the transformation through various production processes of scarce resources into goods and services required by people to satisfy (some of) their needs and wants. The greater the quantity of resources there is, and the more extensively and efficiently they are used, the greater will be the economy's output and, consequently, the more peoples' wants will be satisfied. Unfortunately there is not available any means of measuring directly the degree of satisfaction (or welfare or utility). In the absence of a direct measure, economists have to make do with the imperfect measure of output of goods and services, or rather the value of output.

Prices are used to measure the value that people impute to goods. For example if a person is prepared to pay £5 for a certain article, we must assume that he expects to get from it twice as much satisfaction or welfare as from an article costing him £2·50, and half as much as from an article for which he would be willing to pay £10.

Therefore if we multiply the output of each article by its price or market value

and sum the resultant totals, we shall arrive at some (imperfect) measure of economic welfare. Remember, however, that the methods of measuring activity that will shortly be introduced were not designed to assess welfare or the standard of living, only the output of the economic system.

In the United Kingdom the official estimates of national income and other related figures are published by the Central Statistical Office, generally in August or September each year, in the form of a National Income Blue Book. The first of these was published in 1941. At the time of writing the latest edition available in the series is that published in August 1974 under the title "National Income and Expenditure 1963 – 1973". All the United Kingdom national accounts figures appearing in this chapter have been taken from this publication.

Before we go on, it is worth emphasising that the published figures are only estimates; as the introduction to the Blue Book puts it: "All the value estimates are expressed in terms of a precise number of £ million, but this does not imply that they can be regarded as accurate to the last digit". It would of course be virtually impossible to gather 100% accurate figures.

As we shall see three measures of national output are published. Due to a number of reasons which need not concern us here, the three approaches will not always in practice yield identical results. However as the aggregates are conceptually the same, statistical discrepancies are corrected by means of a balancing item or residual error. Anyone wishing to delve deeply into the basis of the compilation of national accounts statistics is recommended to consult the publication "National Accounts Statistics: Sources and Methods", HMSO, 1968, in which detailed descriptions are given.

MEASUREMENT OF OUTPUT

One of the most widely used approaches to the measurement of economic activity is to calculate the output of goods and services within the economy during some given period.

Measurement of output causes a number of problems, one of which is the "adding-up" problem. When we consider the immense variety of output produced in a typical modern economy we very soon realise that it is impossible to add together such heterogeneous commodities in terms of their physical units of output. We cannot add together lemonade, train journeys, clothes, symphony concerts, petrol, bars of chocolate and economics text-books; such items are "unaddable" or incapable of summation. In order to add these we need some common numéraire or yardstick, and this is present in the form of money in its role as a measure of value or accounting unit.

So we take the quantity produced of each commodity and service, multiply by its average price, and sum the totals to give a measure of the market value of total output. For example consider a simple economy producing only three goods, bread, cheese and beer. National output is calculated as follows:

National output of simple economy

Commodity	Unit	Output	Price per unit (£)	Market Value (£)
Bread	loaf	10,000	0·15	1,500
Cheese	lb	5,000	0·20	1,000
Beer	gallon	20,000	0·20	4,000
Total National Output				£6,500

EXHIBIT 1.1

And so it is with an actual complex economy.

comparison and co-ordination which is allied to that of intelligence. Even to look at an object is an act and by noting whether a young child lets his gaze dwell on the first point that presents itself or whether he directs it so as to include the whole complex of relations, we can almost judge his mental age. When objects that are too distant to be included in the same centring are to be compared, perceptual activity is extended in the form of "transportations" in space, as though the view of one of the objects were being superimposed on the other. These transportations, which thus constitute the (potential) reconciliation of centrings, give place to genuine "comparisons" or double transportations which, by alternating, decentralise the distortions due to one-way transportation. Study of these transportations has drawn our attention to a distinct reduction of distortions with age,[1] that is to say, a distinct improvement in the estimation of size at a distance, and this is self-explanatory in view of the coefficient of true activity which occurs here.

Now, it is easy to show that these decentralisations and double transportations, together with the specific regulations which their different varieties involve, are responsible for the famous perceptual "constancies" of shape and size. It is most remarkable that we scarcely ever obtain absolute size constancy in the laboratory; the child under-estimates size at a distance (taking into account the error of the standard), but the adult almost always over-estimates it slightly! These "superconstancies", which writers have in fact often observed but which they normally pass over as though they were embarrassing exceptions, have seemed to us to constitute the rule, and no fact could better attest the intervention of true regulation in the construction of constancies. Now when we see that infants, just at the age at which this constancy has been noted (although its precision has been greatly exaggerated), indulge in genuine trials, which consist in

[1] Arch. de Psychol., XXIX (1943) pp. 173–253.

illusions shows the existence of modifications with age that would be inexplicable without a close affinity between perception and intellectual activity in general.

Here we must distinguish two cases, corresponding on the whole to what Binet called "innate" and "acquired" illusions, and which we had best straight away name "primary" and "secondary" illusions. Primary illusions are reducible to simple factors of centralisation and are thus dependent on the law of relative centralisation. Now the value of these diminishes fairly regularly with age ("error of the standard", illusions of Delbœuf, Oppel, Müller-Lyer, etc.) and this is readily explained by the increase in decentralisations, and in the regulations which they involve, as the subject's activity when faced with the figures increases. Certainly, the young child remains passive where older children and adults compare, analyse and thus indulge in an active decentralisation which is orientated towards operational reversibility. But, on the other hand, there are illusions which increase in intensity with age or development, such as the weight illusion, which is absent in the grossly abnormal and which increases up to the end of childhood, to decrease somewhat afterwards. But we know that what it requires is simply a sort of anticipation of the relations of weight and volume, and it is clear that this anticipation presupposes an activity which by its very nature increases of its own accord with intellectual growth. Such an illusion, produced by interaction between primary perceptual factors and perceptual activity, may thus be called secondary and we shall shortly be meeting others which are of the same type.

This being so, perceptual activity is distinguished in the first place by the occurrence of decentralisation, which corrects the effects of centralisation and thus constitutes a regulation of perceptual distortions. Now, however elementary and dependent on sensori-motor functions these decentralisations and regulations may be, it is clear that they all constitute an activity of

Between 1965 and 1968 there was considerable speculation that the U.S. government would announce an increase in the official price of gold in order to encourage an increase in the production of newly mined gold and to supplement world liquidity. As a result, central banks lost considerable quantities of gold stocks to the hoards of private speculators, who, in purchasing gold at $35 an ounce hoped to resell it later at say $70 an ounce. To stop any further drain of gold from the international payments system the central banks that were members of the "Group of Seven"[1] agreed not to sell gold except to one another.

Since the conclusion of this agreement in 1968 the central banks have also refused to buy newly mined gold (except in special circumstances) and as a result, greater reliance now has had to be placed upon the key currencies in world liquidity.

The U.S. dollar has, in practice, made the biggest contribution to international liquidity since the last war. The U.S. policy of running balance of payments deficits (mainly on capital account) has pumped dollars into the international payments system. The U.S. debt has been paid by creating dollar balances (deposits) in U.S. banks for overseas residents. These dollars have been accepted because the dollar has until (1971) been convertible into gold by the Federal Reserve Bank of the U.S. Many holders of dollars, however, simply hold them for convenience as the dollar is widely accepted as an international currency and international payments can be effected by making dollar transfers between internationally owned accounts held in the U.S.[2]

However, expansion of world liquidity in this way has its limitations. The provision of international liquidity is not simply a matter of increasing the volume of money in international circulation but also ensuring that people will be willing to hold the increasing quantities of it. A currency such as the dollar is held internationally because holders have trust in that currency, that is to say that it will retain its value, that it can be converted into gold or other currencies and that other currencies will not appreciate in value in relation to it. The strength and therefore the acceptability of the dollar has been seriously questioned in the late 1960s and early 1970s. Continuous U.S. balance of payments deficits have increased the flow of dollars outside the U.S. but the U.S. gold reserves which formed a backing for those dollar balances (providing the "where withall" for conversion of the dollars) have fallen. Thus, confidence in the U.S. ability to convert the dollar fell and willingness to accept the increased flows of dollars from the U.S. therefore decreased. The selling of dollar balances for gold was in fact so great in August 1971 that the U.S. had to suspend convertibility to preserve her reserves.

The degree to which a country like the U.S. can expand world liquidity by running balance of payments deficits and pumping dollars into the hands of people outside the U.S. depends upon the willingness of those people to accept the dollars. A long series of balance of payments deficits may result in so many dollars entering the world payments system that suspicion arises as to whether the U.S. reserves are large enough to meet demands for the conversion of dollars. Secondly, devaluation is always a likelihood in times of balance of payments deficits and thus confidence in the dollar may fall as the deficits continue.

In recent years the problem has been aggravated by the growing strength of less important currencies such as the Deutsch mark and the yen. These

1. Members of the IMF who formulate gold sales policy.
2. Refer to Chapter 26 showing how sterling operates in this way.

have often been shrouded by expectations of revaluation thus making them more desirable, and the dollar less desirable to hold.

Thus, one can see that balance of payments deficits of countries managing key currencies are not always effective ways of increasing world liquidity. Increasing the supply of such currencies often weakens them.

Part Thirteen

INTERNATIONAL TRADE AND MONETARY ARRANGEMENTS

Chapter Twenty-Five

INTERNATIONAL MONETARY PROBLEMS

Reform of the International Monetary System

Of all the reforms introduced since World War II most have simply attempted to improve the operation of the existing system rather than completely reform it. This policy has often been described as "papering over the cracks" and is considered by many as a poor substitute for a much needed total reform of the system.

Complete reform has been held back by lack of unanimity between the major trading powers. All agree that reform is necessary but few agree as to the type of reform. Ideas range from a system of payment based entirely on gold with the elimination of the dollar and sterling as reserve currencies, to a system operating on completely new international reserve units. The latter idea was put forward by Lord Keynes, at the Bretton Woods conference in 1944, and was to be based on an international unit called "bancor". This was a currency which could be issued by an international central monetary authority in accordance with the world's demand for liquidity.

Role of I.M.F. and its Contribution to the Easing of the Liquidity Problem

The International Monetary Fund (IMF) was set up at the Bretton Woods conference in 1944 in an attempt to bring some order and organisation into the international payments system after the chaos that had developed since the abandonment of the "gold standard" in the 1930s.

The IMF is basically a "mutual aid" association having a membership of well over 100 nations.[1] Its functions are broadly two-fold:

1. to engender the international co-operation necessary to conduct a workable international monetary system, and

2. to provide a pool of international reserves which can be used to supplement members' own reserves when they experience balance of payments difficulties or when their currencies need support.

The Bretton Woods agreement insisted that members of "the Fund" maintained fairly fixed exchange rates. Thus, instead of allowing exchange rates to depreciate to ease balance of payments difficulties, the IMF provided its members with currencies to ease their international payments difficulties. This then gave them time to implement domestic deflationary policies to bring their balance of payments into equilibrium.

Operation of the Fund

Each member is alloted a quota. This is a unit on which members' borrowing rights, voting powers and contributions to the IMF are based. The size of a

1. Membership excludes the 'communist bloc'.

member's quota is calculated through a rather complicated formula which takes into account the size of the member's national income, its degree of involvement in world trade and the size of its gold and foreign currency reserves. The U.K.'s *quota* is the second largest and thus makes her a very influential member of the IMF.

The "pool" of currencies held by the IMF, and from which members can make drawings, is provided by members' contributions (in accordance with the size of their quotas). Each member must contribute 25 per cent of the value of its *quota* in "gold" and 75 per cent in its own national currency. When a member runs into balance of payment difficulties and finds his own resources inadequate to meets its needs, it can exercise its right to borrow from the "pool".

Borrowing Rights

Borrowing rights are again governed by the size of the member's quota. Each member can borrow foreign currencies up to 25 per cent of the value of its quota without question. Further borrowing, however, requires the *approval* of the directors of the IMF and is restricted. It is important to note that the borrowing operation is not borrowing in the ordinary sense of the word. As each nation draws currency from the "pool" it pays into the pool an equivalent sum in its own currency. Thus, the more a country borrows from the "pool" the greater the "pool's" accumulation of that country's currency. This brings us to the second limitation on borrowing. A member country can borrow currencies beyond the automatic right of 25 per cent of its quota providing it has the approval of the directors and then only up to the point where the IMF's holding of that country's currency is equal to 200 per cent of the value of its quota. Further borrowing may also be possible if other nations are demanding this country's currency from the "pool". The IMF's holding of the currency may then fall below 200 per cent of the nation's quota enabling it to pay more of its currency into the pool to withdraw more foreign currency (but again only up to the point where the IMF's holding of the borrowing nation's currency is equal to 200 per cent of the borrowing nation's quota).

This system may be more easily understood by looking at the following

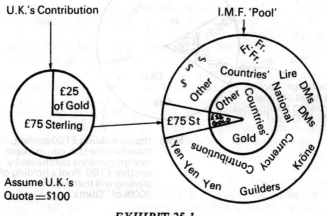

U.K.'s Quota with I.M.F.

EXHIBIT 25.1

highly simplified and hypothetical example: Suppose Britain has been given a quota of $100 and that £1 = $1. Britain's initial contribution to the IMF will, therefore, be £75 sterling *plus* £25 worth of gold as shown in Exhibit 25.1.

Normal borrowing rights would allow the U.K. to draw up to 25 per cent of the value of its quota from the pool without notice. Thus, £25 worth of foreign currencies could be drawn by paying into the IMF £25 sterling. The IMF's holding of sterling would now increase to £100 (the original £75 contribution plus the £25 payment for drawings of that value) whilst its holdings of other currencies would fall as the U.K. makes withdrawals. Note the value of the IMF's holdings of currencies will not change on withdrawal; only the composition of holdings. This is illustrated in the following exhibit.

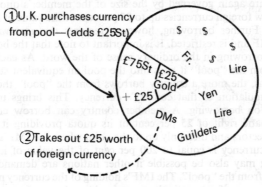

U.K. Borrowing From I.M.F. 'Pool'

①U.K. purchases currency from pool—(adds £25St)

②Takes out £25 worth of foreign currency

EXHIBIT 25.2

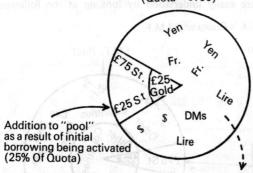

U.K. Borrowing Extended By I.M.F.
(Quota = $100)

Addition to "pool" as a result of initial borrowing being activated (25% Of Quota)

Note : Pool is holding £100 sterling, therefore the U.K. can increase foreign currency purchases by another £100. Pool's holding of sterling will then equal 200% of "Quota".

EXHIBIT 25.3

Assuming that the U.K. now gets the approval of the directors of the IMF to extend its borrowing, it will be able to draw further foreign currencies in exchange for sterling, up to the point where the IMF's holding of sterling is equal to 200 per cent of the U.K.'s "quota" value; that is to say, up to the point where the IMF's holding of sterling reaches £200. Since the IMF is already holding (in this example) £100 worth of sterling, the U.K. could borrow another £100 worth of foreign currencies before its borrowing limit is reached. This is shown in Exhibit 25.3

It is possible, in some circumstances, for borrowing to be extended even further. If, when the limit is reached, another country borrows sterling from the pool this will bring the pool's holding of sterling below 200 per cent of the value of the U.K.'s quota and enables the U.K. to continue increasing its purchase of foreign currencies until it raises the level of sterling to the 200 per cent limit. Exhibit 25.4 attempts to show this situation.

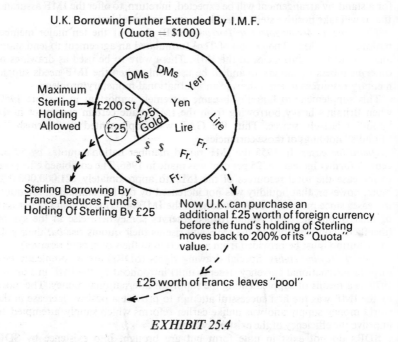

U.K. Borrowing Further Extended By I.M.F.
(Quota = $100)

Maximum Sterling Holding Allowed → £200 St

Sterling Borrowing By France Reduces Fund's Holding Of Sterling By £25

Now U.K. can purchase an additional £25 worth of foreign currency before the fund's holding of Sterling moves back to 200% of its "Quota" value.

£25 worth of Francs leaves "pool"

EXHIBIT 25.4

Other Limitations on Borrowing

All drawings are initially limited to a maximum value of 25 per cent of one's quota in one year and any drawings beyond the automatic 25 per cent of one's quota may be subject to the "borrower" giving the IMF an undertaking that it will take specific steps to improve its balance of payments position. This might take the form of an undertaking by the borrowing nation to control its domestic money supply or introduce an incomes policy.

Repayments to the IMF

Loans from the IMF must be repaid; the repayment including both an interest and service charge. The IMF will normally nominate the currency or currencies

in which the repayment (re-purchase) can be made. Thus, if any member's currency in the pool is in such great demand that the IMF's holdings are below that country's 75 per cent quota subscription, this currency may be a nominated repayment currency. Time periods for repayment are normally over a period of 3 to 5 years.

Other IMF Supplements to International Liquidity

Stand-by arrangements. Since 1952 members of the IMF have been able to ask the IMF for assurances that certain quantities of credit would be made immediately available to them for a particular period without prior negotiation. In practice these rights to draw currencies from the pool will rarely be used. However, the official assurances that currencies are available often help to reduce speculation in a member's currency (for example; the knowledge that the U.K. can borrow currencies to support sterling). Normally, a member asking for a stand-by arrangement will be expected, in return, to offer the IMF assurance that it will take positive steps to tackle its economic problems.

The General Arrangement to Borrow (GAB). In 1961 the ten major member nations of the IMF (The Group of Ten) formulated an agreement to lend stated amounts of their currencies to the IMF. These were to be used as drawings by other members of the group and to be used only when the IMF needs supplementary resources to smooth over an international monetary problem.

This supplement to liquidity became extremely important in the late 1960s when Britain's heavy borrowing from the IMF made certain currencies in the "pool" relatively scarce. Thus the GAB was implemented to replenish the "Fund's" holdings of those currencies.

Quota increases. In 1955 the IMF raised member nation's quotas by 50 per cent. A further increase of 25 per cent was made in 1966. The combined effect was to increase the total resources of the IMF to approximately £21,000,000,000. Note, however, that liquidity was not increased by the full amount of the quota increases since members' contributions to the IMF in terms of gold (25 per cent of their quota increase) would reduce reserves somewhere else in the system (members' contributions to the IMF will rise as their quotas rise *but* their gold contribution must be provided from a reduction in their own gold reserves).

Special drawing rights. Special drawing rights (SDRs) are a completely new form of international currency (reserve unit) introduced by the IMF in January 1970 as a means of supplementing the supply of international money. The move by the IMF was the first successful attempt to provide a positive increase in the world money supply and was unlike earlier reforms which simply attempted to improve the efficiency of the existing system.

SDRs do not exist in note form but are brought into existence by SDR balances created through book-keeping entries credited to member nations' special drawings accounts at the IMF. New allocations of SDRs are normally made annually and the amounts allocated are based on the size of the individual member's quotas. The following allocations have now been made:

Total Allocations to Members
January 1970 – $3,500,000,000 (U.K. $402,000,000)
January 1971 – $3,000,000,000
January 1972 – $3,000,000,000

All SDRs issued, whilst backed by gold, are not convertible into gold. Nevertheless they are often referred to as "paper gold".

The use of SDRs. The IMF expects SDRs to be used when a country has a balance of payments deficit or when it is experiencing a substantial loss of reserves. A nation can activate its rights in two ways, namely:
1. the indirect system, and
2. the direct system.

The indirect system. The initial use of SDRs followed this pattern. A country wishing to use its SDRs would notify the Managing Director of the IMF who would then nominate a country with a substantial surplus in its balance of payments to provide the application country with foreign exchange or gold in exchange for the applicant country's SDRs. The applicant country would then use this foreign exchange for, say, settling some international debt. The SDRs would be added to the donor country's reserves so maintaining their original level. At some later date the applicant country must reconstitute part of these SDRs by repaying foreign currencies or gold to the donor nation.

The direct system. Since SDRs have now become more established and respected many nations are willing to accept them directly into their reserves as settlement of debt.

The merits of SDRs
1. They make a positive contribution to international liquidity.
2. They reduce the need for countries like the U.S.A. to run deficits to supplement liquidity.
3. They can be issued according to the needs for international liquidity.
4. They may eventually replace rather than supplement the present system of reserve currencies and gold.

The problems of SDRs
1. Like all forms of money, success depends upon acceptability. Not all members of the IMF system have fully participated in the scheme.
2. There is a remote chance that excessive issues of SDRs could produce inflation. However, in practice, the issue of SDRs is likely to be strictly controlled.

Raising the Price of Gold as a Solution to International Liquidity Problems
This idea entails the phasing out of key currencies in the international payments system and for the new system to operate with gold (at a greatly increased price) as the sole medium of exchange. We must now examine the likely effects of raising the official price of gold to say $80 per ounce. These can be summarised as follows:

Advantages
1. There would be an immediate increase in the value of world reserves.
2. The mining of gold would be more profitable so bringing more mines (which were previously uneconomic) back into production. The supply of gold to the central banks would, therefore, be increased (assuming they were willing to buy it).
3. Further speculation on rises in the price of gold might cease since a substantial revaluation of the price of gold would make further revaluations unlikely in the short run. Speculators might, therefore, sell their hoards to the central monetary authorities.
4. Removal of national currencies from the payments system would reduce pressures on the nations that operated them.

Disadvantages

1. Nations who keep the bulk of their reserves in gold would probably gain most benefit.
2. Nations politically out of favour with the U.S.A. might stand to benefit most because of their substantial gold reserves, for example South Africa and Russia.
3. Those nations that were good enough to have confidence in the key currencies and kept their reserves in pounds and dollars would gain least benefit.
4. Poorer countries often keep their reserves in key currencies and would, therefore, gain least benefit from an increase in the price of gold. These are often countries with the greatest liquidity problems.

Part Fourteen
INTERNATIONAL TRADE AND MONETARY ARRANGEMENTS

Chapter Twenty-Six
INTERNATIONAL MONETARY ARRANGEMENTS

Sterling Area

The "sterling area" can perhaps best be described as a currency bloc with strong trading ties. It comprises a group of countries (mainly Commonwealth and ex-Commonwealth nations) which conduct a considerable part of their international trade through the medium of "sterling". For over a century these countries have, for one reason or another, found it convenient to hold balances of sterling lodged in bank accounts and other short term investments in the City of London. The balances have come to form an important part of the international payments system with countries holding such balances settling their inter-indebtedness by making payments to each other through their sterling accounts.

Origin of the Area

The origins go back a century or more to a time when the majority of world trade was financed through gold. Gold, of course, was well respected and universally acceptable, but as sterling was convertible into gold on demand many nations not only implicitly trusted it but found it a more convenient means of effecting payment (gold itself was difficult and costly to transport and one also ran the risk of loss through theft).

Growth in the use of sterling as a trading currency was closely parallel with the development of the Commonwealth. During the 19th and early 20th century Britain's trade was predominantly with these countries and naturally enough members of the Commonwealth found it convenient to conduct most of their trade through sterling. Britain, for example, required the raw materials of her Commonwealth partners and effected payment through sterling which increased the sterling balances of these countries. These balances, in turn, were used by the Commonwealth to purchase, from British industry, the capital goods so essential to their economic development. As the demand for U.K. goods expanded so the demand for sterling became more widespread. A highly simplified example of the use of sterling as a trading currency follows:

Let us suppose that Malaysia and Hong Kong hold, in London, sterling balances which they may have purchased from Britain or earned from international trade. Their accounts[1] might, therefore, take the following form:

Malaysia			Hong Kong		
DR		CR	DR		CR
	Balance	£500m		Balance	£500m

1. These may be owned by governments, banks or private individuals.

If Britain purchases rubber valued at £100m from Malaysia the Malaysian's account might be credited with a further £100m so the accounts would now look so:

Malaysia			Hong Kong	
DR	CR	DR		CR
	Balance £500m		Balance	£500m
	From ex-			
	ports of			
	rubber £100m			
	£600m			

Now let us assume that Malaysia purchases trinkets from Hong Kong worth £50m. Payment might be made by transferring £50m from the Malaysian account in London to the Hong Kong account in the same place.

Malaysia				Hong Kong		
DR			CR	DR		CR
To Hong		Balance	£500m			Balance £500m
Kong	£50m	Rubber		Balance	£550m	From
Balance	£550m	exports	£100m			Malaysia £50m
	£600m		£600m		£550m	£550m

Why Sterling was able to Play this Role

Sterling possessed certain qualities which few other currencies displayed at this time. These qualities produced the confidence that was so necessary for its wide acceptance:

1. Sterling was convertible into gold and therefore considered by many as good as gold.

2. Demand for U.K. goods was always high and therefore the demand for sterling was equally high.

3. The rate of exchange for sterling was stable hence the holders of sterling balances stood little chance of suffering a loss through a depreciation of the exchange rate.

4. Britain not only acted as a banker, arranging the finance of world trade but also provided a useful outlet for the investment of surplus funds of new Commonwealth partners, whose own capital markets were usually poor and unsafe. It in fact became the practice that their surplus earnings from international trade be converted into sterling and left in London to earn interest.

5. As Britain had a large and well organised capital market, members of the sterling area were able to raise funds in the City to aid their economic development. Thus many sterling balances grew up as credits to sterling accounts held in London. For example, loans of £10m to Malaysia or £20m to Hong Kong might be shown as such:

Malaysia			Hong Kong		
DR		CR	DR		CR
	Loan	£10m		Loan	£20m

Note: These credits could of course be used to purchase capital goods from the U.K.

Thus. as the size of sterling balances grew so did sterling's capability of financing more and more of world trade.

Formalising of the Area

Until the 1930s the sterling area had operated without much formality. It was then a loose association of countries which conducted a large part of their trade through sterling. The rules of the association were few and were little more than customary practices. The chief characteristic of the area was that it had grown into a "mutual aid association" in which members would exchange their surpluses of foreign currencies for sterling balances and in return acquired the right to convert that sterling into gold and foreign currencies when funds were needed to make payments to countries not accepting sterling. Britain's gold and foreign currency reserves, therefore, became the reserves of the whole area and to which one contributed when in surplus and borrowed from when in deficit.

In 1931, Britain along with many other countries, left the gold standard and sterling was thus no longer automatically convertible into gold. With exchange rates now liable to fluctuate most countries decided to tie their currencies to the "pound" or the "dollar" – those countries choosing the pound sterling as an anchor formally became the "sterling bloc".

In 1939 Exchange Control Regulations applied restrictions to the movement of capital and current payments from sterling area countries to the rest of the world. This action required, for the first time, a registration of sterling area members and thus a rigid delimitation of the area became possible.

Benefits of the Area to the U.K.

Countries hold sterling because they find it both convenient and profitable to do so. However, these benefits do not extend one way. Britain as "banker" to the area also gains some important financial advantages. In return for paying interest on sterling balances deposited in London British banks have the use of this money in much the same way as a commercial bank has the use of its depositors' money. Thus, when the sterling area was generally in surplus with the non-sterling world the inflow of currencies from that surplus flowed into London and were then available for the finance of British balance of payments deficits.

Britain could also re-lend the currency its sterling area partners deposited with it, and earned interest on such loans. In World War II Britain even financed a considerable part of her import bill by giving her creditors sterling balances in exchange for goods. This, as we will see later, had a serious weakening effect on sterling as an international currency.

The Strength of Sterling

The strength of a currency is simply a reflection of the confidence people place in that currency. It is a measure of the willingness or unwillingness of holders

of the currency to continue holding it. Sterling was held by people overseas because they had the knowledge that:
1. the balances will be converted, on demand, into other acceptable currencies, and
2. the balances will maintain their value against other currencies.

Britain's ability to convert these balances (the U.K.'s liabilities) will depend, to a high degree, upon the level of its gold and foreign currency reserves. These provide backing for the balances should the holder of a balance wish to convert his sterling holdings into foreign currencies.

If Britain's reserves were of an equal value to sterling balances the holders of sterling are likely to have reasonable degree of confidence in it. This was very much so before the second world war when Britain's reserves were actually in excess of the holdings of sterling balances.

However, events since this time have produced a situation where sterling balances have grown at a faster rate than the reserves backing those balances. In theory, therefore, Britain has been placed in a position whereby, should all holders of sterling demand conversion of their balances, reserves would be insufficient to meet these demands in the short term. Fortunately most holders of sterling balances are normally content to maintain their sterling balances and as a result the reserves needed to back sterling need not match those balances. However, the wider the gap between reserves and balances the more vulnerable sterling will become – the holder becoming increasingly suspicious of Britain's ability to convert.

Some holders of sterling are likely to be more hesitant about holding sterling than others. Should these people exchange their sterling for foreign currencies, reserves will fall and possibly prompt others to convert whilst currencies are still available. This situation may then develop into one where there is total loss of confidence in sterling, producing the type of "run" on the pound so common in the middle to late 1960s.

Fortunately, not all holders of sterling are likely to withdraw their balances at the first sign of weakness. Many owners of sterling deposits are governments (official sterling) who appreciate the dangers to the international monetary system of a collapse of sterling. However, there have been times when even the most stalwart of sterling supporters have lost confidence during a serious "run" on the pound.

Devaluation and the Pound
A loss of confidence in sterling is sometimes sparked off by rumours of a likely devaluation of the pound. When the British balance of payments has not responded to the traditional treatment, devaluation becomes a likely solution to the problem.[1] Thus, holders of sterling are tempted to sell their balances before the exchange rate is lowered in order to avoid a reduction in the foreign currency value of their investment.[2]

The Reserve/Balance Gap
The growth of the gap between reserves and balances started in World War II. Britain was short of foreign currencies (much needed for the purchase of oil and armaments for the war effort) and so made payments to governments overseas by simply crediting their accounts in London with sterling balances.

1. Only when sterling is operating on a fixed exchange rate.
2. A more detailed account of devaluation will be found in Chapter 23.

Sterling liabilities were, therefore, being created without the U.K. having corresponding assets in the form of gold and foreign currencies to back those liabilities. As it was unlikely that, at any one time, all the holders of sterling would want to convert their balances, it was accepted that this widening of the gap between reserves and balances could be achieved without a loss of confidence in the pound.

In 1966, for example, sterling balances (U.K.'s liabilities) were totalling £4,715,000,000 whilst reserves backing those liabilities were only valued at £1,225,000,000. Sterling was still strong with only a ¼ of its liabilities backed by liquid assets. This situation in principle is very akin to the creation of credit in commercial banking. Here, we know that, should all depositors demand their deposits in cash no bank could pay up immediately as their cash holdings amount to less than 8 per cent of their liabilities or claims on that cash. In both cases success of this system depends upon maintenance of *"confidence"*.

Despite the fact that liabilities can exceed assets without producing a loss of confidence, the wider the gap between balances and reserves the more vulnerable sterling is likely to become. Since the early 1950s the gap has grown larger and the strains upon sterling have grown considerably.

Factors That Weakened Sterling

Some of the major factors responsible for the weakening of sterling are:

1. *Changes in the pattern of trade.* Since the mid 1950s the sterling area pattern of trade has changed considerably. Instead of the sterling area members conducting the bulk of their trade with one another and financing it through sterling, their trading relationships have grown in other directions. Many members of the sterling area have developed strong trading ties with the non-sterling world (U.S.A., Japan, West Germany, etc.) with the result that when deficits have developed with these countries there has been a big demand for the conversion of sterling balances to provide the foreign currencies necessary to finance those deficits. Movements of this type, therefore, have naturally put greater strain on reserves.

2. *Loans and liabilities.* Britain, as banker to the sterling area, has continued its role of providing the sterling area with capital for development. This role is normally effected by the government of the recipient country being credited with sterling (balances) in London. The creation of such balances simply extends Britain's liabilities without producing a corresponding increase in reserves and again makes the latter more vulnerable.

3. *Failure of the area to replenish reserves.* From 1958 onwards many sterling area members began to retain their surplus earnings of gold and foreign currencies rather than follow the customary practice of channelling them to London in exchange for sterling. Many members were also exchanging their balances for foreign currencies to pay for their deficits with the non-sterling world. Few were making any contribution to these reserves, the levels of which were so critical to the strength of sterling. Thus, the combined effect of diminishing contributions to the area's gold and foreign currency reserves and increasing demands upon those reserves, was that sterling was left in a very vulnerable position.

4. *Effects of U.K.'s deficit in sterling.* Further strains in reserves have come from Britain's balance of payments deficits (particularly in the 1960s). These have weakened sterling in two ways:

(a) the running down of reserves to finance the deficits has widened the gap between reserves and balances, and

(b) the fear of devaluation as a possible solution to balance of payments deficits has produced, at times, heavy selling of sterling to avoid capital losses through exchange rate changes.[1]

5. *Sterling and the EEC.* More recently Britain's entry to the EEC has loosened further the trading relationships between the U.K. and the rest of the sterling area. This, coupled with the instability of the pound and the rise of the dollar as a more widely accepted currency, has led to a decline in the importance of sterling as an international currency (and, the sterling area as a currency bloc).

Recent Measures Taken to Strengthen Sterling

1. *Swap Arrangements.* In the middle and late 1960s sterling became subject to a considerably loss of confidence and "runs" on the pound were frequent. Sterling, of course, was still an important international currency and its total collapse would have had damaging effects upon the international payments system. Thus, steps were taken to strengthen the currency through international co-operation. The first move was an agreement in June 1966 by which a group of members of the Bank of International Settlements pledged to provide foreign currencies to support Britain's reserves of gold and foreign currencies when these were being heavily reduced by the conversion of sterling balances. The idea was essentially a form of "window dressing" which involved the bolstering up of reserves in order to stop holders of sterling balances losing confidence in our ability to convert those balances. It was never intended that the finance should be available on a permanent basis but simply to bolster sterling when it was under pressure; however, the agreement was renewed in 1967 and 1968.

2. *The Basle Facility.* In 1968 it became clear that the pressure on sterling was to continue. More countries were selling their sterling balances and taking out foreign currencies and fewer and fewer countries were transferring their surpluses of foreign currencies to Britain and exchanging them for sterling. Thus, a new way had to be found to meet the demands for conversion of sterling balances but at the same time ensure that sterling would still be held widely as an international currency. In September 1968 the Basle facility[2] attempted to achieve this. Under this arrangement Britain could draw $2,000,000,000 worth of dollars and other foreign currencies from the Bank of International Settlements to back up sterling balances when they fell below a certain level. Drawings of this nature would be available in the first three years of the agreement and repayment of the drawings to be made within the 6th and 10th year of this facility.

The funds to supply the facility were to come from borrowings by the Bank of International Settlements in international markets and from deposits of foreign currencies placed with the B.I.S. by central banks of the "overseas sterling area". In addition twelve other nations agreed to provide currencies from their central banks. These sterling guarantees were eventually withdrawn in the budget of November 1974.

3. *Sterling Area Agreement.* In addition to this facility, Britain also negotiated agreements with the sterling area countries whereby we pledged to guarantee 90 per cent of their official balances (90 per cent of their reserves held in sterling) against a devaluation during the life of the Basle agreement. In other words Britain would agree to make payment in sterling to each country to restore the full dollar value of its reserves should we have to devalue the pound.

In return for this guarantee we insisted that the sterling area members should

1. Refer to section on devaluation, page 274.
2. Basle Facility and the Sterling Area, Cmnd 3787.

not maintain less than an individually agreed proportion of their reserves in sterling.

4. *New "Exchange Control" regulations.* The latest move in this strengthening of sterling was a move which has destroyed one of the major unifying features of the sterling area. In June 1972 new exchange control regulations made investment to the overseas sterling area subject to more or less the same restriction as investment to the non-sterling world. In other words, movement of capital to the sterling area was to be subject to Bank of England control.[1]

This measure tended to prevent sterling balances growing in the way described earlier[2] but undoubtedly also ended the sterling area as a formal currency and trading bloc.

1. Exception was made with the Republic of Ireland and Gibraltar.
2. Refer to Page 256.

Part Five

INTERNATIONAL TRADE AND MONETARY ARRANGEMENTS

Chapter Twenty-Seven

The Integration of Economies

One of the most outstanding features of economic development in the post war period has been the movement towards the integration of economies. Most forms of integration have been purely economic and have taken the pattern of two or more countries forming a "trading group" in which goods and services can move between member nations without restriction by tariff or otherwise. At this stage it will be useful to make a distinction between a "common market" (or customs union) and a "free trade area".

Customs Union. This is an union of countries who agree to abolish or reduce all restrictions on trade between themselves but at the same time agree to levy a common external tariff on goods imported from outside the area.

Free Trade area. Trade between members of the area will be free as within the Customs Union, but individual members are left to decide their own duties on imports from outside the area.

TRADING GROUPS

The largest trading group in the western world is the European Economic Community (the EEC) with a population of over 250,000,000. This is followed by the Latin American Free Trade Area (LAFTA) with a population of 225,000,000.

These two, together with the Central American Common Market, the Soviet trading bloc (COMECON) account for some two-thirds of world trade. New trading unions are also being formed and the scope of operation of existing ones is constantly changing. Some of the newest include the East African Community, the Central African Community (UDEAC) and the Caribbean Free Trade Association.

Likely Benefits of Joining a Trade Bloc

Benefits will depend upon the type of trade bloc, its organisation and its size. However, some of the more likely benefits are summarised below:

1. Removal of tariff barriers and other restrictions to trade between members widens the potential market for industry within the area. This wider market could lead to an increase in the scale of operation of many industries and so reduce unit costs of production.

2. As a result of the wider market the efficient firms should expand at the expense of the less efficient. As some nations will have greater potential efficiency in some fields of production than others, greater specialisation of countries might develop, and eventually lead to more effective use of the whole area's resources.

3. Greater specialisation should, therefore, lead to a higher and faster growing national income which, in turn, will generate more investment and growth.

4. If a nation is to develop and maintain modern advanced technological industries in fields such as computers and aircraft, the large markets offered by free trade areas are invaluable. The biggest costs of such industries are normally research and development costs. Thus, a large market may make possible a large output over which these costs can be spread. A small output and heavy fixed costs may make the cost and price of the industry's products prohibitive. Secondly, the large market would produce the revenue and volume of profits necessary to provide the finance for further research and development projects.

The importance of large scale production and large markets in the development of technological industries is well illustrated by the growth of "joint" industrial projects in Europe; these would include the development of Concorde, the European Airbus, and the development of atomic energy for peaceful purposes via EURATOM.

5. Membership of a free trade area removes the protective barriers which shelter domestic industry from foreign competition. It is argued that such barriers breed inefficiency and that exposure to the full force of foreign competition would jolt domestic industry into making improvements in both products and cost.

6. Finally, the movement towards economic unity may lead to political unity. Full political unity of the EEC would produce a very powerful third "power-bloc" whose views would have to be respected by both the U.S.A. and the U.S.S.R.

Development of the European Economic Community (EEC)

After World War II it had become increasingly clear that Western European unity was important to end forever, the conflicts which so often divided the nations of that continent. The first moves towards this unity, however, were economic rather than political. In 1947 the majority of European nations became members of the newly formed Organisation for European Economic Co-operation (OEEC). This was set up so that its members could collectively promote a post war reconstruction and recovery programme, and implement the Marshall Aid Plan (distribution of U.S. dollars aid to help the economic recovery of war-torn Europe).

Whilst this did a lot to bring Europeans closer together in the drive for economic expansion, the real foundations of an integrated Europe were to be laid in 1952 with the establishment of the European Coal and Steel Community (ECSC). This was a plan for European nations to pool their coal, iron ore, steel and scrap resources into a single market with completely free trade in these products between member countries. Although only six countries (France, Belgium, Luxembourg, the Netherlands, West Germany and Italy) joined the scheme it was so successful that members were keen to extend their efforts and produce a community covering integration over a wider range of economic activities. EURATOM, an organisation for the development of the peaceful use of atomic energy, was a further development involving co-operation between these six countries.

However, the most important development resulting from the desire for wider integration was the TREATY OF ROME. This was signed in 1957 and set up the EEC.

Britain was reluctant to join this community on its inception because of her Commonwealth ties and special trading relationships. However, in January 1973 she was admitted along with Denmark and the Republic of Ireland. The market, therefore, now consists of 9 countries with a combined population or market of approximately 250,000,000.

Objectives of the Community

The objectives of the EEC are as follows:

1. To eliminate all tariff barriers and quantitative restrictions to trade between the member nations – the original six having largely achieved this by 1968.

2. To establish a common external tariff barrier on all goods coming in from outside the community. These tariffs were derived from an average of the duties charged by the members of the EEC for particular commodities just before the EEC came into being. Goods coming into the EEC from outside therefore now carry the same tariff whether they enter via France, Italy, or any other member.

3. To provide for the free movement of labour and services; all community workers will have complete freedom to work and reside in any member country. Eventually, members of the professions will enjoy similar privileges when professional standards are unified.

4. To provide for the free movement of capital between member countries. The object here is to make it easy to move capital from one member country to another and thus eliminate the need to meet individual country's exchange control regulations. It is then hoped that a European Capital Market will be formed whereby subscribers and borrowers might come from different member countries.

5. To provide for a common policy in both agriculture and transport. The objective here is to have a farm support policy which is common to every member country and financed from a central fund. Agriculture in the EEC is also to be protected from cheap imports by a system of variable levies and duties.

6. To have a common policy and common rules with regard to the control of unfair trade practices and the regulation of competition. This will mean a system of monopoly laws which will be common to all members. Whilst the U.K. still has its own monopoly legislation the common market law must also be adhered to. Thus, action can be taken against any British company infringing the EEC's rules on monopolies and restrictive practices.

Likely Effects of Britain's Entry

1. Removal of tariff barriers will give the U.K. a market of 250,000,000 compared with her original domestic market of 55,000,000.

This will create greater opportunities for increasing the scale of operations of U.K. industry and possibly lead to lower costs of production and more competitive products. However, it is argued that the greatest advantage will be to those industries where fixed costs are so immense (plant, equipment, machinery, technology costs, etc.) that a high output is essential to hold down unit costs. The aircraft, computer, chemical and electronic industries are ones which will probably derive the greatest benefits from entry. Other industries, where the scale of production has little effect on costs, will gain no special advantage.

While entry to the market will create the potential for lowering costs much depends on whether firms are quick to exploit the advantages. Evidence seems

to indicate that, on Britain's entry to the market, European firms were better prepared for attacking our market than we were to attack theirs.

2. The economic future of the U.K. must rest heavily upon the development of her technological industries. Competition is intense in products that can be easily duplicated, and low wage cost economies are now beginning to excel in this field. However, products which are the result of years of research can not easily be reproduced and tend to give the manufacturer a greater degree of freedom in pricing; an important factor in an economy with high resource costs. The large market of a customs union is important to the growth of these technological industries to provide a :

(i) greater volume of sales over which the heavy research costs can be spread, and
(ii) greater volume of total profits from which research funds can be derived.

3. Entry to the EEC provides British industry with a market which is one of the largest, richest, and fastest growing in the world – see Exhibits 27.1A and 27.1B. This type of market should create an economic environment conducive to rapid industrial expansion and attract a high level of investment in plant and machinery.

4. The EEC is probably a more natural market for the U.K. than the Commonwealth (where Britain's trade has been making up a smaller and smaller proportion of their imports over the past 20 years). Consumer products produced for an affluent society sell better in an affluent market than in a developing country. As one writer put it "It will be 2,000 years, at present rates of growth, before the average citizen of Pakistan will be able to afford a motor car". What hope for the British motor manufacturer? The Commonwealth too has been buying much less from the U.K. and turning to new sources of supply; in particular to Japan and West Germany. A diagramatic illustration of these changing trade patterns can be found in Exhibit 27.2.

The E.E.C. As A Rich Expanding Economy

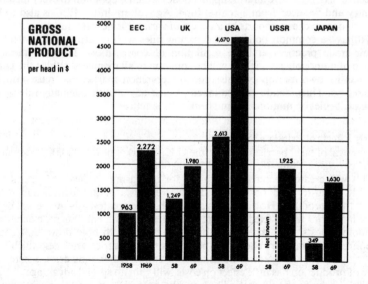

EXHIBIT 27.1A

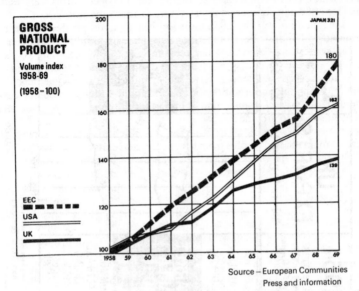

Source – European Communities
Press and information

EXHIBIT 27.1B

5. Removal of tariffs between the U.K. and the EEC countries is, of course, also likely to expose U.K. industry to greater competition. Inefficient firms will rapidly contract or be obliged to seek ways of raising efficiency and reduce costs. The effect generally therefore should be for a more efficient use of national resources and a higher rate of national economic growth.

Likely Problems as a Result of Entry
1. Exposure of our domestic market to the full force of competition from other member countries may cause some of our industries to decline or collapse. Unless steps are taken to improve the mobility of labour in the U.K. serious unemployment may result in some areas, particularly those dependent upon a single displaced industry.
2. The adoption of the Common Agricultural Policy (CAP) has meant a substantial increase in food prices in the U.K. Food makes up about 20–25 per cent of our consumer expenditure and hence price trends of this type are likely to spark off wage demands and produce inflationary spirals.
3. Removal of tariff preferences[1] on imports from the Commonwealth may have further inflationary effects, as much of our food and raw materials still come from these areas.
4. Eventual free movement of capital may starve British industry of its own capital market as more efficient foreign firms absorb funds which might have gone into domestic industry. This may, therefore, have an adverse effect on U.K. industrial growth.
5. The British balance of payments is likely to suffer the effects of entry into the market for at least 5 years beyond entry, as the industrial restructuring necessary

1. Especially low tariffs applicable only Commonwealth goods entering the U.K. (EEC insisted we adopt the common external tariff and removed preferences).

Changing Pattern Of Trade 1964 – 1974

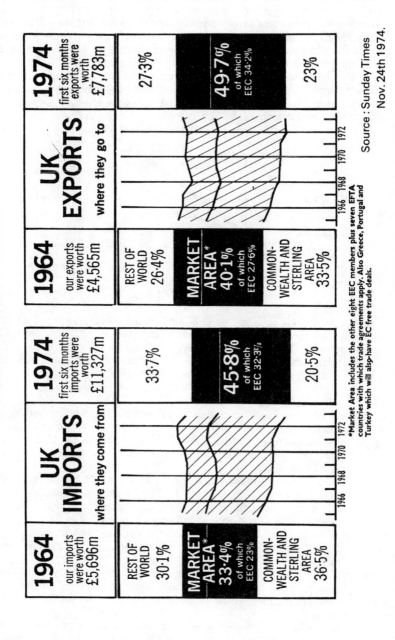

UK IMPORTS where they come from

1964 our imports were worth £5,696m
- REST OF WORLD 30·1%
- MARKET AREA* 33·4% of which EEC 23%
- COMMON-WEALTH AND STERLING AREA 36·5%

1974 first six months imports were worth £11,327m
- 33·7%
- 45·8% of which EEC 32·3%
- 20·5%

UK EXPORTS where they go to

1964 our exports were worth £4,565m
- REST OF WORLD 26·4%
- MARKET AREA* 40·1% of which EEC 27·6%
- COMMON-WEALTH AND STERLING AREA 33·5%

1974 first six months exports were worth £7,783m
- 27·3%
- 49·7% of which EEC 34·2%
- 23%

*Market Area includes the other eight EEC members plus seven EFTA countries with which trade agreements apply. Also Greece, Portugal and Turkey which will also-have EC free trade deals.

Source : Sunday Times Nov. 24th 1974.

EXHIBIT 27.2

to attack the new markets and to face new competition cannot be achieved overnight.

It is impossible to come to any positive conclusion that Britain will do well from entry to the market because of the numerous imponderables. A recent government white paper[1] attempted to measure some of the benefits and detriments but admitted the difficulty of drawing any firm conclusion. All one can say is that entry to the market might create a favourable opportunity for achieving the progress we all desire but success will depend upon how enthusiastically we respond to the opportunities placed before us and how successfully we counter the problems that arise from entry.

1. 'The U.K. and the European Communities' Cmnd 4715, 1971.

Part Sixteen

INTERNATIONAL TRADE AND MONETARY ARRANGEMENTS

Chapter Twenty-Eight

Economic Aid and Developing Countries

Seventy per cent of the world's population are living in countries which can be broadly classified as "developing countries".

THE DEVELOPING COUNTRY

These countries are found in most of the African continent, in Asia, Oceania, the Pacific, the Caribbean and in South and Central America. All such countries tend to display some or all of the following characteristics:

1. The level of income per head of population is extremely low.
2. The greatest proportion of the country's resources lie underdeveloped; usually as a consequence of lack of capital and technological know-how.
3. The population growth has often outstripped the ability of the nation to adequately provide for that population.
4. The traditional way of life tends to be associated almost entirely with agriculture. Industrial development, if any, is often the preserve of non-indigenous peoples.
5. Growth rates are low because of lack of capital. Low incomes result in low levels of savings – often only 1 to 2 per cent of a developing nation's Gross National Product – thus, investment depends upon foreign capital.

All developing countries have the central problem of a cycle of low incomes resulting in low savings resulting in low investment resulting in low incomes, etc. . . . The answer to this problem will vary from country to country but all solutions would involve some form of economic aid.

What is Aid?

Aid consists of contributions, financial and otherwise, made by governments, firms and charitable organisations of developed countries to their "less developed" counterparts for the purpose of helping the latter to expand their growth rates and so increase living standards.

The developed nations' motives for giving aid are often difficult to determine; the real motives often being disguised in a string of moral platitudes. However, some of the following points might be considered:

1. A developed nation may have a sense of moral responsibility to help the less fortunate develop reasonable living standards.
2. Aid may be given with a view to gaining political support from the recipient nation.
3. There may be a desire to repay a nation for the exploitation of its wealth in the past.
4. Aid may be given with a view to creating goodwill which in turn may help the donor nation's export trade in the future.

5. Aid may be given to increase the prosperity of the developing nation and thereby help the expansion of future international trade.

The Need for Aid

Developing economies tend to grow much more slowly than the more developed industrialised economy. Thus the rich and the poor get richer but the rich get richer much more quickly. The problem, therefore, is one of the widening gulf between the rich and the poor. This, though, has probably understated the problem since many developing nations actually become poorer as increases in population more than swallow up any expansion of production.

We must also recognise that the existence of poverty (particularly increasing poverty) in a world of growing wealth can only lead to unrest and discontent.

The problem discussed above was very recently summed up by Robert S. McNamara (President of the World Bank) – "The gap between the rich and poor nations is no longer merely a gap. It is a chasm. On the one side are the nations of the West that enjoy per capita incomes in the $3,000 range. On the other are nations in Asia and Africa that struggle to survive on per capita incomes of less than $100. What is important to understand is that this is not a static situation. The misery of the underdeveloped world is today a dynamic misery, continuously broadened and deepened by a population growth that is totally unprecedented in history."

A major reason for the slow growth of the developing economy is the lack of capital necessary for industrialisation,[1] the latter providing the shortest cut to increased living standards. The source of capital for industrialisation is, of course, savings but in a developing economy income levels will normally be so low that savings make little contribution to the investment needs. The solution therefore must be for these nations to use the savings of people from wealthier nations; these might be received in the form of loans or grants.

Most developing nations find that the greatest strain in their development is balance of payments difficulties. The capital goods and technology necessary for the industrialisation process will have to come from overseas and thus consume large amounts of foreign currency, much of which has to be earned from the uncertain primary product trade (incomes affected by poor harvests, gluts, etc.). Much aid, therefore, is needed simply to ease balance of payments difficulties during the process of industrialisation. Once the nation begins to grow more quickly the growth will tend to become self perpetuating. As income rises so does the accumulation of capital (via savings). This leads to greater application of technology and a higher growth rate still. This, in theory, will reinforce itself further by creating greater opportunities for division of labour and the exploitation of economies of scale.

Lack of capital, however, is not the only drawback to growth in the developing countries. Plant and machinery are ineffective if the labour force is in capable of using them. Hence, education and training and the availability of technical know-how are other vital forms of aid necessary to growth.

A further problem, which has become more pronounced in the last decade, has been the high rates of inflation experienced by the "developed world". This has increased the cost of the capital goods much needed by the developing nations and hence their requirements in terms of foreign currencies. Their

1. The term here meaning the improvement of production processes through the use of technology, machinery and power rather than the replacement of agriculture.

returns from the export of primary products have not provided the increases in earnings necessary to match these increased payments.

Types of Aid

1. *Official government aid.* This consists mainly of economic assistance by way of loans and grants and takes three major forms.

(a) project aid,

(b) non-project aid, and

(c) general aid.

Project aid is assistance given for the importation of capital equipment for specific projects which make up part of a development plan. Such aid might include assistance to construct a dam and install a hydro-electric plant. This aid tends to be largely tied in that the donor country supplies the labour and materials.

Non-project aid is aid basically for the general renewal of capital stock in a developing nation rather than for the further development of the economy. It might also include assistance for the purchase of food, raw materials, and components to be assembled in the recipient country. Again, this type of aid will be tied.

General aid. Balance of payments deficits is the biggest economic headache for the developing country. General aid is therefore often given to help meet balance of payments deficits. In this case, aid is untied.

2. *Private aid.* Some of the most effective aid to developing countries has been made by large private industrial concerns setting up plants in developing countries. Whilst Britain's official contribution has recently been levelling off, private aid has been increasing and filling the gap.

3. *Other forms of assistance.* Development aid tends not to flow lavishly when donor countries experience balance of payments difficulties. However, the following forms of aid go some way to alleviate this problem.

(a) Education,

(b) Technical knowledge and research information,

(c) Population control,

(d) Trade preferences, and

(e) Commodity price agreements.

Education. Much economic aid can be given to developing countries without producing serious effects upon the donor nation's balance of payments. One of the greatest requirements of developing nations is "know-how". This could be provided by a donor nation agreeing to take students from developing nations and training them in the required fields. Should these people return and teach the skills the aid process is further multiplied.

A donor country might also offer *technical knowledge and other research information* which it has developed in its own laboratories. The National Grass Institute in the U.K., for example, provided new strains of grasses to improve grazing in various developing countries. Such action will help growth and at little or no cost in terms of the donor country's balance of payments. This form of aid might also include the lending by the donor country of skilled personnel.

Population control. World Bank studies show that it is the population explosion, more than anything else, which is holding back the advancement of the poor nations. Aid can be given by way of informing these nations of the extent to which population growth is slowing down their potential development, by

providing family planning facilities and research into the most effective way of administering such facilities.

Trade preferencies. Whilst world trade has been increasing the share of the developing nations in that world trade has been decreasing rapidly. It is therefore argued that developing countries should be allowed to sell their goods abroad without having to face tariff penalties.

Commodity price stabilisation agreements. The major exports of developing countries are "primary products". Some countries, in fact, depend almost entirely upon just one primary product for their foreign currency earnings. As the production of many of these products is affected by the vagaries of climate and disease shortages and gluts are frequent and market prices fluctuate greatly. This often has adverse effects upon the developing nation's foreign currency earnings. The United Nations Commission on Trade and Development (UNCTAD) and other international organisations have attempted to get the producers of primary products to form agreements to control levels of production and volumes to be released on to the world markets in an attempt to raise, or at least stabilise earnings. Most agreements, however, have only met with a modicum of success.

EXERCISES

Part One

ESSAYS

1.1 Why is it considered important to measure a nation's economic activity?

1.2 National income figures are often used as an indicator of living standards. Discuss the problems inherent in the use of national income figures as such an indicator.

1.3 Explain the methods by which it is possible to measure a nation's income.

1.4 Discuss the problems likely to arise, and the ways of overcoming them, in the measurement of a nation's income or output.

1.5 What do you understand by the term "gross national product at market prices"? Starting with a GNP market price figure, explain what steps are necessary to arrive at a figure of gross domestic product at factor cost.

1.6 With the aid of suitable diagrams, explain what is meant by the concept of a circular flow of income.

1.7 Discuss the major leakages from, and injections into, the flow of income in a typical economy.

1.8 What are the major components of demand for an economy's output?

1.9 What is the meaning of the term "the consumption function"? What are the factors that determine the level of consumer spending in an economy?

1.10 Explain the term "equilibrium level of income". How is equilibrium income determined?

1.11 What is the multiplier principle? Illustrate your answer with a simple arithmetic example.

1.12 What will be the likely effects on income and employment of (1) a boom in export demand and (2) a successful savings campaign?

1.13 What are the major economic effects of a sustained rise in the general price level?

1.14 Explain what is meant by "cost-push" and "demand-pull" inflation.

1.15 Discuss the ways in which cost inflation may arise.

1.16 Is inflation always undesirable?

1.17 Upon what factors does an economy's rate of economic growth depend?

1.18 How much can labour, as a factor of production, contribute to the rate of growth in an advanced economy such as the United Kingdom?

1.19 What is meant by the growth rate of an economy? Is growth synonomous with improvements in welfare or living standards?

1.20 Discuss what you consider to be the main problems associated with the pursuit of economic growth.

PROBLEMS

1.21 Details of one year's output of a simple economy are given below:

Commodity	Units produced	Unit price (£)
Bread	20,000	0.15
Cheese	4,000	0.40
Beer	30,000	0.20
Machines	2	1000.00

VAT is levied on all output at a rate of 10%. Half of the output of investment goods is for replacement purposes. Net property income from abroad is £500.

(i) What is gross domestic product at market prices?
(ii) What is gross domestic product at factor cost?
(iii) What is net domestic product at market prices?
(iv) What is gross national product at market prices?

1.22 From the information given below concerning a fictional economy in a particular year, calculate:

(i) Total domestic expenditure at market prices;
(ii) Gross national product at market prices;
(iii) Gross national product at factor cost.

Item	£mn
Consumer spending	40,000
Private investment	5,500
Government current spending	13,400
Public investment	4,000
Increase in stocks	100
Exports	7,500
Imports	6,250
Expenditure taxes	5,000

1.23 Label each of the following items as a leakage (L) or an injection (J):
1) Purchase of a British machine by a Manchester textile company;
2) Purchase of a Pentax camera by a Manchester income-tax inspector;
3) Payment of VAT on the above camera;
4) Unemployment pay received by Manchester income-tax inspector's out-of-work brother;
5) Savings put into a building society by mean (thrifty?) Manchester income-tax inspector;
6) Savings put into a Canadian life-assurance company by a meaner (thriftier?) Scotsman;
7) Payment of corporation tax by company referred to in (1) above;
8) Purchase of a ticket for British Airways Kennedy Airport/Manchester Ringway flight by a long-lost American cousin of Manchester income-tax inspector;
9) Government financial aid to an ailing Manchester-based company (not the one referred to in (1) above);
10) Interest received by the gentleman referred to in (5) above.

1.24 Add to the list of items in Problem 1.23 two more, as follows:
11) Income of Manchester income-tax inspector's household – his wife works for the company referred to in (1) above;
12) Expenditure on U.K. goods by above household.

Then design a diagram in which may be shown the flows of income 1–12. Represent the income flows by arrows and label these accordingly. (See Exhibit 1.21 if you are short of ideas!)

1.25 What is MPS when MPC is
1) 0.87
2) 0.75
3) 0.62

1.26   What is MPC when MPS is
1) 0.20
2) 0.31
3) 0.19

1.27   Write the savings functions corresponding to the following consumption functions:
1) $C = Y$
2) $C = 0.87Y$
3) $C = 5 + 0.85Y$
4) $C = \$1500mn + 0.95Y$

1.28   Write the consumption functions corresponding to the following savings functions:
1) $S = 0.2Y$
2) $S = 0.28Y$
3) $S = -40 + 0.3Y$
4) $S = -£500mn + 0.08Y$

1.29   If $C = 100 + 0.8Y$, what are the levels of C and S when
1) $Y = 100$
2) $Y = 200$
3) $Y = 350$
4) $Y = 750$

1.30   What is the value of the simple multiplier when
1) $MPS = 0.2$
2) $MPS = 0.4$
3) $MPC = 0.5$
4) $MPC = 0.7$

1.31   What is the value of the simple multiplier when
1) $C = 0.8Y$
2) $C = £1000mn + 0.9Y$
3) $S = 0.3Y$
4) $S = -\$979mn + 0.25Y$

1.32   Given that aggregate demand consists only of consumption and investment and that $C = 50 + 0.75Y$, what is the final change in national income when there is a change in investment of:
1) 10
2) –16
3) 25
4) –28

1.33   Given that aggregate demand consists only of consumption and investment, what is the final change in national income brought about by an increase in investment of 20, when:
1) $C = 0.8Y$
2) $C = 5 + 0.8Y$
3) $C = 10 + 0.9Y$
4) $C = \$979mn + 0.75Y$

1.34   From the following information calculate
1) APC and APS for each year;
2) MPC and MPS between years 1 and 2 and between years 2 and 3.

	Year		
	1	2	3
Income (£)	4000	4500	5000
Spending (£)	3800	4100	4500
Savings (£)	200	400	500

"TRUE OR FALSE" QUESTIONS

1.35 Gross domestic fixed capital formation is equivalent to the nation's capital stock.

1.36 Transfer payments are excluded from the national income estimates because they are not made for economic activity.

1.37 In the calculation of national income the value of do-it-yourself activities and housewives' services is excluded.

1.38 Gross domestic product means the value of all goods and services produced geographically within an economy during a year.

1.39 Gross national product equals gross domestic product plus output of capital goods.

1.40 Market price GNP equals factor cost GNP plus expenditure taxes.

1.41 Consumer spending is quantitatively the most important component of aggregate demand in the U.K. economy.

1.42 "National income" strictly refers to net national product at market prices.

1.43 MPC = 1 − MPS.

1.44 The multiplier is the reciprocal of MPC.

1.45 MPS is the amount of extra saving undertaken following an increase in income.

1.46 A leakage will reduce the level of national income, other things being equal.

1.47 Capital widening means that an economy's capital stock is growing at a faster rate than its working population.

1.48 Capital deepening improves the capital/labour ratio.

1.49 Gross investment reduces the average age of a nation's capital stock.

1.50 Real per capita GNP or GDP is the best available, though imperfect, measure of a nation's economic welfare.

Part Two

ESSAYS

2.1 What does the marginal product theory assume and state? Why has it been said that it is not suitable for determining the wage level in the "world of the 1970's"?

2.2 The demand for factors are a derived demand. Explain this statement.

2.3 Rent of ability and quasi-rent are forms of economic rent. What is economic rent? Explain why these two types of rent are forms of economic rent.

2.4 Any growth in the British labour force in the last quarter of the 20th century will have to come, mainly, from the female sector. Use statistical material to support your explanation why this is true.

2.5 Occupations are subject to change. Give examples of four occupations that

existed in the early 19th century but are considered to be a declining occupation today and then explain why the decline has taken place.

2.6   How are wages determined in Great Britain?

2.7   Discuss the economic forces that determine the level of wages for unskilled workers (in any industry).

2.8   Why do accountants earn more than their clerks?

2.9   The ultimate stage in settling disputes is the strike or lock-out. Discuss the stages that are available before the ultimate stage is reached.

2.10   Distinguish "real" from "money" wages – use a recent example as background for your answer.

2.11   What is meant by the term "wage drift"? Use a diagram to clarify the definition using time reference points. Examine why the "drift" has occurred.

2.12   Discuss the effects of increased productivity on money wages and real wages during a period of full employment.

2.13   To what extent can *any* trade union increase the wages of its members?

2.14   Define the term "trade union". Discuss the success of unions in achieving at least five specific economic roles at the work place.

2.15   What are the situations in a production line that favour a system of time rates rather than piece rates?

2.16   Distinguish between the pure rate of interest and the gross rate of interest.

2.17   The rate of interest is the rate at which the businessman discounts the future. Explain this statement and then comment upon it.

2.18   "Profit is the reward paid by the community for the services of the entrepreneur." Discuss.

2.19   Discuss the functions of profits in a modern economy.

2.20   Carefully explain the difference between the following:

(i)   economist's profit and accountant's profit, and

(ii) return to capital and return to the entrepreneur.

"TRUE OR FALSE" EXERCISES

2.21   The demand for any factor is a derived demand.

2.22   The price of a factor is *not* affected by the elasticity of demand for that factor.

2.23   The force that operates on demanders for factor service is time.

2.24   The marginal product theory states that the price paid for the use of any factor should be determined by the extra contribution an additional factor makes to production.

2.25   Quasi rent is a special form of "ordinary rent".

2.26   Economic rent is a special term reserved for situations where payments are made to factors which are inelastic in supply.

2.27   The size of the labour force will depend, in the first place, on the number of people that are, by law or nature, able to work.

2.28   The economically active population in Great Britain is approximately 53.56 per cent of the total population.

2.29   Labour is a "homogeneous" factor of production.

2.30   Out of each 100 workers the following is approximately accurate:

        4 in primary production,

        34 in production related to manufacturing, and

        62 in production related to services.

2.31   Wages are paid to labour for their skills and energy which they make available to employers in producing goods and services.

2.32 Wages is a wider term than earnings.
2.33 Assuming there is no inflation – a worker that has an increase in money wages will automatically increase his real wages.
2.34 "Wage drift" simply means that wages are drifting upwards.
2.35 In the 1970s wage levels are generally determined by collective bargaining.
2.36 Voluntary agreements are those reached with government assistance.
2.37 Job evaluation assesses a job and the personal qualities of individuals doing the job.
2.38 Increasing productivity simply means getting more output from the existing factors of production.
2.39 Virtually everything affects productivity – even the smile of a foreman.
2.40 Remove waste and become more efficient.
2.41 From 1962 to 1972 the trend in the number of trade unions was upwards.
2.42 Trade unions, normally, can be classified into four types, namely, Occupational, General, Craft and Industrial.
2.43 Two of the major roles of trade unions is that of promoting the interests of their members and accelerating the economic advance of the nation.
2.44 At the top of the trade union movement stands the Trades Union Congress.
2.45 Interest places a time value upon the money being borrowed.
2.46 Businessmen borrow money today to buy capital goods tomorrow.
2.47 All investment decisions made by businessmen *always* take into consideration the interest to be paid on borrowed money capital.
2.48 DCF means "discounted cash flow" and discount is calculated by:

$$(1 \text{ plus } i)^n.$$

2.49 The prime function of the entrepreneur is risk-bearing and the reward to him for this function is called pure profit.
2.50 Economic profit is an actual calculation of revenue and expenditure based on past transactions.

OBJECTIVE EXERCISES

2.51 Match the following:

a) labour	i) interest
b) land	ii) money
c) capital	iii) profit
d) enterprise	iv) rent
	v) revenue
	vi) wages

2.52 Which of the following is *not* a correct statement?
a) the demand for factors is a derived demand.
b) the demand for one factor will always be equated with the demand for other factors.
c) the demand for factors is a joint demand.
d) the elasticity of demand for the products produced by the factors will affect the demand for factors.
e) the price of factors is determined by the interaction of supply and demand.
2.53 Select the correct statement about "economic rent".
a) it is the same as ordinary rent.
b) is that rent associated with the renting of a house.
c) it is the same as commercial rent.

d)   is associated solely with the factor of production called capital.

e)   may be received by any factor that is fixed in supply in the short run.

2.54   Which of the approximate figures below are correct for the following statement? For every 100 economically active persons in Britain during 1971, and expected for 1991, we would expect to find a breakdown of:

a)   54 men and 46 women   (100 EAP)

b)   58 men and 42 women   (100 EAP)

c)   62 men and 38 women   (100 EAP)

d)   66 men and 34 women   (100 EAP)

e)   70 men and 30 women   (100 EAP)

2.55   Which of the following requirements are *not* normally associated with female dominated occupations?

a)   feeling towards helping others.

b)   sensitive to smell.

c)   softness of touch.

d)   nimbleness of fingers.

e)   speed in handling sewing machines.

2.56   Which of the following statements will *not* increase the "gap" known as the wage drift?

a)   workers pressurise employers to provide more than the wage rates.

b)   greater freedom is extended to workshop bargaining.

c)   companies offer additions to the wage rates to attract scarce labour.

d)   wage rates rise by 10 per cent whereas earnings remain at the same level.

e)   employers in an attempt to keep its present labour force offer additions to wage rates.

2.57   When considering the wage rate difference between one occupation and another which one of the following are *not* taken into account?

a)   one occupation works overtime and the other does not.

b)   one occupation has severer working conditions.

c)   labour is scarce in one but plentiful in the other.

d)   one occupation requires less education and training than the other.

e)   the power of trade unions in one occupation is much greater than in the other.

2.58   Which of the following is *not* correct?

a)   Productivity can be increased simply by increasing the number of units of input.

b)   Productivity can be measured by:

Output divided by Number of workers.

c)   Productivity can be increased by increasing the efforts of each unit of input employed.

d)   Productivity can be measured by:

Output divided by Number of man-hours.

e)   Productivity can be increased by transferring workers from old to new machines with the latest technical advances.

2.59   The Fawley agreement was a productivity agreement which required considerable changes in work practices. Which of the following was *not* specifically mentioned by the Donovan Report?

a)   workers were to allow others to perform part of their work.

b)   manning scales were to be revised.

c)   workers were to perform tasks they had previously regarded as being outside their jobs.

d)   canteen facilities were to be removed.

e) tea breaks were to end.

2.60 Which of the following is *not* an economic role of trade unions?

a) maintenance of full employment.

b) maintenance of the real value of wages.

c) greater liberty for the individual to lead a fuller life.

d) increase the national wealth in real terms.

e) arrange productivity agreements.

2.61 The number of trade unions at the end of 1972 was:

a) between 551 and 575

b) between 526 and 550

c) between 501 and 525

d) between 476 and 500

e) between 451 and 475

2.62 Using a rate of discount of 10 per cent per annum what is the present value of £365 received in two years time?

a) £280

b) £300

c) £320

d) £350

e) £380

2.63 Assuming a firm wishes to continue producing which of the following types of investment are *not* affected by the interest that has to be paid for the use of borrowed money capital?

a) Replacing a plant that has burned down.

b) machine wears out and needs to be replaced.

c) a special Act of Parliament requires all firms to have a sprinkler system for fire prevention.

d) purchasing a new machine with the latest technological advances which is to be added to the production line.

e) purchasing a fire engine because insurance companies refuse to provide insurance if this is not done.

2.64 The reward to the entrepreneur for carrying out the "risk-bearing" function is:

a) normal profit.

b) pure profit.

c) wages of management.

d) salaries paid to managers.

e) economic rent.

2.65 Which of the following statements is true?

a) Profits of the economist are based on past data.

b) Profits of the accountant are based on future data.

c) Profits of the economist are based upon future expectations of revenues and expenditures.

d) Profits of the accountant are based upon future expectations of revenues and expenditures.

e) Profits of the economist are calculated whereas those of the accountant are estimated.

Part Three

ESSAYS

3.1 What is money? What qualities must money possess to satisfy exchange in a modern economy?

3.2 What is understood by the term *money*? Which of the following would you include under the heading of money: (a) coins and notes, (b) cheques, (c) promissory note and (d) money order? Give reasons for your answers.

3.3 Discuss the various ways in which the existence of money facilitates various operations within the British economy.

3.4 Give reasons why coins and bank notes are considered superior to other forms of money (gold, silver, beads, cattle, etc.).

3.5 What functions does money perform in an economy? What effect, if any, has inflation on the performance of these functions?

3.6 Argue the case against the following statement. "To fulfil its functions the value of money must be stable."

3.7 What is credit? If you, a bank manager, were approached by a businessman for a bank loan of £150,000 over a three year period, state in simple terms how you would go about establishing whether or not to provide the loan.

3.8 Clearly distinguish between money and credit.

3.9 Outline the major functions of the commercial bank. How do these differ from those of the merchant bank?

3.10 Explain how a commercial bank "creates credit". What are the chief factors which limit the power of a bank to create credit?

3.11 What is understood by the term "reserve assets ratio"? Examine the significance of this ratio to the commercial bank.

3.12 A banker's lending policy must be a compromise between profitability and liquidity. Explain.

3.13 Discuss the various factors that can cause a change in the total liquid assets of all the clearing banks.

3.14 "Clearing banks can only lend money that others have loaned to them." Discuss.

3.15 What are the major functions of a central bank? Explain its relationship with the banking system as a whole.

3.16 What are the principal functions of the Bank of England? Comment on their relative importance.

3.17 Explain the principal methods by which the Bank of England has controlled the quantity of money within the economy.

3.18 Explain how the Bank of England "supports Sterling" on the international exchange market.

3.19 Explain the special relationship between the Bank of England and the London money market.

3.20 Explain why it was said that the Bank Rate was of little importance to the domestic economy.

3.21 What were the major changes introduced by Competition and Credit Control in 1971?

3.22 What were the results of the changes in the liquidity position of the banks made in 1971 and why was it necessary to introduce the Supplementary Credit Control measures in Dec. 1973?

TRUE OR FALSE EXERCISES

3.23   The importance of money lies not in the goods and services it can buy but in money itself.

3.24   Money can be defined as anything which is generally accepted in the payment for goods and services. In other words, money could be tobacco or cattle or beads.

3.25   Bartering is acceptable in primitive and isolated societies but not normally in the modern communities in the world of today.

3.26   "Money's a matter of functions four, A measure, a medium, a standard, a store."

3.27   The primary or root function of money is considered to be "a standard of deferred payment".

3.28   The function of money termed "measure of value" assists businessmen to calculate gains and losses.

3.29   Credit is defined as an extension of time to pay for goods and services *or* it refers to a transfer of goods or money from one person or business to another person or business with a promise from the debtor that the debt will be repaid at some future date.

3.30   The banker in giving a medium term loan to a business evaluates confidence (that the loan will be repaid) by establishing the borrowers creditworthiness.

3.31   During a period of rapid inflation creditors tend to gain and debtors lose.

3.32   A cheque is not legal tender but it is an instrument used to transfer a sum of money from the banking account of one person to that of another.

3.33   The "clearing banks" are those which are members of the London Bankers" Clearing House.

3.34   Merchant Banks specialise in the acceptance of deposits and the provision of short term loans.

3.35   About 55 per cent of bank deposits are held in current accounts.

3.36   Growth in the use of cheques has greatly facilitated the clearing banks power to create credit.

3.37   Deposits held by the clearing banks at the Bank of England for the purpose of facilitating the settlement of inter-bank indebtedness cannot be regarded as cash by those banks.

OBJECTIVE EXERCISES

3.38   The total amount of money in a country (and economists would tend to agree) consists of:
a)   coins and bills of exchange.
b)   coins and notes.
c)   coins and cheques.
d)   coins and current accounts.
e)   coins and deposit accounts.

3.39   Make the best possible match between column A (various types of possible money) and B (reasons for their being unsuitable).

(A)		(B)
a) bananas	i)	too plentiful
b) beads	ii)	not easily portable
c) copper bars	iii)	lacks durability
d) diamonds	iv)	not widely acceptable
e) skunks	v)	problem of malleability

3.40   Select one of the following which is *not* considered to be a function of money.
a)   it is a measure of value.
b)   it is a standard of deferred payment.
c)   it is widely accepted as a medium of exchange.
d)   it has an intrinsic value.
e)   it is a store of value.

3.41   There are different types of credit; those associated with money and those associated with goods. Which of the following is *not* associated with money?
a)   bank overdraft
b)   hire purchase
c)   cheque
d)   bank bill
e)   bank loan

3.42   Which of the following is *not* legal tender?
a)   a cheque for £4.28.
b)   £3 worth of silver.
c)   a 2p coin.
d)   a £1 note plus a 10p coin plus two 2p coins.
e)   £5 bank note.

3.43   Which statement is *not* correct?
One of the functions of credit is to:
a)   make it convenient for borrowers to settle their debts.
b)   establish a link between savings and investment.
c)   reduce the use of notes and coins.
d)   assist acceptance houses to transfer the use of their name to another firm for trade.
e)   enable farmers to plough their land now and not later.

3.44   Match the types of credit.
a) bank overdraft   i) associated with goods
b) trade bill   ii) associated with money
c) bank bill
d) cheque
e) hire purchase
f) bank loan

3.45   The reserve assets ratio of the Commercial Bank is:
a)   8 per cent of deposits.
b)   12½ per cent of deposits.
c)   14   per cent-of deposits.
d)   15½ per cent of deposits.
e)   28   per cent of deposits.

3.46   Which of the following are *not* part of the Commercial Bank's eligible reserve assets? (More than one answer)
a)   Cash in the till.
b)   Cash at the Bank of England.
c)   Advances
d)   Long term investments.
e)   Treasury bills.

3.47   Which of the following is *not* a clearing bank?
a)   Midland

b) Lloyds
c) Trustees
d) Coutts
e) Barclays
3.48 Advances make up about:
a) 50 per cent
b) 20 per cent
c) 40 per cent
d) 80 per cent
e) 10 per cent
of a Commercial Bank's assets.
3.49 Arrange the following items from a commercial bank's balance sheet in order of liquidity (high to low).
a) advances
b) money at call
c) cash in till
d) local authority bills
e) commercial bills
f) investments
3.50 The number of foreign banks operating in the U.K. is approximately:
a) 20
b) 70
c) 150
d) 170
e) 200

Part Four

ESSAYS
4.1 Examine the major factors influencing economic growth.
4.2 Explain the role of technology in the process of growth.
4.3 "Investment is the engine of economic growth". Discuss.
4.4 Examine the relationship between unemployment and inflation. Attempt an explanation of the changing relationship.
4.5 "It would be folly for government to rely upon the maintenance of margins of unemployment as a means of controlling inflation". Discuss this statement.
4.6 The government has one function and one only to maintain the level of aggregate demand. Explain and discuss.
4.7 What are the major objectives of government economic policy? Explain the difficulty of attaining these objectives simultaneously.
4.8 What is understood by the "Phillip's relationship"?
4.9 What is a demand management policy? Briefly describe the chief instruments of demand management.
4.10 What is the role of incomes policy? What difficulties are likely to be experienced in implementing such a policy?
4.11 Distinguish carefully between structural and cyclical unemployment. What policies might a government pursue to remedy each type – state your reasons for the policies selected.
4.12 Explain the purpose of public expenditure. Why has it grown so rapidly in recent years?
4.13 Why have the rising levels of public expenditure been a problem in recent years?

4.14   What are the main considerations influencing the Chancellor in the formulation of his budgetary policy?

4.15   The original purpose of the Budget was to raise revenue to meet Government expenditure but today it is the major instrument for regulating the economy. Do you agree with this statement?

4.16   Explain the terms "Budgeting for a surplus" and "Budgeting for a deficit". What are the circumstances which make these actions necessary?

4.17   For what purposes, other than raising revenue, may the tax system be used?

4.18   Distinguish between direct and indirect taxation. What are the advantages and disadvantages of each?

4.19   What other criteria would you introduce as amendments to Adam Smith's Canons of Taxation to make them applicable to the 20th century?

4.20   With the aid of diagrams explain the importance of elasticity of demand and supply in the formulation of indirect taxes.

4.21   Criticise the suggestion that a greater proportion of total tax revenues should be raised by indirect taxation.

4.22   Do you consider that indirect taxes are themselves inflationary rather than deflationary?

4.23   What are the major factors influencing a firm's location decision?

4.24   Discuss the major changes which have taken place this century affecting the firm's location decision?

4.25   Explain why the oil refining industry, which was once located on the oil fields, is today predominantly market-orientated.

4.26   Transport costs play an important role in influencing plant location. Discuss.

4.27   Consider the major town of your region. Explain why it was established there and what caused industry and commerce to develop. Is it still attracting industry or is it a declining area? Explain the reasons for whichever comment applies.

4.28   Market forces alone would not have solved the regional problem, consequently it was necessary for the Government to intervene. Comment.

4.29   What have been the main objectives of the U.K.'s post-war regional development policy?

4.30   Explain the major forms of Government assistance in the Development Areas.

4.31   The Hunt Report showed that there was a need for an extension of the Assisted Areas, would you say that there was a need for further extension today?

4.32   In the past Government aid has been given to those areas with unemployment levels above the national average. Do you think that this is reasonable or should other criteria be used?

TRUE OR FALSE EXERCISES

4.33   The quality of life has nothing to do with the standard of living.

4.34   Increasing the length of the working week will unreservedly increase the standard of living.

4.35   Frictional unemployment may be the result of striking trade union members.

4.36   Structural unemployment is essentially caused by falling aggregate demand.

4.37   Fiscal policy involves controlling aggregate demand levels through regulating the lending activities of the commercial banks.

4.38   The economy does not automatically move towards full employment.

4.39   The standard of living involves much more than the acquisition of material wealth.

4.40   The rank order of the objectives of economic policy has *not* changed since 1900.

4.41   In practice perhaps the most convenient measure of the standard of living is national income per head of population.

4.42   Economic growth in simple terms means growth of national output.

4.43   Action that can be taken by a government to help investment is to train and educate the population in their consumption habits.

4.44   The Industrial Training Act 1965 created the incentives to invest in education and training.

4.45   There is no limit to growth.

OBJECTIVE EXERCISES

4.46   The "Phillip's curve" purports to show a relationship between:
a)   unemployment and changes in wage rates.
b)   unemployment and growth rates.
c)   unemployment and balance of payments problems.
d)   all of these.
e)   none of these.

4.47   Which of the following statements is most accurate?
a)   All productivity increases result in higher rates of growth.
b)   All growth is the result of productivity.

4.48   The U.S.A. claims:
a)   one-half
b)   one-third
c)   three fourths
d)   one eighth
e)   one fourth
of her economic growth is the result of investment in education and training.

4.49   Cyclical unemployment is the result of:
a)   falling demand for a particular product which is now being superseded by one having improved technology.
b)   falling aggregate demand levels.
c)   people desiring to change jobs.
d)   strikes in components factories causing workers in an assembly industry to be "laid off".

4.50   Increases in aggregate demand are more likely to cause inflation when:
a)   the economy has spare capacity.
b)   productivity is rising through better methods of production.
c)   the economy is fully employed.
d)   none of the above conditions are in evidence.

4.51   A rise in the price of imported oil is likely in the short run to:
a)   reduce the level of employment in the U.K.
b)   increase the level of employment in the U.K.
c)   leave the level of unemployment unchanged.
d)   increase the level of investment in the U.K.
e)   none of these.

4.52   Public expenditure in 1968 accounted for:
a)   5 per cent
b)   15 per cent
c)   28 per cent
d)   47 per cent
e)   55 per cent
of the Gross National Product.

4.53   Between 1960–1969 Japan invested approximately:
a)   10 per cent
b)   20 per cent
c)   22 per cent
d)   27 per cent
e)   33 per cent
of her Gross National Product.

4.54   Which one of the following factors place the ultimate limit on growth?
a)   investment
b)   technological knowledge
c)   management skills
d)   training of the work force
e)   expenditure by government on goods and services

4.55   Which of the following is *not* considered to be a special type of unemployment?
a)   seasonal
b)   frictional
c)   psychological
d)   structural
e)   transitional

4.56 and 4.57
i)   maintenance of the price of gold
ii)   maintenance of full employment
iii)   stability of prices
iv)   improvement of the standard of living
v)   balance of payments equilibrium
vi)   equality of incomes

From the above select the four that are considered to be the major objectives of economic policy.
a)   i, ii, iii, and iv
b)   i, ii, iii, and vi
c)   ii, iii, iv and v
d)   ii, iii, iv and vi
e)   iii, iv, v and vi

Also using the above details which major economic objectives of government are internal rather than external?
a)   iv, v and vi
b)   iii, iv and v
c)   ii, iii and iv
d)   i, ii and iii
e)   ii, i and vi

Part Five

ESSAYS

5.1   Explain what economists mean by the term "the law of comparative costs".

5.2   "The theory of comparative costs proves that free trade is the best policy." Criticise this statement.

5.3   What is meant by "the Terms of Trade"? How may the terms of trade be measured?

5.4   Show the possible effects of movements in the terms of trade on the balance of payments. Explain with particular reference to the U.K.

5.5   Distinguish carefully between the terms of trade and the balance of trade. How are they related?

5.6   What are the differences between the balance of trade and the balance of payments? Why is it important to distinguish between them?

5.7   If the balance of payments must always balance, how can it ever be said that a country has a deficit or surplus on its balance of payments?

5.8   The U.K.'s visible trade balance is rarely in surplus. Would you agree that this represents failure on the part of British exporters?

5.9   Explain the importance of invisible exports to the British balance of payments.

5.10   How can a country have an unfavourable balance of payments and a favourable balance of trade at the same time?

5.11   Outline the operation of the foreign exchange market.

5.12   What is understood by a "freely floating" exchange rate system? Examine the major benefits and problems of such a system.

5.13   Compare the mechanism of today's exchange rates with those of the 1960s.

5.14   What is understood by the term "gold standard"? Why did Britain abandon the gold standard in 1931?

5.15   Compare international adjustments under the gold standard and the freely floating rate.

5.16   Compare deflation and devaluation as alternative methods of solving balance of payments problems.

5.17   Examine the likely effects of devaluation on the current account of Britain's balance of payments.

5.18   What effect does the devaluation of the "pound sterling" have on sterling balances.

5.19   What is revaluation? Why are nations often reluctant to revalue?

5.20   Trace the origin and development of the Sterling Area. Explain how sterling is used to finance international trade.

5.21   What factors govern the strength of sterling? Why has sterling declined in importance as an international currency?

5.22   How far would you consider 1958 to be the turning point in sterling's role as an international currency?

5.23   Examine the measures taken since 1960 to strengthen sterling.

5.24   Why did sterling become acceptable as an international currency? What benefits did Britain gain from acting as banker to the Sterling Area?

5.25   What justification is there for the growth of "trade blocs"?

5.26   "Trade blocs restrict rather than free trade". Discuss.

5.27   Trade the development of the European Economic Community and outline its chief objectives.

5.28 Outline the merits and problems that have emerged from Britain's entry to the European Economic Community.

5.29 Outline the objectives of the "Treaty of Rome". How far have they been achieved?

5.30 What is understood by the "world liquidity problem"? How far would raising the price of gold solve this problem?

5.31 Examine the contribution made by the International Monetary Fund (IMF) to ease the international payments problems.

5.32 How far might "Special Drawing Rights" (SDRs) be considered the answer to the world liquidity problem?

5.33 Examine the significance of the "Quota" to a member of the International Monetary Fund (IMF).

5.34 "If world trade expands faster than the supply of internationally acceptable currencies then we have a world liquidity problem." Discuss.

5.35 What is understood by the "Basle Agreement"? What contribution did this make to easing the world liquidity problem?

5.36 Distinguish clearly between short and long term solutions to balance of payments problems.

5.37 What is understood by the term "exchange control"? How can this help Britain's balance of payments?

5.38 On what grounds might tariffs be justified as solutions to balance of payments problems?

5.39 Give examples of "non-tariff distortions" to trade. Why have these become a serious problem in recent years?

5.40 Explain the operation of "The General Agreement on Tariffs and Trade" (GATT).

5.41 Outline the chief export services offered by the British government to its exporters.

TRUE OR FALSE QUESTIONS

5.42 Revaluation has the effect of making the revaluing country's exports cheaper in terms of other currencies.

5.43 Both the gold standard and the freely floating exchange rate claim to provide an automatically self balancing balance of payments.

5.44 Freely floating exchange rates break the terms of the Bretton Woods Agreement 1944.

5.45 Since 1950 world trade has increased ten times faster than the supply of internationally acceptable currencies which finance that trade.

5.46 The European Economic Community is the largest trading group in the world.

5.47 Britain donates 10 per cent of her Gross National Product per annum as aid to developing economies.

5.48 Developing economies are those economies which have a low level of income per head of population.

5.49 A nation can borrow up to 25 per cent of its IMF quota without notice.

5.50 The first total allocation of SDRs amounted to $3,500mil.

5.51 A country with a persistently downward floating currency will be experiencing falling import prices.

5.52 Under the gold standard a balance of payment deficit results in an inflow of gold to the deficit nation.

OBJECTIVE EXERCISES

5.53 Devaluation of the pound will:
a) increase the sterling value of sterling balances.
b) increase the foreign currency value of sterling balances.
c) lower the sterling value of the balances.
d) decrease the foreign currency value of sterling balances.
e) none of these.

5.54 Which of the following has made the greatest contribution to world liquidity since world war II?
a) the pound sterling.
b) the Deutschmark.
c) the Yen.
d) the French Franc.
e) the U.S. dollar.

5.55 On becoming a member of the International Monetary Fund a nation will normally be expected to make a gold contribution of a value of:
a) 20 per cent.
b) 25 per cent.
c) 10 per cent.
d) 75 per cent.
e) 100 per cent.
of its quota.

5.56 The percentage of the world's population living in developing economics is:
a) 10 per cent.
b) 30 per cent.
c) 50 per cent.
d) 70 per cent.
e) 80 per cent.

5.57 Which of the following types of aid are most injurious to a donor nation's balance of payments?
a) cash aid.
b) tied aid.
c) aid via transfer of human skills and knowledge.
d) commodity and price stabilization schemes.
e) all of these.

5.58 Developing economies are those economies which:
a) lie solely within the Tropics.
b) lie solely outside the Tropics.
c) have a low level of income per head of population.
d) have no industry.
e) have at least 80 per cent of labour in the service sector of industry.

5.59 Which of the following arrangements was designed specifically to strengthen sterling?
a) the Smithsonian agreement.
b) the Bretton Woods agreement.
c) the Basle agreement.
d) the Treaty of Rome.
e) none of these.

5.60 Britain came off the gold standard in:
a) 1800
b) 1848

c) 1910
d) 1931
e) 1946

5.61   Under the gold standard a nation with a balance of payments deficit
would experience:

a) an outflow of gold.
b) no change in its gold position.
c) an inflow of gold.
d) none of these.

5.62   Eurodollars are:

a) the chief currency of the European Economic Community.
b) U.S. dollars owned by people largely outside the U.S.A. (especially Europeans).
c) U.S. dollars spent by holidaying Americans in Europe.
d) the chief currency of the European Free Trade Area.
e) none of the above.

5.63   The Sterling Area became rigidly delimited in:

a) 1917
b) 1926
c) 1930
d) 1933
e) 1939

5.64   Which of the following areas is free from exchange control regulations
on British investment?

a) Canada
b) France
c) Republic of Ireland
d) Switzerland
e) U.S.A.

INDEX

List of Publications

(Please note that books may be obtained by students direct by mail. There is no charge for inland postage and packing or for sea-mail. Books sent by air-mail will be charged postage)

ACCOUNTING BOOKS

1. **ACCOUNTING: A PROGRAMMED TEXT** by F. Wood, B.Sc., (Econ.), F.C.A., and J. Townsley, B. Com, F.C.A., SBN 85505 000 4.

   A student's first acquaintance with book-keeping and accounting is usually one of learning a number of rules without understanding why the rules have come into existence. This book is intended for anyone studying the subject for the first time, irrespective of whether they are studying for professional accountancy examinations or are managers who want to know the basic fundamentals of Accounting.
   The reader is not expected to accept a mass of rules blindly, instead he is shown the reasoning behind the use of each rule.
   The book also has supplementary questions, with answers, In addition there are also readings which give perspective to the subject.

2. **ACCOUNTING AND FINANCE** by F. Wood, B.Sc. (Econ.), F.C.A., and J. Hellings, B.Sc. (Econ.), A.C.I.S., SBN 85505 001 2.

   This book gives an introduction to Costing, Management Accounting and Computers. Many books make these subjects difficult to understand, but in this book the authors have not seen any virtue in making a topic unnecessarily difficult to learn.
   The topics covered in the book are:

Elements of Costing	Introduction to Pricing Policy
Accounting for Materials	Capital Budgeting
Absorption and Marginal Costing	Capital Structure & Gearing
Job and Process Costing	Fund Flow Statements
Budgeting and Budgetry Control	Control of Working Capital
Cash Budgets	Accounting Ratios
Co-ordination of Budgets	Interpretation of Final Accounts
Standard Costing and Variance Analysis	Accounting & Business Systems
Break-Even Analysis	Introduction to Mechanised
The Electronic Computer	Accounting

3. **ACCOUNTING CASE PROBLEMS** by J. M. Coy, M.Sc., A.A.C.C.A., A.C.I.S., A. C. Clark, B.A. (Econ.), F.C.A., and S. Keers, A.C.M.A. SBN 85505 002 0.

   The use of Accounting in tackling business problems involves far more than being able to draw up Final Accounts or to enter transactions in a firm's records. It is impossible for a student to have a real firm to try out whether or not he makes a good job of using Accounting in the solution of its problems. It is however possible to get much of the feeling of being involved with a real firm if a case problem is used with a class.
   This book is not meant for people studying on their own. It is designed instead to be used with groups of students by a lecturer or other experienced person. The cases cover many of the situations in business where the use of Accounting has anything to offer.

4. **COSTING A PROGRAMMED TEXT** by J. Townley, B. Com., F.C.A., and R. C. McEntegart, B.Sc., F.C.A., SBN 85505 005 5.

This text is intended for all those who are starting Costing. It offers a simple introduction to the subject and covers the following topics:–

Cost and Cost Behaviour	Job and Process Costing
Product and Period Costs	Joint & By Product Costs
Manufacturing Accounts	Budgeting
Accounting for Materials	Standard Costing
The Flow of Costs	Absorption & Marginal Costing
The Treatment of Factory Overheads	Break-even Analysis

By its very nature the programmed text is designed to allow people to work effectively on their own, building up a good basic understanding of the subject. The Book follows the same method as Accounting a Programmed Text which it is designed to follow since it assumes a knowledge of the basic concepts of Accounting.

TAXATION BOOKS

5. **THE ESSENTIALS OF INCOME TAX** by W. E. Pritchard, B.A., F.T.I.I. SBN 85505 014 4.

Written by a Senior Lecturer who was formerly one of H.M. Inspectors of Taxes. It is an introduction to the subject for those people who have little or no previous knowledge of taxation and are studying for examinations. It is written in simple language which it is hoped is easy to understand, unlike many other textbooks on tax which follow closely the language of the legislation and are almost impossible to follow for beginners.

6. **CAPITAL GAINS TAX** by W. E. Pritchard, B.A., F.T.I.I. SBN 85505 015 2.

This is our second book on taxation. It contains a large number of worked examples, and has been written in a style particularly suitable for students.

7. **CORPORATION TAX** by W. E. Pritchard, B.A., F.T.I.I. SBN 085505 011 X.

A companion volume to Essentials of Income Tax by the same author. Written in simple language which it is hoped is easy to understand, unlike many textbooks which follow closely the language of the legislation and are almost impossible to follow for beginners.

8. **CAPITAL TRANSFER TAX** by R. M. Walters, M.A., F.C.A. SBN 085505 017 1.

Written especially for students, unlike most books on this subject which have been written for practitioners.

ECONOMICS BOOKS

9. **ECONOMICS** by Frank Livesey, B.A. (Econ.), SBN 085505 006 3.

The book represents an attempt to bring some business reality into the study of Economics. The book will be particularly useful on courses in Economics for degrees in business studies, professional accountancy and secretarial courses, Diploma in Management Studies, Higher National Certificates and Diplomas in Business Studies, Institution of Works Managers etc.

The book contains a considerable number of numerical and multiple choice questions as well as case problems.

10. **ECONOMICS FOR BUSINESS STUDIES, VOLUME 1** Editor N. L.
Paulus, contributors: B. J. E. Jukes, S. King, N. L. Paulus,
A. G. Whitehouse, SBN 0 85505 013 6.

A book written for the first year of the new (1974) syllabus for Economics
in Ordinary National Certificate/Diploma examinations.
Because of the greater 'business orientation' of the syllabus compared
with traditional economics syllabuses this book is considered eminently
suitable for courses such as Association Certified Accountants, Cost and
Management Accountants, Institute of Bankers, Certificate in Works
Management etc.

11. **ECONOMICS FOR BUSINESS STUDIES, VOLUME 2** Editor
N. L. Paulus, contributors: B. J. E. Jukes, S. King, N. L. Paulus,
A. G. Whitehouse, SBN 0 85505 016 0.

Written for the second year of the new (1974) syllabus for the
ONC/D examinations. Publication August 1975.

BOOKS ON OTHER BUSINESS TECHNIQUES

12. **QUANTITATIVE TECHNIQUES FOR BUSINESS** by N. W. Marsland,
F.C.A., I.P.F.A.   SBN 85505 004 7.

This book has been specifically written for those without a background in
mathematics beyond G.C.E. 'O' level. An increasing number of
Professional and other courses now demand a study of quantitative
techniques and this text has been carefully designed to cover the subjects
in such syllabuses. The topics covered are:–

Linear Programming – General Allocation   Inventory Control Models
Linear Programming – Transportation   Network Analysis
Linear Programming – Assignment   Break-even Analysis
Differential Calculus   Venn Diagrams
Integral Calculus   Queueing and Sequencing
Markov Chains   Simulation
Game Theory   Decision Trees
Regression Analysis   Decision Tables
Evaluation of Capital Projects   Flow Diagrams & Process Charts
Optimum Level of Activity under   Lorenz Curves & Pareto
   Uncertainty   Distributions

The author is a lecturer who specialises in teaching statistics and analytical
methods. He has approached the subject through problems and
the book contains many worked examples. The basic principles and
methods are emphasised which makes the book particularly suitable for
those who require a working knowledge without being specialists in
operations research.

13. **MODERN ANALYTICAL TECHNIQUES** by F. Owen and R. Jones,
SBN 85505 010 1.

Intended as a teaching aid for students who typically come from a very
diverse set of mathematical backgrounds, many with no more than
'O' levels. Suitable for Chartered/Certified/Cost and Management
Accountant Foundation courses, also for various parts of professional
accountancy examinations and for Business Studies courses for CNAA and
National Diplomas and certificates.
Chapter headings: Inequalities: Matrix Arithmatic: Linear Programming-
Simplex-Transportation & Assignment: Probability: Sampling
Theory: Tests of Significance: Quality Control: Dynamic Programming –
Inventories: Simulation: Discounted Cash Flow: Time Series Analysis:
Correlation: Project Planning.